Real-Life Distance Education

Case Studies in Practice

A volume in
Perspectives in Instructional Technology and Distance Education
Charles A. Schlosser and Michael Simonson, *Series Editors*

Real-Life Distance Education

Case Studies in Practice

edited by

Anthony A. Piña
Sullivan University System

Al P. Mizell
Nova Southeastern University

INFORMATION AGE PUBLISHING, INC.
Charlotte, NC • www.infoagepub.com

Library of Congress Cataloging-in-Publication Data

A CIP record for this book is available from the Library of Congress
http://www.loc.gov

ISBN: 978-1-62396-526-6 (Paperback)
       978-1-62396-527-3 (Hardcover)
       978-1-62396-528-0 (ebook)

CONTENTS

PART II

COLLABORATING AT A DISTANCE

PART III

DESIGNING DISTANCE EDUCATION

PART IV

DEVELOPING PROGRAMS

PREFACE

Distance Education in Real Life

Anthony A. Piña and Al P. Mizell

AL'S STORY

You might have asked yourself, "What makes a person want to be an editor of a book about distance learning?" As one of your two co-editors, I feel qualified to answer that question for one of us. Since I was a youngster, I had a strong interest in technology. As an elementary student, I ran the movie projector for the teacher, and then in high school, I did the same plus set up science projects that involved the latest technology; at the time it was hydroponics. I remember in the '40s going to the radio store with the vacuum tubes from my family's radio in my hand to test them in the shop's tube tester to find which ones needed replacing. Then, one day at the radio shop, I saw a poster describing an invention that would replace vacuum tubes—the transistor. After the transistor became popular, it wasn't many more years until those transistors were reduced in size—along with other components—and could be simply printed on a silicon chip. Thus, chip technology was born. This led the way for society to move from the large mainframe computers of the '60s to the personal computer. It also led the way for me to move from traditional audiovisual technology into the computer age.

Real-Life Distance Education, pages ix–xviii
Copyright © 2014 by Information Age Publishing
All rights of reproduction in any form reserved.

During college days, one of the jobs I held was a staff photographer for the Hialeah-Miami Springs Home News—a weekly newspaper. In addition to taking the news photos, I processed them and then pasted up the negatives to burn the metal printing plates for the presses. From this job, paying a tremendous 54 cents an hour (!), it was on to a great job on the night shift at the downtown Miami First National Bank clearing house (paying $1.00 an hour) using wondrous new machines. Once proficient, I competed with a friend to see who was fastest each night to input the correct amounts by touch on the numeric keyboard and then pressing the right button to turn a huge wheel inside the machine to drop the check into the right bank slot—without errors. This was my earliest exposure to one of the forerunners of today's computer processors.

With this background and fondness for technology, I ended up majoring in science and math education, teaching K–12, and eventually going on for graduate work in science education at FSU and then doctoral work in instructional systems technology at Indiana University. At FSU, I decided I wanted to learn about computers but, at that time, the School of Education did not have any computer courses. I found one class in the Library School and got a basic understanding of computers in that course—learning about input, throughput, and output. When doing my doctoral research at Indiana University in 1969 and 1970, I found myself going over to the computer center in the late evenings to avoid the crowds so I could get to the card-punch machines to convert my raw data into Hollerith punch cards. From stacks of these, I could then run my multiple regression and other statistical analysis programs to get the results I sought.

I moved to Maryland in 1970 to join the brand new Howard Community College to become an associate dean in charge of the AV department and the library as well as all faculty development with a focus on the systems approach to creating instruction. Of course, integrating technology into the curriculum was a natural interest for me. I was able to be an early adopter of an electronic student response system in a large auditorium with a connection through a teletype to a mainframe at the main General Electric office for almost instantaneous computing of the data we collected. Why, in ten minutes after we gave a survey or test, we could run the punched teletype tape over long distance phone lines to GE and get the new punched tape back in a few minutes to type out a printed report that we could quickly photocopy (Xerox) to distribute to the participants with a full analysis!

Then, in 1978, when I came to Nova Southeastern University in Fort Lauderdale as Director of Curriculum Design, it wasn't long before the Apple personal computer was released and we purchased a few machines. We set up a lab and began teaching teachers how to use their new tools in the classroom—Lemonade Stand was one of the biggest hits—as was Deer Run a short time later.

From this, came the University Microlab and courses at the different Nova locations around the country. This was a form of distance education although it was conducted in a classroom setting at a distance from the university. A natural outgrowth of this came in 1983 when I was able to create a master's, an educational specialist, and a three-year doctoral program in computer education taught at a distance in a blended format. This will be described in detail in a case study later in the book.

During and after this experience, teachers around the world began experimenting with connecting youngsters over the computer and phone modems. We joined in hosting some of these projects. When Nova purchased a series of high quality compressed video camera stations from PictureTel (now Polycom) and installed them at various Nova sites around the country to teach classes at a distance, I created a project to connect middle and high school students from around the world over video running on an ISDN phone line. Beginning with one school in Sweden and one in Fort Lauderdale, the project grew to offer monthly sessions to ten or more schools with a different educational topic each month and to do it without charge. The project, known as SAXophone, ran for over ten highly successful years. This distance learning project, too, is described in greater detail in a case study further in the book.

So, you can see how the interest of one of your editors began and grew to the point that distance learning became a major focus in his professional career. You may also understand why helping gather and sharing descriptions of a variety of ways to practice and improve distance learning would be of special interest to him and worth the effort to get that information into a form that can be readily shared.

Let's hear from Tony and then you should be as enthusiastic as we have been in reading how these wonderful authors have experienced their special aspects of distance learning. You should find ideas and suggestions from their experiences that can help you do something new and different in your approach to distance learning.

TONY'S STORY

Although I share Al's love for distance learning, our stories are quite different. During my teenage years in the 1970s, rather than being a techno whiz like Al, I was aspiring to join the ranks of Eric Clapton, Jimmy Page, and Carlos Santana as a guitar hero. It was as an undergraduate student at Brigham Young University, that I was introduced to a wonderful field called "Instructional Design and Technology." In 1987, I began my first paid position in my new field: training and certifying preservice teachers in the use of various audiovisual tools and technologies. By the time I left BYU for

Arizona State University at the end of 1990, I had: (a) taught several sections of the technology in education course at the university, (b) designed and taught a computer applications course for a private middle school, (c) attended my first professional conference (the Association for Educational Communications and Technology Convention in Anaheim), and (d) completed a master's degree program in what is now called Instructional Psychology & Technology.

My ASU doctoral studies were interrupted in 1993 by an offer that I couldn't refuse: a position as full-time faculty and the first Coordinator of Education Technology at a California community college (College of the Desert in Palm Desert). During the same year that Al began the SAXophone project (1994), I also started my own journey into distance education by training and supporting our nursing faculty in how to use Picture-Tel videoconference systems, document cameras, and other technologies to teach nursing courses for students at our branch campus in Joshua Tree (60 miles away). Despite the occasional technical glitches, it was a very successful endeavor, with 100% of our remote students earning their nursing degrees and passing their state licensing exams for the RN. This was a great experience, but is not the origin of my passion for distance learning. To understand that, I must shift the focus of this story to my mother.

Teddi Piña was a medical office manager and vocational educator. She believed in setting high standards for those who serve patients in doctors' offices. She served as president of her professional association and was co-author of the clinical and administrative certification exams for medical assistants. She served on the accrediting team of the National Association for Trade and Technical Schools (now the Accrediting Commission of Career Schools and Colleges). Teddi helped put my father, Jack Piña—a law enforcement officer—through three college degrees, while working and raising two children. She earned her own associate degree and pursued a goal of completing a bachelor's degree in vocational education at California State University–Long Beach.

An opportunity for my father to become a police chief meant a move for our family to central California. Fortunately, California State University–Fresno offered the identical degree as CSU–Long Beach, but when my mother sought to transfer into the program, she was told that she would have to establish "residency" at CSU–F, which meant that she would have to take an additional 30 semester units—even though she only needed a few courses to meet the graduation requirements. She was told that it did not matter that her credits had been earned at another CSU campus. This was, after all, a turf issue.

A few years later and prior to her completing her 30 CSU–F units, my parents decided to move back to Southern California (they had discovered that a police chief was more of a politician than a cop). A bidding war between two counties for my father resulted in their relocation to Palm Desert. Fortunately, California State University–San Bernardino had a branch campus in Palm Desert that offered the same bachelor's degree as CSU–Long Beach and CSU–Fresno. Unfortunately, CSU's San Bernardino campus had the same inflexible "residency" requirements as its Fresno campus. When Teddi asked which courses she should take, since she had already completed every course offered by the department, the program chair just shrugged and said "you'll have to take at least more 10 classes from us in anything else that we offer." Since this was the mid-80s and she was not aware of any other options for her chosen degree, she felt as though she had no choice and enrolled in classes at CSU–SB. Tragically, Teddi Piña passed away from cancer before she could finish her last courses to complete her "residency" units for her bachelor's degree. My career as an educational technologist now had new meaning: How technology could be leveraged to transcend the turf boundaries that kept people from achieving their education goals and dreams. This became my passion.

Some months after my mother went "home," I was approached by a faculty colleague for my assistance in building our college's first online course. Web editing software, such as Dreamweaver, was not yet available, so I learned HTML and wrote the code for the course in Notepad. Soon after, I was teaching graduate courses in educational technology for Cal State San Bernardino and using FrontPage to turn my face-to-face courses into hybrid (blended) courses. I began to see that online learning provided opportunities for anytime, anywhere learning that videoconference did not.

At La Sierra University, where I was finishing my doctoral studies, I was given the opportunity to expand the university's graduate certificate in educational technology into a fully online master's degree program. I designed the curriculum, developed and taught several of the courses, and coordinated the program during its successful bid for WASC accreditation and for the next few years.

The year 2004 saw my transition from faculty to administration as we moved from California to Illinois and to a new position as Coordinator of Learning Technologies at Northeastern Illinois University in Chicago. I was tasked with establishing NEIU's online and hybrid learning program and had a great four years developing and teaching online and hybrid courses and helping my colleagues to develop their courses. Between La Sierra and Northeastern, I gained instructional and administrative experience with three different learning management systems (Blackboard, WebCT, and Desire2Learn) and with synchronous platforms such as Elluminate and Wimba. I could see that the true potential of online learning could only be realized through fully online degrees and certificates, not just through individual online courses. Unfortunately, NEIU was not ready to support fully online programs at that time. With my dean's blessing, I interviewed for a position as Dean of Online Studies at Sullivan University, Kentucky's largest private university. Although there were about 200 applicants for the position, it was agreed that I was the right fit for Sullivan and Sullivan was the right fit for me.

I now oversee the academic side of my university's online division, which provides nearly 60 different fully online degrees, certificates, and concentrations to over 1,000 students and online or hybrid courses to an additional 3,000 students each quarter. Many of our students have declared that, due to their work, family, military service, or health situations, they would never have been able to pursue their degrees and achieve their educational and career goals if not for online education. It has been my privilege for the past five years to see numerous lives change for the better. This is "real-life distance education." It continues to be my passion.

I know that my Mother would be pleased.

THE STORY OF OUR BOOK

When we conceived the idea for this book, we realized that there were many well done and useful books on distance education, many of them written by friends and colleagues. Some of these works provided broad-based introductions and surveys of distance education (e.g., Dabbagh & Bannan-Ritland, 2005; Simonson, Smaldino, Albright, & Zvacek, 2012), while others focused upon distance education technologies (e.g., Kats, 2010; 2103), online course design (e.g., Orellana, Hudgens, & Simonson, 2009), faculty issues (e.g., Gannon-Cook, 2010), online teaching methods (e.g., Conrad & Donaldson 2012; Ko & Rossen, 2010), international perspectives (e.g., Jung & Latchem, 2012; Visser, Visser, Amirault, & Simonson, 2012) or applying research-based principles and guidelines (e.g., Clark & Mayer, 2011; O'Neil, 2008). Each of these serves as an invaluable resource to those of us who are involved in distance education.

We determined that we could best serve our professional community by giving a voice to those who practice distance education in "real-life," and having them write about their experiences in distance education using a case-based format. This format includes an introduction, a description of the case study, implications for distance education, conclusions and questions for analysis and discussion. In *Real-Life Distance Education: Case Studies in Practice*, the reader gets to see how distance education was formulated and implemented by the various authors, how well it did (or did not) work in "real life," and provides an opportunity for reflective analysis. As the chapters began arriving from authors from across the globe, nearly all of whom are fellow members of the Association for Educational Communications and Technology (AECT), they seemed to fall naturally into four categories: (a) teaching at a distance, (b) collaborating at a distance, (c) designing distance education, and d) developing programs.

Bruce Harris and Anthony Piña commence the Teaching at a Distance section by exploring both simple and more involved ways in which they have integrated self-regulated learning strategies into their online courses. Next, Michael Barbour and Kelly Unger take us back to school in an investigation of how K–12 teachers strategically use technologies to resolve common communication and instructional issues in English, math, social studies, and science. We then accompany Joanna Dunlap and Patrick Lowethal on an experiential and research-based journey to find the online social presence "grail" (sans Monty Python). Roberta Ross-Fisher leads us to a different "grail"—how to increase online learner motivation—and provides us with a number of ways to incorporate individualized feedback to online learners. This section concludes with Lesley Farmer's experiences incorporating electronic journaling into the online environment, thus allowing students to improve their performance through self-assessment and peer assessment.

Ana Donaldson introduces the Collaborating at a Distance section with a real-world example of what occurs when in-course online collaborations are initiated without clear expectations and when the tasks are put ahead of people. She is followed by Larissa Malopinsky and Gihan Osman, who discuss the various challenges of international collaborations and take a research based-approach to investigate the role that culture plays in knowledge construction, collaboration, and communication. Next, Eunjung Oh, Ying Liu, and Thomas Reeves share ways in which they have implemented authentic learning tasks with collaborative group work to enhance online courses. Finally, Anthony Piña and Julian Scheinbuks discuss the triumphs and challenges of integrating online teaching partnerships between three state universities with very distinct populations and cultures.

Given that most of the authors are members of AECT—the leading professional association for academic instructional design and technology—we were not surprised that Designing Distance Education turned out to be the largest section of the book. This section begins with Lauren Cifuentes, Omar Alvarez Xochihua, & Janine Edwards giving us a look at how various Web 2.0 technologies were used to increase student interaction, satisfaction, and confidence in their skills. Ludwika A. Goodson and In Sook Ahn concentrate on the collaborative and consulting relationships of instructional designers and subject matter experts and how this relationship affects the quality of design. Kim Hosler discusses the pitfalls that occur for both novice and experienced instructional designers who lose focus when they emphasize the media and technology, rather than the instructional purposes for lessons, modules, or courses. E-Ling Hsiao and Xiaoxia Huang delve into activities and technologies used to enhance learner–content, learner–instructor, learner–learner, and learner–interface interactions.

Kathryn Ley and Ruth Gannon-Cook look at how semiotic features can be used in adapting learning management system templates to enhance student perceptions of their online courses. Joi Moore and Camille Dickson-Deane identify the challenges of evaluation in online education, including the difficulty of finding appropriate heuristics and the reliability of evaluators. Linda Simunek, Tatjana Martinez, and Judith Slapak-Barski discuss how the application of sound instructional design principles can be used to improve existing distance education degree programs. Concluding this section, Monica Tracey, Kelly Unger, and Matthew Schwartz lead us through the implementation of a specific type of social media (Ning) and compare it to the most commonly used tools for online education.

Al P. Mizell kicks off the final section, Developing Programs, by taking us back to 1995 and the challenge of creating a world-wide learning network, which led to a decade-long global collaborative partnership of middle and high schools using videoconference technology. The next two chapters address the issue of creating effective faculty professional development. First, Kathryn Ley shows how embedding self-regulated learning support and reducing extraneous cognitive load help to overcome communication challenges in a faculty development program. Xiaoxia Huang, E-Ling Hsiao, and Les Lunce focus their attention on the infrastructure and technologies involved in professional development. Next, Karen Kaminski provides a survey of the various decisions and considerations when planning an online degree program and gives an example of a successful distance education program, while Angela Benson and Andrew Whitworth use the example of a failed initiative to serve as a case study for how to (and how not to) build an effective online program. Brandon Taylor and Rosalind Fielder show how the use of online learning can be an effective way to deliver instructional sessions on library/information literacy to students.

Finally, Al P. Mizell returns to wrap things up by giving us a detailed reflection upon one of the most pivotal events in the history of distance education: the establishment of Nova University's (now Nova Southeastern University) groundbreaking distance education doctoral programs. In the three decades since the inauguration of those first two doctoral programs in the mid '80s, we have now seen online learning become the fastest growing sector of higher education, with nearly one-third of all college and university students enrolled in online courses (Allen & Seaman, 2011).

ACKNOWLEDGEMENTS

Without the efforts of many dedicated professionals, this book would never have come into existence. We wish to acknowledge the Board of the Division of Distance Learning of the Association for Educational Communications and Technology (AECT): Cindy York, Kathryn Ley, Christopher Miller, Ana Donaldson, Tonya Amankwatia, and Maria Avgerinou for giving their endorsement and labors to this project, and also Phillip Harris, Executive Director of AECT, for helping us to realize our desire to donate the royalties from this book to the AECT Division of Distance Learning.

We express gratitude to George Johnson, CEO of Information Age Publishing, for his generous support of the AECT Division of Distance Learning, including the funding of the various IAP-DDL awards and for providing a venue for members of AECT to advance the field and their professional development through publishing opportunities—such as this book. Our gratitude also extends to Michael Simonson and Charles Schlosser, Series Editors, for their timely guidance and help whenever we have had questions or concerns about how to proceed with our first edited book.

Real-Life e-Learning: Case Studies in Research and Practice is a peer-reviewed publication. Therefore, we wish to thank our professional colleagues who gave their valuable time to serve voluntarily as reviewers: Tonya Amankwatia, Tutaleni Asino, Maria Avgerinou, Evrim Baran, Larry Bohn, Charlene Desir, Bruce Harris, Karen Kaminski, Nari Kim, Patrick Lowenthal, Ryan Seilhamer, Delores Smiley, and Cindy York, each of whom reviewed multiple chapters for this book and offered invaluable feedback to the authors.

Speaking of the authors, we wish convey our deep appreciation to each of the authors for their efforts and their patience with a project that took far longer than any of us would have imaged. Please take a moment to read about them in the About the Authors section—it is an impressive list.

Finally, and most important, we wish to thank our supportive and wonderfully indulgent families: Teresa Piña, Heather Piña-Owen, Kellie Piña, Lisa Piña-Schultz, Emily Piña, Serena Piña, Alex Piña, and Al's supportive wife, Mary.

Note: Editors' royalties from the sale of *Real-Life Distance Education: Case Studies in Practice* will be donated to the Division of Distance Learning of the Association for Educational Communication and Technology.

REFERENCES

Allen, I. E., & Seaman, J. (2011). *Going the distance: Online education in the Unites States, 2011.* Babson Park, MA: Babson Survey Research Group.

Clark, R. C., & Mayer, R. E. (2011). *E-learning and the science of instruction: Proven guidelines for consumers and designers of multimedia learning* (3rd ed.). San Francisco, CA: Pfeiffer.

Conrad R., & Donaldson, J. A. (2012). *Continuing to engage the online learning: More activities and resources for creative instruction.* San Francisco, CA: Jossey-Bass.

Dabbagh, N., & Bannan-Ritland, B. (2005). *Online learning: Concepts, strategies and application*. Upper Saddle River, NJ: Pearson Merrill Prentice-Hall.

Gannon-Cook, R. (2010). *What motivates faculty to teach in distance education? A case study and meta-literature review*. Lanham, MD: University Press of America.

Jung, I., & Latchem, C. (2012). *Quality assurance and accreditation in distance education and e-learning: Models, policies and research*. New York, NY: Routledge.

Kats, Y. (Ed.) (2010). *Learning management system technologies and software solutions for online teaching: Tools and Applications*. Hershey, PA: Information Science Reference.

Kats, Y. (Ed.) (2013). *Learning management systems and instructional design: Best practices in online education*. Hershey, PA: Information Science Reference.

Ko, S., & Rossen, S. (2010). *Teaching online: A practical guide* (3rd ed.). New York, NY: Routledge.

O'Neil, H. F. (Ed.) (2008). *What works in distance learning: Sample lessons based on guidelines*. Charlotte, NC: Information Age.

Orellana, A., Hudgens, T. L., & Simonson, M. (Ed.) (2009). *The perfect online course: Best practices for designing and teaching*. Charlotte, NC: Information Age.

Simonson, M., Smaldino, S., Albright, M., & Zvacek, S. (2012). *Teaching and learning at a distance: Foundations of distance education* (5th ed). Boston, MA: Pearson.

Visser, Y., Visser, L, Amirault, R., & Simonson, M. (Eds.) (2012). *Trends and issues in distance education: International perspectives* (2nd ed.). Charlotte, NC: Information Age.

PART I

TEACHING AT A DISTANCE

CHAPTER 1

INCORPORATING SELF-REGULATED LEARNING STRATEGIES IN ONLINE COURSES

Bruce R. Harris and Anthony A. Piña

ABSTRACT

In this chapter, we describe several ways to promote learners' use of self-regulated learning strategies within online courses. Our experiences have shown that incorporating these and similar strategies can help students to be more self-regulated in achieving their learning goals while they complete online courses. In addition, we have found that online courses can be ideal learning environments for teaching self-regulated learning skills to learners. The strategies discussed within this chapter can readily be incorporated into most online courses, regardless of the learning management system being used to deliver the course. However, self-regulation is a complex skill and complex skills take time and practice to learn and to master.

Real-Life Distance Education, pages 3–19
Copyright © 2014 by Information Age Publishing
All rights of reproduction in any form reserved.

INTRODUCTION

In a 2007 review of the empirical literature on self-regulated learning (SRL) in online education, Artino states that, "the highest quality research in online education seems to indicate that providing students with self-regulatory scaffolding can be an effective instructional method—one that instructional designers might do well to consider including as integral to their online courses" (p. 13). Although self-regulated learning (SRL) is most often discussed and studied in traditional, face-to-face environments (e.g., Lindner & Harris, 1992; 1998), a number of researchers have noted that these environments are often not conducive to the development or application of SRL skills (Eastmond, 1996; Loomis, 2000). The primary role for learners in traditional classroom settings has been to receive information, absorb and memorize what is deemed to be of most importance, and then recall the information on a subsequent examination. Although effective learner-content, learner-instructor, and learner-learner interaction can occur in a face-to-face class, the regulation and reflection of learning tends to be under the control of the instructor, rather than the learner (Chang, 2005).

Chang (2005) observes that online learning places additional demands upon learners. "For students, web-based learning is a suitable environment for them to take charge of their own learning, since they can control their own learning process. However, providing students with opportunities to integrate their knowledge through web-based instruction may not be effective if they lack the skills needed to regulate their learning. Thus, strategies that prepare students for the rigors of learning at a distance and increase the probability of retention and success must be put into practice" (p. 217). Retention may be one of the most powerful reasons for incorporating the development of SRL skills into online courses, given the typically higher levels of attrition among online students—particularly first-generation college goers and those with little online learning experience (Moody, 2004; Patterson & McFadden, 2009; Tyler-Smith, 2006; Williams & Hellman, 2004).

The nature of asynchronous online learning environments is such that variables previously under control of the instructor are now controlled by the learner (Dettori, Gianesco, & Persico, 2006; Williams & Hellman, 2004). These include the hour of the instructional delivery, the length of time that it takes to deliver instruction, the amount of practice and review time, and the location of the learner who receives the instruction (Puzziferro, 2008). Jonassen (1995) observes that this changing of roles and tasks between online instructors and learners makes SRL skills more important in online learning environments than they are in the traditional classroom environment.

Harris, Piña, & Lindner, (2002) identified several characteristics of the online learning environment that makes possession of SRL skills necessary for success. These characteristics include: a) the inability of the instructor to receive and process nonverbal cues indicating that the learner may not be understanding or may be having problems; b) the necessity for learners to inform their instructors when they are experiencing difficulties; c) the difficulty of initiating and maintaining social interaction between learners; and d) the managing of busy schedules to include sufficient time for course activities and assignments. Williams and Hellman (2004) state that those who are highly self-regulating tend to set proximal goals, which supports SRL for online environments, given that learners tend to have more freedom of choice with online instruction than they do with face-to-face instruction. Puzziferro (2008), studying the effect of self-regulation behaviors in 815 community college students, found that students engaging in self-regulation had increased academic performance and higher satisfaction in online courses. In two studies involving 476 university students enrolled in online programs, Barnard-Brak, Lan, and Paton (2010) found that students with minimal profiles of self-regulated learned demonstrated poorer academic outcomes (e.g., lower grade point averages).

Learning SRL Skills Online

In a review of several studies that examined SRL skills and strategies within online courses, Harris, Lindner, & Piña (2011) concluded, "While it is true that the development and utilization of SRL skills can contribute to the success of online learners, it is also true that online learning environments are ideal places for individuals to obtain SRL skills and take greater control and responsibility for their learning" (p. 127). For example, Dettori, Gianesco, & Persico (2006) observed that SRL strategies can benefit students who work individually or collaboratively and that online social settings, such as communities of practice (Piña, Sadowski, Scheidenhelm, & Heydenburg, 2008), can be effective environments for obtaining SRL skills. Chang (2005) found that learners' motivation within online courses was enhanced when the courses include SRL strategies to help them self-observe and self-evaluate their effectiveness. The value that learners placed on the instructional material increased, as did their confidence in their understanding and class performance. The learners became more responsible for their own learning, more intrinsically motivated, and more easily challenged.

Graduate students can benefit as they use and adapt SRL strategies to complete tasks and cope with challenges in online courses. Whipp & Chiarelli (2004) found that graduate students in an online technology course utilized a number of traditional SRL skills, including the use of organizers and schedules for goal setting, planning and management; note taking;

charts; reducing distractions and help-seeking from the instructor and peers. They also noted that these students took advantage of the online environment to apply strategies such as planning for technology problems, gauging success by technological performance, interaction with online peers, offline composing, editing and sorting of online discussion forum postings, frequent checks of online grade books, and coordinating online and offline work.

Learning management systems (LMS) like Blackboard, Desire2Learn, Canvas, Sakai, and Moodle, all contain tools that can be used to implement SRL strategies. Piña (2010) provides a list of relevant LMS components, including course announcements, synchronous chat, asynchronous discussion forums, internal messaging, drop boxes, whiteboards, online journals and blogs, wikis, grade books, course calendars, announcements, personal notes, and e-portfolios. An LMS and other Internet-based tools can provide learners with opportunities for communication and collaboration that can support the development of SRL skills and increase student success in online courses (Dabbagh & Bannan-Ritland, 2005; Dabbagh & Kitsantas, 2004).

Harris & Piña (2011) and Chang (2005) have recommended that faculty and instructional designers embed features in instructional materials that encourage learners' self-regulation. The instructor can include prompts within the course that provide guidance to the learners as to when to use various SRL strategies. These strategies and techniques for promoting SRL within an online course will be elaborated in the next section of this chapter.

CASE STUDY

Ideally, students are who effective self-regulated learners systematically direct their thoughts, feelings, and actions toward the attainment of their goals. They are cognizant of their academic strengths and weaknesses, they have a repertoire of strategies they appropriately apply to tackle the day-to-day challenges of academic learning tasks in online courses, and they are self-motivated (Kauffman, 2004; Schunk & Zimmerman, 1998). Unfortunately, our experiences in teaching online courses over the last 20 years has shown that many, if not most, of the students in some courses are not effective self-regulated learners. Many students do not use self-regulated learning strategies that would help them be more successful academically

While there are several reasons to explain why students do not use effective SRL strategies in online courses, our experience has shown there are two primary reasons: a) students have not learned how to use these skills and strategies before entering college; and b) students who have learned effective SRL strategies prior to taking college courses often do not use them because these skills require conscious, mindful effort and students often do not make this effort unless prompted to do so.

For those students who have not learned how to use SRL strategies previous to taking an online course, our experiences and that of others (e.g., De La Paz, 1999; Paris & Paris, 2001; Schunk, 2005; VanderStoep & Pintrich, 2003) have shown that these students can learn these skills if they are motivated to learn. However, a cautionary note needs to be raised. Self-regulation is a complex skill and complex skills take time and practice to assemble and acquire. Nevertheless, we have found that embedding prompts and specific instruction on how to use effective SRL strategies in online courses has empowered students to be more effective self-regulated learners. In addition, we have found that incorporating prompts in online courses to promote students' use of SRL strategies has also encouraged students who have previous learned these skills to use them more frequently and effectively.

In addition to embedding prompts, another strategy that we have found to be effective is to include in the introduction section of the online course a discussion explaining why it is essential for the learners to use self-regulated learning strategies in an online learning environment and why it will make a difference in their academic success. In our online courses we include a discussion that includes many of the principles and concepts presented in introduction to this chapter, such as a) the attrition rates for online courses (i.e., generally online courses have higher attrition rates than traditional face-to- face courses); b) online courses generally require more independent learning; and c) students who are academically successful in online courses tend to be self-regulated. We explain in this discussion that several helps (prompts) have been included in our online course to help the students use self-regulated learning strategies, but ultimately, it is the learner's decision whether or not to use those strategies suggested during the course. We try to clearly explain that the embedded prompts are intended to help students learn to be more effective self-regulated learners; however, if students feel these prompts are a hindrance to their learning, they may choose to skip them or not respond.

As stated previously, online learning environments can be ideal settings to teach students effective self-regulated learning skills and strategies and how to take greater control and responsibility for their learning. This section of the chapter will discuss several techniques and strategies that we have incorporated in online courses for promoting self-regulated learning. The strategies and techniques are grouped into five general categories: a) conditional awareness, b) self-monitoring, c) self-evaluation, d) self-motivation, and e) self-explanation.

Conditional Awareness

Conditional awareness is defined as a student's ability to identify and execute appropriate SRL strategies based on contextual clues in a particular learning situation and context. We try to encourage our students to recognize sources of contextual clues in a course. The most important activity we have done to encourage students to use contextual clues and to be more effective self-regulated learners is to require students to set specific academic goals for a course and to develop a strategic plan to achieve their goals based on contextual clues in the course.

We teach our students that self-regulated learners set goals and develop strategic plans to achieve those goals. Setting a goal will help the students determine how much effort they want to expend related to a particular course. We also explain that setting a goal is critical to using other self-regulated learning strategies, such as self-evaluation, self-monitoring, etc. For example, to effectively use self-evaluation strategies, learners need to have a goal to compare their current performance with to identity any discrepancies and make changes.

To help our students develop these skills of setting goals and making an effective strategic plan, the first assignment in the course requires students to set a goal(s) and develop a strategic plan to achieve that goal. This assignment is included in the introduction section of the course before the students begin the actual coursework. Even though the assignment is worth only a small percentage of the course grade, we have found that students will complete the assignment if points are awarded. Our experience has shown that if points are not awarded for this assignment, most students do not complete the activity.

The assignment requires the students to set at least one goal: a specific grade or score they would like to achieve in the course. We encourage them to set other goals, such as specific knowledge, understanding, or skills they would like to achieve in the course. We stress that the goals should be measurable and include a date to be accomplished (which is usually the same date as the completion date of the course).

The instructions for this assignment also require the students to write a strategic plan to achieve the goal(s) they have established. We teach the students that the strategic plan should not only be specific and detailed, but should also be based on conditional awareness of the course. That is, we encourage the students to evaluate the nature of the course and use contextual clues to determine what specific tasks need to be completed to achieve their goal. One of the best ways to identify these contextual clues is to review the course syllabus. For example, if the student concludes from the course syllabus that the course grade is primarily determined by the scores on multiple-choice exams and quizzes, the learner's action plan would most likely include reading the course materials and textbook chapters for key vocabulary and definitions. The learner may plan to spend a certain amount of time each week to review self-quizzes or study guides well in advance of the exam so he or she will have time to ask the instructor questions and allow time for the instructor's response.

If, on the other hand, the learner concludes from the course syllabus (and perhaps announcements or e-mails from the instructor clarifying his or her assumptions) that a course grade is determined primarily by course projects and assignments, the learner's action plan might include some of the following tasks: a) complete the project or the assignment a week before the due date and submit it to the instructor to get feedback concerning to what degree the project meets the criteria; b) establish a study group with other classmates and have them review the project before submitting it; and c) review sample assignments provided by the instructor.

We also explain in the assignment instructions to look for additional contextual clues in the syllabus that will help them in developing their strategic plan, such as help-seeking information. The course syllabus almost always lists the instructor's office hours so the learner can contact the instructor if he or she has questions. In addition, the syllabus will most likely have information regarding how to contact technical support for questions regarding the course's LMS or for network issues, late assignment policies, how to contact other students interested in working in a study group, etc.

We explain to our students the need to review other course resources for contextual clues regarding how develop an effective strategic plan. For example, our courses include a Getting Started section that includes items such as tips to being a successful online learner, how to order textbooks, how to communication with the instructor and other class members, how to get help using the course LMS, etc. The Getting Started section also includes specific suggestions for controlling the learning environment that would help in developing the strategic plan such as: a) deciding to study at a certain place where distractions are likely to be minimal; b) planning out blocks of time each week for studying; c) if an assignment failed to meet all the criteria specified or to achieve the desired score, how to contact the instructor to seek clarification, etc.

We also clarify in the assignment instructions about various contextual clues in the instructional lessons for the course. For example, for some of our online courses, we have designed the unit lessons so the key vocabulary words and definitions that are important to remember (and most likely to be on the exam) are highlighted in yellow. In addition, the practice test items in each unit focus on the most important concepts and objectives. At the beginning of the lesson, we include specific instructional objectives related to the reading material for that lesson on which they should focus.

Another reason we made this activity an assignment is so we can review the students' strategic plans and give them feedback. Our experience from grading these assignments over the years is that students tend to minimize their strategic plans. Much of the feedback we provided centers around encouraging the students to be more specific and detailed in the strategic plan.

Self-Monitoring

Self-monitoring is defined as students' awareness of their comprehension or performance during or shortly after completing an academic task. We encourage our online students to self-monitor their understanding and performance as they complete course activities and lessons. For example, we have embedded two types of prompts in our unit lessons. For the first type of prompt, we embed self-monitoring prompts at strategic points during the course lessons (usually following several frames of course content) in which the learner simply reads the prompt and chooses whether to respond to the prompt or continue on with the lesson. The learner is not required to type a response to the prompt to advance to the next page. See Figure 1.1 for an example of this type of self-monitoring prompt.

The second type or prompt that we have used is to embed self-monitoring prompts in the course lessons that require the learners to type a

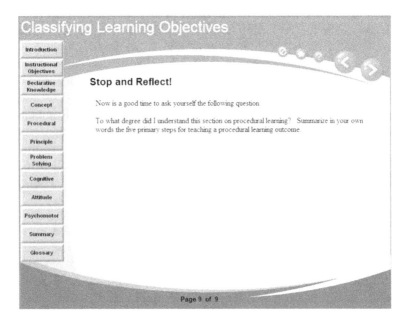

Figure 1.1   Self-monitoring prompt not requiring a written response.

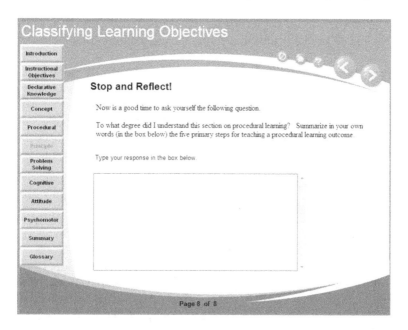

Figure 1.2   Self-monitoring prompt that requires the learner to type a response.

response to the prompt before they can continue to the next page. See Figure 1.2 for an example of a self-monitoring prompt embedded in a lesson that requires the learner to type a response before continuing the lesson. The first technique is rather simple to incorporate in an online lesson that uses a frame-based application, such as PowerPoint or other course lesson development application. The second technique, requiring the learners to actually type in a response to the self-monitoring prompt before they can continue the lesson, usually requires more sophisticated online course development skills than the first technique. We use a web development authoring system to require the learners to type in a response before they can continue to the next page in the lesson. We also wrote the programming code that allowed us to store the learners' responses in a dynamic database so we could review the students' responses to determine the level of thoughtfulness of their responses.

Additional examples of self-monitoring prompts we have incorporated in our lessons include the following:

- "Have I identified all of the key points in this article?"
- "I didn't do as well as I thought I would on the last test. What learning strategies do I need to use to prepare for the next exam, so that I will get an A on the exam?"

- "My attention is beginning to drift. I need to stay focused for the next 45 minutes and then I will take a 10 minute break."

Another strategy that we use to encourage students to use self-monitoring strategies is to encourage the students to review their assignments before submitting them to determine whether their assignment meets all the criteria specified in the assignment rubric. In the instructions section of the assignment drop box of the course LMS, we include some brief instructions reminding the students to review their assignments to ensure it meets all the criteria specified in the assignment rubric. The students see this reminder before they submit their assignment.

Self-Evaluation

Self-evaluation is defined as a student's self-judgment on their performance by comparing it to their goal. Self-evaluation strategies are very similar to self-monitoring strategies; however, self-evaluation strategies differ in that students judge their performance based on the goal they established for themselves at the beginning of the course. Like the self-monitoring prompts, we also include self-evaluation prompts in our course lessons to encourage students to evaluate if their performance is aligned with their academic goal. For example, we use the following self-evaluation prompt at the end of a lesson: "If I were to take a test on this information right now, what grade would I most likely receive?" See Figure 1.3 for an example of a self-evaluation prompt embedded in a lesson from one of our online courses. As Figure 1.3 shows, students actually have to select the grade they think they would receive.

Additional examples of self-evaluation prompts we have incorporated in our lessons include the following:

- "Now that I know my score on this exam, what would I do differently for the next exam to do better?"
- "To what degree am I following the plan I made for achieving my goal?"
- "Why did I do so poorly on the self-test? What misconceptions or misunderstandings do I have?"

We have found that providing ways for learners to evaluate their quantitative progress in an online course is an effective technique for promoting self-evaluation learning strategies. For example, we post the learners' grades (scores) on their graded assignments and course activities in an online grade book so they can evaluate whether or not they are earning enough points to achieve the academic goal they established for the course. The online grade book shows the students how many points they have earned

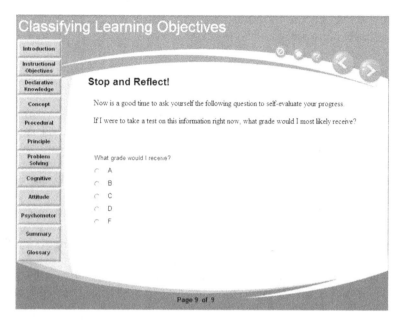

Figure 1.3 Self-evaluation prompt that requires the learner to choose a grade.

out of the total points possible and their current grade percentage at any point in time during the course.

Another technique is to provide self-tests or self-quizzes that learners can complete to help them determine their readiness for taking an exam or quiz. These self-tests are not graded, but are very similar to the exam or quizzes that will be graded. Before learners take the self-test, we encourage them to evaluate how well they think they will perform on the self-test and then compare their estimate with their actual score. This activity gives the learners practice in making more accurate self-evaluations on how well they are prepared for an exam in the future.

Another strategy we use to encourage students to use self-evaluation learning strategies is to require students midway through an online course to submit a self-evaluation report concerning to what degree they are on target towards achieving their academic goal(s) and to what degree they have followed their strategic plan. In this assignment, we ask the students to reflect and report concerning if they feel they will achieve their goal, to what degree are they following the strategic plan they developed, what changes they need to make in their strategic plan or their behavior, etc. We also ask the students to submit a reflection paper at the end of the course. In addition to other questions students respond to in this paper, they respond to such as questions as: a) Did I achieve my academic goal? b) What worked well in my strategic plan and what didn't work well? c) To what degree did I execute my strategic plan? and d) What lessons did I learn from this experience?

Self-Motivation

Self-motivation is defined as students' awareness of their motivation level in regards to achieving their academic goals. We try to encourage students to reflect on their motivation level towards achieving their academic goal and increase their motivation if necessary. Like the self-monitoring and self-evaluation prompts, we also include self-motivation prompts in our course lessons to encourage students to assess their motivation level. For example, we embed the following prompt during a lesson: "How is my motivation right now? If it is low, I need to remind myself that I have been a successful student in the past and that I have overcome difficult challenges on other occasions." See Figure 1.4 for an example of a self-motivation prompt embedded in a lesson from one of our online courses.

Additional examples of self-motivation prompts we have incorporated in our lessons include the following:

- "As soon as I complete the self-test, I am going to reward myself."

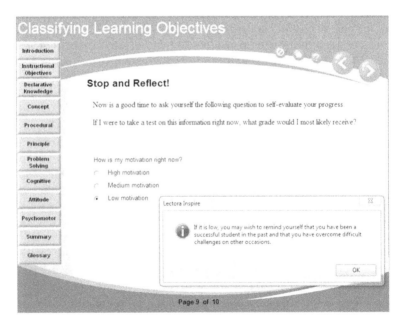

Figure 1.4 Self-motivation prompt requiring learner response and displaying feedback.

- "Even though this article is taking much more time than I anticipated, I am not going to give up until I complete it."

Another way that we try to promote students to use self-motivation strategies is by encouraging students in the introduction section of the course to e-mail the instructor if they find that they are low or lacking motivation at any point in the course. We find that many students feel low motivation during the third quarter of the course. We explain to the students that the instructor can be very helpful in sending e-mails to encourage students and provide individualized help because we have had experiences in previous semesters helping students to regulate their motivation level. Instructors can also help students identify help resources on campus to help them with issues in their lives that may be causing the low motivation levels.

We also provide a help section in the course consisting of several case studies and stories of techniques and strategies that previous students have used to help them stay motivated and follow their strategic plan to achieve their goal. For example, one case study focuses on how a student posted a picture of very nice boat on the side of his computer screen to remind him that he had to do well in his online course in order to get a good job and thus buy the boat he wanted. Another story tells of a student who promised himself a favorite meal at a nice restaurant after he completed each major course assignment.

Self-Explanation

Self-explanation is defined as a type of metacognitive activity wherein students attempt to analyze, clarify, amplify, draw inferences, interpret, and then explicate to themselves the subject matter of the course. We try to encourage students to attempt to generate self-explanations as they study. We also try to avoid the temptation to explain too much to the students in the course materials so they will construct their own understanding and move away from having the instructor do all the work. One way we do this is to provide self-explanation prompts before the summary of a lesson in which students summarize or clarify what they have learned during the lesson. For example, Figure 1.5 shows a self-explanation prompt that students respond to before they advance to the official summary in the lesson.

Additional examples of self-explanation prompts we have incorporated in our lessons include the following:

- "How would I describe the situation, problem, concept, activity, etc.?"
- "What possible implications or predictions can I draw from the information thus far?"

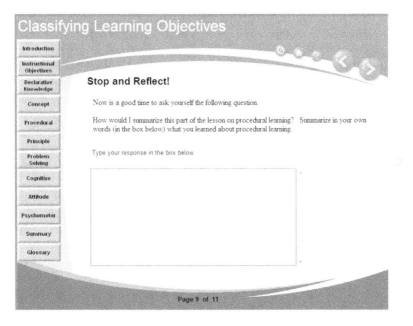

Figure 1.5 Self-evaluation prompt that requires learners to type an explanation of what they learned in the lesson.

- "How would I sum up, interpret, or explain the situation, problem, concept, activity, etc. thus far to someone else?"

Another activity we use to encourage students to use self-explanation strategies is to require students to complete a course reflection paper. Students are asked to do such things as analyze, clarify, amplify, draw inferences, interpret, etc. as they complete the reflection paper. They are also asked to summarize the most important things they learned in the course. In some of our courses, students are required to share their reflections with another person. It is a truism that if you want to learn a skill or subject at a deeper level prepare as though you must teach it to others.

IMPLICATIONS FOR DISTANCE EDUCATION

Our experiences incorporating self-regulated learning strategies in our online courses over the years has shown that instructors can significantly help their students to be more effective self-regulated learners without a lot of effort on their part. Most of the strategies we have described in this chapter do not take a significant amount of the instructor's time to incorporate into their online courses. We hope this chapter has provided some ideas to help instructors get started who have never incorporated self-regulated learning strategies in their online courses. The strategies in this chapter represent just a few of the many strategies instructors can incorporate in their courses to help their students be more effective self-regulated learners. There are many additional self-regulated learning strategies to those discussed in this chapter that instructors can incorporate in their courses that would also have a significant impact on their learners.

Most of our students have given us positive comments and feedback about our integration of SRL strategies in our online courses. A few students have told us that they do not use the strategies we have provided and that they get annoyed with being required to respond to the prompts in order to advance to the next screen—but these comments are rare. Many students have shared with us that they have used the self-regulated learning strategies they learned in our courses in other online courses and it has really made a difference in their academic success.

CONCLUSION

The primary purpose of this chapter has been to discuss several strategies we use in our online courses to promote students' use of self-regulated learning strategies. Our experiences have shown that incorporating strategies such as those discussed in this chapter can help students be more self-regulated in achieving their learning goals while completing an online course. In fact, an online course can be an ideal learning environment for teaching self-regulated learning skills to learners. Most of the strategies discussed in this chapter can readily be incorporated into most online courses, regardless of the learning management system being used to deliver the course. However, as was stated earlier in this chapter, self-regulation is a complex skill and complex skills take time and practice to assemble and acquire. Online instructors who implement the techniques and strategies presented in this chapter will most likely not see a dramatic change in students' self-regulation over short time periods; it is only after considerable and targeted practice accompanied by supportive and specific feedback that self-regulation becomes normative for a given learner (Harris, Lindner, & Pina, 2011).

QUESTIONS FOR ANALYSIS/DISCUSSION

1. Considering your own experiences with online courses, how important do you think it is to promote students' use of self-regulated learning strategies in an online course?

2. What additional (to those discussed in this chapter) self-regulated learning strategies can be incorporated into online courses?
3. How can the construct of self-regulated learning be measured?
4. Which of the strategies and techniques that were described in this chapter do you think would get the biggest bang for the buck?
5. How could an online course be structured and organized to encourage students to teach other students self-regulated learning skills and strategies?

REFERENCES

Artino, A. R. (2007). Self-regulated learning in online education: A review of the empirical literature. *International Journal of Instructional Technology and Distance Learning, 5*(7), 3–18.

Barnard-Brak, L., Lan, W. Y., & Paton, V. O. (2010). Profiles in self-regulated learning on the online learning environment. *International Review of Research in Open and Distance Learning, 11*(1), 61–80.

Chang, M. (2005). Applying self-regulated learning strategies in a web-based instruction: An investigation of motivation perception. *Computer Assisted Language Learning, 18*(3), 217–230.

Dabbagh, N., & Bannan-Ritland, B. (2005) *Online learning: Concepts, strategies and application.* Upper Saddle River, NJ: Pearson Merrill Prentice-Hall.

Dabbagh, N., & Kitsantas, A. (2004) Supporting self-regulation in student centered web-based learning environments. *International Journal on e-Learning, 3*(1), 40–47.

De La Paz, S. (1999). Self-regulated strategy instruction in regular education settings: Improving outcomes for students with and without learning disabilities. *Learning Disabilities Research & Practice, 14*(2), 92–106. doi:10.1207/sldrp1402_3

Dettori, G., Gianetti, T., & Persico, D. (2006). SRL in online cooperative learning: Implications for pre-service teacher training. *European Journal of Education, 41*(3).

Eastmond, D. V. (1996). *Alone but together: Adult distance study through computer conferencing.* Creskill NJ: Hampton Press.

Harris, B. R., Lindner, R. W., & Piña, A. A. (2011). Strategies to promote self-regulated learning in online environments. In G. Dettori & D. Perisco (Eds.), *Fostering self regulated learning through ICT* (pp. 122–144). Hershey, PA: IGI Global.

Harris, B. R., & Piña, A. A. (2011, November). *Five strategies to promote self-regulated learning strategies in online courses.* Paper presented at the annual convention of the Association for Educational Communications & Technology, Jacksonville, FL.

Harris, B. R., Piña, A. A., & Lindner, R. (2002, November). *Facilitating self-regulation in online courses.* Paper presented at the annual convention of the Association for Educational Communications & Technology, Dallas, TX.

Jonassen, D., Davidson, M., Collins, J., Campbell, B., & Haag, B. (1995). Constructivism and computer-mediated communication in distance education. *The American Journal of Distance Education, 9*(2), 7–26.

Kauffman, D. F. (2004). Self-regulated learning in web-based environments: Instructional tools designed to facilitate cognitive strategy use, metacognitive processing, and motivational beliefs. *Journal of Educational Computing Research, 30*(1&2), 139–161. doi:10.2190/AX2D-Y9VMV7PX-0TAD

Lindner, R. W., & Harris, B. R. (1992). Self-regulated learning: Its assessment and instructional implications. *Educational Research Quarterly, 16*(2), 29–37.

Lindner, R. W., & Harris, B. R. (1998). Self-regulated learning in education majors. *The Journal of General Education, 47*(1), 63–78.

Loomis, K. D. (2000). Learning styles and asynchronous learning: Comparing the LASSI model to class performance. *Journal of Asynchronous Learning Networks, 4*(1), 23–31.

Moody, J. (2004). Distance education: Why are the attrition rates so high? *Quarterly Review of Distance Education, 5*(3), 205–210.

Paris, S. G., & Paris, A. H. (2001). Classroom applications of research on self-regulated learning. *Educational Psychologist, 36*(2), 89–101. doi:10.1207/S15326985EP3602_4

Patterson, B., & McFadden, C. (2009). Attrition in online and campus degree programs. *Online Journal of Distance Learning Administration, 12*(2).

Piña, A. A. (2010). An introduction to learning management systems. In Y. Kats (Ed.), *Learning management systems technologies and software solutions for online teaching* (pp. 1–19). Hershey, PA: Information Science Reference.

Piña, A. A., Sadowski, K. P, Scheidenhelm, C. L., & Heydenburg, P. R. (2008). SLATE: A community of practice for supporting learning and technology in education. *International Journal of Instructional Technology and Distance Learning, 5*(7), 3–16.

Puzziferro, M. (2008). Online technologies self-efficacy and self-regulated learning as predictors of final grade and satisfaction in college-level online courses. *American Journal of Distance Education 22*(2), 72–89.

Schunk, D. H. (2005). Self-regulated learning: the educational legacy of Paul Pintrich. *Educational Psychologist, 40*(2), 85–94. doi:10.1207/s15326985ep4002_3

Schunk, D. H., & Zimmerman, B. J. (1998). Conclusion and future direction for academic interventions. In D. H. Schunk & B. J. Zimmerman (Eds.), *Self-regulated learning: From teaching to self-reflective practice* (pp. 225–235). New York, NY: Guilford Press.

Tyler-Smith, K. (2006). Early attrition among first time e-learners: A review of factors that contribute to drop-out, withdrawal and non-completion rates of adult learners undertaking elearning programmes. *Journal of Online Learning and Teaching, 2*(2).

VanderStoep, S. W., & Pintrich, P. R. (2003). Self-regulated learning: From teaching to self-reflective practice. Upper Saddle River, NJ: Prentice Hall.

Whipp, J., & Chiarelli, S. (2004). Self-regulation in a web-based course: A case study. *Educational Technology Research and Development 52*(4), 5–22.

Williams, P. E., & Hellman, C. M. (2004) Differences in self-regulation for online learning between first- and second-generation college students. *Research in Higher Education 45*(1), 71–82.

CHAPTER 2

STRATEGIES FOR OVERCOMING COMMON OBSTACLES IN THE ONLINE ENVIRONMENT

Issues in Virtual School Teaching

Michael K. Barbour and Kelly L. Unger

ABSTRACT

K–12 online learning or virtual schooling has seen substantial growth in the United States over the past two decades. While the practice of virtual schooling has exploded, the availability of research-based best practices to guide teachers working in these environments is lacking. This chapter presents four cases from Michigan Virtual School (MVS) teachers that examine a variety of issues that virtual school teachers face when facilitating K–12 student learning in the online environment, including strategies to provide substantive feedback in English Language Arts, methods for addressing the demonstration of mathematical computations, using Web 2.0 tools to increase interaction in an online environment, and a five-step process for incorporating reading and writing to increase science literacy. Each case follows a similar format, outlin-

Real-Life Distance Education, pages 21–40
Copyright © 2014 by Information Age Publishing

ing *why* the problem exists in the virtual school environment, followed by *what* strategies each MVS teacher uses, and *how* that strategy is implemented in virtual schooling.

INTRODUCTION

K–12 online learning or virtual schooling is growing at an exponential rate in the United States. The first virtual school program began in 1991 (Barbour, 2009), and by 2000 approximately a dozen states had virtual schools (Clark, 2001). In the first national survey of virtual schooling, Clark (2001) estimated there were approximately 40,000 to 50,000 K–12 students enrolled in distance education courses. Less than a decade later, Watson, Murin, Vashaw, Gemin, and Rapp (2012) found there were over 2,000,000 K–12 students enrolled in online courses, with significant K–12 online learning activity in all 50 states and the District of Columbia. Some have even predicted that online learning will encompass half of all of K–12 education by the year 2020 (Christensen, Johnson, & Horn, 2011).

In Fall 2007, the state of Michigan began requiring that all students complete an online learning experience to graduate from high school. This means that there is a potential for any high school teacher within the Michigan education system to be tasked with designing and delivering K–12 online learning content to their students. Yet, Kennedy and Archambault (2012) found that only 1.3% of universities in the United States provided any preparation for their preservice or in-service teacher education students on K–12 online learning. Further, Rice and Dawley (2007) found that less than 40% of all online K–12 teachers in the United States reported receiving professional development before they began teaching online. This indicates a need for teacher education programs to address preservice and in-service teachers' ability to teach in environments that are completely mediated by technology.

At Wayne State University, the revisions required to address this deficit were made in the content of IT6230: Internet in the Classroom. A portion of the new content included incorporating two curricular projects created by Iowa State University: Iowa Learning Online cases and Teacher Education Goes into Virtual Schooling scenarios. This content was piloted in IT6230 and, while it was found to be quite useful, it was also limiting due to its geographic focus. While Iowa is a Midwestern state, its statewide K–12 online learning program focuses on providing opportunity to rural students rather than the greater urban population Michigan's schools serve. This was the rationale for the creation of a series of Michigan-based cases.

This chapter will describe the four Michigan-focused cases created to provide teachers with virtual schooling examples in language arts, mathematics, social studies, and science. The cases were created in partnership with the Michigan Virtual School (MVS)—a division of Michigan Virtual University, using teachers from MVS and pedagogical issues they identified as having faced. The cases presented in the following section will cover the following objectives:

- Discuss potential problems that may arise for virtual school teachers
- Provide exemplary strategies for virtual school teachers for overcoming common problems in K–12 online teaching environments

Each case provides a rationale for the pedagogical issue, a description of the strategies and/or materials utilized by the teacher to overcome the issue, and finally a discussion of the literature related to that online pedagogical issue. The cases are followed by a general discussion of some implications for virtual school teaching and some questions for you to analyze the cases.

CASE STUDIES

In partnership with MVS, the College of Education at Wayne State University created Michigan-focused cases using teachers from MVS and the pedagogical issues they faced. The online teachers were selected by MVS as being teachers who were known within the online program as being effective teachers. Each case provides a rationale for the pedagogical issue, a description of the strategies and/or materials utilized by the teacher to overcome the issue (with links and samples), and finally a discussion of the online pedagogical issue within the literature. This format is the same that was used by the Center for Technology in Learning and Teaching at Iowa State University for the "Good Practice to Inform Iowa Learning Online" cases (Center for Technology in Learning and Teaching, 2013). The purpose of the cases is to provide examples of good practice that can be replicated to support K–12 students and educators with teaching online.

The first case is where we examine three strategies that English language arts teacher Julie Swartz uses for providing substantive feedback to her students. The second case looks at how algebra and calculus teacher Elisha Murphy uses four methods for addressing the demonstration of mathematical computations in the online environment. Strategies for increasing interaction in an online environment are discussed in the third case by examining social studies teacher Jay Bennett's use of Web 2.0 tools. The final case examines science teacher Lorri MacDonald's systematic five-step process for incorporating reading and writing in the online science environment for increasing science literacy.

Strategies for Providing Substantive Feedback in Language Arts in the Online Environment

Subject: English Language Arts
Technology Used: Course Management System, Word Processing and
    Writing Revision Software
Media Files Available at: http://tinyurl.com/wsucase-english

Why?

Providing students with appropriate and timely feedback when they are learning to write, and become successful in the writing process, can be very difficult for a classroom teacher. The difficulty resides in the lack of agreement amongst teachers and researchers on whether the focus of feedback should be on form or content (Fathman & Whalley, 1990). After determining whether to focus on form or content the teacher must then select the appropriate evaluation method. Many times, there is no one method available to assess each student's writing needs. Each student needs to have individualized attention, and the teacher needs to have enough time to provide the kind of substantive feedback that students need to be successful in a language arts curriculum.

In 2001, the United States implemented the No Child Left Behind (NCLB) Act that required testing in reading, writing, and math. States were punishing districts throughout the United States because children were not writing with enough detail. Julie Swartz, online language arts teacher for MVS, claims that today's students "almost write as if they are providing an outline." Students are not providing enough detail in their discussion of topics, and are using fewer paragraphs in their writing.

To combat this issue and broaden children's understanding about what they have written, teachers need to find ways to elevate student engagement with the content, as well as provide meaningful feedback that means something to the student. The feedback must provide students with substantial information so they can expand on their writing, develop a deeper understanding, and be able to engage in a thorough discussion about what they have written.

What?

Julie has been teaching English Language Arts for MVS for approximately eight years, but she has 40 years of classroom teaching experience. As an online language arts teacher, Julie finds it important to discuss with students what they said in their writing. She indicated, "my job is to deepen and broaden their thinking, and [I] need to utilize tools that engage them."

The market is full of tools that allow students to complete course content online or through various technology-mediated software. The problem with many of these tools, according to Julie, is that they don't meet content expectations and they don't provide a real-life person who can supply specific individualized feedback. Studies suggest that feedback, combined with positive reinforcement is a critical component of maximizing performance (Chapanis, 1964; Ilgen, Fisher, & Taylor, 1979; Balcazar, Hopkins, & Suarez, 1985).

How?

Throughout her years in teaching Julie has been able to develop and employ various strategies to provide her students with substantive feedback in her language arts classes. She has successfully transferred these strategies to the online environment for her students at MVS. She is also interested in trying to incorporate programs, like Harvard's Project Zero, into her and other MVS courses. The goal of Project Zero is to "help create communities of reflective, independent learners; to enhance deep understanding within disciplines; and to promote critical and creative thinking" (Project Zero, 2009).

To implement these beliefs, Julie uses three different strategies for providing feedback for her students: (a) the comment feature in a word processor, (b) Quick Write comments, and (c) writing revision software. Her responses must follow MVS's requirements for feedback response times, which indicate that students must receive a response within 24 hours of a message and receive feedback on their homework and assignments within 72 hours.

The comment feature in a word processing program enables Julie to provide substantive feedback on students' grammar, and writing and language mechanics. A rubric is used for each essay and is copied at the bottom of the students' work.

Remarks are provided at the end of the essay focusing on both the content and the assignment requirements. It is important to note that substantive feedback can also be provided in the assignment feature in *Blackboard* or through an e-mail message. However, MVS discourages the use of external e-mail systems with students because the virtual school would not possess a copy of those interactions.

A "Quick Write is a literacy strategy designed to give students the opportunity to reflect on their own learning" (Louisiana Public Broadcasting, 2009). Students are provided short open-ended statements and given only a few minutes to complete them. As such, Quick Writes do not focus on writing mechanics, but rather on students' thoughts and understanding and on the written expression of those ideas. In the Quick Write example provided, Julie asked the students about their feelings and provided them an opportunity to reflect on a situation that they had experienced.

The use of Quick Writes reflects Julie's belief that technology-mediated software doesn't provide a real-life person who can supply individualized feedback and that online teachers need to utilize other pedagogical strategies. The Quick Writes allowed students to reflect on previous situations and things they have learned in the past, and Julie was able to provide personalized feedback for each student's response. The activity also helps to build the online relationship between the student and teacher.

Over a period of 12 months, Julie has altered her use of the Quick Writes in her course. Due to the amount of writing the students were completing, Julie felt it would be better incorporated if she had students relate each assignment to something from their own life experiences. Students now write a paragraph or two offering opinions, examples, description, observations, experiences, etc. as appropriate for all of their writing assignments. Julie tries to choose topics that will connect them to the overall lesson, as a way to build upon the students' existing schema. This allows Julie to use the principles of the Quick Write in a slightly different manner.

Writing revision software is a tool that students can use before they submit work. Julie noted that, "it allows them to plop in their work and then, for example, analyzes and calculates all of the sentences that begin with the word well." The software is intuitive and enables students to see, on their own, where a majority of their errors are originating. Using the software provided students have an opportunity to fix any errors before submitting their work to the teacher.

The writing revision software used at MVS is part of the SAS Curriculum Pathways educational arm. At present, Julie does not require her students to use it. However, she is in the process of incorporating it into several of her courses. She plans to have students use this revision software for every essay assignment in her courses, allowing students to consider making suggested changes before submitting their assignment. Julie also believes non-English language arts instructors would benefit from using the revision editor with their students; as the demand for non-English language arts teachers to focus on writing increases, and many may not have effective strategies to help students revise their writing.

Discussion

There are many technology tools available that allow students to complete online assignments. However, Julie feels that these tools do not often meet the content requirements and lack a real-life person to provide the necessary individualized feedback needed to really deepen and broaden the understanding of the content and writing form of students. To assist in providing the substantive feedback needed to facilitate this understanding, Julie has implemented strategies by using the comment feature in a word processor, implements Quick Write Comments, and suggests students use writing revision software.

While the importance placed on writing has increased in recent years (Yore, Hand, & Prain, 1999), less time is spent on writing instruction (Hurwitz & Hurwitz, 2004; National Commission on Writing, 2003) and students continue to score poorly on writing assessments (U.S. Department of Education, 2007). Interestingly, a survey of employers who hire high school graduates reported that 73% found the writing skills of these employees to be "poor" or "fair" (Public Agenda, 2002). This was likely because only 49% of high school seniors reported completing writing assignments of three pages or greater in length. The systematic approach to writing exhibited by Julie is one way to use the tools provided by the online environment to address these issues and focus on improving students' ability to express themselves in the written format. While this case focused solely on English language arts, these strategies could be used by any subject area teacher who was providing feedback to written work.

Strategies for Showing Computations in Math in the Online Environment

Subject: Math—Algebra, Calculus
Technology Used: Course Management System, Scanner, Equation Editor, Virtual Classroom
Media Files Available At: http://tinyurl.com/wsucase-math

Why?

Teaching and learning math in an online environment has the potential to be extremely difficult for both teachers and students. In a traditional face-to-face math course, students complete handwritten calculations on paper and turn it in to the teacher. The teacher is able to assess the students understanding of computations by reviewing the steps the student has taken. The difficulty students have when trying to "write" in a computation format in an electronic environment increases the challenge of the assessment task for an online teacher and can also become cumbersome for the student. Multiple choice and fill-in-the-blank tests, often used in many self-paced online environments, provide an opportunity for students to cheat or guess the answers without completing any calculations (Blomeyer, 2002). These types of assessment make it difficult for the teacher to assess whether the student understands and can complete the steps required for solving problems.

Students transiting from standard arithmetic to higher-level math courses, such as algebra and calculus, often have a difficult time with the material. These higher-level courses involve symbols, equation solving, and emphasis on relationships (Cavanaugh et al., 2008), which many find challenging. In an online environment students must also acquire technical skills and abilities, as well as have access to the appropriate technology, to represent these symbols and solve these equations. These challenges pose potential burdens to student success in virtual school mathematics courses. In order to address these challenges, Elisha Murphy, a mathematics instructor for MVS, has implemented a variety of strategies to overcome some of these issues with her online algebra and calculus students.

What?

Elisha has taught Algebra 1 and AP Calculus for the MVS for five years as a full-time teacher. Like many mathematics teachers, she states that her online math students fall into three categories: (a) motivated, (b) motivated but lacking the knowledge and ability to complete the work, and (c) unmotivated; with most falling into the latter two categories. In order for Elisha to provide her students an opportunity for success in their math courses, she has developed a series of strategies for students to use when submitting work to demonstrate the computations on their math problems. Specifically, Elisha utilizes four methods that students can use to demonstrate the steps they've taken to solve the problem: (a) students scan their work and attach the file to an e-mail or upload it to the digital drop box in Blackboard, (b) students use the Equation Editor in Microsoft Word, (c) students utilize an agreed upon symbol sheet in a word processor that replaces much of the computational language, and (d) students demonstrate their workings using a synchronous communication tool.

How?

Scanning handwritten math work and submitting it to the teacher as an attachment to an e-mail message is the easiest method for work submission. Elisha models what is expected by providing students with samples of work completed by hand, scanning the document to a computer, and attaching it to an e-mail or posting it in Blackboard. The problem arises when students do not have access to scanners, which often happens when students complete work at home.

Another alternative is to use the Equation Editor for showing the steps for solving math problems. Equation Editor provides a large number of symbol tools and completes much of the formatting for the students by keeping the size of the graphics and numbers consistent. To assist students who are not familiar with this tool, Elisha created an instructional handout. Many students are not familiar with this tool prior to the start of the course, and they choose not to use it because it adds the stress of learning the tool to an already difficult subject (not to mention being an additional topic the teacher would need to cover).

The third method Elisha uses is a symbol key. The symbol key is created and agreed upon by the students, and can be used for submitting work. Specific keyboard keys are assigned to various math symbols that provide the students a quick and easy way to show their computations digitally. It also reduces the students' level of frustration of not having access to a scanner or knowing how to use the Equation Editor.

Finally, Elisha uses a number of synchronous tools to allow her students to demonstrate their computational understanding. For example, she speaks with students online or on the telephone to have them talk through their answers to make sure students are able to verbalize their mathematical processes. Elisha also allows students to demonstrate their work using Adobe Connect Pro, where the teacher and students to communicate in real-time and work through their problems together. This method is sometimes difficult because it often requires access to an electronic pen and tablet, which many students do not have at home or at school. The alternative is to use the mouse to draw calculations; however, this can be very difficult to accomplish. In addition to using the free-hand feature, many synchronous programs also have graphing calculators included as a part of the software or available as an add-on to the virtual classroom.

Regardless of which strategy the students use to submit their written math work, Elisha provides feedback to her students by making handwritten corrections on the student document based on a COST rubric (Correct answer, Organization, Shows work, and Technically correct writing). She then scans the corrected document and e-mails the graded work to her students as an attachment. This rubric is a 5-point grading scale, but also serves as a graphical organizer for students, which allow them to organize their thoughts and also provides a communication tool for the teacher.

Discussion

As students transition to higher-level math courses, it is imperative that they demonstrate the steps in their work because of the increased use of symbols and equations used in these courses. Accomplishing this already difficult task in an online environment can add an extra burden to these students, due to insufficient technology skills, content ability level, and motivation towards the course. An online math teacher needs strategies in place to assist students with overcoming barriers.

At the Virtual School Symposium in 2007, Susan Patrick (President and CEO of the International Association for K–12 Online Learning) indicated that Algebra I and Algebra II were the two highest enrollment K–12 online courses in the United States (Patrick, 2007). One of the reasons for this trend is that almost all jurisdictions in the United States require students to complete at least one full year of mathematics in order to graduate from high school. In their report of eight North Central Regional Educational Laboratory funded studies, Smith, Clark, and Blomeyer (2005) described a study conducted by Ferdig, DiPietro, and Papanastasiou that compared learner outcomes between online and face-to-face education, and whether prediction for online success could be made. The summary of this study described how many of the students who enroll in these online math courses were students who had already failed the course one or more times in the classroom (see Ferdig et al., 2005). This is further evidence that many of these students already find math a challenging subject, without placing additional technology-based obstacles in the students' path. Elisha's experience demonstrates four strategies that online math teachers can use to help students overcome some of the barriers associated with showing the computations necessary to complete their math problems.

Strategies for Increasing Interaction in an Online Social Studies Environment

Subject: Social Studies
Technology Used: Course Management System, Web 2.0 Tools
Media Files Available At: http://tinyurl.com/wsucase-socialstudies

Why?

The normal type of interaction that occurs between teachers and their students in a classroom can be difficult to replicate in an online learning environment. Online teaching is new to most teachers, and many have problems with coming up with ways to effectively interact with their students in order to keep them engaged with the course content. The face-to-face classroom allows teachers to communicate with their students in a variety of ways, ranging from visual and auditory communication to "nonverbal cues such as facial expression, direction of gaze, posture, dress, and physical presence" (Gunawardena, 1995, p. 148). Consistent and effective communication between students and their teacher is necessary if the students are going to have a successful experience, particularly in an online environment that can often be isolating for a student (Swan, 2002).

However, many online teachers and students are also new to the technical tools used in this instructional delivery model. In addition to being new to having to learn how to use a course management system (CMS), many teachers and students often find the CMS communication tools limit their ability to build relationships in the online environment. Teachers need to learn to use a variety of tools and strategies to provide an equal level of interaction with their students as they would receive in a face-to-face environment.

What?

Keeping students engaged and building relationships between students and their teacher in an online learning environment is a specialty for Jay

Bennett. Jay is currently the Instruction and Course Coordinator at MVS, but has been a social studies instructor with MVS for the past nine years. Jay has developed a number of strategies, utilizing a variety of online tools, to put his own personality into the online courses he teaches. He believes it is important for students and teachers in the online environment to create a personal identification with the course and with each other. Increasing that personal touch in the online environment allows all participants to demonstrate who they are when interacting with each other.

How?

For personalizing the course, Jay believes that using avatars, graphics, and audio and video materials can go a long way in terms of introducing yourself to the students. MVS uses Blackboard as its CMS, which allows teachers to post standard announcements, contact information, and teacher pages. Jay also posts some pictures of himself with his family, and other images that would allow the students to get to know him better (e.g., an image of the mascot from his alma mater). Simple images are a great place to begin to allow students to learn a little more about the teacher.

Before starting the actual course content, Jay uses Camtasia to create course tutorials that show the students how to use the CMS. Camtasia is a screen recording programs that allows teachers to create videos of computer screen recordings to illustrate to students how to do specific tasks they will need to complete in the course (examples of similar programs include ScreenFlow and Jing). Then Jay uses podcasts to introduce himself to the students. Podcasts are audio or video recordings that are uploaded to the Internet and streamed via Real Simple Syndication (RSS).

Jay uses these podcasts for the course introduction, teacher information page, and many of the announcements. To record and edit the podcasts Jay uses Audacity—a free, open source software—and then he uses GCast, a free online service, to host those podcasts. Along with the podcasts Jay also provides a written script or, at a minimum, a synopsis of what was said in the podcast in case students are not able to use sound features at their school.

Another way Jay interjects his personality into the online courses he teaches is to use various pictures, movies, voice recordings, icons, avatars, and characters. He also encourages his students to create these as well in order to increase content engagement and build relationships with others in the course. These tools also assist with drawing the students into the content. Jay says, "They add a little snap, a little pop, to the online classroom." Jay often uses these Web 2.0 tools, such as SimpsonizeMe, Blabberize, GoAnimate, Moviestorm, and XtraNormal for course announcements, although they can also be used to cover course content.

After creating these announcements, Jay provides them to his students in one of two ways: (a) by embedding them directly into documents or (b) by providing links to the sites he used to create them. Similar to the podcasts, he also includes the text or a synopsis of the audio with these tools.

In addition to the interactive items that Jay creates on his own, he also makes use of the many existing examples and services that are available on the Internet. One example that Jay regularly uses is the Week in Rap. The Week in Rap is produced every week during the school year to discuss the current events for that week. Not only does it present these current events in rap form, but it also provides an accompanying text that contains links to the stories included in the video. This tool allows Jay to take content many students may find mundane, and present it in a way that is more exciting and engaging to students. Another resource that is available to all MVS teachers, and all teachers for that matter, is the MI Learning Portal at iTunes U, which contains over 200,000 free educational audio and video files.

Finally, Jay also uses more traditional Web 2.0 tools to interact with his students. The Virtual Sociology wiki that Jay has created on Wikispaces is a good example. This wiki was created through an assignment where students had to post one line or fact about a sociologist. As the wiki has been developed over multiple semesters, later students have begun to run out of material from the online textbook that they can add. This has forced students to seek other resources in order to continue contributions to the wiki. This simple assignment of only one line turned into a plethora of information that could be used in other ways throughout the course.

Discussion

Online teaching is a new approach for many teachers, and they need to be sure to employ strategies for engaging their students in the course content, provided consistent and effective communication, and also learn the technology tools used to teach in this environment; they need to be prepared to provide the same interaction online as they would in a traditional face-to-face classroom. This case discussed ways for the teacher and students to add their own personality to the course for increasing interaction among the group.

The Web 2.0 tools used throughout Jay's social studies courses provide an avenue for developing personal identity in the online environment, as well as opportunities to engage and interact with the teacher, content, and other students. Over the past two decades, there have been a variety of possible interactions identified within the online learning environment. Moore (1989) began this process with his identification of the interaction that occurs between the student and the teacher, between students, and between the student and the course content. Later, Hillman, Willis, and Gunawardena (1994) described the interaction that occurs between the student and the CMS and its tools, which was different than the interaction between the students and the actual course content. Finally, Sutton (2001) identified the notion of vicarious interaction or the interaction that takes place when the student watches or lurks while other students interact with each other or the teacher. Through the use of various Web 2.0 tools in his social studies courses, and Jay's belief that online teachers must try to engage their students in a variety of ways, he is able to extend the amount and type of interaction his students have with their teacher, with other students, with the course content, with the CMS and its tools, and in a vicarious manner. Teachers of all subject areas can incorporate these tools in their online environments for increasing interaction and content engagement.

Strategies for Using Reading and Writing in the Online Science Environment

Subject: Science
Technology Used: Course Management System, Concept Mapping and
    Word Processing Software
Media Files Available At: http://tinyurl.com/wsucase-science

Why?

Like many subject areas, it is impossible to teach students everything there is to know about a discipline like science because of the wide array of related fields and sub-fields. Many science teachers focus solely on content, as K–12 science is often organized around content-based fields (e.g., biology, chemistry, physics, etc.), and neglect teaching students how to access, filter, and critically review scientific information.

Science literacy is the application of an individual's scientific knowledge "to identify questions, acquire new knowledge, explain scientific phenomena, and draw evidence-based conclusions about science-related issues" (National Center for Educational Statistics, 2009, para. 3). Other characteristics of an individual's science literacy include viewing science as a form of human knowledge and enquiry, demonstrating awareness of how science and technology shape our world, and showing willingness to engage in science-related issues as a reflective citizen.

Incorporating science literacy can be challenging for teachers because they need to make sure students go beyond memorizing facts. Teachers need to ensure students are able to solve problems, while also incorporating proper language conventions into their responses. The virtual environment poses an additional challenge because teachers and students are not able to directly converse, as in a traditional face-to-face manner, so it is important to incorporate appropriate strategies that require students to "talk" in written format.

What?

Lorri MacDonald has been a classroom teacher, an administrator, and now an online teacher with MVS. In 2008 she was selected as the first MVS Online Teacher of the Year. She teaches the MVS course in forensic science and is currently developing biology courses. Lorri demonstrates that students can be successful when science literacy is incorporated into the content of her online science courses.

How?

In her online courses Lorri guides students through a five-step process to increase students' science literacy: (a) gather information, (b) create a visual organizer, (c) compose a summary, (d) develop a concept map, and (e) conduct a critical analysis. Lorri provides feedback throughout the entire process. Students are provided with a rubric, and Lorri comments on writing mechanics, detail, accuracy of the content, and application, among other criteria.

The process begins with gathering information. Students are provided with a variety of websites and encouraged to explore each site in detail. Lorri usually provides a general graphic organizer to guide students on how to collect or note the specific information (e.g., list the site, its purpose, the important points, etc.).

Next, Lorri requires her students to present their information in a visual manner. Throughout the course, Lorri uses several different styles of visual organizers, depending on the purpose, type of information, and the nature of the task. For example, if Lorri wants the students to simply organize information, the students will usually use a basic table format. If she wants the students to compare and contrast the content, they would often use a Venn diagram. Lorri provides specific written directions and also an audio-based "mini lecture" on different ways to represent information in a visual format. "Mini-lectures" are narrated presentations that are typically six to ten minutes in length. Lorri uses PointeCast to turn these narrated MS PowerPoint presentations into Flash files that students can view online. A written transcript of the audio is included in the PowerPoint notes section, which allows students the option to read and/or listen to the lecture.

The third step for students is to compose a summary. In some instances students may simply summarize the information they found on a specific concept. Other times students may need to summarize cases. An example of a case would be "Murder by the Book," where students make the real-world connection of the importance of soil composition in crime solving. Using these aids completed in the first two steps, students know to search for specific points or clues that will solve the case or find important information. "Science talk" is another strategy used for increasing science literacy, and is recognized for increasing student understanding (McKee

& Ogle, 2005; Winokur & Worth, 2006). Since the course is asynchronous and there isn't really a "talking" component, students post to the discussion board and "talk" about their findings; the idea is to promote understanding and application of the science content to real life situations.

Next, Lorri has the students develop a concept map with definitions for the vocabulary to assist with increasing student understanding of the necessary terms. Students are provided with written directions and another "mini lecture" to help guide them. If students use the definition from the text or Internet verbatim (as opposed to developing their own), she provides feedback such as, "I'm looking for you to construct your own meaning," or "There is no sense in redoing someone else's work, but next time you should develop your own meaning." This type of feedback tells students to extend their own definitions in a comfortable and encouraging environment, and also lets them know they need to work a little bit harder on the next assignment. Finally, it gives them an opportunity for further exploration of the content to further expand their understanding of the specific term in order to develop ownership of the science language (McKee & Ogle, 2005).

Finally, Lorri directs the students to combine the information, visual organizers, summaries, concept maps, and instructor feedback from each of these steps to develop a critical analysis of the content. She instructs her students to decide what is fact and what is opinion, in the process of developing and composing a critical review of the content that is supported by their research. Students submit their assignments as attachments in the course management system. This critical review provides an opportunity for the students to display the major concepts they learned through the assignment. It also gives Lorri a summative assessment tool to evaluate the students' understanding of the overarching concept being taught, and their ability to apply it to a real context.

This sequential process allows students to gather, analyze and synthesize information in a systematic way. This method also provides students an opportunity to mentally organize the information in multiple ways, within the context of real world scenarios.

Discussion

Developing high levels of science literacy in students is a difficult task for teachers. It goes beyond having students memorize facts about content. Instead, teachers must support their students and emphasize all aspects of science literacy. When distance is a factor between the teacher and a student, the task becomes more difficult because they cannot converse directly face-to-face. The online teacher must now include strategies that require students to "talk" in written format to fully encompass the scientific nature of the material. Lorri's systematic five-step process assists students in increasing their science literacy.

The use of writing as a pedagogical strategy to reinforce science concepts has been used in a variety of contexts for more than three decades. One of the best examples of this strategy is the activity of microthemes. Microthemes have been described as an essay that can fit on a 5" x 8" index card (Work, 1979). Essentially, it is a concise form of writing in response to a question or prompt. Several studies into the use of microthemes have found them to be an effective strategy for student learning in science (Ambron, 1987; Collins, 2000; Kirkpatrick & Pittendrigh, 1984; Moore, 1993, 1994). Lorri's use of writing to teach science literacy to online students at MVS is an example that utilizes a similar strategy of having students write in directed ways in a very specific manner to learn scientific concepts. Teachers can use this systematic process in other subject areas as well.

IMPLICATIONS FOR DISTANCE EDUCATION

A major theme that emerges from the four cases is the importance of communication. All teachers in these cases needed to overcome obstacles that impacted the way they communicated with their students. They needed to develop strategies for delivering the course content while making it engaging and for providing meaningful feedback.

A second theme throughout the cases, tied to communication, is the need to use various technology tools for communicating. Not only did the online teachers need to deliver content and feedback through these tools, they had to be able to also deliver instruction for their students on how to use these tools.

In addition to the subject they are teaching, online teachers often fall into the role of teaching multiple content areas, including the subject they are teaching, the tools they are using to communicate, and skills for successful online learning. A third theme among the cases is that these teachers also had to implement strategies that also taught their students had to be successful in online courses. The strategies they implemented not only taught the content, but also demonstrated various ways that they can communicate more effectively in the online environment. These cases demonstrate strategies for overcoming these obstacles in the online learning environment.

CONCLUSION

This chapter focused on various strategies that online teachers from MVS used to overcome obstacles in their online teaching. Using the same format as Iowa State University, researchers from Wayne State University partnered with MVS to develop four cases that addressed pedagogical issues faced by online teachers. Each of the four cases described in this chapter addressed potential problems for online teachers, discussed strategies, tools, and materials used to overcome the problems, and provided a discussion of the pedagogical issue within the literature.

While all four cases underscored the importance of effective communication, each individual case focused on addressing one challenge related to teaching online in the K–12 environment. The language arts case emphasized the need for, and ways to, provide substantive feedback for deepening and broadening student understanding of content and the writing process. Elisha's case discussed methods and tools for assisting students with communicating their computational steps in higher-level math courses. The social studies case supplies various tools that can be used in the online environment to facilitate content engagement and interaction among students, teacher, and content. The fourth case centered on ways to increase science literacy through reading and writing in an online science course.

QUESTIONS FOR ANALYSIS/DISCUSSION

1. How can a virtual school teacher provide substantive feedback in an online environment?
2. What are several ways a virtual school mathematics teacher can have students show computations when submitting their work online?
3. Describe several strategies and/or tools a virtual school teacher can use to increase online student–student, student–instructor, and student–content interaction?
4. What strategies can a virtual school teacher utilize for increasing students' science literacy when teaching in a virtual school environment?
5. What possible factors could affect the successfulness of implementing these same strategies in a different subject area? Different age level? Different students?
6. How, if at all, does using new technology tools for delivering the content interfere with student learning?

DEFINITIONS

K–12 online learning: The generic term to refer to distance education at the K–12 level that uses the Internet.

Virtual school: A supplemental K–12 online learning program where students attend a brick-and-mortar or traditional school and are enrolled in one or more online courses to supplemental their classroom studies.

Cyber school: A full-time K–12 online learning program where the students do not attend a brick-and-mortar school, but complete all of their studies online.

Note: These three terms are often used incorrectly as synonyms.

REFERENCES

Ambron, J. (1987). Writing to impose learning in biology. *Journal of College Science and Teaching, 16*(4), 263-266.

Balcazar, F., Hopkins, F., & Suarez, W. (1985). A critical objective view of performance feedback. *Journal of Organizational Behavior Management, 7*(3–4), 65–89.

Barbour, M. K. (2009). Today's student and virtual schooling: The reality, the challenges, the promise. *Journal of Distance Learning, 13*(1), 5–25.

Blomeyer, R. (2002). *Online learning for K–12 students: What do we know now?* Naperville, IL: North Central Regional Educational Laboratory. Retrieved from http://www.ncrel.org/tech/elearn/synthesis.pdf

Cavanaugh, C., Gillan, K., Bosnick, J., Hess, M., & Scott, H. (2008). Effectiveness of interactive online algebra learning tools. *Journal of Educational Computing Research, 38*(1), 67–95.

Center for Technology in Teaching and Learning (2013). *Good practice to inform Iowa learning online.* Retrieved from http://ctlt.iastate.edu/~vhs/index.htm.

Chapanis, A. (1964). Knowledge of performance as an incentive in repetitive monotonous tasks. *Journal of Applied Psychology, 48*, 263–267.

Christensen, C., Johnson, C., & Horn, M. (2011). *Disrupting class, expanded edition: How disruptive innovation will change the way the world learns* (2nd ed.). New York, NY: McGraw-Hill.

Clark, T. (2001). *Virtual schools: Trends and issues–A study of virtual schools in the United States.* San Francisco, CA: Western Regional Educational Laboratories. Retrieved from http://www.wested.org/online_pubs/virtualschools.pdf

Collins, M. A. J. (2000, April). *Do microthemes improve student learning of biology.* Paper presented at the annual National Science Teachers Association national convention, Orlando, FL.

Fathman, A. K., & Whalley, E. (1990). Teacher response to student writing: Focus on form versus content. In B. Kroll (Ed.), *Second language writing: Research insights for the classroom* (178–190). Melbourne, Australia: Cambridge University Press.

Ferdig, R., Papanastasiou, E., DiPietro, M., Radtke, C., Steiner, S., & Smith, H. (2005, October). *Teaching and learning in collaborative virtual high schools.* A presentation at the annual Virtual School Symposium, Denver, CO. Retrieved from http://www.inacol.org/research/docs/Ferdigetal10-05.pdf

Gunawardena, C. N. (1995). Social presence theory and implications for interaction and collaborative learning in computer conferences. *International Journal of Educational Telecommunications, 1*(2/3), 147–166.

Hillman, D. C., Willis, D. J., & Gunawardena, C. N. (1994). Learner-interface interaction in distance education: An extension of contemporary models and strategies for practitioners. *The American Journal of Distance Education, 8*(2), 30–42.

Hurwitz, N. & Hurwitz, S. (2004). Words on paper. *American School Board Journal, 191*(3), 17–26. Retrieved from http://www.asbj.com/MainMenuCategory/Archive/2004/March/WordsonPaperDoc117.aspx?DID=36636

Ilgen, D. R., Fisher, C. D., & Taylor, M. S. (1979). Consequences of individual feedback on behavior in organizations. *Journal of Applied Psychology, 64*(4), 361.

Kennedy, K., & Archambault, L. M. (2012). Offering pre-service teachers field experiences in K–12 online learning: A national survey of teacher education programs. *Journal of Teacher Education, 63*(3), 185–200.

Kirkpatrick, L. D., & Pittendrigh, A. S. (1984). A writing teacher in the physics classroom. *The Physics Teacher, 22,* 159–164.

Louisiana Public Broadcasting. (2009). *Literacy strategies: The quick write.* Baton Rouge, LA. Retrieved from http://www.litandlearn.lpb.org/strategies/strat_quick.pdf

McKee, J., & Ogle, D. (2005). *Integrating instruction: Literacy and science.* New York, NY: Guildford.

Moore, M. G. (1989). Editorial: Three types of interaction. *The American Journal of Distance Education, 3*(2), 1–7.

Moore, R. (1993). Does writing about science improve learning about science? *Journal of College Science Teaching, 22*(4), 212–217.

Moore, R. (1994). Writing to learn biology. *Journal of College Science Teaching, 23*(5), 289–295.

National Center for Educational Statistics. (2009). *The condition of education.* Washington, DC: Author. Retrieved from http://nces.ed.gov/programs/coe/glossary/s.asp

National Commission of Writing. (2003). *The neglected "R": The need for a writing revolution.* New York, NY: College Entrance Examination Board. Retrieved from http://www.writingcommission.org/prod_downloads/writingcom/neglectedr.pdf

Patrick, S. (2007, October). *Welcome and opening.* A presentation at the annual Virtual School Symposium, Louisville, KY.

Project Zero. (2009). *History of Project Zero.* Cambridge, MA: Harvard Graduate School of Education. Retrieved from http://www.pz.harvard.edu/History/History.htm

Public Agenda. (2002). *What happened to the three "Rs"?* New York, NY: Author. Retrieved from http://www.publicagenda.org/press-releases/what-happened-three-rs

Rice, K., & Dawley, L. (2007). *Going virtual! The status of professional development for K–12 online teachers.* Boise, ID: Boise State University. Retrieved from http://edtech.boisestate.edu/goingvirtual/goingvirtual1.pdf

Smith, R., Clark, T., & Blomeyer, R. (2005). *A synthesis of new research on K–12 online learning.* Naperville, IL: Learning Point Associates. Retrieved from http://www.ncrel.org/tech/synthesis/synthesis.pdf

Sutton, L. A. (2001). The principle of vicarious interaction in computer-mediated communications. *International Journal of Educational Telecommunications, 7*(3), 223–242.

Swan, K. (2002). Building learning communities in online courses: The importance of interaction. *Education, Communication & Information, 2*(1), 23–49.

U.S. Department of Education. (2007). *The nation's report card.* Washington, DC: Author. Retrieved from http://nces.ed.gov/nationsreportcard/

Watson, J., Murin, A., Vashaw, L., Gemin, B., & Rapp, C. (2012). *Keeping pace with K–12 online learning: An annual review of policy and practice.* Evergreen, CO: Evergreen Educational Consulting. Retrieved from http://kpk12.com/.

Winokur, J., & Worth, K. (2006). Talk in the science classroom: Looking at what students and teachers need to know and be able to do. In R. Douglas, M. P. Klentschy, K. Worth, & W. Binder (Eds.), *Linking science and literacy in the K–8 classroom,* (pp. 43–58). Arlington, VA: National Science Teachers Association Press.

Work, J. C. (1979). Reducing three papers to ten: A method in literature courses. In G. Stanford (Wd.), *How to handle the paper load: Classroom practices in teaching English* (80–88). Urbana, IL: National Council of Teachers of English.

Yore, L. D., Hand, B., & Prain, V. (1999, January). *Writing-to-learn science: Breakthroughs, barriers, & promises.* Paper presented at the international conference of the Association for Educating Teachers in Science, Austin, TX (ERIC Document Reproduction Service No. ED441688).

FURTHER READINGS

Barbour, M. K., & Reeves, T. C. (2009). The reality of virtual schools: A review of the literature. *Computers and Education, 52*(2), 402–416.

Cavanaugh, C., Barbour, M. K., & Clark, T. (2009). Research and practice in K–12 online learning: A review of literature. *International Review of Research in Open and Distance Learning, 10*(1). Retrieved from http://www.irrodl.org/index.php/irrodl/article/view/607

Clark, T. (2007). Virtual and distance education in North American schools. In M.G. Moore, *Handbook of Distance Education* (2nd ed.), pp. 473–490. Mahwah, NJ: Erlbaum.

Rice, K. L. (2006). A comprehensive look at distance education in the K–12 context. *Journal of Research on Technology in Education, 38*(4), 425–448.

CHAPTER 3

THE POWER OF PRESENCE

Our Quest for the Right Mix of Social Presence in Online Courses

Joanna C. Dunlap and Patrick R. Lowenthal

ABSTRACT

Social presence theory explains how people present themselves as "real" through a communication medium and is a popular construct used to describe how people socially interact in online courses. Because of its intuitive appeal, educators—including ourselves—have experimented with different ways to establish social presence in their online courses. Over the years we've tried many strategies—from rich threaded discussions to personal one-on-one e-mails to digital stories to using social networking tools like Twitter. Over time, we began questioning how students perceive all of the strategies we use (in other words, what strategies were leading to the most bang for our buck). This case study shares the story of our quest for the social presence grail—from the strategies we use in our courses, to our research on students' perceptions of the effectiveness of these strategies.

Real-Life Distance Education, pages 41–66
Copyright © 2014 by Information Age Publishing
All rights of reproduction in any form reserved.

INTRODUCTION

For years, we have collected students' stories about their "best" learning experiences. The results of analyzing these stories has been consistent in terms of what students see as important characteristics of engaging, memorable, and impactful learning experiences (Dunlap & Lowenthal, in press). At the heart of those experiences are relationships—the connections students have with their teacher and with each other. This isn't surprising. Chickering and Gamson (1987) found that students' relationships with faculty had a direct and significant effect on their level of scholarly engagement; this finding is reflected in subsequent research (for example Kuh, 2002, 2009; Kuh, Cruce, Shoup, Kinzie, & Gonyea, 2008).

Online students, though, often complain about feeling like their professor is absent from the course (Smith & Taveras, 2005). For instance, several years ago, Joni set out to design and deliver the "perfect" online course with lots of rich resources, relevant activities, and authentic/real projects only to receive an e-mail from a student midway through the course complimenting her on the course but asking her, "Where are you?"

Bottom line, social connection—also referred to as social presence—is an important aspect of a successful learning experience. Knowing this, we work hard to make sure we attend to social presence needs in the courses we teach. However, we have found it challenging to establish a consistent and adequate level of social presence in our online courses.

To our consternation, we are never fully satisfied with our social-presence accomplishments. In the following case, we describe our quest for the social presence grail and share the results of our obsession to create engaging, memorable, and impactful learning experiences in our online courses by enhancing social presence. We share several of our strategies, and the results of those strategies based on our research efforts. By the end of this case study, you should be able to

- describe the role of social presence as it relates to student engagement in online courses,
- select strategies to establish and maintain social presence in online courses, and
- analyze the perceived effectiveness of both low-technology and high-technology approaches to establishing and maintaining social presence.

CASE STUDY

Social presence theory dates back to the work of Short, Williams, and Christie (1976). Short et al. defined social presence as the quality or state of being between two communicators using a communication medium. While they originally conceptualized social presence primarily as a quality of a communication medium, later researchers (e.g., Gunawardena, 1995; Rourke, Anderson, Garrison, & Archer, 2001) began to re-conceptualize social presence by focusing more on how people used and adapted to a communication medium than solely on the qualities of a communication medium itself. Then in the late 1990s, Garrison, Anderson, and Archer (2000), building on past research, developed the Community of Inquiry (CoI) framework. They posited that a deep and meaningful educational experience actually consists of three types of presence—teaching presence, social presence, and cognitive presence (Garrison et al., 2000). More specifically, they argued that educators use teaching presence (e.g., instructional design, facilitating discourse, and direct instruction) to develop social presence and ultimately cognitive presence in communities of inquiry (Anderson, Rourke, Garrison, & Archer, 2001).

In the CoI framework, the three presences are interconnected, and in service to each other to create online experiences that lead to student learning; because of its balanced emphasis on teaching, social, and cognitive presence, the CoI framework well reflects the social constructivist view that learning occurs in a social context. This does not mean that social presence cannot naturally occur. Walther (1992) argued 20 years ago that people are social creatures and that given enough time people will find ways to use any communication medium for social purposes. Rather, the CoI framework focuses on deliberate strategies educators use (which it refers to as "teaching presence") to establish social presence in support of and service to cognitive presence and overall student learning.

The CoI framework, though, does not provide much guidance on how to design courses, facilitate discourse, and provide direct instruction to facilitate the development of social presence in support of student learning (Garrison & Arbaugh, 2007). For instance, how many threaded discussions should there be in a course? Should the threaded discussions be full-class or small-group discussions? Should students have specific instructional tasks to accomplish during discussions? Should video be used or not? Educators can make some inferences from the indicators of teaching presence developed by Anderson et al. (2001), but even these indicators lack sufficient detail. So despite its intuitive appeal and overall popularity, online educators continue to experiment with different ways to establish social presence (through "teaching presence") in the courses they teach. For instance, over the years we have experimented with a number of different strategies to establish social presence in our courses ranging from rich and personal threaded discussions to personal one-on-one e-mails to digital stories to recently using social networking tools like Twitter (Dunlap & Lowenthal, 2009a, 2009b, 2010b; Lowenthal & Dunlap, 2010). Now a central concept in online learning, researchers have shown—to varying degrees—a relationship between social presence and student satisfaction (Gunawardena,

1995; Gunawardena & Zittle, 1997; Hostetter & Busch, 2006; Richardson & Swan, 2003; So & Brush, 2008), social presence and the development of a community of learners (Rourke, Anderson, Garrison, & Archer, 2001; Rovai, 2002), and social presence and perceived learning (Caspi & Blau, 2008; Richardson & Swan, 2003). However, research to date (whether grounded in the CoI or not) has not identified which strategies are generally better than others for establishing social presence.

Our Quest Began With Our Teaching

After the "Where are you?" experience, we frequently discussed the challenges of establishing and maintaining social presence in service to student learning in our online courses. It was clear to us that it mattered to students and to us. The absence of social presence abraded the overall aesthetic learning experience and undermined student learning. Therefore, because of the potential payoff in terms of student engagement and learning in online courses, we invested substantial time and energy considering and studying social presence. You could say we became obsessed. We read everything we could find on social presence (whether it was grounded in the CoI or not), we participated in conference presentations and other professional development activities, and we experimented.

We then started trying out different things in our courses. The following pages outline some of the things we have done to establish and maintain social presence in our courses (for those grounded in the CoI framework, these can be thought of as teaching presence strategies).

Introductions

We believe there is a connection between students' comfort and sense of trust and their willingness to share and build the level of personal connection and community needed to establish strong social presence (i.e., sense of being "there" and being "real") in an online course. Therefore, we have spent a lot of time thinking about the best way to conduct introductions—that is, "getting-to-know-you" activities—in our courses. Below are a few examples of the types of strategies we use at the start of our courses.

Teacher Bios

Since we ask our students to share information about themselves, we share a lot of information about ourselves. Besides helping students to have insight into our values, passions, interests, credibility and so on, our sharing models the type and level of sharing we want them to engage in, to set the appropriate tone for social presence and establishing a personal, supporting online learning environment. To this end, we share pertinent resources, such as our teaching philosophies, links to articles we've written, presentations we've delivered, our blogs, and so on (see Figures 3.1 and 3.2).

Student Bios

We approach student bios in a variety of ways. Sometimes we use what we call *the Superhero Powers* strategy (which is described later on in this chapter). Other times we use strategies such as *Aladdin's Lamp, One Extra Hour, Digital Storytelling,* or even a *Photo Roster*. For instance, for *Aladdin's Lamp,* we ask students to respond to the following prompt (or a variation of this prompt, depending on the audience) in VoiceThread (see Figure 3.3):

My Story and Resulting Teaching Philosophy

I have had nine educational experiences in my life (and I'm sure many more) that have shaped me as a educator:

1. When I was in 2nd grade, we constantly sang songs and played dodge ball. This made the 2nd grade a lot of fun, personally meaningful, and engaging.

2. When I was in 3rd grade, we spent a lot of time preparing for and participating in spelling bees. For me, these activities instilled pride and enhanced my self-efficacy about being a successful student.

3. When I was in 5th grade, we turned our classroom into a Revolutionary War-era village, made our own money, grew our own beans, and reenacted the Boston Tea Party. These activities were authentic, but at the time I was more interested in being a pop star (or a veterinarian) so the experience was not personally relevant.

4. When I was in 7th grade, our algebra teacher called us "turkeys" if we got an answer wrong or asked a "stupid" question. This made the experience challenging, encouraged me to study hard, but made me anxious about attending class and negatively impacted my efficacy regarding mathematics.

5. When I was in 8th grade, our geometry teacher spoke very softly and very fast, and wrote his notes and formulas on the chalkboard in the tiniest print. I didn't understand anything in class and never quite understood what was expected from me, but it left plenty of time to daydream about being a pop star (or record producer).

6. When I was in 10th grade, our calculus teacher believed that every student should work at her or his own pace. This experience encouraged intentional learning, autonomy, and self-direction, but no accountability or incentive to challenge ourselves. So, I worked on the same chapter all semester long.

7. When I was in 11th grade, our history teacher was a retired colonel who had served in World War II and the Korean War. His lectures were presented as a series of historical accounts and stories. He took us on fieldtrips to monuments and graveyards. He had high expectations, and we had to take a lot of tests and write a lot of essays. Being with him was an engaging and challenging experience, but the assessment methods lacked authenticity and relevance.

8. When I was a freshman at university, we had a literature professor who taught a course on the influential literature of the 1960s. The books we read were engaging, relevant, and sometimes challenging. One day he told a story about a trip he had taken to Dallas in which he went to the grassy knoll across from the schoolbook repository in order to experience that space. He described how he lined himself up on the knoll until he was in the spot he thought the President's car was when the first shot was fired. With tears streaming down his face he said, "When I finally looked down at my feet to see where I was, I saw that the grass was worn away. I then realized that hundreds, maybe even thousands, of people pilgrimaged to this same spot and did exactly what I did because they were drawn...because they needed to be there." This professor connected with us, inspired us, and made us want to impress him. We were never sure how we were being graded, but we all received an A.

9. When I was an MBA student in graduate school, I had a course with Professor Brown (see my digital story about this experience).

Because of my experience in Professor Brown's course (experience #9), I started to understand how a learning experience that enhances learners' educational opportunities and outcomes needs to have elements from all of the experiences shared above.

Figure 3.1 Joni's story and philosophy.

INTE 6710 ~ Creative Designs for Instructional Materials
Getting to Know Joni

Below are a few items that, if viewed/read, you will get to know me a bit better. I think you will find it helpful -- it will give you more insight on me as an educator. Enjoy, and let me know if you have questions or thoughts based on what you see or read.

Joni's most recent article with Patrick Lowenthal, *Defeating the Kobayashi Maru: Supporting Student Retention by Balancing the Needs of the Many and the One*

    Overview: In this article, Patrick and I share strategies for establishing personal, one-on-one relationships between online students and faculty, to attend to identity, individualization, and interpersonal interaction in support of student engagement and retention. Rather than focus on high-tech solutions, we focus on low-tech solutions — the telephone and e-mail — that all faculty and students have at their disposal. These strategies address the needs of the individual within a learning community by striving for balance between group and individual interactions — between the needs of the many and the one. http://www.educause.edu/EDUCAUSE Quarterly/EDUCAUSEQuarterlyMagazineVolum/DefeatingtheKobayashiMaruSuppo/219103

Joni's presentation, *And now for something completely different*

    Overview: I delivered this presentation in May 2010 at the CU Online Symposium (you will need to scroll down the page to locate it). I am sharing it here because I talk about online teaching, and my thoughts about how to enhance engagement -- it might provide some insight into my approach in this course. It also gives you a chance to see me in action in a setting that we will not experience together -- the classroom or lecture hall.

EdTechTalk Live

    Every Friday (unless I have faculty development commitments to the university), I co-host an EdTechTalk Live show called *Instructional Design Live*. I'm not always the one talking, but it is another way to interact with me. The show is Fridays, from 10-10:30am (MST) -- http://edtechtalk.com/live

Joni's blog, *Thoughts on Teaching*

    For the last few years, I've been sharing my thoughts and ideas about teaching in postsecondary settings in my blog, Thoughts on Teaching. It is important for us all to get to know each other, and for you to get to know me well. This is not always easy to do online. Looking at my blog will give you much insight on my thinking about the teaching-learning exchange that we are engaged in via this course. It will hopefully give you a good sense of what my teaching philosophy is, what I value. Check it out, see what you think, post comments if you are so inclined. [Note: Of late I have been lax in posting to this blog, focusing more on publishing my thoughts in various journals.]

Figure 3.2 Additional information Joni shares with students.

Figure 3.3 Aladdin's Lamp getting-to-know-you activity.

The myth of Aladdin and the Lamp is well-known. It is hard not to imagine what you would do with three wishes, and how best to craft the wishes to make sure you achieve the desired outcome...indeed, that's the rub! Most of you know each other from previous courses, but I don't know you yet. So, instead of asking you to rehash what you already know about each other for my benefit, let's try something different...and hopefully you will learn something new about each other in the process. You now have access to Aladdin's Lamp, and the genie is awaiting your three wishes. Our collective wishes have to be different, so as you consider your three, be sure to check to see what others have shared as their three wishes—no duplication allowed! :-)

The *One Extra Hour* activity is similar. We ask students to consider what they would do if they had an extra hour in the day, and why. Through this sharing (and, we participate too), students learn a lot about the priorities and values of their peers (and us) while also learning about their families and work situations. We use tools like VoiceThread for these strategies because students can share a photo and respond to the prompt using their microphones or webcams. We have found that hearing and seeing each other in this context helps all of us feel more connected.

We also have our students create *Digital Stories* about themselves. We tend to simply ask them to share something about themselves (e.g., What did you do over Winter break?) using an application of their choice (e.g., Microsoft PhotoStory, iMovie, Animoto, VoiceThread). Learning little things about each other through sharing digital stories helps establish social presence in a traditionally text heavy medium (Lowenthal & Dunlap, 2010).

One last strategy we use for student bios is the creation of a *Photo Roster* (see Figure 3.4). While students can attach an image in a threaded discussion or create a "home page" or profile in certain learning management systems (LMS), this results in a disjointed final product. We instead prefer to create one document that has pictures and bio information about each student. By creating a Google Doc and making it editable by anyone, students can quickly login and fill in predetermined information as well as include a photo.

5-Minute Conversations

During the first few weeks of our courses, we also invite students to participate in a 5-minute phone conversation with us (see Figure 3.5). We do this so our students might feel more connected and less distant from us. We have found that these early phone conversations lead to subsequent phone conversations with students for purposes of project brainstorming, content clarification, and formative feedback—and in a much more efficient and personal way than if we had participated in the same exchanges via a threaded discussion.

Bios

INTE 5670 - Spring 2011

Directions: Please find your name below and complete your bio. If you are comfortable with it, please add a picture as well. If your name isn't listed below, just add a column below and add your information. [Note: I (Patrick) simply took the class list which isn't always correct]

Fill in the template as best you can and only include information if you are comfortable sharing it with the class. If an item doesn't apply to you, simply delete it.

Lowenthal, Patrick
website: www.patricklowenthal.com
email: patrick.lowenthal@ucdenver.edu
instant message: patrick.lowenthal@ucdenver.edu (Windows Live)
twitter: plowenthal
google docs acct: patrick.lowenthal@ucdenver.edu
city / state: Westminster, CO

background: Patrick Lowenthal is an Academic Technology Coordinator at CU Online at the University of Colorado Denver. He worked at Regis University in Teacher Education for six years before coming to UCD in 2008. He is a doctoral student studying instructional design and technology at UCD. His research interests focus on instructional communication, with a specific focus on

Figure 3.4   Patrick's photo roster.

Hello everyone, and welcome to INTE 6710! As a starting place, please click on Wk 1 (8/23-29) to see this week's agenda. This week's activities are focused on getting oriented to the course and each other. Please let me know if you have any questions as you move forward with the activities.

Over the next few weeks, I'd like to have a 5-minute phone conversation with each of you. I like to do this at the start of a course so that we might feel more connected, less distant from each other. The agenda -- to hear each other laugh! But, also, to address any questions you may have about the course. If this works for you too, please send me an email with a phone number and some times of day when I might reach you at that number. My email address is joni.dunlap@ucdenver.edu.

I am pleased to be working with you this semester, and am looking forward to our time together.

-Joni

Figure 3.5   Invitation for a 5-minute phone conversation.

Orientations

We also focus on orienting students to our courses much like we do in a face-to-face course. The following are a few "finding-your-way-around" activities we use to help students with course orientation, during the first week and throughout the term.

Orientation Videos

We present short orientation videos, with each video walking students through different aspects of the course shell, learning activities, and projects (see Figure 3.6). Using tools like Jing, we create screencasts showing students all around the course shell. We interject our sense of humor where possible, tell stories, and provide explanations for our design decisions. These videos not only orient students to the course, but to us as well (see this example of a video Patrick used to orient his students to the first unit in his course: http://www.screencast.com/t/MmM3MjM5MjUt).

Course & Syllabus Scavenger Hunt

Videos, though, aren't the only way to orient students to a course. We also use the quiz feature in our LMS to create a course and syllabus scavenger hunt that students submit by the end of the first week. To complete the scavenger hunt, students have to read the syllabus, locate materials, and watch the orientation videos. The results of the scavenger hunt reassure us that students are locating and tracking important course information, and alert us to any misconceptions or confusions that individual students have

Figure 3.6 Example of video orientation.

about the materials so we can immediately reach out to them and provide additional support and guidance.

Weekly Announcements

At the start of each week, we post a new announcement orienting students to the activities of the week, and also send the announcement to students via e-mail (see Figure 3.7). Even though this information exists elsewhere in the course, we like to reach out to students (as opposed to making them log into the course shell) with an enthusiastic and more personal announcement about the week (whether in text format or video). In each announcement, we provide a reminder about how they should focus their time and energy during the week. We also include personal information (e.g., like what we did the week before) and well wishes for a successful up-coming week.

Weekly Agendas

Finally, for each week in the course, we provide students with a week-ly agenda checklist that they can print out to help them track what they should be working on during the week (see Figure 3.8). Again, although

---

Can you believe that it is October? And, we are almost halfway through the semester? I can't...

I really enjoyed reviewing your *Project 1: Presentation Makeover Magic* projects this last week. You each received detailed notes from me – things for you to consider, for revisions and future projects. You may have noticed that although I provided a lot of comments about various aspects of the presentation and design document, I rarely took many points off unless there was a significant issue. I did try to provide clear directions for any revision recommendations, but please let me know if you have any questions. Vague comments from me can be maddening, I know, so be sure to connect with me for clarification, if need be; related, connecting over the phone is always an option if that is helpful. Again, thank you for sharing your work with me, and I look forward to seeing what you do next!

This week, I will send you each a brief email regarding your drafts of Sections 1-6 of the design document for *Project 2: Job Aid Makeover Spectacular* -- a "looks like you are on the right track" note, addressing any issues in the draft that may be helpful to address. As before, please feel free to continue your work on the project while you are waiting for my email -- I'm sure you are all on track, my email will just make it "official". :-)

This week, while you are continuing your work on Project 2, I ask you to participate in two asynchronous discussion activities related to our readings last week. (We will do something similar next week about this week's readings.)

There will be no synchronous Connect session this week. Please see the Week 7 agenda for more information about the next session so you can plan.

Finally, a quick debrief on the Week 6 activities. First, I love the results of the Virtual Paper Bag, Part 2 activity -- so creative, and dare I say fun. :-) I learned a bit more about each of you through this activity, and I hope you learned a bit more about each other too. Also, I hope it helped to play with the idea of comics and graphic novels via this activity, as well as test out a tool or two that may be useful for Project 2.

Regarding the Debriefing David Thomas' Session activity, thank you for your contributions both during the live session with David and in the asynchronous discussion afterward. David always challenges me to think differently about my work, and fun is one of my favorite things to hear him talk about...fun is a big part of what I consider when I design courses and activities (can you see my efforts in this course? ;-)). It is challenging to think about what fun is, and how to incorporate it well -- purposefully in service of the learning objectives -- in stand-alone instructional materials like those we are creating in this course...but it is a good challenge, and I hope all of you are considering as you move on in the course.

Have a great week! See you online!

This weekend, the girls built a couple of estes rockets with their dad, and then met up with friends to fire them off. What a blast! :-)

Figure 3.7 Weekly announcement.

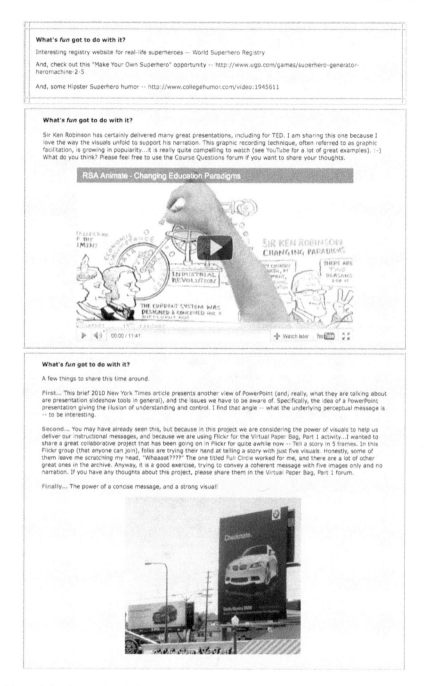

Figure 3.8   Examples of the "What's Fun Got to Do With It?" part of the weekly agendas.

this information exists in the course's master calendar, it helps to have the week's activities laid out in a checklist format. We also use the agendas as another way to help students connect with us by adding personal touches. For instance, Joni includes inspirational artwork and music at the top of each agenda and a "What's *fun* got to do with it?" section at the bottom, where she shares fun and interesting items that are related to the activities of the week.

Personalized and Detailed Feedback

Assessment and evaluation (and the feedback it entails) are difficult aspects of teaching. Whenever possible we strive to provide personalized and detailed feedback to our students to not only improve the learning process but also to maintain our social presence and connection with each student throughout the semester. The following are a few ways that we do this:

One-on-One and Group E-mails

As low tech as it might appear and while it goes against the school of thought that all communication should be kept within the LMS, we are strong believers in the power of one-on-one e-mails (see Dunlap & Lowenthal, 2010c). While we use one-on-one and group e-mails in a variety of ways throughout the semester, we primarily use it as a way to provide personalized detailed feedback with our students (see Figure 3.9).

Hello, everyone! At this point you should have received an individual email from me regarding your peer reviews for course colleagues. A few general notes to keep in mind for the future:

- Make sure that peer reviewers have everything they need to write a helpful review, e.g., guiding questions, original presentation, etc.
- The quality of the guiding questions has a real influence over the quality of the feedback received. So, please do not take lightly your guiding questions for future peer reviews. Make sure they are worded in a way that invites suggestions.
- The quality of the peer-review responses makes or breaks the value of this activity. If the peer-review responses are not helpful, then time and energy has been wasted for all involved. Please be sure to remember the directions for peer-review activities: (a) to include at least one suggestion for improvement for each question, and (b) aim for a review that is 500 words (which actually isn't hard to do if you provide at least one suggestion per question).
- Follow-up with feedback that needs clarification or elaboration. If you do not fully grasp what a reviewer has shared, please do not hesitate to follow-up with them in the threaded discussion or via email. Also, I noticed a few "thank you" posts after reviews were shared...that's nice, I like it. :-)

Thank you for taking the time to complete these reviews. I find that it is helpful to no only receive feedback and suggestions for enhancement, but to see what other people are doing. I hope you found the experience rewarding.

As you process the feedback and put the final touches on your presentation and design document, please let me know if you have any questions. You can connect with me via the course shell, email, or phone (home number is <phone number>, and you are welcome to use it).

I look forward to reviewing your projects next week! Have a great weekend!

-Joni

Figure 3.9   Detailed feedback via a group e-mail.

Video Feedback

Sometimes though, we find the need to provide feedback in a different—high tech—format. For instance, Patrick uses screen recording tools like Jing to provide video feedback to his students on certain assignments in which it is hard to provide feedback in text alone. While cumbersome in that you have to get all set up with your microphone and the software and so forth, students have commented on how valuable it is to hear both the positive and the negative feedback in the tone of our voices.

Reconnecting

In our experience, it is not realistic to get to know people in an online course with one getting-to-know-you activity during the first week of class. Establishing social presence and building relationships and community requires multiple opportunities to share and connect. So, for reconnection purposes, we use activities like the following to reengage students every few weeks.

Superhero Powers

For this activity, we ask students to respond to the following prompt: *What are your superhero powers? What is your superhero moniker? And, how do your superhero powers help you in life?* Using VoiceThread, students share a photo and record their response. Their creative responses are so much fun . . . and help us learn about the assets each student sees as her or his strengths (see Figure 3.10).

Figure 3.10 Superhero Powers reconnecting activity.

Virtual Paper Bag

For this activity, students pick five items that represent who they are and what is important to them. They pull together visual representations of their five items for a virtual paper bag that they share using a tool like Flickr. Once everyone has posted their virtual paper bag, students review each other's, and discuss the meaning of the items. Students learn about each other's passions, values, families, and the like; learn about differences and similarities; and learn each other's stories. This activity helps students feel more connected because of the personal content of the photos and emotion involved in telling their stories.

Soundtrack of Your Life

Another reconnecting activity (and one of our personal favorites) involves having our students create a playlist of six songs: two that represent their past, two that represent their present, and two that represent their planned/hoped for future. Students share their playlists (using a digital jukebox like Grooveshark). They then ask questions about the songs to figure out why certain songs were selected. You can learn a lot about someone from the music they select (Dunlap & Lowenthal, 2010b).

Threaded Discussions

Threaded discussions have been described as the bread and butter of online courses because they are often the primary tool used for student-instructor and student-student communication and interaction (Dunlap, 2009a). They are a great way for students to test their new knowledge, represent their conceptual understanding, and find their professional voices. However, we have found over the years—and the literature supports our experience—that threaded discussions in and of themselves are not inherently good or bad. Rather, their worth typically depends on how they are set up and used in any given course. Therefore, we tend to think a lot about how, when, and why we use threaded discussions to ensure they consistently benefit and support student learning and social presence. The following are a couple of ways we use threaded discussions for social presence purposes:

Non-Threatening Discussions

We don't assume our students know how to effectively use online threaded discussions. For purposes of practicing online discussion (using the tools, protocols, etiquette, etc.), we provide our students with ample opportunities to discuss non-threatening, low-judgmental topics as well as non-course related topics (see Dunlap, 2009a, under Further Readings). For example: We have students visit the Picassohead website (www.picassohead.

com) and create a self-portrait, then submit a link to a threaded discussion forum. Once posted, we encourage students to comment on each other's artwork. We also post entertaining photos (not directly related to the course content) and ask students to share their captions. Student captions for the following image have included:

- Wait please! I do have good news...I just saved tons of money on my car insurance by switching to Geico.
- I can take the giant brain, I can take the claws for hands, but why must you insist on wearing blue leather pants every time we go out?
- Listen, you're a nice guy and have a great personality, but my mother simply won't accept a son-in-law whose brain is on the outside.

Activities like this can help introduce humor into threaded discussions which can be difficult to do—but also can help with social presence (see Figure 3.11).

Discussion Protocols

The same-old-same-old threaded discussion forum format (i.e., instructor posts a question, and each student is required to post an original response and comment on posts from two peers) can be detrimental to social presence and student engagement. Therefore, we use different discussion protocols to ensure the continuing benefit of online discussions while minimizing the potential boredom that comes from threaded-discussion misuse

Figure 3.11   Image used for nonthreatening discussion.

and overuse, and maximizing social presence through student responsibility and engagement (see Dunlap, 2009b, under Further Readings). Discussion protocols also serve to balance student voices, ensuring that everyone in the class has the same opportunity to contribute to the discussion. Finally, discussion protocols provide students with specific roles and directions for how to engage in a productive discussion. An example of a discussion protocol we use is *The Final Post.* Adapted for online discussion from McDonald et al.'s (2003) *The Final Word* protocol, the steps are:

1. Working in a small group of 4–5 students, each student identifies one of the most significant ideas from the reading, illustrated by a quote or excerpt. (Each student should have a backup quote/excerpt in case another student has already posted the same quote/excerpt.)
2. Each student starts a new thread by posting the quote/excerpt from the text that particularly struck her or him. The student points out where the quote is in the text. In approximately 250 words, the student describes why that quote/excerpt struck her or him. (Specify a deadline for the original posts.)
3. Each student responds to that quote/excerpt and what the original student wrote, using approximately 150 words. The purpose of the response is to expand on the original student's thinking about the topic, to provide a different perspective on the topic, to clarify thinking about the topic, and to question the original student's assumptions about the topic. (Specify a deadline for these posts.)
4. After each student in the group has responded to the original post, the first student has the "final word." In approximately 150 words, the original student responds to what has been shared by the rest of the group, offering what she or he is now thinking about the topic, and her or his reaction to what the other students have posted. (Specify a deadline for the "final word" post.)
5. This process continues until everyone has had the opportunity to have the "final word." This means that 4–5 discussions are happening simultaneously within a particular timeframe (e.g., 1 week), or that they are happening one at a time (each discussion over 1–2 days).

Small Groups

Through small-group work and collaboration, students experience and develop an appreciation for multiple perspectives; refine their knowledge through argumentation, structured controversy, and the sharing of ideas and perspectives; learn to use colleagues as resources; and are more willing to take on the risk required to tackle complex, ill-structured problems (Dunlap & Grabinger, 2003). Because of the potential value of small-group work and collaboration on student learning and engagement, and because it is a clear way of involving students in student–student interactions that enhance social presence, we use various small-group and collaboration strategies and activities in our online courses (see Dunlap, 2009c, under Further Readings). Below we describe a few of our activities.

Peer Review

A good way to establish and maintain social presence among students in an online course is through peer review activities. Peer review, while a very authentic activity, is one we find many students struggle with. Therefore, we use a "no penalty" approach to peer reviews:

> The peer review teams are posted in the forum where you will post your drafts of this project. In terms of process, as a starting place, I suggest that you review the project description and assessment tool (not that you already aren't quite familiar) as a reminder of what everyone is aiming for. Please provide your peers with honest constructive feedback on the design of their instructional presentations, answering the five questions they provided to guide your review; **you must provide at least one suggestion for improvement for each question**. Your job as a peer reviewer is to help your peers create the best possible product, so you do them no service if you are not honest and open with your feedback. Be constructive and professional. Please provide 500 words of feedback in response to the five questions each peer asks you to consider. Thank you! [Final note: If when you sit down to do the peer reviews you find that one of your peers has not posted a draft by the due date, then you are not held responsible. The peer who did not post by the due date will lose out on valuable feedback (and points), and you will receive credit for the review regardless.]

"No Jeopardy" Group Work

While many faculty often avoid using group work online to avoid any potential headaches (Wray, Lowenthal, Bates, & Stevens, 2008), we are strong believers in the importance of collaborating with others as well as learning how to effectively work with a group online—not to mention the inherent social presence opportunities when working closely with one's peers. We use "no jeopardy" approaches to collaborative work that allow for a submitted product to be complete without a missing member's contribution. Examples include: each student completes an allocated task that contributes to the final team product and gets the marks for that task; each student writes and submits an individual report based on the team's work on the task/project; each student takes an exam, with exam questions that specifically target the team project, and can only be answered by students who have been thoroughly involved in the project; each student's contribution is assessed via individually-produced evidence such as status reports, journals, time logs, and direct observation; each student produces an individual paper based on the team project.

Document Co-Creation

Finally, we often use Google Docs and Spreadsheets in our online courses to support students' document co-creation activities and enhance social presence. One example of this use is students' co-creation of a *Top-100 List of Design Guidelines* (also called the *What We Know List*), used to support their instructional design work (see Figure 3.12). Developed in Google Docs over the course of the semester, students contribute new design guidelines with supporting citations based on the coursework and readings. By the end of the semester, students walk away with a robust set of design guidelines summarizing the readings that can be used as they continue their design work outside of the course. Google Docs makes it possible for our online students to collectively develop a unique document, each sharing expertise, reviewing each others' contributions for appropriate modifications and redundancy reductions, summarizing and synthesizing what they have learned from the course readings, and reflecting on the value of their individual contributions and the value of the collection of guidelines in general.

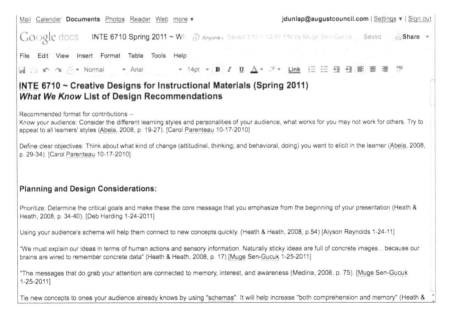

Figure 3.12 Document cocreation activity.

Free-Flowing, Organic Interactions

Last but not least, one of our most recent attempts at establishing and maintaining social presence in our courses involves social networking tools—specifically, Twitter. We began using Twitter (and inviting our students to follow us) because we wanted to have an informal, playful way for our online students to connect with us and each other throughout the day.

On our quest for the social presence grail—as effective as we thought many of the strategies we have previously discussed were—we felt confined within the structure of the LMS. This was exacerbated by the fact that we have been missing the informal, playful banter and chit-chat that is possible when everyone is physically located in the same geographic space. This banter helps students connect with us, and experience our personalities. And, it helps them connect with each other in a more emotional way. Twitter seemed to have potential to further support our social-presence efforts.

Twitter

We invite our students to follow us on Twitter and to follow each other. In addition, we provide a list of people outside of the course who tweet about course-relevant topics to follow as well as a number of publications and professional organizations.

Our decision to use Twitter to enhance social presence in our online courses was reinforced by students' experiences (see Dunlap & Lowenthal, 2009a, 2009b) as well as the plain fact that our communications via Twitter seemed much more natural than logging into our LMS, getting into the course shell, then getting into a discussion forum and posting a message . . . and then waiting for someone to respond later (after she or he has already moved on to other work, thoughts, issues). But unlike many of the other strategies, we found Twitter to be an extremely time consuming strategy so we were left wondering about its effectiveness.

Our Quest Led Us to Dig Deeper

As is clear from the selection of strategies described above, we exert a lot of time and energy on establishing and maintaining social presence in support of student learning in our online courses, using a variety of both low-technology and high-technology strategies. Our sense was always that for the most part it was time well spent—we knew that we were benefiting from our efforts and it seemed that students were as well. For us, we really felt like we were getting to know our students better, and had a closer, more personal and supportive relationship with individual students as opposed to the group (see Dunlap & Lowenthal, 2010c, for more on our efforts to build relationships with individual students in online courses). Even though we believed our efforts were effective, we couldn't help but wonder if maybe there was a social-presence formula for selecting the right strategies for an online course. We were doing so many things to support social presence, maybe we were doing too much? Maybe we didn't have to do all that we were doing (e.g., maybe all the effort we were putting into using Twitter wasn't worth it)? Maybe there was an ideal combination of strategies for achieving the right level of social presence in an online course, and that we were over the threshold and doing more than we needed to? Even though we worked hard to tie the strategies to learning objectives and relevant course content and activities, maybe we were turning students off with all of this social-presence stuff? These were the questions we kept asking ourselves, even though—through informal data collection—students seemed to approve of and value our efforts. Because of these questions, we decided to better track students' feedback, and conduct a more formal study on the perceived effectiveness of the various social-presence strategies we were using in our online courses.

Our goal here is not to report all of the findings of our formal inquiry (see Lowenthal & Dunlap, 2011, for a report of our formal inquiry). However, we hope that presenting a few key findings from our inquiry will help you better understand our quest for the social presence grail. We first began collecting comments from students (e.g., via midterm and end-of-term surveys) about our use of specific strategies to enhance social presence. Our students' comments were consistently positive about many of the strategies described earlier in this chapter. The following are a few examples:

- In general, the discussions helped me feel connected to my course colleagues. The discussions also helped me feel connected to you (Joni). In addition, the feedback I received on my projects helped quite a bit as well.
- The structured discussions that we had always help me, sometimes I may miss a point that someone else may see, so I like that and the various points other students make. I also like the peer review on the projects, I think that helped me feel connected. I think you did a great job with interacting with the discussions and any email I sent you answered quickly, so I felt connected.
- The part of the course that made me feel connected to the other students was the peer reviews. The aspect of the course that helped me feel connected to the instructor was the feedback I received from the instructor and the follow-up email exchanges.
- I really liked being an integral part of reviewing. I felt (especially in certain assignment) that I really got some insight into how the other

students interpreted the assignments and put their own life (either work or other parts of their life) into the assignment.

- I really LOVE twittering with everyone. It really made me feel like we knew each other more and were actually in class together.
- The introductory music activity was absolutely awesome to help in getting to know people. Many of us have worked together the past few semesters, but this helped shed a lot of light of a more personal nature about their lives. I would also say reading and reviewing others assignments and postings also helped indirectly connect....
- The Soundtrack of Your Life: It was a creative way to introduce ourselves to each other that communicated something about ourselves instead of using words. I thought the Google Doc activities were an excellent way to express ourselves freely for others to read freely about our expressions.
- In terms of relating to Joni, I felt your contributions to discussions and commentary were obviously the biggest way to get your thoughts on our work. I would periodically check your blogs to review your thoughts, and the artwork you chose to illustrate each week did give some ideas as to where you are coming from or whom you are.

After analyzing comments like these, we created and administered a survey to systematically investigate students' perceptions of our social-presence efforts. Part of the survey specifically asked students to rate the degree to which different instructional technologies and strategies helped them to connect with her or his instructor. We found that one-on-one e-mails as well as instructor bios were the two highest ranked activities across the courses, followed closely by individualized, detailed feedback; digital storytelling; and the 5-minute phone call. On the other hand, Twitter surprisingly was ranked the lowest.

We also asked students to rate the degree to which different instructional technologies and strategies helped them connect with their fellow students. Digital storytelling and one-on-one e-mails were ranked the highest, followed closely by peer reviews, the virtual paper bag activity, and the soundtrack of your life activity. Again, Twitter was ranked the lowest.

Now we could go on about some of the students' neutral and negative reactions to Twitter but in ways that would be missing our point and beyond the scope of this chapter. What's interesting about this to us is that while we were receiving overall good feedback about Twitter (see Dunlap & Lowenthal, 2009a), when compared to all the other things we were doing, it couldn't compare. This doesn't mean it wasn't effective because overall only a handful of students explicitly stated it wasn't, but it does cause us to question the return-on-investment achieved given the level of time and effort it takes to use a tool like Twitter for social presence purposes.

Finally, we interviewed a small group of students who had high and low overall social presence scores (based on their answers on the survey) in an effort to dig deeper. Three important themes emerged from the interviews regarding what instructors should do to enhance social presence in support of student learning:

- Provide personal, individualized feedback
- Provide opportunities for students to build relationships through (postive) collaborative work and sharing
- Be accessible

Our students reported that it wasn't that our other strategies weren't of value, but that these specific strategies had the "biggest bang for the buck." Finally, all of our students (both those who had a high and those with a low social presence score) reported that they believed social presence was a critical aspect of the online course experience, contributing to their learning, achievement of course-specific learning objectives, and overall professional preparation.

IMPLICATIONS FOR DISTANCE EDUCATION

So where does this leave us on our quest for the social presence grail? Well, our own experiences coupled with our data collection suggest that many if not all of our social presence strategies are effective. Further, our more formal analysis leads us to wonder if low-technology solutions (e.g., personalized, detailed written feedback; one-on-one e-mails; phone conversations) are more impactful than high-technology solutions (e.g., Twitter) in the long run.

When trying to balance workload, which online faculty often have to do (see Dunlap, 2005), it may be more important to attend to these "low-tech" activities rather than others to enhance social presence in online courses. Although there seems to be some clear winners and losers in terms of enhancing social presence, our inquiry suggests that in any group there is a range of preferences, with one strategy not fulfilling the needs of all students. We also surmise that students' perception of social presence isn't enhanced by just one instructional strategy or tool, but instead by a carefully crafted set of instructional strategies and tools that reinforce social presence as a valued part of the teaching-learning experience.

We hope our description of the social-presence strategies we use and the results of our inquiry into how students perceive the effectiveness of social-presence strategies will inform your selection of instructional strategies and tools for enhancing social presence in online courses, and provide insight into why certain strategies and tools are more effective than others.

CONCLUSION

Our personal quest is ongoing—to improve our own online teaching and our students' learning experiences by better understanding where to invest time and energy to get the biggest social-presence bang for the buck. So far our experience coupled with our research suggest that on-going low-tech strategies like one-on-one e-mails and detailed feedback might be more effective than one-time high-tech strategies. We are not about to abandon all of our high-tech strategies nor are we going to ignore future technologies that might help establish and maintain social presence in support of student learning in online courses, but at the same time we think it is important to recognize the power of low-tech strategies and the various needs of learners. The bottom line is that we are obsessed with social presence (whether that be natural ways people adapt to a communication medium or behaviors that result from specific teaching presence strategies) in the courses we teach, and we hope you will become obsessed as well and join us on the journey for the social-presence grail.

QUESTIONS FOR ANALYSIS/DISCUSSION

1. Considering your own experience as an online student or online instructor, how important do you think social presence is in online courses? Why?
2. Given the data results, why do you think students seem to prefer specific social-presence strategies over others? Why do you think students indicate preferring one-on-one e-mails over all other strategies? Why do you think some students indicate disliking Twitter as a social-presence strategy?
3. Given the experience described in this case study, how would you suggest online instructors address social presence needs in their courses? What specific strategies would you recommend they incorporate first, to get the biggest bang for their buck? Why those specific strategies?
4. After selecting specific social-presence strategies to incorporate into your online course, how would you specifically implement and go about assessing the effectiveness of those strategies? Describe your inquiry plan-of-action.
5. How would you approach investigating the role of social presence as it relates to student engagement in online courses?

REFERENCES

Anderson, T., Rourke, L., Garrison, D. R., & Archer, W. (2001). Assessing teaching presence in a computer conferencing context. *Journal of Asynchronous Learning Networks, 5*(2), 1–17.

Caspi, A., & Blau, I. (2008). Social presence in online discussion groups: Testing three conceptions and their relations to perceived learning. *Social Psychology of Education, 11*(3), 323–346.

Chickering, A. W., & Gamson, Z. (1987). Seven principles for good practice in undergraduate education. *AAHE Bulletin, 40*(7), 3–7.

Dunlap, J. C. (2005). Workload reduction in online courses: Getting some shuteye. *Performance Improvement, 44*(5), 18–25.

Dunlap, J. C., & Grabinger, R. S. (2003). Preparing students for lifelong learning: A review of instructional methodologies. *Performance Improvement Quarterly, 16*(2), 6–25.

Dunlap, J. C., & Lowenthal, P. R. (2009a). Tweeting the night away: Using Twitter to enhance social presence. *Journal of Information Systems Education, 20*(2), 129–136.

Dunlap, J. C., & Lowenthal, P. R. (2009b). Horton hears a tweet. *EDUCAUSE Quarterly, 32*(4). Retrieved from http://www.educause.edu/ero/article/horton-hears-tweet

Dunlap, J. C., & Lowenthal, P. R. (in press). What's your best learning experience? Our story about using stories to solve instructional problems. *International Journal of Teaching and Learning in Higher Education.*

Dunlap, J. C., & Lowenthal, P. R. (2010b). Hot for teacher: Using digital music to enhance students' experience in online courses. *TechTrends, 54*(4), 58–73.

Dunlap, J. C., & Lowenthal, P. R. (2010c). Defeating the Kobayashi Maru: Supporting student retention by balancing the needs of the many and the one. *EDUCAUSE Quarterly, 33*(4). Retrieved from http://www.educause.edu/ero/article/defeating-kobayashi-maru-supporting-student-retention-balancing-needs-many-and-one

Garrison, D. R., Anderson, T., & Archer, W. (2000). Critical inquiry in a text-based environment: Computer conferencing in higher education. *The Internet and Higher Education, 2*(2–3), 87–105.

Garrison, D. R., & Arbaugh, J.B. (2007). Researching the community of inquiry framework: Review, issues, and future directions. *The Internet and Higher Education, 10*(3), 157–172.

Gunawardena, C. N. (1995). Social presence theory and implications for interaction and collaborative learning in computer conferences. *International Journal of Educational Telecommunications, 1*(2/3), 147–166.

Gunawardena, C. N., & Zittle, F. J. (1997). Social presence as a predictor of satisfaction within a computer-mediated conferencing environment. *The American Journal of Distance Education, 11*(3), 8–26.

Hostetter, C., & Busch, M. (2006). Measuring up online: The relationship between social presence and student learning satisfaction. *Journal of Scholarship of Teaching and Learning, 6*(2), 1–12.

Kuh G. D. (2002). The National Survey of Student Engagement: Conceptual framework and overview of psychometric properties. Center for Postsecondary Research, Indiana University, Bloomington. Retrieved from http://nsse.iub.edu/pdf/psychometric_framework_2002.pdf

Kuh G. D. (2009). What student affairs professionals need to know about student engagement. *Journal of College Student Development, 50,* 683–706.

Kuh G. D., Cruce T. M., Shoup R., Kinzie J., & Gonyea, R. M. (2008). Unmasking the effects of student engagement on first-year college grades and persistence. *Journal of Higher Education 79,* 540–563.

Lowenthal, P. R., & Dunlap, J. (2010). From pixel on a screen to real person in your students' lives: Establishing social presence using digital storytelling. *The Internet and Higher Education, 13*(1-2), 70–72.

Lowenthal, P. R., & Dunlap, J. (2011, April). Investigating students' perceptions of various instructional strategies to establish social presence. Paper presented at the annual meeting of the American Educational Research Association, New Orleans, LA.

McDonald, J., Mohr, N., Dichter, A., & McDonald, E. (2003). *The power of protocols: An educator's guide to better practice.* New York, NY: Teachers College Press.

Richardson, J. C., & Swan, K. (2003). Examining social presence in online courses in relation to students' perceived learning and satisfaction. *Journal of Asynchronous Learning Networks, 7*(1), 68–88.

Rourke, L., Anderson, T., Garrison, D. R., & Archer, W. (2001). Assessing social presence in asynchronous text-based computer conferencing. *Journal of Distance Education, 14*(2). Retrieved from http://cade.athabascau.ca/vol14.2/rourke_et_al.html

Rovai, A. P. (2002). Building a sense of community at a distance. *International Review of Research in Open and Distance Learning, 3*(1). Retrieved from http://www.irrodl.org/index.php/irrodl/article/view/79/153

Short, J., Williams, E., & Christie, B. (1976). *The social psychology of telecommunications.* London, UK: Wiley.

Smith, G. G., & Taveras, M. (2005, January). The missing instructor: Does e-learning promote absenteeism? *eLearn Magazine,* 1. Retrieved from http://www.elearnmag.org/subpage.cfm?section=tutorials&article=18-1

So, H.-Y., & Brush, T. (2008). Students' perceptions of collaborative learning, social presence, and satisfaction in blended learning environment: Relationships and critical factors. *Computers & Education, 51*(1), 318–336.

Walther, J. B. (1992). Interpersonal effects in computer-mediated interaction: A relational perspective. *Communication Research, 19,* 52–90.

Wray, M., Lowenthal, P. R., Bates, B., & Stevens, E. (2008). Investigating perceptions of teaching online & f2f. *Academic Exchange Quarterly, 12*(4), 243–248.

FURTHER READINGS

Dunlap, J. C. (2009a). Down-and-dirty guidelines for effective discussions in online courses. In P. R. Lowenthal, D. Thomas, A. Thai, & B. Yuhnke (Eds.), *The CU Online handbook. Teach differently: Create and collaborate* (pp. 93–99). Raleigh, NC: Lulu Enterprises. Retrieved from http://www.ucdenver.edu/academics/CUOnline/FacultyResources/additionalResources/Handbook/Documents/GuidelinesEffectiveDiscussions.pdf

Dunlap, J. C. (2009b). Protocols for online discussions. In P. R. Lowenthal, D. Thomas, A. Thai, & B. Yuhnke (Eds.), *The CU Online handbook. Teach differently: Create and collaborate* (pp. 101–105). Raleigh, NC: Lulu Enterprises. Retrieved from http://www.ucdenver.edu/academics/CUOnline/FacultyResources/additionalResources/Handbook/Documents/DiscussionProtocols.pdf

Dunlap, J. C. (2009c). Improving the odds of effective collaborative work in online courses. In P. R. Lowenthal, D. Thomas, A. Thai, & B. Yuhnke (Eds.), *The CU Online handbook. Teach differently: Create and collaborate* (pp. 107–111). Raleigh, NC: Lulu Enterprises. Retrieved from http://www.ucdenver.edu/academics/CUOnline/FacultyResources/additionalResources/Handbook/Documents/EffectiveCollaborativeWork.pdf

Lowenthal, P. R. (2009). The evolution and influence of social presence theory on online learning. In T. T. Kidd (Ed.), *Online education and adult learning: New frontiers for teaching practices* (pp. 124–139). Hershey, PA: IGI Global.

CHAPTER 4

INDIVIDUALIZING FEEDBACK

One Path to Success in a Distance Learning Environment

Roberta Ross-Fisher

ABSTRACT

This chapter discusses the author's challenge of providing academic support to struggling students in an online learning environment; the case study is focused on efforts to elevate student motivation, confidence, and academic success through appropriate feedback tailored to preferred learning styles and principles of adult learning theory. While text-based, audio-based, and video-based feedback was offered, the greatest success came when using video-based feedback.

INTRODUCTION

At the nation's only online competency-based institution, students at Western Governors University (WGU) do not complete traditional coursework, either face-to-face or in a distance learning environment. Instead, they demonstrate their knowledge in a series of carefully planned assessments throughout their program. These assessments require students to utilize

Real-Life Distance Education, pages 67–80

a course of study (similar to what many universities refer to as a syllabus, but typically more in-depth and detailed) and accompanying learning resources to help them think about and apply what they know and can do at all levels of Bloom's Taxonomy. Virtual learning communities are also part of the student learning process; each community is facilitated by one or more academic mentors who possess strong academic and experiential background in the area. These learning communities provide rich, vibrant opportunities for intellectual exchange of ideas, cameraderie, and further study. Discussion boards are active places of conversation, and mentors offer webinars, teleconferences, and chat sessions on a regular basis to provide further student support. For the purpose of clarification, mentors do not *teach* students at WGU; they instead serve as coaches or facilitators of student-led learning.

There are three types of required assessments at this university: the objective competency assessment, the field experience assessment, and the performance assessment. For the purpose of this case study, the performance assessment is most pertinent to the discussion. Upon completion of each course of study, students must demonstrate their understanding of specific standards-based competencies and objectives through a series of applications. These performance assessments vary in scope and nature; some may include the writing of an essay or compare/contrast analysis after reading specified scholarly articles, while others may involve the creation of lesson plans in a particular subject area. Still other performance assessments may require students to synthesize information from a particular field of study or evaluate controversial viewpoints. These performance assessments are stored and submitted within an online management system known as Task-Stream.com and student work is reviewed and graded through comprehensive evaluation rubrics by adjunct University faculty members. Depending on the particular performance assessment, the evaluation rubric is built on three, four, or five competency levels. To progress to the next series of assessments, students must achieve a minimum rating of *Satisfactory, Meets Standard, or Competent,* depending on the level of rubric by which that particular performance assessment is evaluated.

Student work is self-paced as long as they complete the minimum number of competency units per six-month term. Competency units approximate equivalents of semester hours. Undergraduate students must complete at least twelve competency units per term, while graduate students are required to complete at least eight. Some students may experience difficulty in achieving success due to lack of time management skills or challenges with personal organization; others may not know what is being expected of them within a given assessment; still others may not be able to adequately articulate their knowledge in formal written format. Most generally, based on my interactions with students, those who struggle often indicate that they need more guidance, clarification, and feedback in order to be successful.

Primary and Secondary Issues

The primary issue to be covered in the case study chapter will focus on improving student academic success through providing appropriate, varied, and individualized feedback. The secondary issues to be covered will focus on student satisfaction, retention, and an increased feeling of connectedness to the academic mentor as well as to the University at large as a result of the support received through individualized feedback.

An Overview of the Case Study

A select group of students was featured in this case study, each with different cultural and academic backgrounds but with one thing in common: They were each struggling academically. All were seeking initial licensure in either elementary education or special education, along with either a bachelor's or a master's degree. They were all adult learners, trying to juggle family obligations and full-time jobs, and were trying to reach their goal of becoming an elementary or special education teacher. None had ever matriculated into a distance learning environment previously.

Not all students needed my academic support; most were quite self-directed and independent as many adult learners are. However, not all students can be high-performing at first, and some need extra support through a variety of means such as weekly outreach. It was my goal as an academic (course) mentor to provide each of these students with the kind of support that they needed to help them attain success. I set out to learn as much as I could about these students relative to preferred learning styles, interests, motivation levels, comfort level with technology, and so on. As a result of what I learned, I was able to provide feedback tailored to each student. The transformations that took place were truly encouraging to me as a faculty member because I was able to see my students growing on a weekly basis in academic confidence, motivation, and satisfaction with the University as a whole. These students also seemed to develop a higher level of connectedness with me than students who did not receive individualized feedback. Based on my experiences, it is my belief that individualized feedback in a distance learning environment is not only possible, but is very much necessary for increased student success, satisfaction, and retention.

As a result of reading and discussing this case study, the reader will be able to

- articulate the value of individualized feedback in a distance learning environment;
- compare/contrast at least four ways in which to incorporate individualized feedback; and
- evaluate the impact that individualized feedback has on student learning.

CASE STUDY

I served as the course mentor, also known as academic mentor, for the Specific Teaching Practices in the Teachers College at the University for approximately four years. In that capacity, I worked with approximately 1,200 undergraduate and graduate students majoring in elementary education or special education. For students seeking licensure in those areas, the Specific Teaching Practices focus on instructional methods and pedagogy of reading/literacy and language arts; mathematics and science; social sciences; health and fitness; and visual performing arts. In my role as course mentor, I facilitated a virtual learning community where students could come for guidance or clarification about their work; I also provided weekly teleconferences, webinars, and chat sessions on a variety of subject-specific topics related to pedagogy. Additionally, I reached out to struggling students on the telephone and through e-mail offering assistance if needed.

I observed over the years that while I was working very hard and putting in a great number of hours each week trying to help struggling students, I didn't see the kind of results I had hoped for. Some students were still struggling in grasping key concepts and in demonstrating their proficiency as required by established evaluation rubrics; several were taking multiple attempts in order to pass their required work. Nothing I did really seemed to make a significant impact on my students' learning and their academic success, particularly those who were struggling, and I found this disheartening. I tried consulting colleagues. I attended conferences. I engaged in professional and scholarly readings. I even tried using technology-driven communication to connect with my students, such as through weekly greetings and announcements using Voki and Voice Threads. While I received positive comments from students I really didn't see any academic results from those efforts. There just did not seem to be a clear-cut method for helping students to overcome academic challenges, particularly in a distance learning environment, and especially in one that was competency-based and not conducted within the paradigm of a traditional course-based academic model.

I then started thinking about what I already knew regarding how students learn; I thought back to my 16 years as an elementary and middle school teacher and immediately the images of specific students entered my mind. I remembered Jason (all names are pseudonyms), for example, who I had in my kindergarten classroom for two years in a row; that little guy was full of energy—his body always in motion—and I recalled how he got so excited when we used our bodies to make large letters or to act out concepts, and so on. We went outside one day and blew bubbles from soap and I recall Jason getting so excited he could hardly stand it; that was the day he learned about air currents. I then remembered Nadiah, who I had in an eighth-grade gifted class, and how she was so brilliant but yet she could not concentrate on her studies unless she listened to texts in audio format; once she heard the content she seemed to internalize it and could proceed from there. And finally, my mind went back to LeAnne, who was a bright fourth-grader but was very much a visual learner; she often struggled when the teaching style was primarily in a "lecture" format and needed the benefit of having a book, a graphic organizer, or something similar to look at. Without that visual support, LeAnne seemed lost and could quickly become frustrated and just give up on the task at hand.

Learning Styles

My experiences with these K–8 students are in alignment with the classic work of Dunn and Dunn in the area of preferred learning styles (Dunn et al., 1995) as well as with the groundbreaking work of Gardner who explained how all children are smart, but just in different ways (1983). The Dunn and Dunn Learning Styles Model is built upon the notion that students tend to have certain preferences for how they learn based on environmental, emotional, sociological, physical, and psychological stimuli. Within each of those five categories of stimuli, Dunn and Dunn have identified specific elements, which then lead to the identification of specific instructional methods which align with their corresponding stimuli. Gardner's Theory of Multiple Intelligence, in essence, paved the way for the work of Dunn and Dunn, in that Gardner embraced the belief that all students are capable of learning and, moreover, are intelligent in different ways. It is the responsibility of educators, Gardner argued, to determine the specific ways in which each student excels and then adapt teaching methods to align with those forms of intelligence. A meta-analysis of 42 experimental studies based on the Dunn and Dunn Learning Style Model reported that matching instructional methods with students' preferred learning styles enhances academic achievement.

In relation to K–12 learners, Dunn & Dunn observed, "Although some students learn when instruction is provided through strategies that do not complement their learning styles, significantly higher standardized achievement test scores resulted among previously failing students when they were taught with strategies that complemented their learning style preferences" (p. 353). I wondered then: Could this same insight be applicable and appropriate for adult learners? After some degree of contemplation, I concluded that the answer was likely yes—particularly after re-reading the powerful work of Knowles (1984) when he talked about andragogy, and how the principles of adult learning theory really do seem to share substantial commonalities with the pedagogical principles associated with working in a K–12 environment.

Offering Academic Support

This reflective thinking prompted me to reconsider my efforts at helping my students within the Specific Teaching Practices; it occurred to me that perhaps I could offer academic support more effectively if I would tailor that support around my students' individual needs and learning preferences. It was at that point when I decided to focus on the types of feedback that I offered to students, particularly those who were struggling. Given that our University employs a totally online learning environment, I was only able to offer academic support to my students through visual and/or auditory means.

I started by calling students who had been identified as falling behind in their work or whose work submissions required significant revision, or who had contacted me with a question. During the conversation, I engaged the students regarding how they learned best, and what specifically I could do to help them succeed. I took careful notes of the conversations and then went about the task of creating a plan to best meet each student's needs. Patterns tended to emerge, and I discovered that most students indicated that they tended to prefer feedback that was written down in some way; they wanted to be able to see my comments on their screen. I coded these students as "visual" learners. Other students said they needed to hear my voice explaining key concepts or offering advice; I coded these students as "auditory" learners.

From there, I took another look at what those students identified as "visual" learners said to me in our phone conversations; some explained that e-mail or a written document met their needs just fine for various reasons—they either did not have a good high-speed Internet connection or they preferred to print out hard copies of work assignments and feedback. Other students I marked in the "visual learner" category indicated that they wished they could see my face—they indicated that this was one thing they felt was missing in an online learning environment.

Three main categories of feedback and engagement seemed to emerge: text-based, audio-based, and video-based. These three categories seemed to align with Dunn and Dunn's (1995) physical type of stimuli and its corresponding elements (perceptual, intake, and mobility). However, the "adult" and "team" elements of the sociological type of stimuli also seemed to be represented by these three types of feedback, given that I was working with adult learners and that I wanted this approach to supporting their learning to be viewed as a partnership or team effort. I then went about the task of providing feedback as needed to students using these three methods.

For the text-based (written) feedback, I used e-mail, live chat and instant messaging along with the Track Changes feature in my word processing software to provide students with substantive guidance. For the audio-based feedback, I used the free software download Audacity and spoke to the student about key concepts he or she was struggling with; I saved the file in MP3 format and e-mailed it to the student. For the video-based feedback, I used the web conferencing tool the University provides for academic (course) mentors, Adobe Connect Pro; I used the desktop sharing feature so that I could pull up the student's paper or a set of concepts the student was struggling with. I took advantage of the webcam feature so that the students could see my face and hear my voice while they could also see me referring to their papers, graphic organizers of terms, or whatever document in which the students needed academic support. I then recorded the video session and sent a URL link to the student via e-mail so that he or she could view the support session as many times as needed. I conducted the case study over a period of three months with 18 students who were struggling to demonstrate their competency as per the requirements specified in evaluation rubrics for various assignments (performance tasks).

The amount of time it took to prepare the feedback varied based on how complex their specific assignment requirements were and how much they were struggling. However, on average, text-based feedback to a student generally took 5–15 minutes to prepare; audio-based feedback required approximately 15 minutes; and video-based feedback averaged a 15–30 minute commitment of my time because of the additional tools I was employing, plus the need to record the session and then provide the student with the hyperlink to access it. Live video sessions were the most time consuming (20–50 minutes) because I was interacting with the student on the phone while sharing my desktop with him or her. This involved extended conversations and question/answer time.

Results

The results were interesting to me; I found that when I used the text-based feedback, many times I would never receive a response from the student; other times I would receive a quick note saying, "Thanks!" or something similar. Occasionally there would be a follow-up question from the student and we would then continue the conversation either through e-mail or by telephone. The audio-based feedback seemed to yield a few more responses from students; they seemed to like hearing my voice as I walked them through a challenging performance assessment. However, it wasn't until I started experimenting with the video-based feedback that I felt I hit academic pay dirt; the e-mails and phone calls starting pouring in from students expressing both surprise and gratitude for my assistance. I even had some students who said that they loved the combination of hearing my voice and seeing my face on their computer screen, and they expressed delight at the realization that I was a "real person" in their online learning environment. A sampling of some comments I received is provided here:

> Thank you so much for the videos!!! They are just what I need. I find sometimes I need the audio/visual component to understand a concept.

> Thanks again for the great video. I like your video about [the] Fry graph and about objectives. I learned something from you. Thanks a lot.

> I can confirm it—I pay better attention to these presentations than I do the written ones—joking aside—I do read but I enjoy this (it adds depth).

> Just wanted to drop you a line and tell you how great it is of you to do these videos! This was more what I was expecting when I signed up to an online college.

> You are the best!!! Online schooling is so challenging for me. I like the feel of being in a classroom and listening to the teacher (weird, I know). Sometimes these tasks are so confusing in their wording, but your videos make things so clear and it feels as though I'm in the classroom having things explained to me directly. I appreciate them so much; I appreciate you!

> This gives me more confidence to come to you if I get stuck on anything! Keep up your great efforts in helping us students! They haven't gone unnoticed!

> I'm a visual learner and it helps me to see what you're talking about. This helped me to get myself in gear and get motivated.

> Hello there Dr. Ross-Fisher. I just wanted to give you some positive feedback on your task clarifications! I am sure that I can honestly say for all of us that we are deeply thankful for all the extra work that you put in for us students sitting here looking blankly into Taskstream! You really should teach a community board class or something to share with others your ideas. So thank you and you are doing an AWESOME job!

> The video was extremely helpful! I wish I could get feedback on all my work like the ones you presented . . . life would be so much easier! Thanks for taking the time and going out of your way to help!

Two data points for you: 1. Because of your method—emails, phone calls, and videos—I "get" what you are writing much quicker than I do with some others when I email—so, while I know it took you time and risk to do the videos and take time to call me—I think it's paying you back (a lesson/method for me! to remember); 2. The videos saved you from another email from me—I was struggling to move ahead on a Vocabulary Lesson—went to the video file—3 minutes into the video I turned it off—with the two ah ha moments I needed.

A student had been struggling with a task for a very long time, and her motivation level was very low. I took the following notes about my work with her:

Met with S. today in Adobe Classroom with webcam; shared desktop & reviewed directions for a task. She absolutely loved it and was motivated by it. She commented that she thinks she is the type of learner that benefits from that face-to-face interaction and she felt that she got it today using this format. UPDATE: Student submitted this task for grading within an hour of my session with her!!

A mentor of one of the students I assisted sent me the following e-mail:

During our appt. yesterday she specifically expressed how helpful you have been already. She said she "loved-loved-loved" the audio-visuals that you provided to clarify the TaskStream instructions. She said you are a definite keeper. So thank you and keep up the great work with our students. We all appreciate it so much! J

As stated previously, this is just a sampling of the feedback I received, and the greatest reactions were to the video-based feedback model. Not only did students become more actively engaged, but I noticed that their motivation levels increased during my phone calls and interactions with them and even more importantly, their academic success improved as evidenced by the reduction in revisions needed on their work. An examination of results from one assignment deemed particularly challenging revealed that struggling learners did benefit from the extra support through tailored feedback. Out of the 208 students who completed the assignment during the three-month time frame, an average of 68% of students was able to pass it on the first or second attempt as compared to 62% of struggling students within that group. Thirty-three percent of the entire group required three or more attempts in order to pass as compared to 38% of the struggling group. While the lowest performing students still lagged behind, I believe that their understanding was supported through my individualized feedback in order to help them perform at about the same success rate as their peers who were not deemed to be struggling.

IMPLICATIONS FOR DISTANCE EDUCATION

As has already been suggested by this case study, the implications for current and future distance education teaching and learning models are significant. Prompt, substantive feedback to students is an essential element of their academic growth as well as to their overall level of satisfaction with online courses in general and the university as a whole. Furnborough and Truman (2009) found that the quality of feedback also has an impact on student motivation levels. Student motivation, as we know, impacts retention and graduation rates. Bonnel (2008) went even further and shared that a lack of appropriate feedback sometimes leads to students feeling abandoned by their faculty member or academic mentor and these feelings can even lead to course failure.

Furnborough and Truman also offered some interesting insights about online students regarding feedback; they noted that those students who tend to be the most successful seem to have a tolerance for ambiguity and that they tend to feel a personal sense of empowerment relative to their own learning. However, it is my view that distance learning models should be created and implemented in such a way to accommodate the needs of *all* students, not just those who have a natural predisposition for a feedback model that presupposes ambiguity and independent learning.

While student feedback is most commonly found in text-based format there are, as I have discussed above, distinct advantages to offering a combination of feedback methods including text-based, audio-based, and video-based formats. However, regardless of the specific methods employed, students engaging in a distance learning experiences have certain expectations relative to the quality of feedback that they receive from their faculty member. For example, in his work with nursing students in an online environment, Price (1997) found that students expected their feedback to be helpful and clear, to provide a justification for the grade that was awarded, and what the specific strengths and weaknesses of the work were. Rather than trite or ambiguous remarks such as "Good job!" or "A good try—but still needs work," students would prefer to be told precisely in what ways their work was strong, or conversely, what they could do to improve the quality of their work; this applies not just to students who submitted work of average or below quality but also for those high-performing students.

One way to help faculty members produce such feedback is to use well-constructed rubrics during the evaluation process; these instruments can have a powerful impact not only on student success but also on teacher effectiveness; I discussed this in detail in my article, "Developing Effective Success Rubrics" (Ross-Fisher, 2005). The message conveyed when providing feedback to students should always be positive and supportive, yet honest and specific. Furthermore, there should always be suggestions either for further enhancement of work, or suggestions for extended learning opportunities. These suggestions could even come in the form of thought-provoking, open-ended questions tailored to the student's work.

Ros i Solé & Truman (2005) offered an interesting perspective that feedback should promote students' self-correction, and that it should represent a two-way communication between the faculty member or academic mentor and the learner. The authors warn against feedback simply becoming a one-way directive from the faculty member to the student without the latter using that information to self-evaluate and self-correct future work samples. This is a fascinating view, and one to be considered further. For example, a model could be created whereby the faculty member would provide video feedback, and then the learner would reciprocate by responding to the faculty member's comments in like manner; a virtual conversation (asynchronous or even synchronous, if logistically possible) could then be experienced with both parties engaging in a rich, thoughtful, and reflective dialogue that might results in greater student learning and satisfaction.

Another recommendation is for students to provide feedback to their peers within an online learning environment. Groves and O'Donoghue (2009) experimented with this model in their online seminar, and reported that students found "... the opportunity to provide feedback a satisfying and rewarding experience" (p. 145). While the authors reported some variation with regard to student satisfaction, overall this proved to be a positive element of their course. I would not recommend it as the sole source of feedback that learners receive, but it could certainly serve as one source of information designed to stimulate their thinking and deepen their learning.

It is clear that all students need and deserve prompt, substantive feedback in an online learning environment. Hyland (2001), however, pointed out that the need for quality feedback may be even greater for students whose native language is not English. The author even suggested this might be an area in which further research may need to be conducted in order to learn how to serve English language learners in the best way possible by stating, "Although feedback plays such a crucial role in distance education, it is largely unexplored in a distance language learning context. We therefore need to look more closely at the feedback offered to distance language students (p. 233). Hyland went on to say that since most feedback offered to students taking online courses tends to be text-based, many students who are already struggling to read or write in a new language may not find this format supportive of their needs. That is why it is important to offer students a variety of feedback options, including text-based, audio-based, and video-based comments from the faculty member as discussed in the case study above. This view is supported by Annison (2002), who learned as a result of her action research project that videoconferencing seemed to yield the greatest results for her students over other more traditional feedback methods. Williamson et al. (2000) shared one faculty member's experiences in using a synchronous textchat software application as one method for providing feedback to his students; learners were even able to interact with the faculty member in real time through the same textchat application by clicking options such as "...faster, slower, perfect, and please review" (p. 57). This helps to keep students actively engaged and more involved in their own learning, which in turn elevates motivation levels and promotes higher academic success.

In light of the insights gained from the experiences of others such as those cited above as well as through my own experiences, it is recommended that the impact of feedback on student motivation, learning, and satisfaction serve as the focus of future research studies, since there is still much to be learned about this topic. In turn, faculty members need to continue to share what they have learned from their experiences, both successes and failures. It is through this growing body of knowledge, coupled with thoughtful contemplation and collaboration that clarity can be gained about virtual feedback and its role in producing an excellent experience for students.

CONCLUSION

As I learned from working with my students, the benefits of individualized feedback are numerous; I witnessed (virtually) students who felt discouraged and disconnected become motivated, enthusiastic, and engaging with peers and with me. I was delighted when I observed students who were struggling and even some at risk for academic failure experience breakthroughs. Those students started taking the initiative for their own learning, and they began asking questions and seeking feedback, because they saw what a difference such behaviors made to them as learners. I am pleased to report that each of the students whose comments were featured above was able to successfully complete his or her respective programs, and they are now licensed teachers. I can think of no better source of professional satisfaction than to see students that I assisted now in a position to offer support to their own students.

With all the benefits of this approach of individualizing feedback, there are two main concerns that I have when considering scalability and access. First, not all students have the same level of technology skills, nor do they have the same access to high-speed Internet connections. Both audio and video-based feedback require a significant amount of bandwidth to work properly. A few students reported frustration that they were not able to access my feedback from their home computers because they had dial-up Internet service; those students ended up having to use a computer at their local public library or at a family member's home. This was a workaround, but it was not ideal. For students in these situations, text-based or telephone-based feedback may be the only viable alternatives.

The second concern about using video-based feedback relates to the time involved in its creation. It is, for obvious reasons, much faster to generate feedback that is text-based; audio feedback requires a little more time but it is still not significant after becoming comfortable with the software. Moreover, crafting the video-based feedback that I want to share with my student, then recording that feedback and finally, sending the link to the student via e-mail does take several minutes. Upon reflection, however, the amount of time it took to create each of those types of feedback for struggling students really did not differ from the amount of time I have spent in the past working with students in traditional face-to-face universities. When those efforts yield the kind of positive results that I received from my students, the time invested in creating individualized feedback tailored to specific learning preferences is without question well worth it and I made the conscious decision to make this sacrifice of time to enhance the learning experience of my students without hesitation or regret.

QUESTIONS FOR ANALYSIS/DISCUSSION

Potential questions that could be used by readers to analyze the issues, problems, and solutions presented in my case study are as follows:

1. What are the factors affecting the problem(s) related to this case?
2. Could the techniques used in this case study be applicable to my own teaching situation? Why or why not?
3. How could I improve upon what the author has done in this case study?
4. What are the potential drawbacks to providing individualized feedback in a distance learning environment?
5. What are some other benefits to students, educational programs, and the community at large that might result from the approach used in this case study?
6. How might data be collected in order to more fully explore the advantages and disadvantages of providing individualized feedback to students enrolled in distance learning programs?
7. What are some of the emerging technologies that should be considered in solving the problem(s) related to the case?

REFERENCES

Annison, J. (2002). Action research: Reviewing the implementation of a distance-learning degree programme utilizing communication and information technologies. *Innovations in Education and Teaching International 29*(2), 95–106.

Bonnel, W. (2008). Improving feedback to students in online courses. *Nursing Education Perspectives, 29*(5), 290–294.

Dunn, R., et al. (1995). A meta-analytic validation of the Dunn and Dunn Model of Learning-Style Preferences. *Journal of Educational Research, 88*(6), 353–362.

Furnborough, C. , & Truman, M. (2009). Adult beginner distance language learner perceptions and use of assignment feedback. *Distance Education, 30*(3), 399–418.

Gardner, H. (1983). *Frames of mind.* New York, NY: Basic Books.

Groves, M., & O'Donoghue, J. (2009). Reflections of students in their use of asynchronous online seminars. *Educational Technology & Society, 12*(3), 143–149.

Hyland, F. (2001). Providing effective support: Investigating feedback to distance language learners. *Open Learning, 16*(3), 233–247.

Knowles, M. S. (1984). *Andragogy in action: Applying modern principles of adult learning.* San Francisco, CA: Jossey-Bass.

Price, B. (1997). Defining quality student feedback in distance learning. *Journal of Advanced Nursing, 26,* 154–160.

Ros i Sole', C., & Truman, M. (2005). Feedback in distance learning programmes in languages: Attitudes to linguistic faults and implications for the learning process. *Distance Education, 26*(3), 299–323.

Ross-Fisher, R. (2005). Developing effective success rubrics. *Kappa Delta Pi Record, 41*(3), 131–135.

Williamson, C., Bernhard, J., Chamberlin, K. (January 2000). Perspectives on an internet-based synchronous distance learning experience. *Journal of Engineering Education, 53–61.*

CHAPTER 5

USING NARRATIVE INQUIRY FOR ONLINE EDUCATIONAL ASSESSMENT

Lesley S. J. Farmer

ABSTRACT

In an effort to study assessment as an element in the scholarship of teaching, the investigator incorporated online narrative inquiry into her library media management course. Students electronically posted and shared reflections about three course-related critical incidents they experienced that semester. A content-analysis matrix was developed to capture: source of conflict/program, source of support, resolution, and demographic information. Central management issues were human relationships, resource management, and administrative details. The main sources of support were administrators and fellow teachers. Electronic journaling enabled students to self-assess areas for improvement; and assess peers' situations and problem-solving approaches. Journals helped instructors to assess students' areas of concern, how students solved critical issues, and the degree to which course content dealt with the critical events. The activity also fostered a sense of a community of practice, and helped link academic coursework and field experience.

Real-Life Distance Education, pages 81–91
Copyright © 2014 by Information Age Publishing

INTRODUCTION

Assessment serves as a core activity in course implementation, both for student and instructor improvement. Specifically, assessing student work on a formative basis helps instructors to diagnose student process and gaps in learning. This information can be used to modify course delivery as well as provide feedback for students so they can make their own adjustments in learning approaches. Students can also self-assess their experiences and learning. When shared, these reflections can be used to help students understand concepts through contextualization and generate knowledge. Reflections can also be reviewed by colleagues to provide peer coaching. Instructors can analyze student self-assessments to identify individual and class trends in understanding and application. Moreover, instructors can triangulate the assessments to determine student self-efficacy.

With the incorporation of communications technology, students and instructors can interact more actively and preserve their thinking processes more easily. Work can be posted and shared quickly and efficiently. Conversations about academic topics can continue throughout the course regardless of in-class time constraints. Ideas can be preserved. As a result, assessment can be more effective.

Theoretical Context

By its nature, much of the formal preparation for school librarianship melds theory and practice. Increasingly, service learning and field experience comprise central components of this academic program. Service learning, in particular, allows students to test the veracity of theories in real-life contexts as well as apply abstract knowledge to concrete situations. Indeed, most state and NCATE (National Council for Accreditation of Teacher Education) standards require field experience. Under the NCATE School Library Media Specialist curriculum standards, the reviewers ask for description of practicum experiences: "the information here should show how candidates are given opportunity to practice teaching the skills and knowledge specified in the standards" (American Association of School Librarians, 2003, p. 26).

To ensure that the learning circle is complete, those same real-world experiences need to be processed and generalized conceptually. Reflective journaling provides a means for students to critically analyze their life experiences, framing theory contextually. When students share these reflections, they can then compare both their experiences and their conclusions in order to draw valid inferences across contexts (Boud, 2001) and generate knowledge (Flavell, 1977). This exercise has been recommended specifically for library science preparation (Yontz & de la Pena McCook, 2003) and more generally for professional development (Schon, 1983). Technology optimizes this process because students can access, analyze, and respond to peers' entries at their convenience. In her review of journaling for learning, Moon (1999) posits several other benefits: development of questioning attitude and critical thinking skills; means to understand one's own learning process; increased intellectual involvement; increased self-empowerment and responsibility for learning; and alternative means of self-expression

In terms of research methodology, drawing from experience to deepen understanding of the theoretical may be linked to naturalistic inquiry: "research that focuses on how people behave when they are absorbed in genuine life experiences in natural settings" (Lane, 2002, chapter 10, p. 1). The underlying premise is that social context influences what occurs, so inquiry may be validly pursued in natural settings. Moreover, personal interpretation is impossible to escape. Students who journal about their experiences exemplify autoethnography; i.e., they examine their own lives. Instructors acting as researchers are engaging in ethnography as they discover social acquired and share shared understandings.

Within naturalistic inquiry, reflective journaling combines biographical methodology and narrative inquiry. The biographical aspect arises from exploring one's own experiences. The narrative aspect is derived from the "story making" used to construct meaning from experience. By sharing journals, students and instructors link life experiences and generate shared knowledge. Assessment of such journaling enables both student and instructor to examine the effects of milieu and strategies on the learner, and to identify interventions to optimize future practice.

Case Objectives

In an effort to study assessment as an element in the scholarship of teaching, the researcher of this case study incorporated narrative inquiry into her library media management course. Specifically, she had students write about three course-related critical incidents that they experienced that semester. This exercise served as a basis for: (a) identifying possible reasons for differences among student performances and (b) reviewing course content and delivery.

In the case study, the journaling activity focused on critical incidents: identifying and analyzing key events. Boud (2001) further asserts that reflection after an event can be particularly valuable because it enables the learner to revisit an experience and link it with information and insights gained since the time of the original incident. Indeed, the very act of selecting a specific event among other occurrences serves as an assessment task in the same way that one identifies the key phrase or most important fact in an essay, particularly if the learner justifies the basis for that selection. Furthermore, in describing the main issues of the event, tracing the decision-making process, and identifying the main points learned, the learner hones metacognitive skills and helps build a personal knowledge base that can be shared with others.

Finally, journal writing provides a means for self-assessment, which contributes to the body of evidence demonstrating professional competence. Furthermore, it recognizes each individual's responsibility and involvement in a community of practice. Boud (1999) states:

> We cannot expect students to become competent professionals unless they learn to be actively involved in constructing and reconstructing notions of good practice as they proceed. It is important to note though, that the practice of self-assessment does not imply that this engagement is an isolated or individualistic activity. It commonly involves peers, makes use of teachers and other practitioners and draws upon appropriate literature. (p. 123)

In terms of narrative inquiry approach used in distance education, the following case study provides an opportunity to explore ways to incorporate narrative inquiry into online courses, administrate and analyze narrative data, and act upon narrative data analysis.

CASE STUDY

This case study investigated student self-reporting of critical events related to issues of school library media management. The following research questions guided the analysis:

- What do students consider to be critical management issues?
- How do students solve critical management issues?
- How does a student's academic preparation and employment status impact the critical event in terms of identification and solution?
- How does the curriculum impact the critical event?
- How do the critical events and their discussion change over time?

Methodology

Students in the library media center management class were asked to write up three critical events related to the course. They were to submit them at the end of the first, second, and third month of the semester course, with the intent that students would discuss current issues. The directions for the reports were as follows: "Identify three critical events related to library management. For each, write a narrative that describes the event; states why it is critical; states what you decided, and the basis for your decision; and states what you learned. If you are a classroom teacher, think about your interactions with the library/librarian. If you are not in a school setting, interview a librarian about a critical event."

Students submitted their work online, and were asked to read and respond to one other student's submission. They were graded on completing each aspect of the task. The instructor responded to each student's critical event, and read all of the replies, commenting on about a third of them.

At the end of the semester, the students' work was archived for further study. A matrix was developed to capture the following data: source of conflict/program, source of support, and resolution. Captured demographic data included: employment status, number of years working in a school or other type of library, presence of other library staff, years of classroom teaching experience, and library media courses taken. From the investigator's first reading of the submission, entries were categorized in alignment with the course content; topics not covered in the course were categorized separately. Entries were then coded according to the categories and problem-solving process, noting the author. The investigator performed a content analysis on the matrix to identify trends, and to cross-reference the data (both the topic as well as the process) with the course delivery.

Findings

Thirty-two students submitted critical events, as shown in Table 5.1 below. Of those, half worked in a school library: between a few months to ten years. The number of years of teaching experience ranged from none to 32, with a median of 12 years. Eight students were male; seven were non-Anglo.

Student choice of topic depended on current employment activities, current course activities, and response or "resonance" with other students' submissions; students who submitted their events early sometimes impacted the topics that other students chose to write about. A semester was not long enough to discern significant growth in means of solving management problems, although students did mention the use of policies that they had learned about during the course. Gender and ethnicity did not seem to affect the choice or discussion of the critical event.

Critical events identified were ranked as follows:

1. Human relationships
2. Resources
3. Administration
4. Technology

TABLE 5.1 Respondents' Identification of Critical Event Issues

Critical Event	Issue	Number
Human relations (n= 32)	With classroom teachers	15
	With students	8
	With students	3
	With administrators	2
	With student aides	1
	With library staff	1
	With public librarians	1
	With community members	1
Resources (n=21)	Selection/ordering	9 (2 not solved)
	Circulation	4 (1 not solved)
	Lack of resources	3
	Textbooks	2
	Challenged materials	2
Administration (n=16)	Facilities use	5 (1 not solved)
	Budget	4 (1 not solved)
	Policies	3 (1 not solved)
	Scheduling	2
	Book fair	1
	Theft	1
Technology (n=6)	Appropriate use	3
	Automation	1
	Printing	1
	Access	1

Issues dealing with research projects tended to be identified by those with less experience, while budget issues were identified by more experienced librarians. The main issues for practicing librarians were human relationships with teachers and materials selection, which also implicated other staff. Typically, a teacher's behavior negatively impacted library service (e.g., over-scheduling classes, not supervising students, not returning materials). On the other hand, students who were classroom teachers sometimes complained about negative behavior on the part of their librarians. In general, critical events focused on outside elements that affected library service rather than library service that impacted other constituencies; the students were usually in a reactive stance.

A few of the topics instigated multiple responses and extensive discussion: the *Sports Illustrated* swimsuit issue (about the same number on either side of the issue in terms of access), excessive computer printing, scheduling of library use, appropriate computer use (specifically looking at inappropriate sites), other negative library behavior by students or teachers, and policies related to job status (four students were laid off).

Seven problems were not resolved successfully. In one case, the student had taken a course related to the problem; in two cases the topic was covered in the course; in four cases the student had not taken a course related to the problem. Three students had never worked in a library, three were in their first year in the library, and one was in his or her second year in the library. One had no teaching experience, but another had over 20 years' teaching experience, so that factor was apparently not significant.

Sources for help in solving the problem were ranked as follows:

1. Administrators
2. Fellow teachers
3. Self
4. Policy
5. Library media specialist

Employed librarians tended to consult administrators. All of the students who thought that administrators (particularly principals) were a significant factor in solving the problems had been working in libraries. Basically, they saw administrators as a source of power: to call meetings that would enable the librarian to negotiate with stakeholders, and to support and back up the librarian's decision. On the other hand, when administrators were the source of the problem, then it was hard to confront them; one person used policies, and another solicited the help of a powerful parent. Experienced librarians also tended to use: policy to solve problems, parents, fellow teachers, and themselves. They seemed to be good negotiators, able to solve problems directly with their colleagues as partners. Not surprisingly, most students sought site support, and were more successful at that level. About half the time when a student who was a classroom teacher sought help from the site librarian, the issue was resolved satisfactorily.

In examining what they learned from the incidents, 12 students cited the need for effective communication as the most important factor. Second in importance was principal support, mentioned by seven students. Third in rank was collaboration, noted by five students; classroom teachers were particularly struck with the impact of collaboration. Three mentioned the usefulness of observation, two praised student aides, and other factors noted by individuals included planning, training, and positive attitude.

In terms of the process itself—reflecting on critical management events— students thought that the activity was useful and enlightening. They were able to see how the coursework applied to their settings, and how problems they encountered could have been solved more easily once they learned library management skills and knew more resources. They particularly liked reading peers' reflections because (a) they found that others had similar problems so did not feel isolated or "strange" and (b) they were given good tips that they could use if a similar problem arose for them. Several course activities were found to be particularly applicable to their critical events: the use of policies, collaborative practices, the examination of facilities, and budgetary processes.

Discussion

This study focused entirely on the analysis of written reports about critical events. As such, it does not account for class time oral discussion of critical events. Furthermore, one of the program's master's degree candidates conducted an action research project that entailed interviewing first-year school librarians, so additional data was gathered from that activity but not included in the present discussion. It should also be noted that the study investigator co-taught the course with two other lecturers, and after the first class interacted with the students only via telecommunications. Thus, she used the information from the critical events to provide overall feedback to the students and other instructors via e-mail. Those instructors were then able to use that information to help detail their own content that they delivered in subsequent class sessions.

The critical events chosen significantly aligned with the course content. Students seemed to choose events that did indeed reflect management issues. Course discussions and peer postings often led to the choice of critical event to report. However, some of their events were not covered sufficiently in the course to help them in their practice; some assistance arose through the online discussions, however. In a few cases, the issue was one that was dealt with in another course, (e.g., technology, selection, reference and information literacy). There was no significant relationship between topic and timing within the semester.

In those cases where students did not resolve their incident successfully, they tended to have neither the relevant course background nor library experience. On the other hand, having had the relevant coursework alone or having worked in a library without the underlying coursework did not *guarantee* that an issue would be solved satisfactorily; some factors were outside the students' control.

It was hoped that the online journaling of critical events would help students bridge their coursework with their daily careers. Furthermore, the investigator hoped that the identification of and response to critical events would inform course development. Thus, based on the reflections, the investigator recommended that the course content would be modified as follows:

- Add explicit discussion on collaboration/negotiation/advocacy with administrators and parents.
- Add face-to-face time on advocacy and negotiating skills, including role-play and other simulations.

- Add explicit discussion on adult development and organizational behavior.
- Explicitly link curriculum with student research projects.
- Explicitly link specific policies with specific management issues rather than group policies together.
- State which other courses deal with specific management issues.

To optimize the use of critical events, these actions are suggested:

- Have students help build the class agenda based on critical events findings.
- Have students explicitly identify how their coursework helps them solve actual management issues.
- Archive in-class discussion of critical events; compare the in-class and online discussions.
- Conduct follow-up focus groups to reveal other management issues.

IMPLICATIONS FOR DISTANCE EDUCATION

Critical event journaling constitutes one viable way to uncover and deal with relevant issues in an online environment. Similarly, the increasing emphasis on communities of practice and knowledge management provides a venue for using critical event reflection and sharing. In the process, articulation between academic preparation and professional growth can be bridged more seamlessly.

The case study affirmed the viability of online narrative inquiry. Asynchronous online learning environments are just as effective as face-to-face interaction—or even more so because students can take their time to articulate and reflect on their experiences. Furthermore, peer comments can also be done in a thoughtful way. Obviously, journals record a student's thoughts, unlike oral class discussion, and the online venue facilitates sharing.

In the final analysis, having students write about critical events online impacted learning in the following ways:

- It facilitated discussion of issues in a safe, supportive environment.
- It provided a positive means to articulate and analyze effective practice.
- It facilitated a community of practice whereby students with prior academic and work experience helped neophyte professionals.
- It helped contextualize theory and transition from practice to concept.
- It blurred the lines between class and online time.
- It helped identify curricular areas that needed more extensive coverage.

CONCLUSION

Reflective journaling of critical management events was a useful course delivery method and assessment vehicle. It also facilitated a sense of a community of practice, extending interactivity beyond formal class time. Posting identified issues of importance to students, and provided a means to share concerns and effective problem-solving techniques. Students had control of the content and presentation so they could assume more responsibility for learning as well as determine the extent that they wished to reveal themselves.

In essence, journaling acted as a means for *students* to (a) self-assess their areas of strength and weakness, (b) assess peer situations and problem-solving approaches, and (c) assess content areas that needed addressing. On the part of instructors, journals helped them to (b) assess students' areas of concern, (b) assess how students solved critical issues, and (c) assess the degree to which course content dealt with student-identified critical events.

The length of time, focus on one assessment method, variability in student response, and population limitations constrain the investigator's license to generalize findings. However, the process has been insightful and provides a foundation for further study.

QUESTIONS FOR ANALYSIS/DISCUSSION

This case study investigated student self-reporting of critical events related to issues of school library media management. The following research questions guided the analysis:

1. What do students consider to be critical management issues?
2. How do students solve critical management issues?
3. How does a student's academic preparation and employment status impact the critical event in terms of identification and solution?
4. How does the curriculum impact the critical event?
5. How do the critical events and their discussion change over time?
6. How does technology impact narrative inquiry?
7. What are some emerging technologies that should be considered in using narrative inquiry?

DEFINITIONS

Autoethnography: Examining one's own life.
Narrative inquiry: Process of gathering information for the purpose of research through storytelling.

Naturalistic inquiry: Research that focuses on how people behave when they are absorbed in genuine life experiences in natural settings.

REFERENCES

American Association of School Librarians. (2003). *Program standards: School library media specialist preparation.* Washington, DC: National Council for Accreditation of Teacher Education.

Boud, D. (2001). Using journal writing to enhance reflective practice. In L. English & M. Gillen, (Eds), *Promoting journal writing in adult education* (pp. 9–18). San Francisco, CA: Jossey-Bass.

Boud, D. (1999). Avoiding the traps: Seeking good practice in the use of self assessment and reflection in professional courses. *Social Work Education, 18*(2), 123–137.

Flavell, J. (1977). *Cognitive development.* Englewood Cliffs, NJ: Prentice-Hall.

Lane, D. (2002). *Theory and research methods.* Lexington: University of Kentucky.

Moon, J. (1999). *Reflection in learning and professional development.* London, UK: Kogan Page.

Schon, D. (1983). *The reflective practitioner* London, UK: Temple Smith.

Yontz, E., & de la Pena McCook, K. (2003, Winter). Service-learning and LIS education. *Journal of Education for Library and Information Science, 44,* 55–68.

PART II

COLLABORATING AT A DISTANCE

CHAPTER 6

E-COLLABORATION CHALLENGES

J. Ana Donaldson

ABSTRACT

Though the literature stresses the importance of effective online collaboration, it is often a challenge when students are juggling busy schedules and online course work. This case looks at an actual situation where misunderstandings and diverse expectations led to student and instructor frustrations. The case is presented as an example of the importance of creating an effective collaborative relationship, clearly stating expectations for interaction, and recognizing the challenges inherent to this communication process. The case includes facilitator guidelines and examples of correspondence between the participants.

INTRODUCTION

LaToya and Neda were graduate students who were new to online courses. Several tasks were assigned to the pair for the first portion of the course. The 16-week course was divided into eight two-week modules. Everything went fine for the first module, but by the second 2-week module, the instructor was receiving e-mails of complaint from each student. By the third module, there was open confrontation between the two students. Both

Real-Life Distance Education, pages 95–105
95

students requested the instructor to intervene. The case objectives for discussion focus on the following items:

- Discuss the importance of clearly stated expectations in an online interaction.
- Identify the necessary elements for creating an effective collaborative relationship.
- Categorize a learner's priorities that encourage or create challenges for effective online interaction.

CASE STUDY

A graduate course entitled *Performance Management and Technology* at a Midwestern university had been recently moved online. Sixteen students signed up for the spring course and the instructor, Dr. Helen Peterson, was anticipating teaching the course for the second time using the online format that had worked successfully during the previous semester.

This was LaToya Robinson's first semester returning to college after graduating with a bachelor's degree from the same university 10 years earlier. She was a single mother living 75 miles away from the University. LaToya was not able to join the class when they met for the first evening on campus because of her work schedule, child care issues, and the distance. She had not met anyone in the program or even the instructor prior to this course. This was her first online course, and she was anxious about balancing her demanding work schedule, the unknowns of an online graduate program, and the issues of raising her young daughter.

Neda Farouk was a graduate assistant in the master's program and a busy mother of three boys. Her husband was supportive of her commitment to do well in the program. She had worked as a dental assistant for several years and was teaching courses at the local community college. She was hoping to make a career change and to excel. This was Neda's second semester in the program but her first time taking an online course. She met many of the other students on the first evening when they discussed expectations and got acquainted on campus. This new learning environment was exciting but Neda was concerned about working collaboratively. In the past, several group projects had ended in frustration, with Neda taking the lead when the other students did not contribute sufficiently to the final deliverable.

During the third week of a 16-week course, the two women were asked to work together for the next two two-week modules. Their task was to report their consensus on the assigned discussion questions regarding several case studies. A new case was assigned at the beginning of the next two-week module. The first week required each student to post her personal views on the case in the online discussion area. By the second week, the assigned pair was to come to consensus and take turns e-mailing to the instructor their shared responses on the assigned case study. This was to be the pattern for the next 2 modules.

The first module went well, as both students worked on understanding the expectations for the tasks and learning to analyze a case study using detailed guidelines provided by the instructor. Neda took the initial lead for posting the consensus of their responses. She was a bit disappointed when the instructor advised her that she had reported the pair's individual comments without comparing or contrasting their views. This was a new approach for Neda. She promised herself to do better on the next module. There was some confusion regarding where to post the individual responses. Both women subsequently agreed that posting to Google Docs would allow for simplified interactions. Neda had used Google Docs successfully in a previous course to post collaborative group documents for discussion and updating.

As assigned, LaToya took the lead for the second module. It was a hectic week at her place of employment with an announcement of expected layoffs. Also, late in the week, her daughter was diagnosed with asthma. In spite of these stressful situations, LaToya was able to make the initial individual posting's due date of Sunday evening with two hours to spare. After completing the posting, she noticed that Neda's posting had appeared six days earlier. Work got even more demanding the next week as half of LaToya's work team received a termination notice. She was one day late posting her response to Neda's week-one posting. After reviewing Neda's work, LaToya posted the consensus with special attention to comparing and contrasting their views. Later on Sunday night, LaToya went back to retrieve her consensus report for posting to the instructor only to find that Neda had drastically edited the posted document. This development angered LaToya. She felt that Neda had questioned LaToya's competence. After thinking about this situation, she felt it might be best to contact the instructor immediately to ask for a new partner. It obviously was not going to be a successful partnership since Neda questioned everything LaToya wrote.

At the beginning of the third shared module, Neda wrote the instructor requesting that she be assigned a new partner. She explained to Dr. Peterson that LaToya's repeated postings at the end of each week had not provided the necessary time for a response. With Neda's demanding work, school, and family schedules, she felt that it was imperative to have a partner with the same commitment to meeting deadlines. Neda felt better after sending the e-mail to the instructor but was wondering if online courses were the best format for her.

This case study presentation ends at this point with several unresolved issues. Of immediate concern is the necessary action by the instructor:

- What should Dr. Peterson's response be to this stressful situation?
- Should the students be assigned a new team member?

- Would it be better for these individuals to work independently at this point in the course?

Of long-term concern is how this situation might be avoided in the future.

The following questions are provided to focus the discussion on the important elements of this case. The subsequent sections of this case provide additional resources to enhance the discussion (refer to Appendix A) and an overview on the implications and lessons learned from this actual experience.

IMPLICATIONS FOR DISTANCE EDUCATION

Online instructors often focus on the content elements of a course without considering the importance of student or faculty interactions. The craft of developing effective collaborative relationships is often learned through trial-and-error experiences. Understanding the adult learner and providing a structured approached to enhance engagement is critical to online success. The Phases of Engagement model (Conrad & Donaldson, 2011) is a suggested methodology for implementing a structured approach for creating a collaborative learning environment.

Of value to the instructor is the question of when an intervention should occur and at what level. In this situation, the professor turned the situation into a learning "opportunity" for the two students by requesting that they resolve their differences by working together.

CONCLUSION

This case study demonstrates a situation where establishing a collaborative relationship between students was placed second to the completion of course tasks. Without clear expectations, the students and the instructor experienced a high level of frustration. The case discussion questions are provided to focus on how this situation might have been avoided. Facilitator resources are included with the case for an additional level of understanding on how the situation developed and was resolved. This case is truly an example of how one can learn from one's mistakes.

QUESTIONS FOR ANALYSIS/DISCUSSION

1. What are the hurdles that you see facing these two participants? What steps might have been taken earlier in the process to avoid the existing confrontational situation?

2. Refer to the Phases of Engagement model (http://phases.wetpaint. com/page/Phases+of+Engagement+Model). What steps were taken or omitted in establishing an effective relationship between these students?

3. The theory of andragogy (Knowles, Holton, & Swanson, 2005) addresses the needs of adult learners. How did the interaction between the students in this situation demonstrate characteristics of adult learners? What could have been done to strengthen the learning environment based on these principles?

4. How are online interactions different from those that might be experienced in a face-to-face situation? List three positive aspects and three potential challenges.

REFERENCES

Conrad, R., & Donaldson, J. A. (2011). *Engaging the online learner revised: Activities and resources for creative instruction.* San Francisco, CA: Jossey Bass.

Knowles M.S., Holton, E.F. III, & Swanson, R. A. (2005). *The adult learner: The definitive classic in adult education and human resource development* (6th ed.). Boston, MA: Elsevier.

ADDITIONAL INFORMATION
APPENDIX A

This case is an example of one instructor's failure to establish communication and expectation guidelines for participants. Even though both students were dealing with family and work issues, their expectations and timelines differed greatly. There also was a cultural difference that influenced their interactions.

LaToya was the first in her family to attend graduate school. As an African American single mother raising a sickly child, she found herself wanting to make a difference in the world. One of her challenges was trying to discuss issues with a group of students whom she had never met. She also was not sure of Dr. Peterson's expectations of her students. LaToya had learned at an early age that it was advantageous not to trust strangers and that any level of respect needed to be earned.

Neda had moved with her family from Saudi Arabia five years before and was from a family of university professors and engineers in her home country. As this was her second semester as a graduate student, she had already had classes with fellow students in this program. She also was very comfortable with her professors and did not hesitate to stop by Dr. Peterson's office whenever she had a question.

Dr. Peterson had taught this course many times in the past but this was only the second time she taught it online. In other online courses, she had assigned students to work in pairs for the second and third weeks of class. Students were then moved into a four to five member student team. The first assignment of the newly formed group was to create a group contract that specified when to post and how to deal with peer lateness or absences. For the first time, Dr. Peterson kept the student pairing for six weeks into the semester, omitting the contract regarding posting considerations. There was no problem with the other groups. However, LaToya's and Neda's multiple e-mails, phone calls, and level of frustration convinced Dr. Peterson that any subsequent group work needed to be supported with earlier group contracts or posted guidelines.

The following e-mails indicate the level of frustration, the instructor and student interactions by e-mail, and the final resolution. Of note is that Dr. Peterson held her ground and turned the situation into a "learning" moment for everyone involved, including her. Listed below are e-mail exchanges in the order received and answered:

From: Neda
Sent: 9/8:00–6:00 PM
Subject: Frustrated

Dear Dr. Peterson,

I'm extremely frustrated with the assignment due tonight that needed collaboration. I suggested google doc and LaToya said it's fine. I sent the document to you to see everything done so far by me and NO collaboration. She said that she'll do her part last night, but there is nothing there and no response to my emails!!! what should I do?

—Neda

*   *   *

From: Dr. Peterson
Sent: 9/8–8:10 PM
Subject: RE: Frustrated

Neda,

It takes two to collaborate. You need to contact LaToya and ask her how she wants to handle this in the future. I suggest you set a date for the next collaboration task with enough time to discuss. Your grade will not be affected by her lack of interaction at this point. If it becomes necessary I can step in but I would like to see if the two of you can come to an agreement first.

—Dr. Peterson

*   *   *

From: Neda
Sent: 9/8–9:04PM
Subject: Frustrated

High priority

Dear Dr. Peterson,

I understand. Thank you.

—Neda

*   *   *

From: LaToya
Sent: 9/10–7:23 PM
Subject: Partner Work

Hi Dr. Peterson,

I was wondering if there is another person/group I could work with. I received an email from Neda tonight regarding the re-submission of the consensus and I personally don't like when someone tries to portray me as not wanting to follow through on my work. She's a little overbearing and I think she needs to understand that yes we are students, but we also lead lives. The way she may handle something is definitely not a way someone else may. I definitely can understand where she's coming from, but at this point I think the tension and frustration on my part will be greatly diminished if I could work with someone else. I work fine with Becky, so I'm quite sure it may just be the situation for now. If you have any input, I'll gladly accept it, but I don't like to be belittled or have someone second guess my role as a student because I know my potential and I know what I want to achieve. Thanks.

—LaToya

*   *   *

From: Dr. Peterson
Date: 9/10–10:54PM
Subject: RE: Partner Work

LaToya,

I understand that course expectations can differ greatly between students. You will be in another group as of Module 3 so if you can hang in there for one more week with Neda we all can get through this stage together. I talked about the contract tonight in the chat. By explaining in detail expectations of each group member in advance, I believe this situation would never have gotten to this point. I'm at fault by not also doing a dyad [two member team] contract. I will speak to Neda and ask for more understanding on her part in light of your participation. The chapters talk about team building and effective interactions. I ask for your patience as the class progresses. If you want to discuss this more, please let me know.

Something also to keep in mind is that your communication has been through words without the visuals or tone of voice that often softens a message. I'm sure that her words were from her concern on meeting deadlines and were not intended to wound or hurt. Please see this as a learning opportunity when working online. Communication is always the key to success.. :-) I look forward to your response . . .

—Dr. Peterson

*   *   *

From: LaToya
Sent: 9/13–12:47PM
To: Dr. Peterson

Subject: RE: Partner Work

I definitely understand what you're saying which is why I've been so patient thus far. I've talked to her on the phone before so I'm sure her wording in her emails may be said in a different manner if we spoke. I also know from the last project we worked on that she preferred to be able to meet face to face at the university to work, which didn't work for me. So that may be an issue that can be better for her because I understand that we do a lot of group work and it is hard to try and figure each other out just by typing each other.

As far as the group participation, I know that I put equal work in, I had called her and she said she was busy until later on that night so yes for the last assignment we did not finish it until a little after ten which is a little nerve wrecking. I continued to work on it until she joined in on the google doc & it seemed that everything I wrote, she questioned it and I ended up removing a lot of the information I had typed prior to her joining in the google session. That did bother me a little bit, because I did feel like she thought my writing wasn't good enough to include, which I know wasn't the case. I do agree with the contract because some people need that and I think in this instance we did. I don't have any harsh feelings over this situation, but I also don't want to be looked at as a person who doesn't value my education or any other persons. She has stated she is very busy and I'm sure it's likewise for everyone else in this class and I definitely understand that communication is a big key. Out of my four years undergrad, this isn't the worst group situation I've been in, but I do recognize that maybe for her it may be easier to have someone that she can meet face to face with.

Thanks for following up with me on this.

—LaToya

*   *   *

From: Neda
Sent: 9/13–4:24 PM
Subject: google Doc

Hi LaToya,

Did you make the necessary changes in the google Doc? I don't know about your schedule but with my extremely busy schedule I really can't afford doing everything on the last day! I hate to sound pushy, but I think doing it earlier will help both of us with all the new assignments we need to do. We need to re-submit it by Tuesday the latest.

Thank you,

—Neda

*   *   *

From: LaToya
Sent: 9/13–8:05 PM
Subject: RE: google Doc

Neda,

Ok, well first of all I don't like doing things at the last minute either. No I have not made changes to it because I have been focusing on doing my other work first. My schedule is just as busy if not as busy as yours, and both being adults I definitely don't need reminders on when work is submitted. She submitted the email on September 10th about fixing it & I didn't hear anything from you until the 12th, so now that it's Sun. I don't see the reason for panic. It's due Tues. just like our other new work. I'd rather focus on what new work needs to be submitted now and get that in then I plan to look at that since we already completed it and know what to do. I will notify you once my part is completed.

—LaToya

*   *   *

From: Neda
Sent: 9/13–10:39 PM
Subject: RE: google Doc

LaToya,

I won't send you reminders if you don't like them. I just thought is less pressure on both of us if the big assignments are done before the due date (unlike the last one). Even if it's one day prior, because you never know what happens. I'm looking forward to working with you during the semester and would appreciate more feedbacks and chats if there is any problems or concerns. Thank you,

Neda

* * *

From: LaToya
Sent: September 13–11:18 PM
Subject: RE: google Doc

Neda,

This has been completed (Chapter 6 Redo).

*I'm not saying that I don't like reminders, I think it was just how it came off at first when I read it. Although I read over your email a few times I still felt kind of attacked. As I mentioned I don't like waiting for the last minute on things, but if something comes up that's the way it may have to be. I don't want to lower my grade by not getting something completed and I definitely don't want to harm anybody else's. It is really hard to just work online and I realize that especially with our day to day lives and I also know that the way one may perceive the words of an email is not the same as if it was coming from that's person's mouth. I'm very open to scheduling a day or two as soon as we get a new assignment to come to an agreement of when to have our parts done by and still leave a couple of days to look it over. This being the first assignment, there's a lot to learn from and hopefully change. Let me know what you think.

Thanks,

—LaToya

* * *

From: Neda
Sent: September 13–11:47 PM
Subject: RE: google Doc

Yes! going back to the first email i sent, it sounds like I'm emailing my husband or something; sort of in rush, no tone or emotions is sensed from it and i didn't realize that and i thank you for noting that. I try to sound better in the future. And i agree, there is a lot to learn from this whole online experience. Thank you for your response. Talk to you later :-)

—Neda

P.S. You may also call me at xxx-xxx-xxxx

Final Student Comments

Neda discussed this case study with Dr. Peterson and agreed that it provided an accurate description of the situation. Here's LaToya's response to this case study:

Hi Dr. P,

I have been able to read over this quite a few times over the past few days so I think I'm comfortable with the message being presented and what you have written. I think everything looks good and I like that enough background is provided to see where we both are coming from based on our prior upbringing/experiences. The information regarding my history is right on.

The only thing that came to mind regarding me that I thought would be helpful in knowing why I reacted the way I did is that my overall educational experience had a lot to do with it. Growing up in Iowa, I was always a minority because my mom didn't send us to schools that our black friends or family members went to. Those schools were viewed as the trouble schools that didn't take pride in producing a good education for minorities so I had to get accustomed to proving to people that I valued my education because off the bat they didn't think that. Since elementary school I can remember standing up for my reasoning of doing work and solving problems and taking a stand to show people that my ideas and how I did work was just as good as they thought they could do. Undergrad was a big eye opener for me because there was always a person who thought their way was the best way and I'd often find myself forcing people to add in my thoughts which ultimately would be correct. It would be the same response "Oh we're so glad you added that in because that was a big part of the assignment"...so that's my short soapbox on how I became so defensive when it came to collaborative work. BUT as I stated, I think it's good and it allows room for thinking. So I approve and hope it can be a learning experience for others as it was to me. Please let me know if you'd like any more information or have any other questions.

Thanks,

—LaToya

CHAPTER 7

FACILITATING WITH THE LEARNER IN MIND

Strategies for Cross-Cultural Online Collaboration

Larissa V. Malopinsky and Gihan Osman

ABSTRACT

In this chapter, we share the experience of a partnership project between several Azerbaijani and U.S. higher education institutions focused on integrating learner-centered pedagogical approaches in designing online curricula. We first examine the challenges of cross-cultural collaboration focused on applying learner-centered pedagogy and social learning strategies in online course design, and then introduce recommendations formulated by the partner teams for addressing these challenges. This study seeks to advance educators' understanding of the critical epistemological differences that may (a) impact cross-cultural collaboration focused on designing online curricula and (b) challenge implementation of the learning experiences aligned with social constructivist principles in culturally diverse educational contexts.

Real-Life Distance Learning, pages 107–138
Copyright © 2014 by Information Age Publishing
All rights of reproduction in any form reserved.

INTRODUCTION

The rapid growth of online learning worldwide and adaptation of constructivist pedagogy and social learning methods for online instruction have created a need for studying cultural influences on both online interactions and the design of online learning environments. A grant from the U.S. Department of State provided the three-year partnership opportunity between Indiana University, the Azerbaijan State Economic University (ASEU), and the Azerbaijan Research and Education Network Association (AzRENA). The partnership focused on two goals: developing online teaching capabilities in Azerbaijani universities and introducing learner-centered pedagogical concepts as part of the movement to Western style education supported by the Azerbaijani government and leading academic institutions in Azerbaijan.

Since gaining independence in 1991, Azerbaijan, a former member of the Soviet Union, has been seeking to build a democratic, market-oriented society and introduce change in its educational system. Although important directions for reforming education have been provided by the legislation, the transitional process has been challenging (Loxley & Julien, 2005). The economic difficulties experienced by Azerbaijani society in recent years resulted in a rapid decline of participation in education and training while the demands for skilled workers grew under the new economic initiatives (ANHD Report, 2003). Although still in its infancy, online education in Azerbaijan brings new educational opportunities and the potential for overcoming some of these difficulties. In particular, it offers the potential for addressing three educational goals: (a) provide access to education in rural areas, thus stemming the movement of people to the cities, (b) allow citizens to maintain employment while going to school, thus making education more economically viable; and (c) provide a vehicle for educational reform through introducing learner-focused interactive pedagogical approaches (Bagirov, 2001).

The technological infrastructure is growing rapidly in Azerbaijan, with several higher education institutions already possessing considerable technology infrastructure. Thus, distance education is less of a technology issue and more about a need for understanding and gaining experience in the design and delivery of learner-centered online courses that can be adopted and scaled up in culturally diverse contexts.

Partnership Project

The partnership project was implemented over the course of three years. It started with the analysis of the Azerbaijani faculty readiness to teach at a distance, individual and institutional barriers to adoption of online instruction, and an examination of technological capabilities of Azerbaijani universities. The results of the analysis affirmed the technological readiness and pointed to the need to support faculty in (a) adopting effective online pedagogical approaches, (b) designing and delivering online curricula, and (c) managing and evaluating online learning processes. The project plan, developed by the United States and Azerbaijani collaborating institutions to achieve these goals included:

- Training a group of Azerbaijani experts in the area of online instructional design and pedagogy, through their participation in an Indiana University certification program. These experts would provide consulting and online program support for faculty at participating Azerbaijani universities.
- Integrating learner-centered instructional methods in the certification program activities, thus allowing the group of Azerbaijani trainees to experience the new pedagogical strategies that they would be implementing at the local universities upon completion of the certification program.

The certification program, in which the Azerbaijani participants were students and the U.S. participants were facilitators, included both courses delivered online during the academic year and workshops at both Indiana University and the Azerbaijan State Economic University during the summer. There were six semester-long online courses that focused on instructional design, learner-centered pedagogy, online facilitation, evaluation of online student leaning and program effectiveness, online curriculum delivery platforms, and instructional consulting. All instruction was learner-centered and it was delivered as a structured design workshop with an emphasis on group activities, discussions, and student analysis of teaching and learning issues. The students, supported by the U.S. facilitators, practiced designing instructional activities to serve as models for future online courses in those Azerbaijani universities that were planning to implement online curricula in the near future.

During the first year of the program, it became evident that differences between the Azerbaijani and U.S. teams were impacting the collaborative design process and student learning. The issues arose around the differences in understanding how teaching should be structured and managed. The impact of those differences was evident not only in the sample designs that partnering teams were building together, but also in the workshop interactions and communication preferences of the Azerbaijani trainees and the U.S. facilitators. At first, these differences were documented informally. As the project progressed, the authors, who were the facilitators in the project, realized that systematic study of those differences was necessary for gaining a better understanding of the challenges and developing strategies for addressing them. We anticipated that culture might be an important variable to consider in that examination.

CASE STUDY

The research study formulated by the end of the first project year aimed at advancing understanding of the critical aspects of designing and delivering online instruction that may be impacted by the cultural differences of collaborating teams. The study focused on (a) analysis of the potential cultural impact on interactions between the two teams during the design workshops, (b) examination of the cultural challenges experienced by the Azerbaijani group as they were applying learner-centered pedagogy in their designs of online learning activities, (c) exploration of the causes for differences related to managing the learning process, making design decisions, and sustaining collaboration during group-based activities, and (d) formulation of strategies for addressing cultural challenges to enable more effective collaboration and knowledge transfer between the partner teams.

Theoretical Framework and Relevant Research

The online educational process is thought to require teaching and learning approaches that differ from face-to-face instructional context (Easton, 2003; Mandernach, Gonzales, & Garrett, 2006; Moore & Kearsley, 2005). In the traditional classroom, the teacher's role has been often seen as that of transmitting knowledge to students and assuming responsibility for directing the learning environment (Cowan, 2006). However, researchers suggest that online instructors should allow students to adopt a more central role in their own learning (Barrett, 2006). They further argue that the online instructors' performance is measured by their ability to facilitate self-directed student work and foster active collaboration among students (Chang & Fisher, 2003; Craig, Goold, Coldwell, & Mustard, 2008).

Teaching and learning processes, like all other human activities, are seen as grounded in the unique social practice of the cultures involved (Alfred & Nafukho, 2010; Pratt & Nesbit, 2000). This assumption holds true for both traditional and online educational settings. Empirical studies provide multiple examples of how learning and collaborative work may be affected by the cultural differences in the following epistemological domains: (a) perception of social positions and power relationships between teachers and students (Dhindsa & Fraser, 2003; Hofstede, 2001; Paulus, Bichelmeyer,

Malopinsky, Pereira, & Rastogi, 2005); (b) cognitive strategies applied for processing information (Boykin & Bailey, 2000; Liu, Liu, Lee, & Magjuka, 2010; Winzer & Mazurek, 1998); (c) the concept of self in relation to independent thinking, competitiveness, and collaboration with others (Kanu, 2005; Morris & Peng, 1994); and (d) dependency on support and direct guidance in managing one's own learning process (McLaughlin, 1996; Rutherford & Kerr, 2008). Fundamentally, these cultural differences impact the interpretation and valuing of learning content, the learning process, and the pattern of interaction between students and instructor and among learning peers. Moreover, epistemological dissonance in a cross-cultural learning group can make it challenging for representatives of different cultures to establish effective communication and manage their collaborative activities (Hofstede, 2001; Zaida, 2004).

Various conceptualizations of culture suggest that it is a dynamic entity characterized by distinct beliefs, attitudes, and behavioral patterns which are accepted and expected by the dominant groups of a society and which differentiate one human group from another (Hofstede, 1991, 2001; Triandis, 1995). In the past decade, an increasing number of researchers have recognized the need for serious cultural analysis in the context of international educational collaboration. Scholars focusing on transnational knowledge transfer, that is, the exchange of pedagogical concepts and their applications between two different countries, suggest that the concepts and methods that proved effective in the country of origin might meet resistance and even result in failure of transfer in the receiving country (Elenkov, 1998; McLaughlin, 1996; Penny, Ali, Farah, Ostberg, & Smith, 2000; Zajda, 2004). In addition to the epistemological differences, researchers emphasize the relevance of the curriculum transferred from one educational context to another as being a critical factor in the successful knowledge exchange (Huysman & de Wit, 2002). Western universities often attempt to transfer their educational solutions without taking into consideration the dominating values and beliefs and the environmental constraints that make specific educational interventions difficult for the developing systems to adapt (Bagirov, 2001; Zajda, 2004).

Language is another crucial factor that influences cross-cultural learning situations (Altbach, 2004; Hofstede, 2001). Recent research suggests that the students' limited foreign language ability impairs their potential to fully understand the concepts being taught in that language, thus forcing them to resort to memorization and recitation as coping strategies (Kanu, 2005; Zajda, 2004). Therefore, differences in language proficiency levels may present additional barriers to adaptation and transfer of new concepts and processes from one cultural context to another (Osman & Herring, 2007).

Cultural differences may amplify the challenges of implementing learner-centered instructional approaches in an online classroom. Students belonging to cultures with established instructor-focused and highly structured academic environments often find themselves disadvantaged in unstructured learning situations that the online educational space presents (St. Amant, 2005; Gunawardena, Nolla, Wilson, Lopez-Islas, Remirez-Angel, & Megchun-Alpizar , 2007; Usun, 2004). In order to succeed as online learners, students are expected to work within minimal guidelines, plan and manage their online tasks and resources, actively seek collaboration with peers, and systematically reflect on their learning experiences (Hong & Jung, 2010; Mazzolini & Maddison, 2006).

Research suggests that the cultural context in which learning takes place provides implicit structures and rules about the way people work together and solve problems as they deal with issues of change, either through the integration of new elements into existing cultural structures or by adapting new structures to fit with the elements in their existing environment (Chen, Hsu, & Caropreso, 2006; Morse, 2003; Schein, 1992; Triandis, 1995). The analytical framework provided by Hofstede (1991, 2001) and Trompenaars and Hampden-Turner (1997) allows for structured analysis of cultural differences and enables formulation of strategies focused on meaningful and sustainable adaptation of new learning designs within culturally different "ecosystems." This framework of "cultural dimensions" refers to the key indicators of predominant and observable behaviors in specific social situations, such as making decisions or managing people and tasks.

Researchers argue that among the cultural dimensions, the following indicators are the most challenging for the adaptation of collaborative, learner-centered approaches:

> *Power Distance*—The extent to which individuals at lower levels of a cultural hierarchy accept their lack of autonomy and authority.
> *Individualism*—An emphasis on one's own goals as opposed to the goals of the greater collective.
> *Uncertainty Avoidance*—The extent to which risk and ambiguity are tolerated.
> *Achievement vs. Ascription*—Recognition of a person's status based on their professional skills and achievements as opposed to their seniority position, gender, or economic worth.
> *Specific (low-context) vs. Diffuse (high context) Orientation*—The degree to which personal matters and relationships are mixed, or interfere, with the work-related tasks (Hall, 2000; Hofstede, 2001; Trompenaars and Hampden-Turner, 1997; Van Hook, 2007).

The participants of the study discussed here represented the Turkish culture, shared by several ex-Soviet states including Azerbaijan, as well as by Iran and Pakistan (Akpinar & Merkert, 2000; Hofstede, 1986). Drawing on

Hofstede's (1986) and Trompenaars' (1997) cultural dimensions, the researchers argue that the Turkish culture is grounded in tradition characterized by the dependence on the authority, high intolerance to ambiguity, and reliance on structured processes (Akpinar & Merkert, 2000; Gunawardena, 1996; Kanu, 2005; Murphy, 1991; Usun, 2004). Students in the Turkish culture are expected to manifest obedience, speak only when addressed, and avoid challenging a teacher, especially in a group setting. Open disagreements between peers and challenging peer ideas are perceived as manifestations of personal disloyalty. Such dynamics between teachers and students have been observed in the cultural contexts that tend to be collectivist in nature and characterized by high power distance, low uncertainty avoidance, and ascriptive orientation (Bodycott & Walker, 2000; Hofstede, 1991; Trompenaars, 1997). Usun (2004) and Kanu (2005) argue that representatives of such cultures may be challenged in unstructured learner-centered situations: Adult professionals would avoid compromising their authority position and risking "losing face," while students would likely reject the role of teacher as facilitator and would be reluctant to take initiative in structuring their own learning process.

Research Questions

Our first-year project experiences confirmed observations provided in the cross-cultural studies mentioned above. As most of the project activities took place at a distance, the Azerbaijani students immediately found themselves in the role of online students for whom they were designing their first online course. They were thus challenged not only by the task of designing learner-centered instruction for online delivery, but also by the collaborative, peer-based working style practiced by the U.S. facilitators during the online sessions. Those early experiences suggested the relevance of cultural differences to our project environment and their potential impact on the challenges we experienced when working together. Therefore, the framework of cultural patterns, or dimensions, was used for analyzing the results of our study guided by the following research questions:

- What are the challenges experienced by the project partners in the process of collaborative design of online learner-centered instruction?
- Which cultural differences are relevant to understanding the challenges?
- Which strategies can be used to respond to those challenges to ensure successful design of the online learner-centered instruction and effective online collaboration between the project partners belonging to different cultures?

Methodology

A case study approach with mixed methods of data collection and analysis was utilized (Creswell, 2003; Stake, 1995). Although the most common criticism of case studies is that their results do not allow statistical generalizations, Yin (2003) argues that the case study is the preferred method for investigating complex real-life phenomena leading to analytical generalizations or theory development.

The Azerbaijani participants included five members of the core Azerbaijani partner team, all employed by the project partner organizations and entrusted with development of the first Distance Learning Center in Azerbaijan. Additionally, we analyzed the survey responses from 46 faculty members representing Azerbaijani universities that formed the AzRENA consortium. The U.S. participants included two senior faculty members and two doctoral students, all with expertise in instructional design and distance education. The U.S. participants were the online facilitators in the certification program designed for their Azerbaijani partners. They also managed all aspects of the project. The U.S. participants designed and led the research study discussed in this chapter. Since some of the research instruments were administered to the U.S. team and asked about their facilitation experiences, their role in the research project was that of the participant-observer.

The study data was collected for 12 weeks during the second year of the partnership project and included surveys, transcripts of weekly online chats, pre-and post-chat questionnaires for students and facilitators, and semi-structured interviews with students. The Azerbaijani team who worked directly on the certification program in the United States provided responses to the pre- and post-chat questionnaires and interviews. They also responded to the survey that addressed epistemological beliefs and possibilities for implementing learner-centered online curricula in Azerbaijan. The faculty members from AzRENA universities were asked to respond to a survey that focused on the potential barriers to implementing distance learning in their country as well as their usage of and beliefs regarding learner-centered teaching strategies versus teacher-centered instruction. All research instruments were developed in both English and Russian, and two Russian native speakers verified the translation accuracy. Russian is the second official language in Azerbaijan and is still prevalent in Azerbaijani higher education institutions.

Faculty Survey

A survey soliciting information about perceived barriers to implementing online programs in post-secondary Azerbaijani institutions was administered to 46 faculty members of the universities that participated in our project. The survey section focusing on potential epistemological barriers was included in our analysis. Eight Likert scale items were used to elicit information about respondents' beliefs about teaching and learning and the strategies they used, or regarded as good practice, in the classroom.

Student Survey

An epistemological beliefs questionnaire was distributed to the Azerbaijani team at the beginning of the data collection period. Thirty-two items were adapted from 10 subscales of Schommer's (1990) epistemological beliefs survey. Inclusion of items was based on judged relevance to the learning context. All items used a five-point Likert scale. Two to five items were chosen from each of the following ten subscales: Seeking single answers; Avoiding integration; Avoiding ambiguity; Knowledge is certain; Ability to learn is innate; You cannot learn how to learn; Success is unrelated to hard work; Learning the first time; Learning is quick; and Concentrated effort is a waste of time.

Pre- and Post-Chat Questionnaires

These questionnaires were administered to both Azerbaijani students and the U.S. facilitators before and after each chat session for 12 weeks, the period allocated for the data collection of the current study. The pre-chat questionnaires were administered two days prior to each online discussion session. In the pre-chats, the students were asked about their learning experiences gained in the past week, as well as their challenges and learning needs. Facilitators were asked about their understanding of the students' learning needs, and they were prompted to share their facilitation strategies for the upcoming discussion.

The post-chat questionnaires, administered immediately after the online discussions, asked students to evaluate facilitation methods and the relevance of the discussion topics to their learning needs. The facilitators were requested to reflect on the dynamics of the chat session and provide their interpretation of the usefulness of the topics discussed to the needs of their students. The facilitators were also asked to provide comments for changes to their approach to be considered in future discussions.

Chat Transcripts

Transcripts for each of the 12 one and a half hour, weekly synchronous online discussions were collected. Although the main sessions were conducted in English, learners at times exchanged private messages in Russian with the main instructor. The chats focused on learner-centered instructional design applied in the context of creating the first online course, which was one of the main goals of our partnership project.

Student Interviews

The semi-structured interviews were conducted with all Azerbaijani students at the end of the 12-week data collection period. They included the questions soliciting students' reflections on their online learning experiences and collaboration with the U.S. partner team. The students were also asked to share their plans regarding application of learner-centered design principles in their future development of online programs for Azerbaijani universities. Each interview lasted approximately 60 minutes. All interviews were conducted in Russian and audio recorded, and their transcriptions were translated into English for analysis.

Analytical Procedures

We approached the analysis of the challenges from epistemological, social interaction, and learning management perspectives, using Hofstede's (1986, 1991) and Trompenaars and Hampden-Turner (1997) frameworks of cultural dimensions to interpret those challenges. These researchers have examined the cultural dimensions across many countries and provided scores for each country to indicate their relative position on each dimension. In using these frameworks, we hypothesized that the cultural dimensions on which Azerbaijan and the United States differed substantially would be relevant to interpreting the differences we identify. Further, we limited the number of cultural dimensions applied in this study to those which, according to the studies of cross-cultural knowledge transfer, may indicate the points of dissonance between representatives of different cultures regarding their views of teaching and learning: power distance; individualism; uncertainty avoidance; achievement versus ascription, and specific versus diffuse orientation (Akpinar & Merkert, 2000; Bodycott & Walker, 2000; Hofstede, 1991; Kanu, 2005; Paulus et al., 2005; Usun, 2004).

Since Azerbaijan was not included in Hofstede's and Trompenaars' studies, we used Iran and Pakistan (available in Hofstede's data), and Russia (available in Trompenaars and Hampden-Turner data) as proxies for Azerbaijan. Iran and Pakistan share the characteristics of the Turkish culture with Azerbaijan, and have similar geographical, historical, and religious contexts. Russia shared the same educational system, and for over 70 years these two countries were highly integrated politically, economically, and culturally as members of the Soviet Union. Researchers have found that the U.S. and Pakistan/Iran are widely separated on three out of five dimensions that were the focus of this study: power distance, individualism, and uncertainty avoidance, while the United States and Russia were widely separated on all five dimensions selected for the study.

Survey responses were analyzed quantitatively. The interviews and chat transcripts, and responses to the pre- and post-chat questionnaires, were first independently reviewed by two researchers to identify emergent themes and then group those themes into categories. Emerging themes were subsequently modified until an agreement on more than 96% of categorized data was achieved. The resulting three high level categories reflected major groups of challenges:

- Adaptation of learner-centered pedagogy for online instruction
- Online communication and collaboration between students and instructors as well as among peers
- Students' management of their online learning process

Credibility and trustworthiness are the primary criteria for establishing the validity of qualitative study (Lincoln & Guba, 1985). We ensured credibility by grounding our inquiry into the framework of cultural dimensions and focusing observations, interviews, and questionnaires on the phenomena related to the cultural attributes. Trustworthiness was established by triangulating findings from the various data sources and researchers' debriefing (LeCompte & Goetz, 1982). Every item in each of the three categories was extensively discussed by researchers from the cultural perspective and alternative causes were explored.

Results

Our study findings are discussed here in terms of the three categories and themes identified in the previous section. The framework of cultural dimensions serves as the theoretical framework that guides our interpretations of the findings.

Adaptation of Learner-Centered Pedagogy for Online Instruction

Our collaborative design sessions revealed challenges experienced by the Azerbaijani team related to understanding and application of learner-centered methods in designing online instruction. Students' initial struggle with the learner-focused concepts prompted the researchers to examine differences in beliefs about learning and expectations regarding teacher-student roles in classroom interactions. Two themes addressing epistemological beliefs were identified: (a) concept of the learning process and (b) the teacher's and student's roles in the educational process.

Pratt identified differences in epistemological beliefs as a major factor impacting the success of cross- cultural collaboration (Pratt & Nesbit, 2000). Research on epistemological beliefs has characterized a dimension with one end anchored in a belief that knowledge is fixed and is directly transferred from teacher to student. This is an absolutist view. At the other end of the dimension is the relativist, who believes that knowledge is constructed by a learner, grounded in social interactions, and based on evidence and context.

The responses to the adaptation of Schommer's (1990) epistemological beliefs questionnaire (Table 7.1) suggests that the Azerbaijani team was more comfortable with the absolutist view in contrast to the learner-centered pedagogy that reflects a relativist perspective. The students agreed that learning happens fast and that there is only one right answer ($M = 2.250$, $SD = 1.732$). They were uncomfortable with ambiguous learning situations and believed in the certainty of knowledge ($M = 2.625$, $SD = 1.479$). The learners reported an even stronger agreement with statements that indicate a tendency to avoid integration of knowledge from different sources and across contexts ($M = 2.250$, $SD = 0.935$).

The results of the survey administered to the Azerbaijani faculty were consistent with the responses provided by the core team (Table 7.2): the majority of respondents' strongly agreed or agreed with 6 of the 8 statements aligned with the teacher-centered instructional methods.

The survey responses were consistent with both facilitator and student comments. The facilitators noted that learners seemed to be confused, sometimes even frustrated when asked to undertake a specific task without a detailed instructional "recipe." This was true even after students received substantial guidance, both individually and through online group discussions. The lead facilitator, "Jane," repeatedly expressed dissatisfaction with

TABLE 7.1   Results of Epistemological Beliefs Questionnaire (Schommer, 1990)

Code	Category	Items in Each Category	Mean	Standard Deviation
A	Seek single answers	11	2.455	1.396
B	Avoid integration	8	2.188	0.765
C	Avoid ambiguity	5	2.050	0.873
D	Knowledge is certain	6	2.417	1.232
E	Depend on authority	4	2.000	0.842
F	Do not criticize authority	6	2.542	1.030
G	Ability to learn is innate	4	1.500	0.540
H	Can't learn how to learn	5	2.900	0.742
I	Success is unrelated to hard work	4	3.813	0.774
J	Learning the first time	3	2.333	1.127
K	Learning is quick	5	2.200	0.908
L	Concentrated effort is a waste of time	2	3.625	1.237

TABLE 7.2   Results of Epistemological Beliefs Questionnaire

Questionnaire Items	N	Mean	Standard Deviation	Orientation
Professors know a lot more than students	46	2.33	1.097	Teacher-centered
A quiet classroom is generally needed for effective learning	46	2.04	1.173	Teacher-centered
Students are not ready for meaningful learning until they have acquired basic knowledge in the discipline	46	1.74	.855	Teacher-centered
It is better when the professor decided what activities to be done	46	1.96	1.095	Teacher-centered
Student projects often result in students learning all sorts of wrong knowledge	46	3.35	1.178	Teacher-centered
Students should help establish criteria on which their work will be assessed	46	3.04	1.414	Student-centered
Instruction should be built around problems with clear, correct answers	46	2.17	1.018	Teacher-centered
Teaching facts is necessary to provide the foundation for more advanced learning	46	1.80	.582	Teacher-centered

the outcomes of the chat sessions: "I believe our students just want to guess the 'right' answer, fix the designs following our instructions, and be done with it." "Sabir," one of the Azerbaijani students, talked in his interview about the confusion among the Azerbaijani team members who could not immediately accept a relationship of equals between them and their United States facilitators:

> The differences between our approaches were very noticeable. The discussions were more like between partners, and it was sometimes confusing. In Azerbaijan, there is always a teacher and there is always a student—there are clear boundaries between them. The teacher tells the student what to do. Everything is pretty formal.

The preferences for teacher-centered instructional methods grounded in prior learning experiences were naturally reflected in the designs the Azerbaijani team proposed for the online course co-constructed with the U.S. partners. Although the students appreciated their empowered voice as learners in the certification program and understood learner-centeredness at the conceptual level, they rarely focused on the learner in their own designs of instruction. The following quote by "Helen," the second facilitator, reflects the facilitators' efforts to help them make that shift:

> The discussion focused on clarifying learner's goals was very beneficial for our students; we need to reinforce the importance of thinking about learner goals

through the next chats. I have the impression it was the first time they discussed the course from learner's perspective, through learner's eyes...They constantly came back to the teacher's perspective when proposing specific design. What makes my facilitation especially difficult is that the students expect one ready solution to the ill-structured design tasks. They ask for a template, algorithm, and there is none. Each design situation is unique and grounded in the specific context. Certainly, there are design principles, but what they want is prescription.

Jane added to this observation by noting that the students "insisted on designing the course as memorization and reciting of content," and they were reluctant to "let learners decide what to do in the course." In his interview, Emin explained students' insistence on more pronounced teacher-centered approaches in the course design:

We have to remember that our teaching styles are different, and we need to make some changes to the courses we've designed in the U.S. In our system, educational process is about a teacher who has a specific program to deliver. Most of our faculty use lectures and seminars and do not use problem-based teaching. Everything is outlined and prescribed.

Another member of the Azerbaijani team, "Afet," added that in a typical Azerbaijani classroom "the students are required to record what the teacher said, and follow those records." The deference to the teacher extended to the relationships between the Azerbaijani design team and the faculty members of those universities whom the students were to consult after completing our certification program. Despite their growing expertise in online design and their position as future online learning consultants for Azerbaijani faculty, the students repeatedly mentioned that it was not their job "to tell faculty how to define the course goals, the designers cannot challenge a faculty member, they need to design whatever he wants" (Sabir, interview transcript).

The belief in the authoritative role of the teacher is consistent with the findings of cross-cultural research studies discussing the high levels of power distance and uncertainty avoidance in the cultures with an established didactical approach to teaching (Hofstede, 1991; Morse, 2003; McLoughlin, 2007; Kanu, 2005). Ill-structured nature of the learner-centered instructional methods can be uncomfortable for the students from those cultures since they expect very structured guidance from the teacher, and the constructivist approach can be viewed as unprofessional or undermining the role of an instructor. For example, after returning from the second summer session in the United States to his students in Baku, Sabir tested the new approach in the classroom and reflected on the progress:

My students are in their fourth year, they already do not believe that a class and a teacher can be interesting—they come to class just to spend time. I started using the approach learned from you: challenging the students and selecting the topics that can trigger a discussion and sharing perspectives. I have to use it cautiously because it is not considered a "serious" teaching approach here.

Communication and Collaboration

The majority of learning activities in the online certification program and summer design sessions was structured as projects that required team effort. The rationale behind group-based learning is grounded in the notion of social construction of knowledge, the process where individuals are exposed to multiple perspectives, share their experiences and expertise, and negotiate meaning (Gredler, 1997; Lave & Wenger, 1991; Rogoff, 1990; Vygotsky, 1978). Distributing roles and responsibilities and co-managing resources in a cross-cultural learning environment can be challenging (Forsyth, 1999; Paulus et al., 2005), but it is a necessary aspect of successful online collaboration (Craig et al., 2008; Zhang, 2007).

The relationships of the Azerbaijani team with their U.S. facilitators were complex. Socially, both team members developed trusting, friendly, and caring attitude towards each other. They spent considerable amount of time together outside the classroom during summer sessions learning about each other's cultural and religious traditions, and social and family life. During the online work periods they were frequently in touch through e-mail and Skype (online chat) technology, updating each other on the local news and chatting about casual matters. However, the students' beliefs about the superior status of the teacher as the source of knowledge and the object of respect affected their interactions with the U.S. facilitators inside the classroom. The students were ready to occasionally ask a clarifying question, but they shied away from openly doubting the concepts introduced by the facilitators or reflecting on the facilitators' performance. When inquired about this, Emin explained: "Nobody wants to criticize a teacher. Why? I guess this is how we are brought up; it is against our mentality. Our U.S. mentors are still teachers, even though we all are on the same level here."

Students' reluctance to question the authority of the facilitators persisted even in situations when facilitators stepped down from their official teaching roles and participated in discussions as regular team members. Facilitator Jane noted:

> The students agreed with us even if they were not convinced or seemed not to understand what we were saying. In order to learn, they need to ask more questions. If they do not share their issues, we wouldn't know what they're struggling with.

Having to respond to the teammates' ideas also came as a great difficulty for Azerbaijani students. The assignments that required evaluation of the peer designs or performance during the online discussions facilitated by the students were perceived as the most challenging: only six out of 48 required reflective summaries were submitted after the chats. When asked to elaborate on the reasons for not submitting the reflection notes, Afet explained:

> Reflection was difficult to us. Let's say, the facilitator is my friend, and it is very difficult for me to write about her, even if I know for sure that she will never read my notes about her. How can I report on my friend?!

Another student, Emin, highlighted superior knowledge of subject matter and seniority of a teammate as other reasons for their reluctance to challenge peers:

> We did make some progress when you showed us how to reflect on process without focusing on personalities, but it is still a very difficult task for us. According to our mentality, if someone performs the task incorrectly, I will not be talking about it. He [Anar] is the senior instructor back in Baku—I won't criticize him—what if he knows the subject better than me?

These concerns about the threat to the peer and teacher loyalty can be linked to diffuse and ascriptive cultural traditions, where people have difficulty separating personal relationships from the tasks they are charged with. Being pragmatic, or particularistic in Trompenaar's terms, learners value loyalty and would rather choose to abandon the task than risk being blamed for criticizing a friend or a teacher.

Aycan et al. (2000) suggest that the rules of high power distance and ascriptive societies do not approve when less experienced team members challenge the ideas of peers with the higher social or professional status thus showing disrespect for their views. However, the authors of this study believe that the students' behavior could be explained not only by their values and prior cultural experiences, but perhaps also by the lack of skills necessary for participating in critical and analytical discursive practice, and especially for producing written critiques. A few submitted reflection papers did not offer any in-depth analyses of strengths and weaknesses of the proposed design solutions or critical reviews of peer participation in project activities. The following succinct statement submitted by Anar after one of the online chats represents a typical feedback on peer performance: "I think everybody worked very well last week and during the chat. We focused on the design of the course problem section. Following useful advice of our instructors we completed our work successfully."

It came as a surprise that the same students who were reluctant to critically evaluate the work of their peers preferred to work independently. This preference is perhaps most clearly exemplified in the students' parallel efforts in preparing a conference presentation focused on the project activities. While the U.S. team consulted each other in developing a set of introductory slides, the Azerbaijani team, when given responsibility for the main presentation on their country's educational system, chose to work in parallel and develop individual versions of presentation, then compare them and select a "winner." Facilitator Jane noted in her interview that the students "did not want to work together on the draft, and as a result we got four versions all differing in format, style and design, and each person insisted on his/her version. When we asked them why they did not work together on the draft, Sabir explained that they wanted to compete and select the best presentation. The Azerbaijani students all recognized their difficulty in collaborating with peers and noted how it was not a familiar practice:

> We have to be more understanding of each other. Now, everyone pushes their own ideas and thinks that it's the best idea out there. I think we definitely need to learn how to work as a team and also we have to remember that we are a team (Emin, post-chat questionnaire).

The research recognizes that high-context, collectivist academic traditions grounded in content-based learning with emphasis on formal assessments make little emphasis on transferable knowledge and peer interaction (Morse, 2003; Rutherford & Kerr, 2008). Moore et al. (2006) describes the case when students representing collectivist, high-context cultural group were reluctant to participate in group projects and discussions out of fear that they would say something inappropriate or make a mistake that would reflect badly on their team. Certainly, the cultural context alone may not fully shape the dynamics of classroom interactions, and the diversity of students' personal learning styles and preferences as well as their prior academic experiences must also be taken into consideration when planning collaborative learning activities. Nevertheless, both instructors and designers of online learning experiences may expect that students from high-context, collectivist cultures would prefer a certain degree of formality, identical assessments for all, precise instructions, and competition in learning (Dunn & Marinetti, 2007; Liu, 2007).

In the context of our study, gradual and careful introduction of new collaborative approaches worked well; the students felt increasingly more comfortable exchanging ideas with others and working as a team:

> Last week our instructors gave us a very interesting assignment. We were switching roles, and every one of us was acting as a chat manager. We were

able to see the mistakes of others, and better understand what it takes to manage a team. I learned a lot from this assignment (Sabir, post-chat questionnaire).

Managing Learning Process

Learning at a distance can present unique challenges to anyone regardless of their cultural background, as online interactions lack the non-verbal cues, rely on technology that may impair the amount of communication motivation and skills to work with minimal support toward fulfilling the learning goal (Curtis & Lawson, 2001; Paulus, 2003; Osman & Herring, 2007). However, self-directed learning strategy and ability to proactively seek information and manage learning resources are all necessary attributes of the successful online learning experience (Craig et al., 2008; Liu et al., 2010). Two groups of challenges related to managing online learning process emerged from our project experiences: students' ability to independently structure their work and students' time management.

The data revealed that the U.S. facilitators and Azerbaijani students initially had different expectations regarding the amount of support or "scaffolding" required for students to organize their learning process and reach the goals for each of the project's milestones. One of Sabir's pre-chat comments indicates confusion with the assignment when students were expected to set their own goals and work towards them: "I am not very happy that the last week was more of a "weekend." There were no concrete assignments. We were just asked to reflect on our designs and provide the rationale why we made certain design decisions."

While the students seemed to be confused when given less "prescriptive" assignments, they rarely asked facilitators for clarification. Thus, Jane noted "the students often just assume they got the assignment right, they would spend substantial time working on the task without requesting feedback, and they would get surprised, even upset, if I pointed at something that needed change." Such difference between facilitator and student expectations regarding management of one's own learning process has been addressed by cross-cultural researchers examining diffuse vs. specific cultures (Trompenaars & Hampden-Turner, 1997; Hall, 2000; Rutherford & Kerr, 2008). They argue that representatives of cultures with predominantly diffuse (also referred to as "high-context") orientation depend on nonverbal, situational, and contextual cues as opposed to explicit information preferred by people from specific, or low-context, cultures. Liu (2007) and Dunn and Marinetti (2007) found that students from diffuse, or high-context cultural groups tend to ask fewer questions than their North American peers who prefer to be more direct, explicit, and expressive in their interactions with both instructors and classmates. Hofstede (1991) and Trompenaars and Hampden-Turner (1997) found that the diffuse, or high-context cultures also tend to exhibit high power distance characteristics. Therefore, students' view of the instructor as an authority figure who "knows best" also may have contributed to the challenges related to management of student learning activities.

Time management was another point where the students and facilitators experienced some dissonance. The online weekly sessions always had interesting starting dynamics: a lengthy greeting ritual when every student welcomed his or her peers and facilitators individually, asking specific questions about families, health, weather, and other social matters. An analysis of chat sessions revealed that socializing took approximately 30% of the time allotted to the discussion session needed for the partner teams to work on the project tasks (Osman & Herring, 2007). The U.S. facilitators frequently expressed concerns with the slow pace and overly lengthy socializing periods, mostly because of the limited time allocated to chats and the amount of content to cover:

> I get impatient sometimes to move right to the task, and I know I need to learn to appreciate personal conversation more. Overall, I do not mind at all to discuss personal matters as it makes us closer, but I am just concerned that we cannot accomplish what's planned because the chat time is so limited (Helen, post-chat questionnaire).

While the facilitators thought that socializing took too much of the online class time, the Azerbaijani students felt that facilitators were too business-like and direct: "I don't know if it is allowed or not, but to step away from the subject for a bit, have a joke, not to rush through the discussion" (Sabir, post-chat questionnaire).

This difference in managing the time planned for the task-related activity validates the observations made by other cross-cultural researchers (Hall, 2000) who reported communication difficulties between individuals from individualistic, and specific, or low-context cultures that prefer a direct and precise communication model and those coming from diffuse, or high-context cultural environments with predominantly collectivist values. In learning situations, specific-oriented teachers or students tend to keep socializing to the minimum and get straight to the task, while representatives of diffuse cultures expect to allocate substantial time to building personal relationships and demonstrating respect (Trompenaars & Hampden-Turner, 1997). Different expectations of the classroom dynamics may put a strain on cross-cultural collaborative work and lead to potential interpersonal or group conflicts (Paulus et al., 2005).

Language-Related Challenges

Our analysis of the challenges would be incomplete without a brief discussion of the impact of language on the dynamics of our collaboration and student learning of new educational concepts. As English language was used as primary language for all project communication and design work, Azerbaijani students had to deal not only with unfamiliar subject matter but had to discuss the concepts and present their design solution in a foreign language. Facilitators, in turn, had to do a lot of guessing of what specific comments or suggestions meant. No doubt that a certain amount of distorted interpretations of the online knowledge exchange took place, and some ideas simply got lost in translation.

Language as a constraining factor is emphasized in most studies that focus on cross-cultural communication and knowledge transfer (e.g., Harzing & Maznevski, 2002; Osman & Herring, 2007). It becomes especially important in online environments, where teachers and students are separated, and the most common way of communication is written text submitted either through electronic mail or in the form of synchronous and asynchronous exchange. The authors writing on the issues of "expatriate" education to developing countries (e.g., Zajda, 2004) argue that researchers communicating in the national language of the country receiving new educational methods and technologies would be able to more adequately asses the level to which innovative concepts are understood, accepted, and integrated into local practices.

The synchronous mode of communication (chat) initially proved to be a substantial barrier to student comprehension and interaction. As such, chats were often conducted in Russian during the early stages of training. Although students were gradually becoming more comfortable using real-time communication, our Azerbaijani colleagues did not recommend the use of synchronous tools for the discussion of content, thus echoing numerous research observations (e.g., Kanuka & Garrison, 2004; Ko, 1996). Students advocated limiting the use of chat to management of online work, such as clarifying assignments, resolving technical issues, and negotiating deadlines. This preference may or may not be attributed to the cultural context of our students. There is no doubt that synchronous communication presents some degree of uncertainty through its fast pace and inability to prepare in advance for the arguments presented by peers, characteristics that students from high uncertainty avoidance culture may find quite uncomfortable. At the same time, such resistance may come from limited language proficiency as well as limited experience using asynchronous tools. While it may take time and effort to integrate new forms of communication into the daily work with the students who feel more comfortable taking notes and preparing their assignments in advance, we believe that the immediacy of synchronous formats has the potential for facilitating more effective knowledge construction, dynamic questioning, and more balanced participation.

Discussion

Cross-cultural differences in educational contexts are sometimes over-powered by the general assumption that learning is a "well-defined, standard experience across cultures" (Jones, 2008, p. 2). However, the findings of this study and numerous more in the literature (e.g., Kanu, 2005; Lun, 2010; Osman & Herring, 2007) underscore the important role culture plays in knowledge construction, collaboration, and communication. Rather than ignoring or working despite the culture, cultural differences need to be acknowledged and considered in both design and delivery of learning experiences for global audiences.

Developing and applying cultural competence becomes especially important in educational reform projects such as the one discussed in this chapter where the impact of culture does not stop at the boundaries of the collaborating team, but extends to the broader community that this project seeks to serve. The goal delineated for the Azerbaijani team, discussed in the study, for example, was not only to embrace student-centered learning, but also to eventually transfer what they have learned among the wider academic community that mostly adheres to Azerbaijani cultural values. Accordingly, those in charge of facilitating learning and collaboration on cross-cultural projects concerned with educational change had to device strategies that would help both achieve the short-term goals of training the partner team and make the desired reforms more adopted by the wider Azerbaijani educational community.

Several culture-sensitive strategies were employed by the U.S. facilitating team to enable more effective adoption and transfer of new teaching and learning methods by their Azerbaijani counterparts. These strategies targeted three major categories of challenges that our study has revealed.

Adaptation of Learner-Centered/Constructivist Pedagogy for Online Instruction

The original approach to introduce the Azerbaijani team to learner-centered instructional principles was to fully immerse them in learning opportunities that were entirely constructivist and learner-oriented. Learners were confused by this method of teaching and were resistant to accept it as a pedagogy that would work in general and in the Azerbaijani context in particular. Our approach to counter the challenge was multifaceted. Facilitators encouraged the Azerbaijani team members to systematically reflect on their learning and focus their reflection on learning experiences and the instructional methods as opposed to mere recollection of the content being covered. Partner teams systematically engaged in comparing and contrasting learner-centered activities and instructional events that employed information transmission models. Facilitators engaged learners in instructional activities that demonstrated a learner-centered approach and invited discussions of the value of these activities in terms of attitudinal and learning benefits. Facilitators used every opportunity to collaborate with the Azerbaijani team on designing instructional solutions grounded in learner-centered theoretical frameworks and establishing links between theories and design decisions. Sharing best practices in teaching and learning and discussing the extent to which specific instructional strategies could be applied in the Azerbaijani classroom context was another strategy that proved to be useful in "bringing home" the concept of learner-centered instruction. Finally, the U. S. team encouraged their Azerbaijani partners to share ideas on how to involve their own students in setting learning and performance outcomes for themselves.

Although the facilitators continued offering activities that were ill-defined and constructivist in nature, the instructional scaffolds that were inserted were more explicit and well-defined to address the learners' need for structure. The use of these scaffolds was decreased as the project progressed. We also divided design tasks and assignments into smaller units and provided more opportunities for monitoring and feedback.

Communication and Collaboration

Influenced by social constructivist notions of learning, the U.S. team designed most instructional opportunities to involve teamwork, collaboration, and open communication (Vygotsky, 1978). However, it became obvious early on that our Azerbaijani students were uncomfortable with such forms of interaction. Accustomed to the information-transfer tradition of teaching, in which the teacher is the source of knowledge, the team did not see much value in the team approach, and desired more structured, formal, and competitive tasks (Dunn & Marinetti, 2007; Liu, 2007). They also resisted questioning or providing feedback to their instructors or to older members of the team. Once the behavior was understood, the U.S. team engaged in a number of explicit as well as immersive opportunities to address this challenge.

Explicitly, we discussed our observations and differences in expectations with the Azerbaijani team. We listened to their concerns, deeply rooted in a culture that focused on face-saving behavior, loyalty to peers, and respect to those higher in status. But we also explained the value assigned to teamwork, relativistic epistemologies, and argumentation in western cultures, and underscored their importance as integral precursors to learning.

We also immersed learners in activities that entailed collaboration, negotiation, and the exchange of perspectives at the very core. We provided a safe culture for critique and learning in which knowledge is regarded as tentative and disagreements in perspective are seen as opportunities for growth. During class discussions, the U.S. team modeled multidirectional critique by challenging the ideas of our peers as well as those "higher in power." We also engaged learners in debates on controversial subjects. These debates presented excellent opportunities for developing students' critical thinking as well as legitimizing discursive practice and argumentation. We also asked students to reflect on these activities and their impact on learning and used these reflections as springboards for deepening their understandings. Finally, we encouraged social activities developed a peer relationship and spirit of fellowship between teachers and students.

Managing Learning Process

Striking the balance between the guiding role of a teacher and students' responsibility for managing their own learning process was a strategy adopted by the U.S. facilitators both in their classroom work with the Azerbaijani team and in the online designs that were collaboratively developed for implementation at Azerbaijani universities. Very early in the project, the facilitators recognized that a compromise must be made in terms of how much "ill-structuredeness" can be used to ensure that the designs inspired by the learner-centered principles are feasible to implement in the local academic context. A combination of instructor-led presentations, individual projects, and student-led discussions formed a design framework that the Azerbaijani team was comfortable to apply when developing online courses for their local audiences.

Facilitators also considered the students' need for more direct guidance coming from their earlier educational experiences, and developed several approaches for addressing that need: engaging the student in role playing, team-based facilitation of discussion sessions, using real-life examples and visual metaphors—all focused on gradual removal of support and enabling students' independent work in the course. Educators facilitating such transition from teacher-focused to learner-centered paradigm must be patient; even with the appropriate amount of support, students' continue struggling with developing independent learning habits. Helen commented: "Although our students exhibit some progress, I believe they still have not internalized these design concepts. They literally copy our notes from last summer or our comments from the chats to their design drafts, sometimes just slightly rephrasing them" (Helen, post-chat questionnaire). Similar observations, when the students copied the instructors' same examples to their papers, were reported by Kanu (2005) in her work with Pakistani teachers and earlier by McLaughlin (1996), who conducted teacher education research in Papua New Guinea.

Instructional scaffolding, or temporary support framework that gets reduced as students' competencies develop, provides necessary structure to students coming from cultures where people feel uncomfortable in new environments, including new learning situations (Hofstede, 1986; Kanu, 2005; Vygotsky,

1978). As much as the Western facilitators from uncertainty-accepting societies would like to see such students succeed, it is important that they find an appropriate balance between continuous support and learning challenge while advancing their students' independent learning and critical thinking skills.

Time management challenges were addressed using multiple strategies. Both teams worked toward finding a balance between their styles in order to get the work done. Facilitators developed and communicated structured agendas for the online meetings in advance. The agendas included topical questions to address and proposed times. Specific time periods were allocated to address personal matters during the online discussions, and separate forum spaces were created where students could discuss any non-project related matters with their facilitators.

Language Challenges

In order to overcome the language barriers, a number of measures were implemented in the project. A substantial component of the course was offered in asynchronous formats to allow learners to move at their own pace through the readings and assignments. Content was provided in simplified English. Also, the students were allowed to submit some of their assignments and reflections in Russian, which they were proficient in. Having a facilitator who was a native Russian speaker proved to be another valuable strategy as it allowed for immediate, context-specific clarification of utterances offered by both learners and facilitators.

Study Limitations

Several limitations of the study should be noted. First, it would have been beneficial to follow the process of adaptation of new pedagogical concepts by Azerbaijani students during all three years of the project as opposed to the 10-month collaborative work during the second project year. However, the research activities during the first year would have been negatively impacted by the students' limited knowledge of English, and the third year involved different activities: the students were starting to facilitate other faculty in Azerbaijan rather than working with the U.S. partners in the structured environment of weekly discussion and design sessions.

Second, students' English language proficiency required for the quick expression of ideas, responding to questions, and synthesizing the information was limited, especially at the beginning of the project. Limited language skills made the students frustrated with their inability to keep up with the pace and forced them to use electronic translators that made the discussions very ambiguous and left the facilitators, who were unaware of the translators, puzzled with students' responses. It would be interesting in future research to examine whether the use of the students' native language (in our case, Azeri) facilitates more effective knowledge transfer of new educational concepts.

Although the Azerbaijani faculty responses to the survey were included in our analysis, interactions with only one cultural group of students were studied in-depth. Although consistent with the case study approach, the number of students and facilitators was small, and it limited our ability to provide broader generalizations about the patterns of cultural dynamics between the two partner groups representing different cultures.

Yet another limitation was related to the difference between the researchers' observations of the classroom dynamics and how those dynamics were presented in the students' reports. It seems that students' responses were constructed to please the researchers rather than accurately describe what happed during the working session. Aycan et al. (2000) attributes this phenomenon to the diffuse, high power distance cultural contexts, where communication is structured in a more socially desirable way as opposed to reporting simple facts. Although in our project, we had an opportunity to triangulate the results obtained from students' reports by observing classroom interactions and analyzing written discourse, some of the student responses, especially those related to their progress in terms of adapting new methods and practices, may have been more optimistic than the reality.

Despite the limitations discussed above, this research provides an opportunity for those U.S. educators who are involved in international collaboration to critically reflect on the transfer of pedagogical knowledge into different cultural contexts. In-depth upfront analysis of the enabling and constraining forces that characterize the cultural framework of the partner team is necessary for developing an understanding of the degree to which new educational practices can be implemented.

IMPLICATIONS FOR DISTANCE EDUCATION

The issues of diversity, multiculturalism, and globalization increasingly become the foci of online curriculum development projects (Rutherford & Kerr, 2008). Challenged by the learning needs and communication preferences of diverse cultural audiences, online instructors and curriculum developers are seeking to address many critical questions grounded in cross-cultural contexts: How to build and deliver an online course that would facilitate deep learning of a multicultural audience? How do the U.S. educators need to formulate or adjust their teaching strategies to be able to effectively teach in an online space? Should different teaching methods and learning approaches be offered to cater to online learner groups that belong to different cultures? Multiple recent studies acknowledged the differences between the U.S. distance education philosophy grounded in the principles of social learning and student-instructor partnership and other global cultures, in which the hierarchical relationship between instructor and student, and success in examinations form the scope and goals of educational practice (Liu, 2007; Shattuck, 2005; Dunn & Marinetti, 2007; Al-Harthi, 2005; Hong & Jung, 2010). As Moore et al. (2006, p. 15) alluded: "Constructivist-based pedagogy couched in the highly interactive communication can be a lonely place for an international online learner whose cultural experiences are different."

Our attempt in this study to highlight the challenges of cross-cultural online collaboration that may be attributed to cultural differences aimed at contributing to the development of greater understanding of the role of cultural attributes in global educational contexts. Our three-year partnership experiences taught us very important cross-cultural lessons that may provide insights and guidance to those U.S. researchers and practitioners who are involved in international distance education projects or teach in cross-cultural online spaces. Thus, when planning a cross-cultural learning initiative, U.S. participants may consider expanding their preparatory activities beyond linguistic proficiency and knowledge of the local educational systems and include development of cross-cultural competence that would enable them to critically interpret and adapt new cultural knowledge. When working with global audiences, online faculty and developers of online curricula, to be effective, must accommodate diverse cognitive styles and communication genres and demonstrate flexibility in selecting and applying instructional methods.

Our partnership experience also transformed our understanding of a culture as a static concept. In our daily interactions with the Azerbaijani partner team, our cultures seemed to mesh, integrate, and evolve into a new framework of negotiated meanings. Agar (2002) describes this transformation as a building of a new definition of culture through experience and dialogue with others and by integrating the differences between two cultural paradigms into a "coherent connection of differences."

Although the results of our study are not meant to generalize to other contexts, and we realize that every cross-cultural project is unique and highly specific, we believe that our experience should provide useful insights for educators with similar design and research agendas and assist them in developing effective collaboration and knowledge transfer strategies.

CONCLUSION

Applying the framework of cultural dimensions presented some challenges with reference to the "cultural profiles" of countries with transitional economies and politics, such as Azerbaijan. An important concern that is frequently brought up in the recent research literature focused on applying Hofstede's and Trompenaars' cultural indicators is that globalization and rapid socio-economic development of developing countries, such as Azerbaijan, often have a cultural impact, making the initial cultural "assessments" of these societies to some extent obsolete. Thus, Naumov & Puffer (2000) noted the decrease of power distance and uncertainty avoidance levels and increase of individualism and masculinity in post-Soviet Russia with the transformation of the country into a market-oriented society and the greater emphasis on individual decision-making. It is logical to assume that the countries of the former Soviet bloc have been experiencing similar cultural changes, although more studies are needed to capture these changes. Moreover, we recognized that the issues encountered in this collaborative project could not be explained exclusively by the differences in cultural values and traditions. Such powerful factors as Azerbaijan's political climate, existing educational policies, available technology infrastructure, and technical skills of teachers and students are all expected to have an impact on the rate of adoption of learner-centered pedagogy and online education. All of these variables must be taken into consideration when transferring educational ideas, methods, and practices to a different cultural environment. More research is, however, needed to examine the impact of the above barriers to the integration of innovative teaching technologies into existing pedagogical practices and identify the factors that may contribute to the success of initiatives similar to our project.

QUESTIONS FOR DISCUSSION

The following questions have been formulated for the follow-up discussion of the case introduced in this chapter:

1. What other factors, besides cultural differences, might have contributed to the challenges discussed in this case?
2. What additional or alternative approaches would you recommend to address the challenges discussed in this case? Provide your argument in support of the recommended strategies.
3. What are the most critical socio-cultural factors that need to be considered when implementing online curricula in countries where distance education practices have not yet been established?
4. What strategies can be applied by online facilitators working with representatives of multiple cultural groups enrolled in the same course?
5. What emerging technologies may be considered the most effective for facilitating knowledge exchange in cross-cultural distance education initiatives?
6. How would you use the findings of this study if you were working on a similar project that involves educational institutions from different cultures?

REFERENCES

Agar, M. (2002). *Understanding the culture of conversation.* New York, NY: Perennial.

Akpinar, M., & Merkert, R. (2000). *Turkey–Westernizing Muslim country: Bridge between two cultures.* Unpublished manuscript. Retrieved from: http://www.ricomerkert.de/uni/Turkey-Westernizing_ Muslim_Country.pdf

Alfred, V. M., & Nafukho, F. M. (2010). International and comparative examination of adult and continuing education. In C. E., Kasworm, A. D., Rose, & J. M. Ross-Gordon (Eds.), *A handbook of adult and continuing education* (pp. 93–102). Los Angeles, CA: Sage.

Al-Harthi', A. S. (2005, March). *Globalization of distance education: Implications for access, social stratification, interconnectivity, and cultural imperialism.* First International Conference on Globalization and Education in Washington State University.

Altbach, P. G. (2004). Globalization and the university: Realities in an unequal world. *Tertiary Education and Management, 10,* 32–33.

Aycan, Z., Kanungo, R. N., Mendonca, M., Yu, K., Deller, J., Stahl, G., & Khursid, A. (2000). Impact of culture on human resource management practices: A ten-country comparison. *Applied Psychology: An International Review, 49*(1), 192–220.

Azerbaijan National Human Development (ANHD) Report, 2003. Retrieved from: http://www.un-az.org/undp/nhdr2003/content_eng.html

Bagirov, H. (2001). The birth of Western University. *Azerbaijan International, 9*(4), 38–78.

Barrett, K. R. (2006). *Gender and differences in online teaching styles.* In E. Trauth (Ed.), Encyclopedia of Gender and Information Technology, Vol. 1 (A-G), (pp. 372–377). London, UK: Idea Group.

Bodycott, P., & Walker, A. (2000). Teaching abroad: Lessons learned about intercultural understanding for teachers in higher education. *Teaching in Higher Education, 5*(1), 79–94.

Boykin, A.W., & Bailey, C. (2000). *The role of cultural factors in school relevant cognitive functioning: Synthesis of findings on cultural contexts, cultural orientations and individual differences* (Report 42). Washington, DC and Baltimore, MD: Howard University and Johns Hopkins University, Center for Research on the Education of Students Placed At Risk (CRESPAR).

Chang, V., & Fisher, D. (2003). The validation and application of a new learning environment instrument for online learning in higher education. In M. Khine & D. Fisher (Eds.), *Technology-rich learning environments: A future perspective* (pp. 1–20). Singapore: World Scientific.

Chen, S. J., Hsu, C. L., & Caropreso, E. J. (2006). Cross-cultural collaborative online learning: When the west meets the east. *International Journal of Technology in Teaching and Learning, 2*(1), 17–35.

Cowan, J. (2006). Introduction. In J. O'Donoghue, *Technology supported learning and teaching: A staff perspective* (pp. 1–13). London, UK: Idea Group.

Craig, A., Goold, A., Coldwell, J., & Mustard, J. (2008). Perception of roles and responsibilities in online learning: A case study. *Interdisciplinary Journal of E-Learning and Learning Objects, 4.* Retrieved from http://ijklo.org/Volume4/IJELLOv4p205-223Craig510.pdf

Creswell, J. (2003). *Research design: Qualitative, quantitative, and mixed methods approaches.* Thousand Oaks, CA: Sage.

Curtis, D. D., & Lawson, M. J. (2001). Exploring collaborative online learning. *Journal of Asynchronous Learning Networks, 5*(1), 21–34.

Dhindsa, H. S., & Fraser, B. J. (2003). Culturally-sensitive factors in teacher trainees' learning environments. *Learning Environments Research: An International Journal, 7*(2), 165–181.

Dunn, P., & Marinetti, A. (2007). Beyond localization: Effective learning strategies for cross-cultural e-learning. In A. Edmundson (Ed.), *Globalized e-learning cultural challenges* (pp. 255–266). London, UK: Information Science Publishing.

Easton, S. S. (2003). Clarifying the instructor's role in online distance learning. *Communication Education, 52*(2), 87–105.

Elenkov, D. (1998). Can American management concepts work in Russia? A cross-cultural comparative study. *California Management Review, 40*(4), 133–156.

Forsyth, D. R. (1999). *Group dynamics* (3rd ed.). Belmont, CA: Wadsworth.

Gredler, M. E. (1997). *Learning and instruction: Theory into practice.* Upper Saddle River, NJ: Prentice-Hall.

Gunawardena, C. N. (1996, November). *Designing learner support for media-based distance education.* Paper presented at Turkey First International Distance Education Symposium (pp. 271–280). Ankara, Turkey: MONE-FRTED.

Gunawardena, S. N., Nolla, A. C., Wilson, P., Lopez-Islas, J. R., Remirez-Angel, N., & Megchun-Alpizar, R. M. (2007). A cross-cultural study of group process and development in online conferences. *Distance Education, 22*(1), 85–121.

Hall, E. T. (2000). Context and meaning. In L. A. Samovar & R. E. Porter (Eds.), *Intercultural Communication: A Reader* (9th ed., pp. 34–43). Belmont, CA: Wadsworth.

Harzing, A.W., & Maznevski, M. (2002). The interaction between language and culture: A test of the cultural accommodation hypothesis in seven countries. *Language and Intercultural Communication, 2*(2), 120–139.

Hofstede, G. (1986). Cultural differences in teaching and learning. *International Journal of Intercultural Relations, 10,* 301–320.

Hofstede, G. (1991). *Cultures and organizations: Software of the mind.* London, UK: McGraw-Hill.

Hofstede, G. (2001). *Culture's consequences: Comparing values, behaviors, institutions, and organizations across nations.* London, UK: Sage.

Hong, S., & Jung, I. S. (2010). The distance learner competencies: A three-phased empirical approach. *Educational Technology Research and Development, 51*(1). doi: 10.1007/s11423–010–9164–3.

Huysman, M. H., & de Wit, D. (2002). *Knowledge sharing in practice.* Dordrecht, Netherlands: Kluwer Academics.

Jones, M. (2008). International students' cross-cultural experiences of learning. *International Journal of Asia-Pacific Studies, 4*(2), 39–72.

Kanu, Y. (2005). Tensions and dilemmas of cross-cultural transfer of knowledge: post-structural/ postcolonial reflections on an innovative teacher education in Pakistan. *International Journal of Educational Development, 25,* 493–513.

Kanuka, H., & Garrison, D. R. (2004). Cognitive presence in online learning. *Journal of Computing in Higher Education, 15*(2), 30–49.

Ko, K.-K. (1996). Structural characteristics of computer-mediated language: A comparative analysis of InterChange discourse. *Electronic Journal of Communication, 6*(3).

Lave, J., & Wenger, E. (1991). *Situated learning: Legitimate peripheral participation.* Cambridge, UK: Cambridge University Press.

LeCompte, M. D., & Goetz, J. P. (1982). Problems of reliability and validity in ethnographic research. *Review of Educational Research, 52*(1), 31–60.

Lincoln, Y. S., & Guba, E. G. (1985). *Naturalistic inquiry.* Newbury Park, CA: Sage.

Liu, X., Liu, S., Lee, S., Magjuka, R. J. (2010). Cultural differences in online learning: International student perceptions. *Educational Technology and Society, 13*(3), 177–188.

Liu, Y. (2007). Designing quality online education to promote cross-cultural understanding. In A. Edmundson (Ed.), *Globalized e-learning cultural challenges* (pp. 35–59). London: Information Science.

Loxley, W., & Julien, P. (2005). *Information and Communication Technologies in Education and Training in Asia and the Pacific.* Asian Bevelopment Bank Report. Retrieved from: http://www.adb.org/Documents/Reports/ICT-Education-Training/ict-education-training.pdf

Lun, V. M.-C. (2010). *Examining the influence of culture on critical thinking in higher education.* Doctoral dissertation, Victoria University of Wellington, Australia.

Mandernach, B. J., Gonzales, R. M., & Garrett, A. L. (2006). An examination of online instructor presence via threaded discussion participation. *Journal of Online Learning and Teaching, 2*(4). Retrieved from: http://jolt.merlot.org/vol6no4

Mazzolini, M., & Maddison, S. (2006). The role of the online instructor as a guide on the side. In J. O'Donoghue, *Technology supported learning and teaching: A staff perspective* (pp. 224–241). London, UK: Idea Group.

McLaughlin, D. (1996). Who is to retrain the teacher trainers? *Teaching and Teacher Education, 12*(3), 285–301.

McLoughlin, C. (2007). Adapting e-learning across cultural boundaries: A framework for quality learning, pedagogy, and interaction. In A. Edmundson (Ed.), *Globalized e-learning cultural challenges* (pp. 223–238). London, UK: Information Science.

Moore, M. G., & Kearsley, G. (2005). *Distance education: A systems view* (2nd ed.). Belmont, CA: Thomson Wadsworth.

Moore, M., Shattuck, K., & Al-Harthi, A. (2006). Cultures meeting cultures in online distance education. *Journal of E-Learning and Knowledge Society, 2*(1). Retrieved from http://www.jel-ks.it/archive/02_05/Methodologies1.html

Morris, M. W., & Peng, K. (1994). Culture and cause: American and Chinese attributions for social physical events. *Journal of Personality and Social Psychology, 67*, 949–971.

Morse, K. (2003). Does one size fit all? Exploring asynchronous learning in a multicultural environment. *Journal of Asynchronous Learning Networks, 7*(1), 37–55.

Murphy, K. L. (1991). Patronage and oral tradition: Influences on attribution of distance learners in a traditional society (a qualitative study). *Distance Education, 12*(1), 27–53.

Naumov, A., & Puffer, S. M. (2000). Measuring Russian culture using Hofstede's dimensions. *Applied Psychology: An International Review, 49*(4), 709–718.

Osman, G., & Herring, S.C. (2007). Interaction, facilitation, and deep learning in cross-cultural chat: A case study. *The Internet and Higher Education, 10,* 125–141.

Paulus, T. M. (2003). *Collaboration and the social construction of knowledge in an online learning environment.* Unpublished doctoral dissertation, Indiana University, Bloomington.

Paulus, T. M., Bichelmeyer, B., Malopinsky, L., Pereira, M., & Rastogi, P. (2005). Power distance and group dynamics of an international project team: A case study. *Teaching in Higher Education, 10*(1), 43–55.

Penny, A. J., Ali, M. A., Farah, I., Ostberg, S., & Smith, R. L. (2000). A study of cross-national collaborative research: Reflecting on experience in Pakistan. *International Journal of Educational Development, 20,* 443–455.

Pratt, D. D., & Nesbit, T. (2000). Discourses and cultures of teaching. In A. L. Wilson & E. Hayes (Eds.) *Handbook of Adult Education* (pp. 117–131). San Francisco, CA: Jossey-Bass.

Rogoff, B. (1990). *Apprenticeship in thinking: Cognitive development in social context.* New York, NY: Oxford University Press.

Rutherford, A. G., & Kerr, B. (2008). An inclusive approach to online learning environments: Models and resources. *Turkish Online Journal of Distance Education, 9*(2). Retrieved from: http://tojde.anadolu.edu.tr/tojde30/pdf/article_2.pdf.

Schein, E. (1992). *Organizational culture and leadership.* San Francisco, CA: Jossey-Bass.

Schommer, M. (1990). Effects of beliefs about the nature of knowledge on comprehension. *Journal of Educational Psychology, 82,* 498–504.

Shattuck, K. (2005). *Glimpse of the global coral gardens: Insights of international adult learners on the interactions of cultures in online distance education.* Unpublished Doctoral Dissertation, The Pennsylvania State University.

Stake, R. (1995). *The art of case research.* Thousand Oaks, CA: Sage.

St. Amant, K. (2005). Online education in an age of globalization: Foundational perspectives and practices for technical communication instructors and trainers. *Technical Communication Quarterly, 16*(1), 13–30.

Triandis, H. C. (1995). *Individualism and collectivism.* Boulder, CO: Westview.

Trompenaars, F., & Hampden-Turner, C. (1997). *Riding the waves of culture. Understanding cultural diversity in global business.* (2nd ed.). New York, NY: McGraw-Hill.

Usun, S. (2004). Factors affecting the application of information and communication technologies (ICT) in distance education. *Turkish Online Journal of Distance Education, 5*(1). Retrieved from http://tojde.anadolu.edu.tr/tojde13/articles/usun.html

Van Hook, S. R. (2007). *Application of transcultural themes in international classrooms.* (ERIC Document Reproduction Service No. ED495063).

Vygotsky, L.S. (1978). *Mind and society: The development of higher mental processes.* Cambridge, MA: Harvard University Press.

Winzer, M. A., & Mazurek, K. (1998). *Special education in multicultural contexts.* Upper Saddle River, NJ: Prentice Hall.

Yin, R. K. (2003). *Case study research: Design and methods* (3rd ed.). Thousand Oaks, CA: Sage.

Zajda, J. (2004). Cultural transferability and cross-cultural textbook development. *Education and Society, 22*(1), 83–95.

Zhang, J. (2007). A cultural look at information and communication technologies in Eastern education. *Education Technology Research and Development, 55*(3), 301–314.

CHAPTER 8

SUPPORTING ADULT LEARNERS' AUTHENTIC LEARNING EXPERIENCE BY OPTIMIZING COLLABORATIVE GROUP WORK IN DISTANCE LEARNING COURSES

Eunjung Oh, Ying Liu, and Thomas C. Reeves

ABSTRACT

The target audience of this case study is current and future faculty interested in designing and teaching distance learning courses for learners in higher education institutions. The case involved adult learners' collaborative group work in an online evaluation course in which authentic tasks comprised the major pedagogy. A guiding principle for the overall study was that adult learners working in groups collaboratively to complete authentic tasks constitute a pedagogically strong approach to satisfy their needs for professional development. This case study is nested within the context of a two-year multi-phased design research project; it reports major challenges learners encountered during group work on authentic evaluation projects and what supports and scaffolding successfully resolved those challenges.

Real-Life Distance Education, pages 139–158

INTRODUCTION

The Internet has become the preferred technology for learning and teaching at a distance. The merits of online learning stem from the fact that it provides education opportunities to people who might otherwise have no access, and it allows all students to learn with greater flexibility in time, place, and study modes. These inherent advantages of Internet technology, coupled with the constant need for adult learner education (Merriam, Caffarella, & Baumgartner, 2007), have led to the spread of online education through higher education. Online learning also makes it possible to distribute specialized professional development opportunities originally available at specific locations more widely. Evaluation is one such area.

Evaluation is an applied field and evaluation education is resource intensive (Trevisan, 2004). Teaching evaluation involves much more than a solid knowledge base of theory and methodology. The paramount goal for evaluation education is to prepare students to be competent professional evaluators possessing the necessary theoretical knowledge and practical skills to conduct successful evaluation projects. Some explicit knowledge and skills can be acquired through classroom learning in relatively straightforward ways, but the capacity to apply evaluation knowledge and skills appropriately must be gained through experience (Hurley, Renger, & Brunk, 2005). Similar to other practical fields, incorporation of experiential opportunities has been vital for teaching evaluation (Darabi, 2002; Kelley & Jones, 1992; Trevisan, 2004). Unfortunately, not all institutions and organizations can afford the resources necessary for students to learn evaluation through practical opportunities, particularly in online learning environments.

Context

The context for this case study is the development of a new online evaluation course offered by the College of Education at a large southeastern U.S. university. The professor, also an expert evaluator, has taught this graduate class for nearly 20 years in a face-to-face setting. The course has been successful, well known not only in the home institution but also at other institutions. For several years, the professor received requests for a distance version of the course from faculty and students around the globe unaffiliated with the host institution.

In the evaluation course's face-to-face setting, the instructor relied on a constructivist view of learning and emphasized the value of practical experience in learning evaluation. The primary pedagogy has always been "authentic learning tasks" (Herrington, Reeves, & Oliver, 2010). Course activities involved the real-life task of evaluating a specific e-learning product (e.g., a web-based course or an interactive multimedia training module) for a real client. The overall process included preparing an evaluation plan, implementing it, and writing a final report with all tasks accomplished by collaborative groups of two to four people. Collaborative group work was integral to fulfilling the course and project objectives.

The instructor stressed the importance of ensuring that the new distance learning course would be as effective as the face-to-face version and that it also would employ authentic learning tasks as its primary pedagogy. To provide an equivalent quality of learning experience for learners, an educational design research (McKenney & Reeves, 2012) team comprised of the instructor and two Ph.D. students identified supporting students' distance group work on evaluation projects as a major pedagogical goal in the course. Thus, the case described herein sums up the processes and outcomes of a two-year multi-phased educational design research project. The overall study was guided by the principle that adult learners working in groups collaboratively to complete authentic tasks constitute a pedagogically strong approach to satisfy their needs for professional development.

Educational design research usually pursues two goals simultaneously, i.e., solving a real world problem and contributing generalizable knowledge (McKenney & Reeves, 2012). The authors conducted this educational design research study to achieve twin goals:

- To design and implement an online evaluation course that maximizes the opportunities for adult learners to have a meaningful learning experience through authentic learning tasks and collaborative group work.
- To identify reusable design principles and strategies to optimize collaborative group work among adult learners when working on complex authentic learning tasks in online learning environments in general.

Theoretical Perspective

To provide students located in multiple institutions in the U.S. and other countries with ample opportunities for developing the knowledge base and practical experience needed for learning evaluation, the research team created an online learning environment that integrated two major theoretical design considerations: authentic learning tasks and collaborative group work.

Authentic Learning Tasks

Authentic learning is believed to have multiple benefits for learners, especially for those in online environments (Herrington, Reeves, & Oliver, 2010). Use of real-life, authentic tasks is central to this learning model because they enable learners to make connections between academic learning and their lives. The authentic tasks learning model has the following distinctive characteristics:

- Authentic tasks have real-world relevance.
- Authentic tasks are ill-defined, requiring students to define the tasks and sub-tasks needed to complete an activity.
- Authentic tasks comprise complex activities to be investigated by students over a sustained period of time.
- Authentic tasks provide the opportunity for students to examine the task from different perspectives, using a variety of resources.
- Authentic tasks provide the opportunity to collaborate.
- Authentic tasks provide the opportunity to reflect.
- Authentic tasks can be integrated and applied across different subject areas and lead beyond domain-specific outcomes.
- Authentic tasks are seamlessly integrated with assessment.
- Authentic tasks create polished products that are valuable in their own right.
- Authentic tasks allow competing solutions and a diversity of outcomes. (Herrington, Reeves, & Oliver, 2006, p. 237)

The use of authentic learning tasks as a primary pedagogy is most appropriate due to the application-oriented nature of evaluation. People who write about teaching evaluation often advocate authentic pedagogical practices that can foster effective application and transfer of evaluation knowledge and skills (Alkin & Christie, 2002; Febey & Coyne, 2007; Hurley, Renger, & Brunk, 2005; Lee, Wallace, & Alkin, 2007). Course projects and practicum experiences have been commonly used in evaluation courses (Trevisan, 2004). Even though these learning activities may not meet every criterion listed above, they normally reflect most of the key features as they occur under the supervision of a real client, involve real field work, result in a final evaluation report supported with data, and require collaboration between multiple people (cf. Darabi, 2002; Hurley, Renger, & Brunk, 2005; Kelley & Jones, 1992; Trevisan, 2004). This online e-learning evaluation course was specifically designed to help students gain knowledge and skills eventually transferrable to future work requirements.

Collaborative Group Work

In online courses, using authentic learning tasks optimizing collaborative group work is usually essential because few authentic tasks are tackled by a single learner. Collaborative group work is widely used in adult education (Smith, 2005). It is also a popular pedagogical approach in online learning (Jonassen, Lee, Yang, & Laffey, 2005). For adult learners, group work is fundamental to an effective and meaningful learning experience because students not only discuss concepts and processes, but also must enact these ideas to produce outcomes similar to those they are likely to perform in their actual lives. Additionally, use of collaborative group work can help adult learners in many areas including mastery and retention of material, quality of reasoning strategies, process gains, and transfer of learning (McConnell, 2006). Moreover, working with others also allows learners opportunities to refine the skills they need to work together to achieve important goals throughout their lives.

Knowledge of how to support collaborative group work in teaching evaluation, even in the context of face-to-face instruction, is limited. Indeed, there is little discussion of pedagogical frameworks of any kind in the evaluation teaching literature (Oliver, Casiraghi, Henderson, Brooks, & Muslow, 2008; Trevisan, 2004). Moreover, although there are considerable benefits in using group work for accomplishing real-world projects, it is certainly challenging for online learners communicating at a distance as they work together to achieve common goals (Roberts & McInnerney, 2007).

Case Objectives

The literature discussed above shows that using authentic learning tasks and collaborative group work is promising for teaching evaluation. However, to successfully apply these pedagogically sound approaches online requires many more considerations due to the distinctive characteristics of online environments. Thus, we present our case study as an example to provide guidance for current and future instructors interested in designing and teaching distance learning courses for learners in higher education institutions. This case study emerged from a multiyear educational design research initiative undertaken by the authors. Readers of this case study will be able to

- perceive how adult learners can work at distance as a group to accomplish authentic evaluation projects,
- anticipate the challenges and problems distance learners may confront in such a authentic learning environment, and
- identify ways instructors can effectively support adult learners in this type of authentic learning environment.

CASE STUDY

Educational Design Research and Case Study Approach

The case in this study can be defined as adult learners' collaborative group work in an online evaluation course where the major pedagogy involves authentic learning tasks. The research team examined what really happens when adult learners work online as a group to accomplish authentic evaluation projects using a case study approach nested within an overall educational design research approach (van den Akker, Gravemeijer, McKenney, & Nieveen, 2006). Design research is defined as "a systematic but flexible methodology aimed to improve educational practices through iterative analysis, design, development, and implementation, based on collaboration among researchers and practitioners in real-world settings, and leading to contextually-sensitive design principles and theories" (Wang & Hannafin, 2005, p. 6).

Educational design research aims to accomplish the dual goals of improving practice in specific local settings and developing reusable design principles that capture the essence and patterns of teaching and learning in local settings and can be applied in other settings. Educational design research is not a single research method on its own: rather, it is a paradigm or genre for exploring and answering research questions (Kelly, 2006). The techniques and methods for design research are still evolving (McKenney & Reeves, 2012). Educational design researchers typically incorporate multiple data collection methods borrowed from multiple research traditions, depending on the goals and emerging requirements of the research project (Edelson, 2002; Wang & Hannafin, 2005).

A case study method was applied in this design research project for several reasons. First, case study is a suitable design when researchers are particularly interested in understanding the process and asking "why" and "how" types of questions (Merriam, 1998). Second, case study in education is useful when researchers are interested in investigating educational innovation (Merriam, 1998). Case study methods allow researchers to deeply investigate and understand a case in real-life situations, yielding a rich description of a complex phenomenon, and presenting readers with many insights. Third, the characteristics of case study—*particularistic, descriptive, and heuristic* (Merriam, 1998, p. 29)—sync up well with the characteristics of educational design research. Both case study and design research investigate particular and specific situations or phenomena. As the focus of a case study is a case, design research's focus is a specific educational problem in a specific local setting. Case study provides rich, vivid, and thick descriptions as a part of its research outcomes, and this provides the information to guide the iterative design and redesign efforts required for successful design research.

Methods/Processes

The overall guiding question of this case was "How can successful collaborative group work be supported in an online learning environment?" The following subquestions were asked:

- What challenges do learners encounter when they work in groups in online learning environments?
- What supports or scaffolding do learners need during the group work process?

To investigate these questions, the design research proceeded in the four stages Bannan-Ritland (2003) delineated in her Integrative Learning Design model: (a) exploration, (b) enactment, (c) implementation, and (d) dissemination. The project lasted for two years from summer 2007 to spring 2009. The four stages often overlapped with each other because the design research proceeded in a cyclic manner with an activity in early stages often influencing activity in later stages. Figure 8.1 presents the overall process of this design research project.

We launched the first online course in the spring 2008 semester. For three semesters, 33 graduate students from 13 institutions in six countries representing 13 nationalities worked in different time zones and brought diverse cultures into the course. During the implementation stage, all data collected were used by the researchers to make decisions about the kinds of interventions to provide and whether to introduce them in the same iteration the data were collected or in the following one. The major criteria for design and implementation refinement during these three iterations focused on (a) the quality of students' learning outcomes such as their evaluation plans, final reports, and individual quizzes; and (b) the quality of students' group work processes and level of satisfaction with their collaborative group work. Findings from these data were also used to refine the overall course's design framework and the design principles supporting the course.

Data were collected using four primary methods: (a) semi-structured interviews, (b) surveys (i.e., course evaluations), (c) archival data, and (d) online observations (see Table 8.1). By using multiple data sources, the

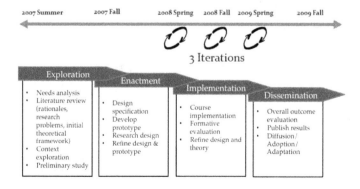

Figure 8.1 The overall educational design research process.

TABLE 8.1   Data Collection During Implementation Phase

Phase (Weeks)	Focus	Primary data collection
Pre-group work (W1-3)	Background information Prerequisite knowledge & experience	Student Profile Survey Evaluation skills inventory First student interviews Interaction among members (i.e., E-mails, Wikis, Group forums)
During-group work (W3-16)	Characteristics and work styles of the groups Initial challenges Initial understanding of the project and group members Group work process	Evaluation plan Instructor feedback Interaction among members (i.e., E-mails, Wikis, Group forums) Team and process assessment Second student interviews (Informal) Instructor interviews
Post-group work (After W16)	Overall experience/reflection Group work process Critical factors for success Suggestions for improvement	Evaluation report Instructor feedback Self/Peer evaluation Third student interviews Instructor interview

researchers tried to achieve a thorough understanding of students' collaborative group work processes as they worked on evaluation projects at a distance using data from multiple sources and perspectives.

As noted above, three iterations of the online evaluation course were studied. Figure 8.2 depicts the complete research process during one iteration.

For data analysis, four tools were used: MS Word, MS Excel, SurveyMonkey, and NVivo 8.0. Interviews were transcribed in MS word and transferred to NVivo. Survey results were first organized in SurveyMonkey using the data analysis function and downloaded and managed using MS Excel. Archival and observation data were managed in MS Word. Qualitative data were analyzed using techniques borrowed from grounded theory perspectives (Merriam, 1998; Strauss & Corbin, 1998).

Design and Implementation of the Course

For this case study, the design and implementation of the third iteration of the online course, the most successful semester, is presented. The course was delivered in an asynchronous manner because students were located in multiple time zones. The course management system was the open source Moodle course management system. Figure 8.3 presents the third iteration Moodle site. The instructor posted weekly activities, guidance, and resources. Each week, students studied textbook readings, evaluation case studies,

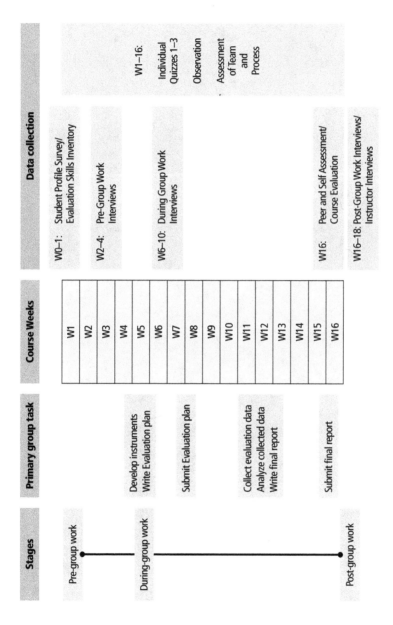

Figure 8.2 Overview of research process during one iteration.

Figure 8.3 Screen capture from course Moodle Site Version 3.0.

and a prerecorded PowerPoint lecture individually, and contributed to the Weekly Forum in which the instructor posted questions or ideas for discussion. Students were also asked to freely share their reflections or introduce new discussion topics. Several course guidelines were provided, both at the beginning of the course and through weekly announcements.

The principal authentic task in the course was a semester-long evaluation project. The instructor assigned groups of three or four students to work with specific real-world clients. Each week, the instructor sent out announcements using the Course News Forum, posted activities and resources, and asked discussion questions regarding evaluation. The questions were associated not only with readings but also with the students' group work process to provide task-oriented scaffolding. The instructor also communicated with student teams via e-mail, sending additional announcements and encouragement, answering questions, and giving feedback on group efforts. The two course facilitators, who were also members of the research team, attended the first two synchronous online group meetings to provide support and answer questions.

In terms of tools, the course management system, Moodle, provided a Group Work Forum and Group Wiki for collaboration. Students were also encouraged to use Skype for synchronous meetings. E-mail was the most frequently used tool for communication. For writing, students used Google docs and MS Word review functions. The Moodle Survival Guide and Wiki guide were provided during the first and second weeks. For grading purposes, assessment was based on their evaluation plans, reports, individual quizzes, and participation. For individual evaluation, each student's participation, quiz grades, and results of self and peer assessments were considered. For the group portion, evaluation plans and final evaluation reports were assessed using rubrics.

Major Challenges and Support Provided

During the three iterations of the course involving 33 students, a number of challenges arose. The three challenges that were major issues in all iterations across all groups were communication, differences in expectations, and learning about evaluation.

Communication

During the first iteration, students identified communication in particular as the greatest challenge. Evidence of communication problems was clear from observations of students' interactions via e-mail and on the course website, as well as from participant interviews.

During the second iteration, communication was improved to a great extent and was more functional; however, delayed communication and lack of response on the part of some group members caused frustration among others in the group and delayed the overall group process. With design and implementation improvements, communication in all groups during the third semester was quite smooth, and additional challenges regarding communication were not identified.

According to Paulus (2009), in collaborative learning environments, where students need to establish a common ground, students may have communication difficulties on four levels:

- Contact (indicating they are willing and able to continue the interaction)
- Perception (indicating they are willing and able to perceive the message)
- Understanding (indicating they are willing and able to understand the message)
- Attitudinal reaction (indicating they are willing and able to react and respond, accept or reject the message). (p. 229)

In online environments where students do not know or see their group members and the instructor, it may be unrealistic to anticipate that adult learners naturally know how to communicate with each other actively and work together effectively to learn the essence of evaluation and complete the project. To design and implement the course to optimally support students' communication, our efforts fell into three categories: (a) facilitate communication, (b) establish a strong sense of community and help students develop a sense of belonging to their groups and the class, and (c) provide a variety of technologies that everyone can use.

We sought to establish a sense of presence so that communication and interaction among students could be more active and collaborative, and yield better learning outcomes. To facilitate students' communication, we utilized multiple strategies. First, throughout the semester we strove to provide strong instructor and facilitator presence via weekly announcements, frequent check-ins, invitations for individual meetings, participation in discussions, and guidance during the first two group meetings. Second, our efforts to enhance the quality and quantity of course discussions also helped facilitate communication. Once social presence was established as a whole group, it became easier to elicit immediacy of online interaction within groups. Third, modeling optimal communication behaviors, styles, and methods was important. We found that our adult learners still needed guidance because many of them were new to online learning environments, online communication, or collaborative group work using different tools, or they were unaware of optimal communication methods among their group members. Many online learning studies suggest that explicit facilitation of online groups is important for guiding students to effectively learn and work together online (Paulus, 2009). Fourth, groups were assigned considering time zones. The response time in online groups is a critical factor to the online interaction because when one group member does not respond promptly enough to establish common ground and move the project forward, other group members, in particular the sender, perceive less social presence (Tu & McIsaac, 2002).

To enhance communication and students' collaboration, it is important to establish a strong sense of community and help students develop a sense of belongingness to their groups and to the whole class. Kirschner and Kreijns (2004) claimed that for computer supported collaborative learning to be successful, social interaction among participants is a prerequisite. However, Kreijns, Kirschner, and Jochems (2003) argued that social interaction fails to occur in distributed learning groups (DLGs) in CSCL environments because instructors tend to take social interaction for granted and restrict social interaction to cognitive processes. Since online learners tend to experience a greater sense of disconnection and anonymity and sense less individuality in and awareness of the personalities of others, it is important to design diverse—both on-task and off-task—opportunities and contexts for them to interact with each other and encourage social relationships. We used the following specific strategies: (a) providing opportunities for students to form impressions of co-members through an ice-breaking activity and promoting the development of social relationships, (b) providing social spaces and contexts for both individual groups and the whole class throughout the semester, and (c) encouraging a culture of knowledge sharing and open communication.

Providing a variety of technology that everyone can use and access is important. Haythronthwaite, Kazmer, Robins, and Shoemaker (2000) recommend providing multiple modes of communication to support students' abilities to engage in cognitive and social interactions and to develop a community of learners at a distance. We used the following strategies to help students learn to use different online communication technologies: (a) providing group spaces and encouraging use of transparent communication within groups; (b) promoting group writing and editing tools; (c) providing both synchronous and asynchronous tools, even though the course itself was asynchronous without virtual class meetings; and (d) giving overt guidance for students to take advantage of the tools in proper ways because their levels of proficiency with technology were different.

Differences in Expectations Regarding Commitment and Product Quality

During the first iteration, a number of students had personal situations such as natural disasters, unexpected moves from one country to another and serious illness or loss of family members. These events forced these students to leave the course for a period of time and prevented them from completing an equal share of the work required to accomplish the authentic task. During the second iteration, when communication issues were resolved to a great extent, differences in expectations regarding commitment and product quality, and consecutive actions created the greatest challenges and frustration across the groups.

Although all students reported they had at least a fairly high level of motivation, there were differences in individual participation. Participation in this online group work could be demonstrated by responsiveness in asynchronous communication, active synchronous communication, and actual contributions to the group outcome. The variations in the degree of participation mostly came from differences in expectations regarding commitment levels toward the course and perceptions of satisfactory product quality. These differences created challenges within the groups, especially for the more motivated and engaged members. Behaviors causing frustration for other group members included delayed or lack of responses to e-mails, no-shows at multiple meetings, and a reluctance to contribute as much as others expected. One group had to be divided into two smaller groups after the members simply stopped talking.

The instructor's expectation for students in this course was successful completion of the evaluation project in a professional manner that met the client's needs and students' substantial learning about evaluation during the process. Learning about evaluation can be achieved individually, but the project had to be completed collaboratively. Therefore, individual contributions to collaboration are important (Hathorn & Ingram, 2002). The specific strategies used were (a) authentic evaluation projects with real-life relevance to students that certainly helped students' intrinsic motivation; (b) assessment strategies including self- and peer evaluation that strengthened the extrinsic motivation of students to actively learn about evaluation and to participate in group work; (c) clarification of instructor expectations regarding the learning outcome, commitment, and performance at the beginning of the course, which set a standard and prevented potential conflicts and challenges within groups; and (d) the sharing of student expectations and goals and establishing common objectives and rules. It is important for groups to explicitly negotiate common ground (Paulus, 2009) so that the group members can establish and share "mutual understanding, knowledge, beliefs, assumptions, presuppositions, and so on" (Baker, Hansen, Joiner, & Traum, 1999, p. 33). For example, during the first meeting, students not only introduced themselves and selected a leader, but also discussed ground rules for teamwork.

Time Management

The authentic learning tasks involved external stakeholders such as clients and evaluation participants. For the students who also had other academic, professional, and personal commitments, to work with each other and these stakeholders at a distance required sophisticated time management and organization skills. They had to have a clear project timeline to adhere to, as well as to be flexible with uncontrollable factors such as weather-delayed data collection or participant recruitment difficulties. During the first and the second iteration, even though students expressed their concerns about time management, they were more concerned with communication and less responsible group members. Once those issues were resolved in the third iteration, most groups' concerns were about whether they could complete their work on time.

To avoid student haste to complete this large-scale project in the last weeks of the term, it was important to help them effectively and efficiently manage and organize their work process. First, we found it useful for online groups to select their leaders because the project involved significant communication with the client and among group members, and organization of tasks and documents. During the first and second iterations, some groups had challenges with ineffective leadership such as not knowing how to manage group work processes at a distance or lacking technology proficiency. Therefore, for the third iteration, we looked at students' profile surveys and intentionally assigned in each group at least one or two people with online learning experience and desirable online group work experiences, although it was still the members' responsibility to select a leader. We provided guidance on selecting a group leader and specified the roles and responsibilities a leader should have. Second, providing an overall timeline of projects and all the milestones at the beginning of the collaboration helped the students. Even though to receive a grade, only the evaluation plans and reports were required to be shared with the client, there were several smaller, additional tasks students had to achieve. Thus, it was important for students to know how much time they had and how many tasks they needed to complete. Third, it was important to mentor, coach, and guide groups on how to work with clients and to intervene between the clients and the group, if necessary. The instructor as an expert evaluator helped students initiate their projects by finding and connecting clients with the groups. Although most clients were cooperative and eager to know the evaluation results, project processes were often delayed due to the clients' busy schedules. So, occasionally the instructor had to intervene between the clients and the groups to push the process forward, as well as model communications and resolutions. Fourth, having groups hold regular synchronous meetings and share meeting minutes was important. Sometimes, groups did not have much to discuss, but having a weekly meeting to check on the progress helped groups move forward without undue procrastination. Also, students sometimes needed to share their frustration with each other about delayed or difficult processes. In addition, having meeting minutes posted in an open space helped the instructor and facilitators see where groups were and determine how they could assist students. Table 8.2 summarizes the design principles and strategies that emerged from this educational design research study to support collaborative group work in this type of online course.

IMPLICATIONS FOR DISTANCE EDUCATION

Experiential learning has been the most widely used approach in traditional face-to-face evaluation courses. When we decided to offer an evaluation course online, we were not limited to more traditional academic approaches such as lectures or online discussions of readings. The particular pedagogical approach we used, authentic learning tasks, was determined by the content and context. If an authentic evaluation project and students' collaborative group work could be effective approaches for students to learn evaluation online, the role of instructors and designers was to discover how to make it happen.

We believe that this case is sufficiently mature through three iterations of design, implementation, data collection and redesign processes to have strong applicability and generalizability for other online courses our readers might design and teach. Our case is particularly informative for those who aspire to incorporate complex authentic learning tasks and collaborative group work in distance courses.

Our students were mostly Instructional Technology or similar majors who were likely to be familiar with teaching and learning with technology and were assumed to have some online learning or group work experience. Nevertheless, they still needed clear guidance on how to learn and work together online and required specific advice on tools, resources, group work, and leadership. Although only the three major challenges our students experienced are discussed in this chapter, we believe they are among the most common challenges many instructors could experience in both face-to-face and online classes.

CONCLUSION

Increasingly, institutions of higher learning have been developing online education programs, and enrollments in those online learning programs in the United States have been steadily growing as administrators and online teaching faculty believe that online courses are important to meet students' needs for life-long learning (Allen & Seaman, 2011). However, a criticism exists on whether the quality of online learning is actually fulfilling the real

TABLE 8.2   Design Principles and Strategies for Supporting Students' Online Collaborative Group Work

Principles	Design and Implementation Strategies
1. Facilitate communication	• Provide strong instructor and facilitator presence in various ways • Enhance quality and quantity of course discussion • Model optimal communication behaviors, styles and methods • Assign groups considering time zones
2. Establish strong sense of community and help students have sense of belongingness to their groups and the class	• Use strategies to help students form impressions of each other and promote the development of social relationships • Provide social spaces and contexts throughout the semester • Establish culture of knowledge sharing and open communication
3. Provide a variety of technology everyone can use	• Provide group spaces and encourage their use • Provide group writing and editing tools • Provide both synchronous and asynchronous tools • Provide overt guidance for students to take advantage of the tools in proper ways
4. Enhance individual motivation, accountability, and engagement for active participation in group work	• Use authentic evaluation projects with real-life relevance to students • Incorporate a variety of assessment strategies • Share instructor's expectations regarding learning out-come, commitment, and performance • Have students share their own expectations and goals and establish common goals and rules during the first group meeting
5. Help students effectively and efficiently manage and organize their work process	• Have groups select a group leader and provide guidance regarding the roles and responsibilities of leader • Provide the overall timeline of projects and all the milestones to complete projects at the beginning of group work • Mentor, coach and guide groups on how to work with clients and intervene between the client and student groups if necessary • Require groups to have regular synchronous meetings and share meeting minutes

needs of students. We believe that pedagogy is more critical than technology for making learning meaningful. We hope our two years of effort on this case will assist readers who desire to offer more engaging and authentic learning experiences to their students.

QUESTIONS FOR ANALYSIS/DISCUSSION

1. One of the major challenges faced by groups of students working online to complete authentic learning tasks is engaging each group member in completion of the tasks. Some group members described in this case study definitely made minimal contributions, whereas other members assumed far more responsibility than they should have. What could the instructor and course designers have done to ensure more equitable distribution of the workload? What could be done to facilitate group members reconciling their different expectations while ensuring that course requirements are fulfilled?

2. Authentic learning tasks of the kind described in this case study depend heavily on having good communication between student groups and their clients. Breakdowns in communication sometimes occur. Who should take primary responsibility for resolving such miscommunications, e.g., the student group, the instructor, or the clients? How can such miscommunications be reduced in the first place?

3. Although group accomplishment of authentic learning tasks was the primary pedagogy used in this course, students also had individual responsibility for additional academic tasks such as weekly readings and quizzes. How can these academic tasks be more authentically woven into the overall learning environment within a distance course of this kind? When group projects play a central role in the course, how can the course assessment activities be designed to more accurately reflect individual students' learning?

4. What new technological tools can be enlisted to improve course communication, collaboration, and assessment?

REFERENCES

Alkin, M. C., & Christie, C. A. (2002). The use of role-play in teaching evaluation. *American Journal of Evaluation, 23*(2), 209–218.

Allen, I. E., & Seaman, J. (2011). Class differences: Online education in the United States, 2010. Retrieved from, http://sloanconsortium.org/publications/survey/class_differences

Baker, M., Hansen, T., Joiner, R., & Traum, D. (1999). The role of grounding in collaborative learning tasks. In P. Dillenbourg (Ed.), *Collaborative learning: Cognitive and computational approaches* (pp. 31–63). Oxford, UK: Pergamon.

Bannan-Ritland, B. (2003). The role of design in research: The integrative learning design framework. *Educational Researcher, 32*(1), 21–24.

Darabi, A. (2002). Teaching program evaluation: Using a systems approach. *American Journal of Evaluation, 23*, 219–228.

Edelson, D. C. (2002). Design research: What we learn when we engage in design. *Journal of the Learning Sciences, 11*(1), 105–121.

Febey, K., & Coyne, M. (2007). Program evaluation: The Board Game: An interactive learning tool for evaluators. *American Journal of Evaluation, 28*(1), 91–101.

Hathorn, L. G., & Ingram, A. L. (2002). Online collaboration: Making it work. *Educational Technology, 42*(1), 33–40.

Haythornthwaite, C., Kazmer, M. M., Robins, J., & Shoemaker, S. (2000), Community development among distance learners: Temporal and technological dimensions. *Journal of Computer-Mediated Communication, 6*(1), 1

Herrington, J., Oliver, R., & Reeves, T. C. (2006). Authentic tasks online: A synergy among learner, task and technology. *Distance Education, 27*(2), 233–248.

Herrington, J., Reeves, T. C., & Oliver, R. (2010). *A guide to authentic e-learning.* New York, NY: Routledge.

Hurley, C., Renger R., & Brunk, B. (2005). Instructor learning from a challenging fieldwork evaluation experience: Perspectives of a student and an instructor. *American Journal of Evaluation, 26*, 562–578.

Jonassen, D. H., Lee, C., B., Yang, C, -C., & Laffey, J. (2005). The collaboration principle in multimedia learning. In R. E. Mayer (Ed.), *The Cambridge handbook of multimedia learning* (pp. 247–270). New York, NY: Cambridge University Press.

Kelly, A. (2006, March). Professor of educational psychology, George Mason University, interview (Is design-based research a method on its own?) Video file retrieved from http://projects.coe.uga.edu/dbr/expertinterview.htm

Kelley, J. M., & Jones, B. J. (1992). Teaching evaluation by doing it: A multiple-utility approach. *Evaluation and Program Planning, 15*, 55–59.

Kirschner, P.A., & Kreijns, K. (2004). Designing sociable CSCL environments: Applying interaction design principles. In J.W. Strijbos, P.A. Kirschner, & R.L. Martens (Vol. Eds.), *Computer-supported collaborative learning: Vol 3. What we know about CSCL and implementing it in higher education* (pp. 241–263). Boston, MA: Kluwer Academic.

Kreijns, K., Kirschner, P. A., & Jochems, W. (2003). Identifying the pitfalls for social interaction in computer-supported collaborative learning environments: A review of the research. *Computers in Human Behavior, 19*, 335–355.

Lee, J., Wallace, T. L., & Alkin, M. (2007). Using problem-based learning to train evaluators, *American Journal of Evaluation, 28*(4), 536–545.

McConnell, D. (2006). E-Learning groups and communities. Berkshire, UK: *The Society for Research into Higher Education & Open University Press.*

McKenney, S., & Reeves, T. C. (2012). *Conducting educational design research.* New York, NY: Routledge.

Merriam, S. B. (1998). *Qualitative research and case study application in education.* San Francisco, CA: Jossey-Bass.

Merriam, S. B., Caffarella, R. S., & Baumgartner, L. M. (2007). *Learning in adulthood: A comprehensive guide* (3rd ed.). San Francisco, CA: Jossey-Bass.

Oliver, D. E., Casiraghi, A. M., Henderson, J. L., Brooks, A. M., & Muslow, M. (2008). Teaching program evaluation: Three selected pillars of pedagogy. *American Journal of Evaluation, 29*(3). 330–339.

Paulus, T. M. (2009). Online but off-topic: Establishing common ground in small learning groups. *Instructional Science, 37*(3), 227–245.

Roberts, T. S., & McInnerney, J. M. (2007). Seven problems of online group learning (and their solutions). *Educational Technology & Society, 10*(4), 257–268

Smith, R. O. (2005). Working with difference in online collaborative groups. *Adult Education Quarterly, 55*(3), 182–199.

Strauss, A. L., & Corbin, J. M. (1998). *Basics of qualitative research: Techniques and procedures for developing grounded theory* (2nd ed.). Thousand Oaks, CA: Sage.

Trevisan, M. S. (2004). Practical training in evaluation: A review of the literature. *American Journal of Evaluation, 25*(2), 255–272.

Tu, C.-H., & McIsaac, M. (2002). The relationship of social presence and interaction in online classes. *The American Journal of Distance Education. 16*(3). 131–150.

Van den Akker, J., Gravemeijer, K., McKenney, S., & Nieveen, N. (Eds.). (2006). *Educational design research.* London, UK: Routledge.

Wang, F., & Hannafin, M. (2005). Design-based research and technology-enhanced learning environments. *Educational Technology Research & Development, 53*(4), 5–23.

CHAPTER 9

EXPERIENCES IN CROSS-INSTITUTION ONLINE TEACHING COLLABORATIONS

Anthony A. Piña and Julian Scheinbuks

ABSTRACT

In this chapter, we discuss the case of the first four years of a program to create online teaching collaborations between rural, suburban, and inner-city universities with distinct racial and cultural student populations. Faculty members who were new to the experience of teaching online, collaborated with more experienced instructors through a team approach to instructional design and teaching. Many of the online teaching partnerships utilized a combination of synchronous and asynchronous online technologies. Students at the three universities learned how to be effective online learners as they interacted with each other in virtual classrooms and discussion forums. As a result of these partnerships, faculty became more confident and capable using technologies to teach a diverse student population and the curriculum was enhanced by the addition of new courses.

Real-Life Distance Education, pages 159–176
Copyright © 2014 by Information Age Publishing
159

INTRODUCTION

The Online Teaching Partnership (OTP) was a program that had its genesis in the idea that higher education institutions and their faculty and students would benefit by working together on compatible goals. Synchronous and asynchronous technologies can be used to transcend the limitations of time, space, and location (Scheinbuks & Piña, 2010b) and, in fact, this has been the primary purpose for distance education since long before the advent of digital delivery (Simonson, Smaldino, Albright, & Zvacek, 2012).

Collaboration between universities and faculty is certainly not a new concept and partnerships between universities and faculty in different countries have demonstrated that distance education can be a helpful tool in breaking down barriers existing between different countries, races, and cultures (Hodgkinson & Holland, 2002; McIsaac, 2002; Summers & Tronsgard, 1999). However, significant cultural differences can exist between higher education institutions within the same city or state (Piña & Scheinbuks, 2008).

In this chapter, we discuss the case of the first four years of a program to create online teaching collaborations between rural, suburban, and inner-city universities with distinct racial and cultural student populations. Faculty who were new to the experience of teaching online collaborated with more experienced instructors through a team approach to instructional design and teaching. Many of the online teaching partnerships utilized a combination of synchronous and asynchronous online technologies. Students at the three universities learned how to be effective online learners as they interacted with each other in virtual classrooms and discussion forums. As a result of these partnerships, faculty became more confident and capable using technologies to teach a diverse student population and the curriculum was enhanced by the addition of new courses. Both faculty and students unfamiliar with distance education came to the realization that effective teaching and learning can occur outside the classroom. In the words of one of the teaching teams, "we learned most from each other" (Scheinbuks & Piña, 2010b, p.1).

CASE STUDY

From its inception in 1972 the Higher Education Cooperation Act (HECA) has provided a means to promote collaboration and increased access to higher education through partnerships between and among Illinois colleges and universities (IBHE, 1974). In 2002, the IBHE awarded a HECA grant to fund a collaborative effort between two public universities, the University of Illinois at Springfield (UIS) and Chicago State University (CSU).

The purpose for the grant was to promote the use of online learning to reach previously underserved student populations (IBHE, 2005). Chicago State University had recently begun offering online courses and its faculty was largely inexperienced in online instructional design and teaching. At the University of Illinois, online learning was becoming an important part of the university's mission, with numerous courses and entire degree programs developed for online delivery (Oakley, 2004). Unlike CSU, UIS had taken the steps to ensure the institutionalization of distance education at the university (Piña, 2008). The HECA-funded project allowed UIS to provide advisement, training, and staff development activities to CSU (Mc-Curdy & Schroeder, 2005a).

Both institutions saw value in expanding the scope of the partnership. The Office of Distance Learning at Chicago State University had a goal to expand the quantity of its distance learning offerings and to develop online teaching expertise among its faculty. The Office of Technology-Enhanced Learning (now the Center for Online Learning, Research and Service) at UIS had a goal to extend the University's outreach beyond its borders to a more diverse student population (McCurdy & Schroeder, 2005b).

In 2004, the original HECA proposal was expanded into the Online Teaching Partnership (OTP) program between CSU and UIS, allowing for online collaborations between individual faculty and students at the two universities. In 2005, the partnership was expanded to include Northeastern Illinois University, an urban campus with a larger and more diverse student population (Scheinbuks & Piña 2010a). Table 9.1 lists the characteristics of the three institutions. Goals of the OTP partnership were fourfold:

- Increase student exposure to technology.
- Train faculty to use technology to enhance face-to-face and blended courses.
- Enhance the curricula at the partner universities.
- Encourage and provide a rich learning experience to a diverse student population.

TABLE 9.1 Institutions Participating in Collaborations (After Scheinbuks & Piña, 2010a)

Institution	Locale	Enrollment	Student Population
University of Illinois-Springfield	Rural	4,900	Predominately White
Chicago State University	Urban	7,200	Mostly African-American
Northeastern Illinois University	Suburban	12,000	Diverse with a significant Latino population

University of Illinois-Springfield

Nestled among the cornfields not far from the state capital in central Illinois, the University of Illinois at Springfield (UIS) is a small, rural campus with a predominantly white student population of just over 5,000. Its online program, established in 1997, has been highly successful, with 17 fully online degree programs and an annual student enrollment growth of 30% (Schroeder & McCurdy, 2005). Retention of students in online courses at UIS is equivalent to that of students enrolled in face-to-face courses (Oakley, 2004; University of Illinois-Springfield, 2013). Training, development, and technical support for online courses and faculty has been provided by the UIS Office of Technology-Enhanced Learning (OTEL). In 2007, the University was awarded the 2007 Sloan-C Award for Excellence in Institution-Wide Online Teaching & Learning (Sloan Consortium, 2009). In 2008 the Center for Online Learning, Research and Service and the New Century Learning Consortium were established to further the University's e-learning leadership and outreach goals to educational institutions across the country (Center for Online Learning, Research & Service, 2013).

Chicago State University

Chicago State University is an urban inner-city campus in the southern end of the country's third largest city, with the largest minority student population in the state. More than 80% of CSU's student population of 7,200 is African American. When the partnership with UIS was established, CSU had a developing distance learning program that offered several online courses, but no online degrees. CSU's instructors were less experienced in teaching within a virtual environment than those at UIS. Training, development, and technical support for online courses and faculty were provided by the CSU Office of Distance Learning (Scheinbuks & Piña, 2010b).

Northeastern Illinois University

Northeastern Illinois University (NEIU) is an urban public campus on Chicago's north side with a student population of approximately 12,000 (about the same as UIS and CSU combined). NEIU is recognized by *US News and World Report* as the most racially and culturally diverse campus in the Midwestern United States, with a population that is 29% Hispanic, 10% African American, and 9% Asian (U.S. News, 2011). Unlike UIS and CSU, NEIU did not have a dedicated distance learning department and did not offer any fully online courses or online degree programs when it joined the partnership. Training, development, and support services for faculty participating in the OTP were provided by NEIU's Center for Teaching and Learning (Piña & Scheinbuks, 2007).

Infrastructure and Support

The nature of the OTP involved the establishment of mentor-mentee relationships in planning and implementing the instructional partnership. The faculty partners did not always assume exclusive roles of mentee and mentor, but shared these roles as they exposed each other to their strengths and weaknesses (Gatliff & Wendel, 1998). Those with more confidence in using technology in their teaching or great experience teaching online served as mentors for the other faculty members. However, sometimes the professors with less technology or online experience were the primary subject matter experts and served as content mentors for their peers. This cross-mentoring dynamic was particularly effective for partnerships whose courses spanned different disciplines.

A faculty partnership was established when the partners agreed to the extent of collaboration (full semester or unique units). The partners cooperated to develop a syllabus containing assignments meeting the individual course objectives and the goals of the partnership. These were supported by an agreement to team teach and facilitate student activities and research in both synchronous and asynchronous modes. Students enrolled at their own university, so that there were no conflicts related to tuition and participation in programs leading toward a degree or certification. The instructors assigned by that institution were responsible for evaluating their own students' efforts (Scheinbuks & Piña, 2010a). Instructors who participated in the online teaching partnerships were eligible to receive a stipend, which varied according to the length and extensiveness of the collaboration.

The project was made publically available on the UIS-sponsored Online Teaching Partnership website, where faculty members at the member universities made contact and provided information about the disciplines in which they taught and their specific topic areas of interest. Once faculty members had contacted each other and determined that they wished to collaborate, they notified the support office at their respective institutions to prepare a proposal for an online teaching partnership.

The Office of Distance Learning at CSU, the Office of Technology Enhanced Learning at UIS and the Center for Teaching and Learning at NEIU provided primary instructional and technical support for members of the partnership. This support included assisting faculty in the development of proposals, training in the use of technology, administering the learning management systems and virtual classrooms, dissemination of information, preparing reports, and troubleshooting.

Technologies

Some of the participating faculty had prior experience teaching online or in using technology within their face-to-face courses, while others had little or no experience and required training and mentoring. The Blackboard learning management system (LMS) was used by all three institutions for asynchronous instruction, communication, and interaction. The most common LMS tools used within the partnerships were uploading course content, class announcements, threaded discussion forums, assignment management, quizzes and assessments, and the online grade book (Piña, 2013).

To provide interactive real-time instruction, such as two-way audio, application and desktop sharing, whiteboards, live PowerPoint presentations, and interactive polling and quizzing, UIS and CSU each provided the use of their Synchronous Classroom System (SCS). The SCS used for the OTP project was Elluminate Live! [*Note:* In late 2010, Elluminate was acquired by Blackboard and the product is now known as Blackboard Collaborate (Piña, 2013).] These technologies were made available to both faculty and students, to assist in developing and completing joint assignments and discussions by the support organizations at each institution.

Since administrative and management rights and authority for the LMS and SCS resided at the same departments that provided the primary support for the online teaching partnerships, each partnership could be assigned to a joint Blackboard course administered by one of the campuses. Students and partner faculty from both campuses were enrolled into the joint course. Both faculty members were given full instructor privileges in the course. Some instructors chose to use the group feature in the LMS to separate students from the two institutions for grading purposes, but all of the courses used tools in the LMS to allow all of the students to interact with each other and/or complete joint assignments (Piña & Scheinbuks, 2007).

Collaborations

The faculty and students participating in the collaborations were of diverse ethnic, racial, socio-economic, educational, and technological backgrounds. The demographics of the students tended to reflect those of the geographic area in which their institution was located. UIS students tended to be white, middle-class, and rural; CSU students tended to be African American and from Chicago's south side. NEIU students tended to be more racially mixed, with about 40% of Latino ancestry. It was expected that this mix of diverse backgrounds would enhance teaching and learning for all the collaborative groups studied (Piña & Scheinbuks, 2008). Nine teaching collaborations that were implemented and completed during the initial four years of the online teaching partnership are shown in Table 9.2 below. The collaborations consisted of two faculty members, each one from a different university (Scheinbuks & Piña, 2010b).

Technology in the Curriculum and Cooperative Education

This collaboration between two professors from different departments within their respective colleges of education provided an opportunity for both faculty members to develop a unique assignment unit for all members of the collaborative class. The class consisted of students who had varying experiences, backgrounds, and cultural differences. Students from CSU were pre-service education majors and the students from UIS were in-service educators. They were divided into several research groups, which included students from both UIS and CSU. Group discussions were facilitated in real time by the use of the SCS.

Due to the differences in student service background, the concerns of CSU students were different than those of the UIS students. The groups worked well together in a professional manner and carried out a series of surveys of concerning technologically advanced high schools in three areas: Northern Illinois, Central Illinois, and the Greater Chicago area. The extent of the study was novel for this class and had an impact on reaching class

TABLE 9.2 Online Teaching Collaborations: Lead and Partner Institutions and Courses

Lead Institution	Course	Partner Institution	Course
UIS	Technology in the Curriculum	CSU	Cooperative Education
UIS	Internet and American Life	CSU	Special Topics in Technology & Education
CSU	Creative Writing	UIS	Black Women Authors
NEIU	Technology for School Leaders	CSU	Cougar Academy for Future Teachers
UIS	Science Teaching Methods	NEIU	Environmental Studies
NEIU	Human Resource Development	CSU	Educational Leadership and Technology
CSU	Educational Leadership	UIS	Educational Leadership
NEIU	Latino & Latin American Studies	UIS	Public Administration
CSU	Introductory Biology Health	CSU	Second Life

objectives for the course. The students learned to effectively use the SCS in working well together by complementing each other's skills and interests. In conclusion, the students felt that the collaboration between the classes was a rewarding experience that enhanced learning.

Internet and American Life and Special Topics in Education

This collaboration allowed a UIS professor of communications to mentor another in online pedagogy as their students collaborated in an online course environment. CSU students and a CSU instructor were enrolled within a UIS Blackboard course shell. Activities were also shared by using the SCS. The faculty agreed to a common syllabus with similar expectations for both UIS and CSU students. Readings of the *Pew Charitable Trust Project* served as the basis for student discussion of their own experiences. In describing the tone of the class, one of the instructors (UIS) noted, "The perspectives reflected in the discussions were far more rich with the addition of the CSU students. Extended exchanges were common as the students sorted through the impact of the Internet on such aspects of American life as health care, government, elections, and education" (Schroeder & McCurdy, 2005).

The collaborating CSU faculty member provided a different but relevant perspective. As time progressed, he developed experience and confidence in the role of an online collaborative faculty member and began to recognize some significant differences in the computer literacy and online course expectations between CSU and UIS students. Other CSU online faculty confirmed these observations. The CSU faculty member adapted this UIS course to offer it as a new CSU course, thus expanding the CSU curriculum.

Creative Writing and Black Women Authors

This collaboration gave a unique opportunity for both faculty members who were interested in Black women authors to create a unit for discussion between their two classes. In preparation for this unit, both classes were assigned to read *Mama Day*, by Gloria Naylor and view the film, Julie Dash's *Daughter of the Dust*. Real-time collaboration and discussion occurred in two sessions using SCS. The software permitted considerable input from most members of both classes. In addition, there were several sidebar conversations (implemented by written chat that related to the ongoing speaker's discussion). Students reported that they had enjoyed the collaborative sessions and felt that it helped them understand the issues and relative to the novel, *Mama Day*. Both instructors were excited about the results of the collaborations and indicated that they would be willing to collaborate again.

Technology for Prospective Teachers and Technology for School Leaders

In this collaboration, one of the instructors, an administrator and faculty member in instructional technology, was able to mentor the other, a young teacher education instructor, concerning the implementation of pedagogical techniques used with technology. The two faculty members had agreed to a blended learning approach where a component of the collaboration was asynchronous using the LMS for online discussions between students in the two courses and synchronous lessons, where the instructors provided live step-by-step instruction in the creation of instructional materials using the SCS and PowerPoint software in both linear and non-linear formats. In implementing the synchronous presentations and exercises, the presence of faculty members to assist students was an important issue in providing a successful student experience.

A breakdown in communication occurred as a result of instructional assignment changes at Chicago State University. As a result, the class of pre-service teachers at CSU was replaced by a class of pre-college students who were interested in entering a career in education—unbeknownst to the NEIU instructor. The students at NEIU were graduate students who were principally professional educators in the last stages of their master's degrees. As a result of the gap in communication, some miscalculation occurred in developing collaborative assignments that would be equally useful and beneficial to both classes. In reality, both classes had a very unique experience in understanding the differences in the capabilities and maturities of the collaborative class. The collaboration was also a challenging experience for both instructors who had to do some "on the fly" adaptation of their instruction to match the backgrounds of the students in each of the classes. The pre-college students tended to be a bit overwhelmed, while the graduate level students were amused and understanding of their younger colleagues located on the other side of the city.

Environmental Studies and Science Teaching Methods

Both classes in related disciplines provided an opportunity for the faculty members to focus on various points of views related to the collaboration. The CSU class had a greater focus on the development of instructional techniques related to the various scientific disciplines, particularly environmental sciences. The NEIU class provided students at that institution with an opportunity to fulfill their general education requirements for an undergraduate degree by being exposed to real environmental issues and understanding how these can be studied to resolve environmental problems. The instructors agreed upon a syllabus that provided an opportunity to collaborate and team-teach their students for three different units or areas.

The first was related to the development of concept maps as an approach to relating scientific concepts. Various biological concepts were studied and concept maps were developed relative to the regulation of the biosphere through a process called homeostasis. Life forms interact with environmental factors to produce a self-regulating system. A movie clip was used to illustrate the concept. A classroom activity was designed in which an interactive free computer program CTOOLS was used for producing the concept maps. Students from both classes evaluated each other's maps in terms of the overall effectiveness of organizing new information. The CSU class in terms of how the use of these maps could enhance learning in a high school classroom setting analyzed the learning process.

The second unit involved a class visit to the Green Technology Center in Chicago. This city-operated center provides information about how to pursue and develop green technologies. This outing permitted students in both classes to meet and interact. Up to this point, the students interacted asynchronously. This outing allowed the students to meet their counterparts in the teaching partnership and interact on a different level. Many of the students in the environmental studies class have considered developing a career in education. This interaction was helpful for them to meet potential role models of students who were actively pursuing these objectives.

The third unit developed from concepts that had been discussed from the second unit. The second unit related to green technologies and the absence of hazards, while the third unit dealt with an understanding of hazards and how they affect the environment. Discussions of how hazards affect the environment were done synchronously using the SCS. The NEIU instructor demonstrated an Air Emissions Modeling Program (ALOHA) to assist responders to emergency events. An understanding was developed of the issues related to such an environmental catastrophe. Students were then given similar problems for analysis and to develop strategic approaches for resolving these problems. As a result of the immersion into this model, each class developed different take-home lessons. The CSU students used this as a model to develop an instruction plan while the NEIU students used this as a model for understanding issues related to toxic accidents.

The students were queried about each of the three units. Their responses were positive and helpful in assessing learning associated with each of the units. Students were enthusiastic about the collaboration and said that they would participate in additional courses using similar formats. The two instructors were not experienced at using online technologies for instruction prior to the course and while they found some of the technology to be challenging initially, they were able to master a wide range of synchronous and asynchronous applications.

Human Resource Development and Educational Leadership

This was an instance where a teaching partnership had been planned and one of the instructors' courses did not have sufficient enrollments to be offered that semester. In its place, another course was selected after the semester had begun. The original full-semester partnership was modified to four weeks of collaborative instruction.

This partnership provided two faculty members the opportunity to collaborate in teaching two different courses, one offered by the Department of Human Resource Development at NEIU and the other by the Department of Educational Leadership at CSU. Students in the NEIU were undergraduates who were interested in training and development in business and industry settings, while the CSU students were studying the integration of technology into school curriculum and instruction. Both courses were blended courses, which implemented both asynchronous activities using the LMS and synchronous sessions using the SCS. This teaching partnership involved a number of collaborative events. One was a discussion forum related to interviews with technology coordinators at local K–12 school districts by the CSU class. Both classes discussed the results of several research findings and proposed an optimal type of arrangement for a local K–12 institution. The students discovered that some of these institutions were lacking in technology (implicating a digital divide) while others were well supported. Students compared and contrasted K–12 technology training and support with that provided in industry settings.

A second asynchronous unit dealt with the advantages and disadvantages of online verses blended learning modalities. The discussions indicated that both are appropriate, but the blended class would be the most acceptable to the group. They discussed what types of learning should take place in synchronous verses asynchronous sessions. A further discussion related to recent research on the use of mobile technology, such as iPods, PDAs, MP3 players and cell phones by minority students and Caucasian students. The finding that minority students tended to use the advanced features of mobile technology at higher rates than Caucasian students led students from both courses to conclude that mobile delivery of online content should be a priority of minority-serving institutions (Rainie & Keeter, 2006; Rainie & Madden, 2005).

A synchronous presentation of the history of distance learning in the state of Illinois was presented using the SCS followed by a discussion of the presentation using the tools made available by the SCS. At the conclusion of the course, both of the instructors and the students concluded that, despite the rocky start of the partnership, it was a success and the instructors were looking forward to future collaborations with each other.

Educational Leadership and Educational Leadership

This partnership gave the two faculty members an occasion to collaborate in teaching two educational leadership classes at the graduate level located at different institutions separated by distance. The UIS class was populated with graduate-level in-service teachers and the CSU class contained undergraduate-level pre-service teachers. The instructors were experienced in offering both blended course and online course modalities. The instructor at UIS had stronger technology skills than did the instructor at CSU. The instructors developed a syllabus for their respective classes that had designated both asynchronous activities (2–3 weeks) and synchronous activities (3 weeks). The asynchronous activities were implemented easily and the students appeared to enjoy the interactions between members of both classes. Two of the three synchronous sessions using the SCS were successfully implemented. The instructors interacted well in planning the collaboration as well as interacted well in the various collaborative sessions with the students.

The instructor of each class was responsible for setting the standards and objectives for their respective classes and evaluating their own students. Although the objectives for the two courses differed somewhat, the instructors agreed upon the objectives for the collaborative sessions. Students were queried both at midterm and at the end of the course by survey to obtain feedback concerning the collaboration. The students indicated that they enjoyed the collaborative activities and felt that the collaboration added a dimension to the content of the course. The extra dimension was related to student backgrounds—UIS is an institution located in rural Illinois while CSU is located in the Chicago urban area. Both students and faculty felt that their experiences were valuable in that they were able to obtain unique information and understanding relative to their diverse backgrounds. Both faculty members have presented papers at conferences based upon this collaborative experience.

Latino and Latin American Studies and Public Administration

A proposal for a semester-long partnership focusing on diversity (the Barrio in Latin-American communities) was submitted during the spring semester. During this semester, the faculty team planned the nature of the course collaboration, which was implemented during the fall semester. Since a course on this topic did not exist at UIS, the faculty member proposed a new course that met UIS general education requirements so that it could be scheduled for the fall semester.

The partnership focused initially on the development of web resources to study the Barrio. To accomplish this goal, an introduction to the use of technology to link the classes together was provided within the first 2 weeks. During the third week, a lecture/discussion was presented to both classes on "The Meaning of Context" relative to the study of the Barrio. The demographics of Chicago and the state of Illinois were examined in lecture/discussion using the SCS. Students were involved in discussion forums within the LMS that were related to the nature of the Barrio. Following these discussions, students were assigned to propose research projects based upon the course's introductory sessions. These research projects were discussed during the fifth week of the partnership.

After the initial two-week technology introduction period was complete and the team-teaching of the course content commenced, it became clear to the two faculty partners that their teaching styles were not compatible. One instructor was very meticulous in his preparation and delivery and preferred instructor-led discussions, while the other one preferred to "go with the flow" and allow the instruction and discussion to be led by the students. Ultimately, these two styles proved to be incompatible and it was agreed that the collaboration would end after five weeks and the two courses would be developed and offered independently for the remainder of the semester. Feedback from the students indicated that they were unaware of the difficulties between their two professors and assumed that the course was designed for collaboration at the beginning only. Students from both courses rated them highly, which reflected positively on the professionalism of the faculty involved.

Introductory Biology Health and Second Life

This collaboration provided an opportunity to enhance an introductory level biology class focused on issues related to sexually transmitted diseases. The objectives of the course are to make the issues of contracting and treating these diseases meaningful to the minority student audience at CSU. Collaboration was begun between CSU and UIS, in partnership with the Illinois Department of Public Health's Brothers and Sisters United Against HIV/AIDS (Illinois Dept. of Public Health, 2009), to enhance learning by immersing the students in the course into the virtual worlds of Second Life. Some students in the class were familiar with Second Life and had developed avatars, while others accessed it for the first time to develop their new avatars. With the assistance of UIS Office of Technology Enhanced Learning, our students were introduced to the virtual instructional world of UIS Second Life Island. The process of enrolling students into Second Life was cumbersome because of issues related to the selection of avatar names.

Students in the class were given access to the BASUAH Ambassador training site to learn and review basic information about sexual diseases. The course also provided a unique focus promoting the attitude of education the public about problems surrounding these diseases. Many of the students were excited about the opportunity to become BASUAH ambassadors and looked forward to educating their community within the confines of community and state organizations. The class utilized this experience to develop skits so that they could role play how they would meet the challenges of educating members of the community about sexual disease issues. The presentations and skits were recorded on the SCS and then converted to a format so that these could become available in the BASUAH instructional area within the UIS SL Island.

Results

To gauge the impact of the online teaching partnerships, interviews were conducted with the collaborating faculty, support personnel, and a sample of students enrolled in the courses. Student comments from Blackboard discussion forum questions and end-of-course evaluations were also analyzed. Faculty who participated in the online teaching partnerships agreed that it promoted a well-rounded education that provided access to a diverse student population. It also afforded opportunities for faculty to enhance and develop teaching skills by learning how to apply new technologies and how to teach on asynchronous and synchronous online learning environments. Although most of the participating faculty had some experience with the LMS (Blackboard), only four had ever used the SCS (Elluminate). At the end of their collaborative experience, every one of the instructors expressed that they felt confident to teach using either a learning management system or a synchronous virtual classroom in their teaching. They praised both Blackboard and Elluminate for having a relatively gentle learning curve and for having few technical glitches. Faculty rated the experience of collaborating and team teaching as exhilarating and motivating, with the caveat that the collaborators must be compatible in their goals and teaching styles (Scheinbuks & Piña, 2010a; 2010b).

One of the greatest advantages indicated by the faculty was that online technologies can be used successfully to bring together and teach students who are racially and culturally diverse and that the interactions between students at the different institutions enhanced the courses. They also considered the new courses that were developed as a result of the project to be a very tangible success. All of the faculty participants—including those in the least successful partnership—stated that they would be agreeable to participating in future collaborations of this kind and that there was great potential for a state-wide initiative with more participating institutions (Scheinbuks & Piña, 2010a; 2010b).

Students likewise held positive views of the online teaching partnerships, mirroring the faculty comments about the utility of both Blackboard and Elluminate. They commented that the technology enhanced their learning experience. They particularly enjoyed the ability to access materials at any time, view their grades, upload their homework, interact with and query their instructors, and interact with other students. This agrees with findings by Educause on how students utilize and value LMS features (Kvavnik & Caruso, 2005). Although students praised the ability to interact and work with students at the partner institutions and that they would like to do more inter-institutional collaboration, they did not tend to acknowledge that they were interacting with students of different races, backgrounds or rural versus urban locale. This was taken as a positive indicator that an online teaching partnership can bring diverse students populations together successfully (Scheinbuks & Piña, 2010a; 2010b).

The directors of the support centers at the three institutions were also pleased with the positive results of the project and its impact upon the participating faculty and students. They also discussed some of the challenges involved in establishing and implementing the online teaching partnerships. These included funding delays from the IBHE, difficulty in publicizing the program to faculty, scheduling conflicts, changes in teaching assignments, and low enrollments in a few of the courses that prevented some collaborations from taking place. However, they acknowledged that the increase in technological competency of the faculty, the positive reviews of the students and the enhancements to curriculum more than made up for the difficulties that were experienced (Scheinbuks & Piña, 2010a; 2010b).

IMPLICATIONS FOR DISTANCE EDUCATION

The OTP leverages the strengths found in distance education, including the ability to take advantage of the freedom from time and space limits (Simonson, Smaldino, Albright, & Zvacek, 2012). The implications of OTP for distance education are that the challenges and complexities of development, management, support and participation in distance teaching and learning become even more acute when multiple institutions, disciplines, and a diversity of faculty and students are added. To make inter-institutional online programs successful requires—first and foremost—the right people in the right positions. Faculty involved in online teaching partnerships must be willing to serve as peer mentors and/or learners. Teaching online requires a different skill set than teaching face-to-face. They must have the ability to compromise and trust the other partner.

- Faculty who are willing to serve either as peer mentors or as learners (e.g., online teaching and class management skills; use of the LMS and SCS).
- Faculty who can establish a partnership of compromise and trust with someone from a different institution (and, perhaps a different discipline) and determine the roles of the members of the partnership.
- Faculty who are willing to devote the time and effort to become competent in the use of technology for distance learning.
- Leaders who are knowledgeable about their institutional policies, politics, and possible barriers to collaborations (e.g., turf wars) and have the authority and diplomacy to overcome the barriers.
- Leaders who have authority over the delivery systems (LMS, SCS, etc.).

- Leaders who have the ability to coordinate, evaluate, and write about the program (particularly if it is a multi-year program with annual reporting requirements).
- Training and support personnel to keep the systems running well and provide the faculty with the skills to use the necessary tools.

CONCLUSION

Although the initial OTP grant-funded project has concluded, a number of activities have grown out of it. The participating faculty members continue to use synchronous and asynchronous technologies in their online, blended, and web-enhanced courses. Several of the participants have delivered papers and presentations at local and national conferences based upon their experiences with their collaborations (Schroeder & McCurdy, 2005; Piña & Scheinbuks, 2008). Both instructional and noninstructional collaborations between the three partner institutions and others in the region are being facilitated by means of SLATE, a community of practice of leaders and faculty from over 60 institutions who share an interest in technology and distance learning (Piña, Sadowski, Scheidenhelm, & Heydenburg, 2008). The New Century Learning Consortium has been established with funding by the Alfred P. Sloan Foundation to continue to work of the OTP to colleges and universities across the United States and beyond. Initial partners of the Consortium include: California State University-East Bay, Chicago State University, Louisiana Tech University, Oakland University, Southern Oregon University, University of Illinois-Springfield, and University of Southern Maine (Center for Online Learning, Research and Service, 2013). Online teaching partnerships can be a viable and effective way to build virtual bridges across races, cultures and institutions.

QUESTIONS FOR ANALYSIS/DISCUSSION

1. What were the problems or issues addressed by the Online Teaching Partnership?
2. Most institutions offer some kind of technology training to faculty. Is the Online Teaching Partnership an effective way of training faculty to use technology? Why or why not?
3. Are both synchronous and asynchronous technologies essential to accomplish the goals of the OTP?

4. Learning management systems, like Blackboard, and virtual class-room systems, like Collaborate, are very expensive. Are there any other technologies that could be used to accomplish similar goals?
5. Included in this chapter was a discussion of an unsuccessful partnership. Why did the partnership fail and what could have been done to avoid the failure?
6. How can a program like OTP be institutionalized after the grant cycle is over?

ACKNOWLEDGMENT

This chapter is a revision of Scheinbuks & Piña (2010a; 2010b), in honor of the late Julian Scheinbuks.

REFERENCES

Center for Online Learning, Research and Service. (2013). *New century learning consortium (NCLC).* Retrieved from http://www.uis.edu/colrs/learning/gettingstarted/NCLC.html.

Gatliff, B., & Wendel, F. C. (1998). Inter-institutional collaboration and team teaching. *The American Journal of Distance Education, 12*(1), 26–37.

Hodgkinson, M., & Holland, J. (2002). Collaborating on the development of technology enabled distance learning: A case study. *Innovations in Education & Teaching International, 39*(2), 89–94.

IBHE. (1974). *Progress through collaboration: A report on the higher education cooperation act.* Springfield, IL: State of Illinois Board of Higher Education.

IBHE. (2005). *State of Illinois Board of Education: Higher Education Cooperation Act, fiscal year 2005 application.* Springfield, IL: State of Illinois Board of Higher Education.

Illinois Dept. of Public Health. (2009). Brothers and sisters united against HIV/AIDS. Retrieved from http://www.basuah.org/

Kvavnik, R., & Caruso, J. (2005). *ECAR study of students and technology 2005: Convenience, connection, control and learning.* EDUCAUSE Center for Applied Research, Boulder, Co.

McCurdy, S., & Schroeder, R. (2005a, June). *Achieving diversity through online interinstitutional collaborations.* Paper presented at ED-Media World Conference on Educational Multimedia, Hypermedia and Telecommunications, Association for the Advancement of Computing in Education, Montreal, Quebec, Canada.

McCurdy, S., & Schroeder, R. (2005b, August). *Inter-institutional collaboration in the delivery of online learning.* Paper presented at the annual Distance Teaching and Learning Conference, Madison, WI.

McIsaac, M. S. (2002). Online learning from an international perspective. *Educational Media International 39*(1), 17–21.

Oakley, B. (2004). The value of online learning: Perspectives from the University of Illinois at Springfield. In J. C. Moore (Ed.), *Elements of quality online education: Into the mainstream*. Needham, MA: Sloan Consortium.

Piña, A. A. (2008). Factors influencing the institutionalization of distance learning in higher education. *Quarterly Review of Distance Learning 9*(4), 427–438.

Piña, A. A. (2013). Learning management systems: A look at the big picture. In Y. Kats (Ed.) *Learning Management Systems and Instructional Design: Metrics, Standards and Applications* (pp. 1–19). Hershey, PA: Information Science Reference.

Piña, A. A., Sadowski, K. P, Scheidenhelm, C. L., & Heydenburg, P.R. (2008). SLATE: A community of practice for supporting learning and technology in education. *International Journal of Instructional Technology and Distance Learning 5*(7).

Piña, A. A., & Scheinbuks, J. (2007, October). *Creating a culture of technology through inter-institutional online teaching partnerships*. Paper presented at the Convention of the Association for Educational Communications & Technology, Anaheim, CA.

Piña, A. A., & Scheinbuks, J. (2008, April). *Spotlight session: An e-learning partnership between racially and culturally different institutions*. Paper presented at the Technology in Education (TechEd) Conference, Ontario, CA.

Rainie, L., & Keeter, S. (2006). *How Americans use their cell phones*, Washington, DC: The Pew Research Center.

Rainie, L., & Madden, M. (2005). *Podcasting catches on*. Washington, DC: Pew Research Center.

Scheinbuks, J., & Piña, A. A. (2010a). Building virtual bridges with online teaching partnerships. *International Journal of Instructional Technology and Distance Learning 7*(6), 3–14.

Scheinbuks, J., & Piña, A. A. (2010b). Online teaching partnerships in diverse socioeconomic institutions. In S. Mukerji & P. Tripathi (Eds.) *Cases on Technological Adaptability and Transnational Learning: Issues and Challenges* (pp. 27–41). Hershey, PA: IGI Global.

Schroeder, R., & McCurdy, S. (2005). *Inter-institutional class collaborations online*. Paper presented at the Midwest EDUCAUSE Conference, Chicago, IL.

Simonson, M., Smaldino, S., Albright, M. J., and Zvacek, S. (Eds.) (2012). *Teaching and learning at a distance: Foundations of distance education* (5th ed.). Upper Saddle River, NJ: Prentice Hall.

Sloan Consortium (2009). 2007 Sloan-C excellence in online teaching and learning awards. Retrieved from http://www.sloan-c.org/aboutus/awards.asp.

Summers, A., & Tronsgard, B. A. (1999). Designing and administering a collaborative international course using distance technology. *Online Journal of Distance Learning Administration 2*(3).

University of Illinois-Springfield (2013). *UIS online course completion rates*. Retrieved from http://www.uis.edu/colrs/about/history/completionrates.html.

U.S. News & World Report (2011). Choosing a school: Campus ethnic diversity. *America's Best Colleges*. New Hudson, MI: U.S. News & World Report.

PART III

DESIGNING DISTANCE EDUCATION

CHAPTER 10

APPLYING WEB 2.0 FOR LEARNING WHILE AVOIDING COGNITIVE OVERLOAD

A Challenge

Lauren Cifuentes and Omar Alvarez Xochihua

ABSTRACT

A graduate level, online course, Computer Graphics for Learning, was taught to 10 students using Web 2.0 tools including blogs, wikis, image galleries, RSS feeds, interactive desktop videoconferencing, and the Blackboard course management system. By adopting a variety of Web 2.0 tools, the instructors intended to enhance cognitive flexibility while controlling for potential cognitive overload in students. The class consisted of nine modules and seven assignments involving production of instructional graphics. Assignments had corresponding rubrics. Students used the tools to post, critique, and revise each other's work. They spent an unfortunate amount of time dealing with novel technical issues as opposed to focusing on course content. However,

Real-Life Distance Education, pages 179–195

they used Web 2.0 tools to facilitate each other's technical competence and applied multiple strategies to self-regulate and adjust to the complex, innovative learning environment. They increased their skills both with Web 2.0 tools and with development of computer graphics for learning.

INTRODUCTION

In a graduate level course, Computer Graphics for Learning, the instructor and two fellow researchers immersed course content and interactivity in Web 2.0 tools including blogs, wikis, image galleries, RSS feeds, interactive desktop videoconferencing, and the Blackboard course management system. They felt that Web 2.0 technologies would support a student-centered environment and expected that the read/write tools would empower students to generate, share, and edit course content as never before. The course was delivered to 10 students who never met face-to-face throughout a 15-week semester. The authors investigated the impact of Web 2.0's provisions for two-way communication, user contribution, dynamic and nonproprietary content, and social networking among the community of learners that they hoped would form around course content. The researchers sought to describe the instructor's design and development processes, students' learning outcomes, and students' regulation of their own learning in this complex learning environment.

The term, Web 2.0, was coined by O'Reilly (2005) to describe the new read/write capabilities and functional characteristics of the Web. Early platforms for the Web, referred to as Web 1.0, are characterized by centralized, one-way communication. They were used solely to deliver content, and users were not able to contribute to the pages viewed in Web 1.0. Such content on the Web is rarely updated, is static, and there is little reason to revisit a site once a user has received its messages. Only the author of the site can contribute to or revise site content, as all information on Web 1.0 is proprietary.

By contrast, Web 2.0 is characterized by two-way communication between the site itself and users. Anyone with Internet access can contribute to a Web 2.0 site. Therefore, the content of Web 2.0 sites is dynamic; Web 2.0 pages are constantly changing as multiple contributors and visitors revisit these sites to access new information and to update content. Web 2.0 sites are nonproprietary in that they allow users, as well as the site's author, to create new content and functionalities and share them with other users. Wikipedia is an example of a Web 2.0 site in that users can interact with and change the content that is dynamic and nonproprietary. Wikipedia (n.d.) defines Web 2.0 as "a social phenomenon embracing an approach to generating and distributing Web content itself, characterized by open communication,

decentralization of authority, and freedom to share and re-use content."
These Web 2.0 technologies can empower instructors to create student-centered learning environments as never before because read/write tools empower learners to generate, share, and edit course content.

Two compatible theories framed the development of the Computer Graphics for Learning course. Cognitive flexibility and cognitive load theory provide direction for instructional designers. The first emphasizes the importance of providing learners with multiple representations of content in order to increase those learners' cognitive structures. Cognitive load theory, on the other hand, indicates that simultaneous presentation of multiple representations of content may interfere with learning because of potential overload of learners' mental processes.

The overall problem is that, when incorporating the power of Web 2.0 applications in instructional environments, instructional designers face the challenge of finding balance between providing sufficient stimulus for flexibility (Spiro, Feltovich, Jacobson, & Coulson, 1995) and limiting stimulus to avoid overload (Paas, Renkl, & Sweller, 2003). Quality instruction facilitates cognitive flexibility without creating cognitive overload. Given the tension between the course design implications of these two theories, we sought insight into students' experiences in a course delivered exclusively through Web 2.0 with its nonlinear, complex, intertwined, and dynamic content.

Case Objectives

- Describe advantages and disadvantages of incorporating Web 2.0-based activities in instruction.
- Describe design features of online instruction that helps learners achieve cognitive flexibility without experiencing cognitive overload.
- Describe online instruction that simultaneously challenges students by providing multiple representations of content and supports their self-regulation for learning.

CASE STUDY

The online course, Computer Graphics for Learning, was designed to acquaint students with the full range of computer graphics production capabilities for developing instruction. The course was intentionally designed to promote cognitive flexibility while providing structure and guidance to minimize cognitive overload. This case was previously discussed in Cifuentes, Alvarez-Xochihua, & Edwards, (2011).

Theoretical Framework for Course Design

Spiro, Feltovich, Jacobson, and Coulson's (1995) cognitive flexibility theory offers a set of recommendations for the development of instructional hypertext programs to promote successful learning of difficult subject matter. Spiro proposes that hypermedia environments offer unlimited opportunities to present nonlinear, complex, intertwined media and content. Designers are advised by the theory to build virtual landscapes, full of rich representations of knowledge in many forms. While linear environments have what Spiro calls a "reductive bias," hypermedia environments such as Web 2.0 promote cognitive flexibility because they simultaneously afford multiple representations of knowledge, social interactivity, and collaborative construction of objects. Anderson (2007) states that read/write Web technologies have powerful ideas at their core that are changing the way some people interact through: (a) individual production and user-generated content; (b) the "power of the crowd"; (c) availability of data on an epic scale; (d) a structure or architecture of participation; and (e) an openness which involves control, access, digital rights, and open-sourced applications that lend themselves to further development and enhancement by Internet users. For the instructor who wants to create a constructivist learning environment and promote cognitive flexibility, these ideas all provide a rationale for adopting the read/write Web for course delivery. Thus, the instructors felt that students would benefit from the opportunities to see, build, and share multiple representations in a Computer Graphics for Learning course.

Cognitive load theory suggests that preliminaries to learning, such as transitions between media or delivery systems or between representations of content, actually interfere with learning and that effective instructional material facilitates learning by directing learners' cognitive processing toward activities directly related to their learning (Paas, Renkl, & Sweller, 2003; Sweller, van Merreinboer, & Paas, 1998). Increased extraneous load has negative consequences to learning. One suggested example of ineffective instruction provided by Paas et al. is when learners are required to mentally integrate disparate sources of mutually referring information such as separate, redundant text and diagrams. The authors claim that such "split-source information" generates too heavy a cognitive load. Open Web 2.0 environments cannot be controlled to avoid presentations of "split-source information." In addition, the extraneous task of learning Web 2.0 technologies can negatively affect learning in an online course by excessively increasing cognitive load. As Hannafin, Hannafin, and Gabbitas (2009) state, in Web 2.0 environments:

> ...the potential for increased and largely unregulated resources alters the [predictability] of cognitive demands associated with resource access and use.

Designers are unable to account for individual cognitive demands in advance since the context of learning is often spontaneous and the availability and use of resources [evolves] continuously. (p. 769)

Instruction delivered in Web 2.0 is, therefore, at risk of creating cognitive overload.

Sweller, van Merreinboer, and Paas (1998) assert that "cognitive load imposed by instructional designs should be the preeminent consideration when determining design structures" (p. 262) and they recommend a variety of ways to present instructional content to reduce cognitive load during learning. For instance, they advise instructors to integrate multiple sources of information related to the same content to avoid splitting students' attention and thus interfering with cognition. They also recommend an emphasis on goal-free problems, worked examples, and completion problems while increasing tasks germane to learning goals and eliminating extraneous tasks. Mayer and Moreno (2003) describe nine ways to reduce cognitive load in multimedia learning: off loading, segmenting, pretraining, weeding, signaling, aligning, eliminating redundancy, synchronizing, and individualizing. These methods are each thoroughly discussed in their article and can be attended to as one designs instruction.

Given the potential chaotic experiences of students in Web-2.0-based courses, structured course designs and explicit guidance can help manage working memory demands (Zajicek, 2007). Although design features such as specified objectives may diverge from constructivist principles, they may be applied in Web 2.0-based courses to help students manage cognitive load without compromising their abilities to construct knowledge.

In addition to intentionally designing to support cognitive flexibility and control for cognitive overload, instructors can provide guidance to learners to help them self-regulate their learning in Web 2.0-based courses, thereby controlling their own cognitive load (Northrup, 2001). Distance learners are most successful when they take responsibility for their own learning by seeking information, setting goals, pacing themselves, organizing and transforming content, keeping task lists and monitoring efforts, seeking social assistance from peers, and revising content to build understanding (Zimmerman & Martinez-Pons, 1995; Zins, Weissberg, Wang, & Walberg, 2004).

Computer Graphics for Learning: Course Design

Goals for the course were that each student achieve the following capabilities: demonstrate proficiency with major computer graphics production software and associated hardware devices; develop graphic materials designed for specific educational applications, including visualization of facts and concepts and creation of animations, presentations, and web graphics; summarize the theoretical foundations that support the appropriate use of graphics in instruction; and generate materials that apply the most appropriate design principles for a given instructional situation.

Goal analysis helped the instructors identify specific performance objectives that would help students achieve the goals. Those objectives were divided among projects and rubrics were developed for assessing students' project work. The rubrics were included in the course syllabus so that students knew what was expected of them and the specific criteria by which their work would be assessed. In compliance with the Web 2.0 open source philosophy that emphasizes shared cognition, students were able to see each other's work and learn from each other's submissions. Due dates were set for each project, but at any time in the semester students were allowed to revise and resubmit their projects for a higher grade.

To provide structure, the course was divided into nine units, each of which included readings and exercises from Lohr (2008) and design and development projects incorporating principles learned. Unit one introduced students to drawing and painting tools and selection strategies in Photoshop; students explored representation strategies on a continuum ranging from concrete to abstract representation. In unit two, students explored ways to digitize data. In unit three, they explored functional design principles and representation strategies. In unit four, students developed visual examples and nonexamples of concepts (Cifuentes, McKintosh, & Douglas, 1997). In unit five, they applied principles of graphic composition. In unit six, they explored desktop publishing. In unit seven, they represented quantitative data in multiple ways to convey different messages through selective data analysis, photo manipulation, and stylistic embellishment (Cifuentes, Myers, & McKintosh, 1998). Unit eight introduced students to the power that motion can bring to instructional messages. And in unit nine, students developed trigger visuals for Web delivery (Cifuentes & Dylak, 2007).

Student assignments involved development of a cohesive series of representations, visualization of an example and a nonexample of the same concept, development of a brochure and a newsletter, visualization of a complex concept, representation of quantitative data, and development of a trigger video. Each assignment had a corresponding rubric. Web 2.0 was leveraged for social product construction, critique, and negotiation of meaning. Students posted their projects in Facebook portfolios using Slates. They RSS-fed their work both to their instructor for assessment and to their classmates to learn from each other during and beyond the scope of the course semester. They were allowed to revise and resubmit any project at any time in the semester. They each made four contributions to a wiki entitled "Visual Literacy." They also posted their trigger videos to an online photo gallery, named "Seeing Culture," that was designed to enhance visual literacy and understanding of visual culture through an efficient display for sharing visuals (Cifuentes, Carpenter, & Bulu, 2008). Lastly, students participated in a desktop videoconference webinar on ethical uses of blogging using Centra software. The hour-long, audio-based discussion involved continuous and simultaneous presentation and recording of ideas through PowerPoint and the chat tool that comes with Centra. Students were able to see each other's work, and feedback was given by the instructor through the rubrics as well as through frequent correspondence responding to posts.

While the instructor of record had taught Computer Graphics for Learning online via the Blackboard course management system for several years, this was the first time for incorporation of blogs, a wiki, an image gallery, RSS feeds, and interactive desktop videoconferencing in that course. The content of the course remained the same as in previous semesters, with the distinguishable variable being adoption of the Web 2.0 tools for meeting course objectives. Students were assigned to use the same text, work toward achievement of the same objectives, work on most of the same assignments, and generate the same products. For instance, rather than post graphics that they had developed in the Blackboard system (where they would be deleted at the end of the semester), they posted their work in a portfolio that each created in Facebook where they could publicly comment on and edit each other's work and in an image gallery that allowed them to categorize their own and others' images according to cultural dimensions. The only entirely new assignment involved collaborative construction of the visual literacy wiki.

Methods for Exploring the Case

We framed the case investigation by asking the following questions: 1) What were the impacts of design features applied to this Web 2.0-based course on students' mastery of Web 2.0 tools, their learning outcomes, and their satisfaction with assignments? and 2) How did students self-regulate in the complex environment?

Ten students and three co-instructors/researchers participated in the course. Two of the students were male and eight female. They ranged in age from 24 to 56 and included two African Americans, one Kenyan, one Taiwanese, one Hispanic, and five Whites. The instructor of record, another researcher/professor, and one doctoral student designed the course and investigation in advance of the semester and acted as participant observers throughout the semester (Spradley, 1980).

The five data sources included design and development documents collected during course development and delivery, the course retention rate, transcripts of student discussions in the various Web 2.0 applications, a pre and postcourse survey, and student-written narratives of critical incidents during the semester. The data were subjected to qualitative analyses not only after the data were gathered but also throughout the process of data collection. The five data sources and three interpreters of the data provided for rich description. Triangulation, peer debriefing, and member checks established credibility (Lincoln & Guba, 1985). The three investigators compiled the data and conducted the data analyses together serving as peer debriefers. To assure credibility and trustworthiness of findings, member checks were conducted ten months after the course was over. Participants received an e-mail with a summary of our findings and a request to respond if modifications were appropriate. No one requested modifications.

Results

Course design and development documentation revealed that the design, development, and implementation activities required to translate an online course to a course leveraging Web 2.0 technologies is a substantial task for instructors. Each instructor had a great deal to learn about pedagogically sound approaches to integrating Web 2.0 in courses and therefore conducted a literature review on the topic. In addition to design recommendations to support cognitive flexibility and control cognitive load, the following, among other readings, provided guidance regarding methods for scaffolding student learning and assessing outcomes in Web 2.0 environments: Anderson (2007), Beldarrain (2006), Driscoll (2007), Dunlap, Sobel, and Sands (2007), Godwin-Jones (2006), Lightner and Willi (2007), McNabb (2006), Oliver (2007), Raman and Olfman (2005), Solomon and Schrum (2007), and Resta and Laferriere (2007). In addition, each instructor needed to gain technical skills. Fortunately, their institution provided support for wiki, blog, and podcast development and for desktop videoconferencing using Centra software. Even with three instructors for the course of ten students, the instructors each stayed busy teaching the course throughout the semester.

Positive Outcomes of the Course

Time spent by instructors paid off in student satisfaction. Critical incident reports and comments in discussions revealed that students were generally satisfied with the course and felt that the most effective course design feature was the timely, positive, encouraging, and easy-to-access interactions among classmates and instructors. One student offered, "I have really enjoyed the positive attitude of this class," and another stated, "The class has been a tremendous success personally and professionally." In addition, explicit ties among concepts in readings and assignments as well as fair and clearly described weighting of points toward grades in rubrics contributed to enthusiastic engagement in course activities. One indicator of student satisfaction was that the retention rate for the course was not outside the typical retention rates for graduate level courses at the University, including those delivered through distance learning technologies.

Students' reports of their Web 2.0 skills before and after the course showed that they generally felt their skills improved with wikis, blogs, social networks, desktop videoconferencing, course management systems, and online photo galleries (see Table 10.1).

According to students' self-reports, they learned how to use both Web 2.0 technologies and computer graphics in the course and students reported an increase in proficiency with major computer graphics production software and associated hardware devices. Student reports indicated that prior to the course one was a novice, five were beginners, three were intermediate, and one was an expert. After the course, the novice moved up to being a beginner and the five beginners increased their skills, with three rating themselves as intermediate and two as proficient. Those three who had rated themselves as intermediates reported increasing skills toward proficiency; and the one expert before the class continued to see himself as expert (see Figure 10.1). When asked what percentage of their computer graphics skills they learned as a direct outcome of the course, the ten responses were: 90%, 85%, 80%, 75%, 75%, 65%, 45%, 40%, 15%, and 2%. Each student reported gaining competence and flexibility with PowerPoint, Photoshop, Centra, and Facebook. According to one of the students, "Adobe Photoshop is a wonderful tool that can be extremely productive when one knows how to use it, as I now do."

Among the important outcomes of the course were peers learning how to critically evaluate each other's work and how to facilitate each other's technical competence. The instructors observed that, in Facebook, students

TABLE 10.1   Number of Students' Self-Assessments of Mastery Before and After the Course

	Wikis	Blogs	Social Networks	Desk-top VC	CMS	Photo Galleries
Expert	0/0	0/1	0/1	0/0	2/2	0/0
Proficient	1/6	1/6	1/6	1/3	3/6	1/4
Intermediate	2/3	1/3	1/3	1/4	4/2	1/3
Beginner	3/1	4/0	4/0	3/2	0/0	3/1
Novice	4/0	4/0	4/0	5/1	1/0	5/2

Note: Numbers of student ratings are reported as before/after.

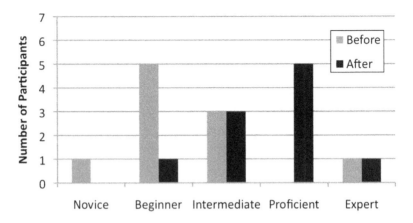

Figure 10.1 Self-reported computer graphics proficiency before and after the course.

began the semester by being excessively complimentary with each other, responding to requested feedback on assignments, comments such as "Looks really good!" "The concept related drawing is priceless!" or "Great job! Loved the animation." When one instructor emphasized to the students the value of critiquing their peers' assignments, students began to make comments such as "Tell me what you truly think . . . not just what I would want to hear!" One student, after giving feedback remarked, "Thanks, you are the best e-learning pals and feel free to ask the same of me (even if I have to fix something)." Students then began to give more constructive feedback. For instance, one commented on the work of a fellow student saying that their message could be improved by moving text lower on the screen. The helpful attitude that formed among the learners was exemplified when, in response to a student's concern about the integrity of fonts, a student coached: "To assure that a font used on one machine will show in a ppt or doc on another machine—embed the fonts. . . . To do this, click on . . . , etc." Eighty percent of the students reported seeking social assistance from peers (classmates or friends).

The students consciously regulated their learning in the course, indicating that they adopted several self-regulation strategies. All reported seeking information from the library, the Web, peers, or instructors. Nine of the students set goals, planned their studies, and paced themselves during project development. Eight organized and transformed content by creating outlines or concept maps, kept task lists and monitored their efforts, sought social assistance from friends, and reviewed content more than once. Seven students used a self-evaluation strategy. Six structured their environments to facilitate studying (e.g., turned off the television or radio). Five students gave themselves rewards for successes during their coursework, and one intentionally rehearsed and memorized content.

Issues Generated by Adoption of Web 2.0 Technologies

Although the course provided features of well-designed instructional environments such as performance objectives, guidance toward those objectives, elicitation of generative responses, and feedback directly related to those responses (Simonson, 2009), leveraging Web 2.0 in the course threatened learners' senses of organization. For instance, the course wiki and blogs were designed for user generation of content, but lacked an implicit content structure beyond the wiki outline of topics and a chronological posting. One student shared her experience with Facebook: "Facebook is not for my generation; I'm starting to feel very old. . . . There is no structure except that you have to invite people to be your friend before they can see your information . . . I didn't know where to go half the time." Although they were given tutorials for each application, the lack of structural support for the learning process within each Web 2.0 environment led students to communicate with each other and share ideas about just where and how to make course entries.

The multiple technological problems with Web 2.0 tools that students encountered took time away from their efforts to master instructional message design skills. For example, in Centra they had difficulty configuring the client software and establishing the audio capability. For some students, Facebook presented challenges in setting up an account; uploading files; and establishing an e-mail domain, groups, Slates, and RSS feeds. Students agreed that the Wiki software was not intuitive and they were irritated that they had to learn some html labels.

Most of the students expressed some discomfort with working on the Web for learning. After the class was over, 40% reported being distracted in general by links on the web, and 30% expressed difficulty focusing their attention in the class. All students indicated that they felt that they could overcome computer related problems and use electronic resources well enough to get information for class assignments.

Critical incidents revealed that learning Flash overwhelmed the majority of the students and, as a whole, they did not leave the class with a high level of competence with that software. One student wrote, "I am torn between rating [our experience with Flash] as a success or failure. I believe it was a failure." Another said of the assignment to develop an instructional trigger visual in Flash, "It seems like all of the successes I have experienced throughout this course and on assignments have come to a screeching halt with this one piece of software." When asked through SurveyMonkey if "navigation for the course [was] clear, simple, and friendly," seven students moderately agreed, two slightly agreed, and one strongly disagreed. One student who was satisfied with the course in general, complained, "Every time we started something new it took me so much time to be proficient. For example, making a Facebook page took me a good part of a day. It was hard just getting familiar with each new computer operation."

Content analyses of online course discussions in the various arenas revealed that dealing with novel technical issues took an inordinate amount of time from their focus on course content. For instance, during the videoconference, 40% of the comments were about the videoconferencing technology itself rather than the topic of the videoconference that we called "Ethical Issues of Blogging." Due to the multiple applications adopted, students spent time in transitioning from one software program to another. One student who had persisted and felt competent by the end of the class commented, "Applying a lot of time to a concept did not always guarantee that I would improve at that skill. Sometimes I would spend many hours trying to create graphics and at bedtime I would realize I just didn't even get anywhere." One student expressed the difficulty she was having learning Flash with, "this one has me feeling like a failure and wanting to just quit!" However, another student revealed her cognitive flexibility in response to the difficulty she was having with Flash by saying, "I feel that [the course] was a success in making us think outside the box and find another program [as a few did to fulfill the assignment] which is more user friendly."

According to students' self-assessments of their depth of understanding versus surface understanding, students perceived themselves as having neither surface nor deep understanding at the end of the semester, except for one student who sees himself as sophisticated, profound, masterful, insightful, and wise in generating such messages. The student who rated his levels as high is the one who perceived himself to be an expert before the course and reported learning only 2% of his graphics skills from the course; he did not attribute his deep level of understanding to course experiences. The majority of students reported achieving moderate levels of understanding of design of computer graphics for learning and generally became developed, perceptive, able, considered, and thoughtful in generating lessons with visual instructional messages.

IMPLICATIONS FOR DISTANCE EDUCATION

Web 2.0 adoption appears to have substantially increased the cognitive load for extraneous content such as dealing with technical problems. Rather than simply serving as vehicles for learning content, use of Web 2.0 technologies created a steep learning curve and tool-use had to become part of the course content. Cognitive load theory indicates that learning both Web 2.0 applications and content simultaneously splits students' attention and contributed to cognitive overload in this case. Increased cognitive load interferes with students' abilities to deeply learn content as it did in this computer graphics course. This interpretation of the findings supports the assumption in cognitive load theory that extraneous cognitive load has a negative impact on learning.

While Web 2.0 technologies interfered with deep learning, they may have contributed to learners' cognitive flexibility by providing students with representations of knowledge in many forms through the opportunity to see each others' ways of addressing the projects in the course, incorporating each others' ideas into their project solutions, and revising their products based upon what was learned through social networking. By experiencing graphic message design in multiple Web 2.0 platforms, learners had the opportunity to see the conceptual interrelatedness of ideas and their interconnectedness as stressed by cognitive flexibility theory.

Students in this course used social networking tools to self-regulate. We had adopted Web 2.0 tools with the belief that, because they are broadly used and afford social construction of meaning for cognitive flexibility, they could facilitate deep learning of computer graphics. While deep learning as a result of this course did not seem to occur, it is possible that deep learning will subsequently occur through continued social networking.

Descriptions of students' experiences advance knowledge regarding how Web 2.0 technologies might be used by instructors. In addition, they provide guidance for instructional designers as they design and implement read/write Web technologies in instructional environments. Based on previous literature and our experiences with this case, we recommend adopting Web 2.0 technologies cautiously in order to avoid cognitive overload and enhance cognitive flexibility:

- Differentiate assignments according to learners' prior experiences in Web 2.0. Add Web 2.0 applications gradually for students who are Web 2.0 novices and provide tutorials and just-in-time technical support. These suggestions correspond with Mayer and Moreno's (2003) suggestion to individualize instruction.
- Scaffold self-regulation and direct learners' cognitive processing. A first step is to maintain a personal presence in courses through frequent e-mails to students that provide regular feedback. Those e-mails should remain positive and encouraging while including constructive criticism germane to course content. This suggestion corresponds with that of Mayer and Moreno (2003) to pretrain and signal students, weeding out extraneous content, in order to enhance transfer and reduce extraneous processing.

- Develop rubrics that clarify expectations for each assignment and use those rubrics to give feedback. This suggestion corresponds with instructional design theory.
- Provide for continuous online discussions among peers regarding readings and assignments; encourage peer cooperation and feedback; provide a separate forum for peer exchange of technical help.
- Most importantly, students should be able to apply the Web 2.0 philosophy by seeing each other's work, critiquing each other, and having opportunities to revise and resubmit work based upon peer and instructor feedback. These suggestions correspond with Gunawardena, Hermans, Sanchez, Richmond, Bohley, and Tuttle's (2009) suggestion to build communities of practice with social networking tools.

CONCLUSION

We conclude that Web 2.0 tools can be applied to help learners meet the goals of self-regulated deep learning and cognitive flexibility when course design attends to cognitive load and when students are provided with guidance in self-regulation. Although students did experience cognitive overload in the course under study, their abilities to work through and manage the chaos indicate that through course design and the application of self-regulation strategies students can indeed learn in the context of multiple Web 2.0 tools. The students actually had two mutually exclusive sets of objectives—course-content objectives and the unstated objectives of Web 2.0 tool use. Being able to apply Web 2.0 for learning is an important goal that aligns with the goals of the course under study. Perhaps what students learned about applying Web 2.0 tools for social learning compensated for what may have been lost through cognitive overload in their progress toward prespecified objectives. In a course where Web 2.0 use itself is totally extraneous to course content, the opportunities for social construction of knowledge afforded by Web 2.0 adoption might not be worth the increased cognitive load. However, we argue that in today's world, where Web 2.0 literacy is important, learning to use Web 2.0 to meet course goals is germane to most content areas.

Although a body of literature suggests that students are already sophisticated in finding, synthesizing, contributing to, and integrating information using Web 2.0 (Collis & Moonen, 2008), our findings indicate that students would benefit from more training in how to use Web 2.0 tools to support their own learning. Such training would decrease their experience of cognitive overload in courses that leverage Web 2.0 while increasing their cognitive flexibility.

We believe that our quandary regarding requiring students to apply Web 2.0 tools will become a nonissue soon enough as students become more agile with Web 2.0 technologies. However, until students have gained sophistication in using Web 2.0 technologies, learning activities in which students use Web 2.0 should be structured and scaffolded with tutorials to avoid cognitive overload and enhance cognitive flexibility. As with word processing in the 1980s and use of the Internet in the 1990s, facility with Web 2.0 technologies for learning will increase over time until it becomes commonplace. At that point, we hope that Web 2.0 will be so well integrated into learning environments that educators will be able to assume Web 2.0 literacy.

The Internet shows great potential for enhancing collaboration among people, and the role of social media has become increasingly relevant in recent years. Students' learning experiences increasingly include social networking. The construction of students' social networks, the evolution of these networks, and their effects on the students' learning experiences in a university environment should be further examined. Deep learning from, and self-regulation in a course result, in large part, from course design features. Studies need to be conducted to provide evidence regarding the impacts and effects of specific design features that enhance learning and metacognition. We specifically recommend further investigations exploring the design features of learning environments that apply Web 2.0 tools to promote cognitive flexibility without cognitively overloading students.

QUESTIONS FOR ANALYSIS/DISCUSSION

1. What might be the disadvantages of using Web 2.0 for learning in an online course?
2. Given the complexity of the Computer Graphics for Learning course content, what might be the added value of leveraging Web 2.0 capabilities for learning in an online course?
3. How might Web 2.0 applications be applied in online courses to build cognitive flexibility?
4. What design features might be included to avoid cognitive overload in online courses that leverage Web 2.0 applications?
5. How might students be encouraged to regulate their own learning in an online course involving so many different platforms?
6. Based upon this case, instructional design theory, and your own experience, what recommendations can you make to online instructors who adopt Web 2.0 applications in their online courses?

REFERENCES

Anderson, P. (2007, February). What is Web 2.0? Ideas, technologies and implications for education. *JISC Technology and Standards Watch*, 1–64.

Beldarrain, Y. (2006). Distance education trends: Integrating new technologies to foster student interaction and collaboration. *Distance Education, 27*(2), 139–153.

Cifuentes, L., Alvarez-Xochihua, O., & Edwards, J. C. (2011). Learning in Web 2.0 environments: Surface learning and chaos or deep learning and self-regulation? *Quarterly Review of Distance Education, 12*(1), 1–21.

Cifuentes, L, Carpenter, B. S., & Bulu, S. (2008). An online collaborative environment for sharing visual culture. *Journal of Visual Literacy, 26*(2), 133–150.

Cifuentes, L, & Dylak, S. (2007). Trigger visuals for cross-cultural online learning. *The International Journal of Continuing Engineering Education and Lifelong Learning, 17*(2/3), 121–137.

Cifuentes, L., McKintosh, K., & Douglas, J. (1997). What's wrong with this picture? Creating nonexamples in Adobe Photoshop. *Learning and Leading With Technology, 25*(2), 58–61.

Cifuentes, L., Myers, L. J., & McKintosh, K. (1998). Selective data analyses, photo manipulation, and stylistic embellishment for honest message design. *Journal of Visual Literacy, 18*(2), 165–174.

Collis, B. & Moonen, J. (2008). Web 2.0 tools and processes in higher education; quality perspectives. *Educational Media International, 45*(2), 93–106.

Driscoll, K. (2007). Collaboration in today's classrooms: New web tools change the game. *MultiMedia & Internet@Schools, 14*(3), 9–12.

Dunlap, J. C., Sobel, D. & Sands, D. I. (2007). Designing for deep and meaningful student-to-content interactions. *TechTrends, 51*(4), 20–31.

Godwin-Jones, R. (2006). Emerging technologies: Tag clouds in the blogosphere: Electronic literacy and social networking. *Language Learning & Technology, 10*(2), 8–15.

Gunawardena, C. N., Hermans, M. B., Sanchez, D., Richmond, C., Bohley, M., & Tuttle, R. (2009). A theoretical framework for building online communities of practice with social networking tools. *Educational Media International, 46*(1), 3–16.

Hannafin, M., Hannafin, K., & Gabbitas, B. (2009). Re-examining cognition during student-centered Web-based learning. *Educational Technology Research and Development, 57*(2), 767–785.

Lightner, S. B., & Willi, C. (2007). Team-based activities to promote engaged learning. *College Teaching, 55*(1), 5–18.

Lincoln, Y. S., & Guba, E. G. (1985). *Naturalistic inquiry*. Newbury Park, CA: Sage.

Lohr, L. (2008). *Creating graphics for learning and performance: Lessons in visual literacy*. Upper Saddle River, NJ: Pearson.

Mayer, R. E., & Moreno, R. (2003). Nine ways to reduce cognitive load in multimedia learning. *Educational Psychologist, 38*(1), 43–52.

McNabb, M. (2006). Navigating the maze of hypertext. *Educational Leadership, 63*(4), 76–79.

Northrup, P. (2001). A framework for designing interactivity in Web-based instruction. *Educational Technology, 41*(2), 31–39.

O'Reilly, T. (2005). What is Web 2.0: Design patterns and business models for the next generation of software. *Communications & Strategies, 1*(17).

Oliver, K. (2007). Leveraging Web 2.0 in the redesign of a graduate-level technology integration course. *TechTrends, 51*(5), 55–61.

Paas, F., Renkl, A., & Sweller, J. (2003). Cognitive load theory and instructional design: Recent developments. *Educational Psychologist, 38*(1), 1–4.

Raman, M. R., & Olfman, L. (2005). Designing knowledge management systems for teaching and learning with wiki technology. *Journal of Information Systems Education, 16*(3), 311–320.

Resta, P., & Laferriere, T. (2007). Technology in support of collaborative learning. *Educational Psychology Review, 19*(1), 65–83.

Simonson, M. (2009). Best practices for designing distance education and the U-M-T approach. In Rogers, P. (Ed.), *Encyclopedia of distance learning* (2nd ed., pp. 181–187). Hershey, NY: Information Science Reference.

Solomon, G., & Schrum, L. (2007). *Web 2.0 new tools, new schools.* Eugene, OR: ISTE.

Spiro, R. J., Feltovich, P. J., Jacobson, M. J., & Coulson, R. L. (1995). *Cognitive flexibility, constructivism, and hypertext: Random access instruction for advanced knowledge acquisition in ill-structured domains.* Hillsdale, NJ: Erlbaum.

Spradley, J. P. (1980) *Participant observation.* Florence, KY: Wadsworth, Thomson Learning.

Sweller, J., van Merreinboer, & Paas, F. (1998). Cognitive architecture and instructional design. *Educational Psychology Review, 10(3), 252–296.*

Wikipedia. (n.d.). Web 2.0. Retrieved from http://en.wikipedia.org/wiki/Web2.0

Zajicek, M. (2007). Web 2.0: Hype or happiness? In *Proceedings of the 2007 international cross-disciplinary conference on Web accessibility (W4a)* Banff, Canada (Vol. 225, pp. 35–39).

Zimmerman, B. J., & Martinez-Pons, M. (1995). Self-monitoring during collegiate studying: An invaluable tool for academic self-regulation. In P. R. Pintrich (Ed.) *Understanding self-regulated learning,* (pp. 13–28), San Francisco, CA: Jossey Bass.

Zins, J. E., Weissberg, R. P., Wang, M. C., & Walberg, H. J. (Eds.). (2004). *Building academic success on social and emotional learning: What does the research say?* New York, NY: Teachers College Press.

CHAPTER 11

CONSULTING AND DESIGNING IN THE FAST LANE

Ludwika A. Goodson and In Sook Ahn

ABSTRACT

The online course design process in this case study demonstrates how improvements in learning can occur with a consulting process and course template design that addresses three issues: (a) context of learning, teaching, and course content; (b) analysis of "significant learning" to redefine learning outcomes; and (c) corresponding alignment of technology, instructional strategies, and content to expand the students' opportunities for an authentic updated worldview and context of cultural diversity. This case study shows how the *roles* of an instructional designer and subject matter expert interacted to deal with online course design and content dilemmas and, thereby, overcome limitations inherent with learning from the textbook in a classroom environment. This case study further illustrates how the online course architecture, defined within an "opening page template" and "quizzes," accommodated anticipated content changes and shifted learning from *lower-level, culturally biased* to *higher-order, culturally diverse* outcomes.

Real-Life Distance Education, pages 197–220
Copyright © 2014 by Information Age Publishing
All rights of reproduction in any form reserved.

INTRODUCTION

Consulting and designing in the fast lane resulted from the schedule demands of a new faculty member and role responsibilities of an instructional designer at a university's teaching and learning center. Within two weeks of the first meeting of the faculty member and the instructional designer, they would: (a) build two modules and launch the first of these in a new online course, (b) produce a template for the design of the remaining modules, and (c) stay one week ahead of the students for the duration of the term.

Instructor Context

The instructor had been hired to teach courses in fashion design, had previously taught at an art college, and had been an owner and designer in a business involved in every level of the fashion industry from designing and sourcing materials, through negotiating prices, selecting distribution channels, and pricing finished products, to organizing fashion shows. Those experiences produced practical knowledge that could help in creating authentic learning experiences. This level of expertise was as yet unknown to the instructional designer.

After less than a week on campus, the instructor stopped by the instructional designer's office to ask for support in placing a fashion design course online. The instructor had never taught online and was unfamiliar with online learning tools. The instructor's primary language was not English and the instructor was asking for additional support to ensure high quality communication within the anticipated online course discussions with students. This also was the instructor's first time to meet an instructional designer.

Meanwhile, the instructor was becoming acquainted with a new city as well as a new campus, attending orientation, completing forms, meeting with program administrators, learning about expectations for service and research as well as other teaching responsibilities, locating university resources, making contact with a university mentor, and unpacking and organizing family responsibilities.

Nonetheless, because of scheduling demands, the instructor had made a firm decision to deliver the course online in the current term, a course that would begin in the following week. Students would meet in a classroom with the instructor at the start of the term and for two proctored tests.

Instructional Designer Context

At the time of this case study, the instructional designer's responsibilities included work with an academic writing circle, a creative writing circle, weekly faculty development workshops, a faculty course development retreat, consultation for other courses, classroom teaching observations, and special projects.

Previous work in online course design and educational research, training, and assessment prepared the instructional designer for collaborative design with the full expectation that art, craft, and science coexist and strengthen the quality of instructional design (Davies, 1991; Gram, 2010; Greenberry, 2004; Oh & Reeves, 2010). The instructional designer had never studied fashion design, but had an appreciation for the complexity of design elements because of prior experiences in artwork and Feng Shui design principles.

The following set of professional practices guided the work of course design, development, and production in this case study. Although later editions for references cited with these practices have been published, it is the earlier editions that most deeply shaped these professional practices.

- *Practice 1:* Begin by describing "significant learning" for students in the course. Dee Fink provided a practical guide for this first stage of analysis (Fink, 2003, 2007, 2009; Fink & Fink, 2009).
- *Practice 2:* Define competencies for the learners and use them to guide selection of teaching and assessment strategies. An older but rock-solid example comes from Davies (1973), who not only described, but explicitly modeled this practice in his book on competency-based learning. While many scholars list this practice as part of instructional design, more recently Campbell, Schwier, & Kenny (2009, pp. 650, 655) took it a step further in showing it to be a critical relational practice in the role of learner advocacy.
- *Practice 3:* Use systematic course development and production procedures. In early professional practice, when the instructional designer gave detailed feedback in a small-group field trial for the model that Dick and Carey were developing (1978), the need for clear course production procedures had already become extremely evident. Later, the instructional designer (Andrews & Goodson, 1980, 2011) completed a comparative analysis of about 40 models of instructional design, the commonalities of which emphasized this systematic approach, an analysis republished in Anglin (2011).
- *Practice 4:* Build conditions for different types of learning. This practice first began with a book on *Conditions of Learning* (Gagné, 1970) and later *Principles of Instructional Design* (Gagné & Briggs, 1974, 1979), brought into its fifth user-friendly edition with authors Gagné, Wager, Golas, and Keller (2004). The inspiring concepts in these books led to studies in a doctoral program and meeting Briggs, who challenged the instructional designer to figure out:

"How do models of teaching fit with models of instructional design?" Approaches to conditions for learning were later influenced by the ARCS model for creating conditions that foster student motivation to learn (Keller, 1999, 2008, 2011). The practice was further developed when reviewing strategies that work for learning higher order thinking and problem-solving skills in a couple of projects with colleagues (King, Goodson, & Rohani, 1998; King, Rohani, & Goodson, 1997). Finally, the writings on models of teaching (Huitt, 2003; Joyce and Weil, 1972; Joyce, Weil, & Calhoun, 2009), together with the question from Briggs, increased attention to teaching models that lend *fidelity of the learning context* to the target environment in which knowledge and skills will be used, e.g., jurisprudential model for teaching law.

- *Practice 5:* Use layout and graphic design principles to make instructional text easier to understand. Although many studies have been influential about effective web design practices, it was Hartley (1994, 1996) who provided a research-based framework for making decisions about font, spacing, and other attributes for ease of navigation and comprehension. Web-based learning requires equal attention to layout and graphic design elements (Knupfer & McIsaac, 1992; Pomales-Garciá & Liu, 2006; Webster & Ahuja, 2006).

- *Practice 6:* Use a flexible user-centered style of consulting in the course design and development process. This practice was first influenced by Davies (1981) and was strengthened, not within the study of instructional design, but by others who focused on clarity of the relational communication process (DeYoung, 1996; Denning & Dargan, 1996; Gram & Tovar, 1991; Kuhn & Winograd, 1996; Schön, 1987; Schön & Bennett, 1996), consulting as a strategy for knowledge transfer (Jacobson, Butterill, & Goering, 2005), and the kind of flexibility in transformational practice needed in organizational change strategies (Walsh, Crisp, & Moss, 2011). Within the particular context of instructional design, Keppell (2001) offered the consulting perspective that most closely matches the one used in this case study.

Course Content

The course subject was the aesthetics of fashion design. The instructional designer began by asking for the opportunity to review the course syllabus and textbook. The syllabus had a bare skeleton—what would be "significant learning" for students was unclear. The textbook pages unveiled a series of white female "body types," placement of plus-sized figures in an "other" category, and tips on personal wardrobe analysis. Yet, this university emphasized respect for cultural diversity and active learning informed by scholarly practices. The instructional designer noted the stereotypes and that such limited content did not seem to fit with university expectations or for broader goals suggested in the syllabus.

Important questions about content remained unknown. Did the new faculty member select this textbook? If selected by someone else, did it nonetheless express the instructor's focus? Was this the only set of course materials? To expand resources for discussion, the instructional designer searched the Internet to find lists of competencies of fashion design aesthetics. These lists would be used to ask if the instructor would expect similar competencies in the course. Meanwhile bookstore ordering procedures had already made the textbook available to students.

Design Challenges

At this stage, the instructional designer had more questions than answers. How could the instructional designer (ID) approach questions about content with the instructor, who by role definition had academic responsibility and was the subject matter expert (SME)? Along with the need for quality of design, what kind of template or prototype could work to speed up development and production? Would the SME be interested in formative evaluation? How could timely revisions be made?

If the course was to be taught online, it would need to be ready for launch within two weeks in spite of what was still unknown, and in spite of what seemed like too many questions. Keeping these questions in mind, it was time to set priorities focused on what would be needed before beginning the design for the online course structure and activities:

- Learn more about the context of learning and teaching.
- Discover and analyze the significant learning expected for the students.
- Align technology choices with instructional methods and content.

CASE STUDY

The course development pace would be intense. The best production outcome might be to provide just-in-time delivery of course materials. Nonetheless, instead of leaping into production, the ID began by engaging the instructor as a new acquaintance, not just as SME.

Within this approach, answers about significant learning would be needed:

1. What was worth caring about in the "aesthetics of fashion design?"
2. What are the most important concepts and why do they matter?
3. Who are the students? One culture or diverse? Both male and female?
4. What would be important and relevant to them?
5. How and why would they apply what they learn?
6. How would the course address the broader goal of helping students to learn how to learn and to learn how to think?

These kinds of questions are an adaptation of Dee Fink's approach to instructional analysis (Fink, 2009; Fink & Fink, 2009). They also support front-end analysis in the steps of systematic course development (Dick, Carey, & Carey, 2004; Gagné, Wager, Golas, & Keller, 2004), including the dimension of cultural analysis (Saxena, 2011).

Learning, Teaching, and Course Content

The next meeting of the ID and SME began with a welcome, a warm cup of coffee, a comfortable chair, and questions starting with "How are you doing? Sugar? Please sit here. Now, help me to understand a little more about your course." The process was informal with listening, responding, and guiding. The tone and style expressed high regard for the SME role and as the one with control over course design decisions (Keppell, 2001; Kuhn & Winograd, 1996). Table 11.1 shows the exploratory communication and rapid unfolding of the SME vision.

The SME and ID began searching for examples of art and objects that have inspired fashion design. With key word searches, in just a few moments, they had found an image of Gustav Klimt's "The Kiss" and the "Tree of Life" (Featuring Gustav Klimt). Then with another key word search of "Klimt AND fashion," they found examples of fashion inspired by this art style at The Artist Workshop Community (Evening Dresses inspired by Gustav Klimt), and at the Style.com website (Rachel Comey menswear). The search for a man's example was harder, but successful, and revealed the power of the web to open up the world of fashion design.

This was a moment of creative and intellectual spark with both glimpsing the possibilities for an exciting course design while also leaving this meeting with something concrete and with inspiration for further thinking to prepare for the next meeting. They would look ahead in planning the course, collecting representations of male, female, cultures, and lifestyle fashions.

Opening up the worldview also would help to overcome the limited exposure to the apparel industry available in the local community, with only one mall, limited brand names and styles, a few traditional downtown shops, and a couple of grocery and drug stores. Yet, even in a large urban area, students still

TABLE 11.1 Exploratory Communication About Course Content and Vision

Q. Did you develop this syllabus?
A. No. It was given to me to use for teaching this course.

Q. Did you select this textbook?
A. No. It was assigned along with the syllabus.

Q. Alright. Have any other course materials been selected for use with this textbook?
A. No.

Q. Who will be the students in the course? Will it be only females, or do males take the course?
A. At least one male will be in the course.

Q. Do you expect the students to be from just one culture? Or do you think there will be students from several, maybe from different countries?
A. It's a mixed group of students. Some may be from other countries.

Q. What else can you tell me about the students in this course?
A. They are mostly sophomores and juniors. And, they are majoring in fashion design and merchandising.

Q. Okay. That makes a difference. How's the coffee?
A. This is the best coffee I've ever had!!! I want to know how did you make it? (This train of thought would be picked up later and the SME would buy dark roast beans and an espresso machine with a steamer.)

Q. Let's take a closer look at the textbook now. Look. This is an image of a white woman. FLIPPING PAGES, and this is what we see throughout the pages of the book. It looks like this is about making wardrobe choices, tips on how to match a student's body type and what to wear, not what to design. And the book puts the larger-sized women in an "other" category; there is one dark-skinned woman in the lingerie section. When I look at the syllabus, it looks like there could be more to aesthetics of fashion design, but I'm wondering if this is what you really mean when you say "aesthetics of fashion design" or do you mean something else?
A. No, it's a lot more than that.

Q. Alright, then, let's say you want a student to design something. What are the "big ideas" they would need to use? What do they have to think about? What would make it "fashion" and not something just put together to cover a body? What are the elements of "aesthetics?"
A. Several things. Shape. Line. Form... (The ID made notes, then cycled back to ask for meanings and examples of each concept.)

Q. If you wanted students to learn the key concepts of fashion design aesthetics, so that they would learn how to think about aesthetics, where would you begin?
A. Inspiration. I'd want them to know what inspires the aesthetics of fashion design.

Q. Alright, then let's start there. Tell me more about what you mean. Give me an example... Give me another example... (As each example was mentioned, the ID made notes, then used the examples for further development of learning activities and a course template.)

would not be able to fully access global markets (Global Fashion News, n.d.; Hergeth, 2005; Easters, 2012; Hazel, 2008). Online links would open up this world, and with course design, could lead to powerful learning.

It also became clear that the SME had a broad sensitivity to cultural diversity and its need for representation in fashion design. In support of this sensitivity, it may be worth noting that population growth has been projected to make minorities the "majority by 2042" (America.gov, 2008, p. 2); this grouping includes "Hispanic, Black, Asian, American Indian, Native Hawaiian, Pacific Islander, or mixed race," (p. 3). Frey (2011), Day (n.d.), and Pew Research Center (2012) report similar projections.

Analyzing Significant Learning

Rather than the limited perspective of the textbook, the SME hoped that the course would inspire students to extend their knowledge under their own steam after completing the course and that the course would help the students to get the jobs they want. The course would help students to develop a vision and disposition toward the aesthetics of fashion design in a way that would serve them as they engaged in the highly competitive workplace. Students would be able to combine key concepts and elements of aesthetics into the process of creative fashion design.

As a result of this vision, the course would become an in-depth investigation of aesthetics and how aesthetics applies to the roles of the fashion and apparel industry professional. Students would come to know both the theory and practice of aesthetics in apparel. Students would need practice in identifying and classifying concepts and have assignments that would challenge them to create designs using the concepts they studied.

The ID began pulling together features for the course design:

1. Students would need to learn concepts before application of rules (Gagné, Wager, Golas, & Keller, 2004).
2. Using the concept attainment model (Joyce, Weil, & Calhoun, 2009) would mean a focus on definitions and examples of content, categorizing examples, and forming and applying concepts.
3. Once concepts were well learned, students would be able to combine them in rule-using applications through a blend of inquiry and inductive thinking methods, and develop problem-solving skills (Kapp, 2011; King, Goodson, & Rohani, 1998; King, Rohani, & Goodson, 1997; O'Neill & Hung, 2010).

The content challenge in applying these instructional strategies would be to choose language that would produce systematically clear concepts without losing the *gestalt* of the design process (Berglin, Cederwall, Hallnäs, Jönsson, Kvaal, Lundstedt, Nordström, Peterson, & Thornquist, 2007). Discussions and quizzes would engage students in more than "body type" and "wardrobe choices"—they would focus on using a fashion-context professional style with direct relevance, informed reasoning, and responsiveness to the concepts. Content would be rich with diversity and relevance to their professional goals, they would have choices like those of a fashion designer, and the course organization and layout would give them reliable consistency and structure—all of which would support their motivation to learn (Keller, 2008, 2011).

Students would be able to accomplish the following major objectives:

1. Explain and apply the various concepts of aesthetics (explicitly identified in the modules).
2. Identify and apply design concepts of individual textiles and apparel styles.
3. Analyze and evaluate the interconnection of apparel and other forms of aesthetic experience.
4. Analyze and apply basic aesthetic concepts to figure styles, visual displays and promotional information.

This course design would gain momentum with alignment of goals, activities, feedback, and assessment. Table 11.2 shows the major shift in the course vision.

Aligning Technology Choices

ID guidance addressed how to collect and integrate content from Web and news sources; integrate images into web pages; efficiently use the learning management system (LMS); broaden cultural representation as well as domestic and global perspectives; integrate active learning and advance organizers in main points and discussions (a format issue for the course's "opening page"); review, analyze, and give feedback on online

---

TABLE 11.2   Course Vision Shift

Textbook Vision	New Course Vision
Wardrobe Selection: Form and fashion for personal body type, review of one's closet space, shopping and tailoring for one's own body type, and selection of undergarments and accessories.	*Fashion Design Aesthetics:* Sources of inspiration and using elements of line, texture, form, color, balance, emphasis, rhythm, complexity, and novelty in authentic contemporary fashion design.

discussions and quizzes; construct an online survey for formative evaluation; and collect, analyze, and respond to evaluation data. Table 11.3 shows some of the major design challenges for which online tools provided direct solutions.

TABLE 11.3   Teaching Challenges and Online Solutions

Limited Textbook Focus

Problem:

- Focus on one's personal body type (rather than design elements)
- Gender bias (showing women only)
- Very low diversity of cultures (mostly white, all same sleek hairstyle)
- Examples were out of date, out of fashion, did not allow a grasp of the concept of design, and lacked the freshness and excitement of changes in fashion

Online Solution:

- Add images of males, as well as females
- Add images of diverse cultures
- Focus on design elements, rather than personal body type
- Expand sources of inspiration
- Elicit examples from students themselves
- Create a course template to allow updates of examples to reflect changes in fashion

Restricted Fashion Context

Problem:

Limited design perspectives (rural location, few stores)

Online Solution:

- Add web links to multinational fashion hubs (beyond the local region)
- Add examples from different fashion lines and designers
- Update with access to fast-changing domestic and international markets

Restricted Class Time

Problem:

- Few students give examples and explanations in class discussions within the available time period—no opportunity to know what other students are thinking
- Corresponding feedback is limited to the focus of a few

Online Solution:

- Post discussion questions, with images when appropriate
- Direct ALL students to answer questions, add new examples, and explanations
- Review weekly discussion postings and then add end-of-module review and summary for students

Course Management Efficiencies

Problem:

In traditional class structure with office hours, instructor deals with student emails and messages that take away time from learning (questions about grades, schedules...)

Online Solution:

- Create an "Online Office" for questions, comments, and answers that all can view
- Use electronic grade book to post and confidentially report student grades

---

Course Template Development

The timeline could be met more easily with a course template that could structure organization of course content. This would involve discussing how students learn, determining what architecture could be used immediately and could apply to every module, and creating a structure that could be updated with changes in fashion lines.

Emerging requirements included:

1. The course would need to be explicitly organized, have navigation ease for students and instructor, and include interactivity for learning.
2. The schedule of course production would need to be met, with periodic "tickling" to prompt preparation for upcoming meetings.
3. Implementation requirements would include web site creation, access to technical support tools, and creation and uploading of course components.
4. Delivery, especially in the first few weeks, would involve course monitoring and formative evaluation, reminders of teaching activities, support for responding to discussions, collection of student feedback, and testing and assessment analysis.
5. The course architecture would need to include purpose and objectives for each module with a focus on key concepts, prompts for providing examples, questions to guide student thinking, questions to discuss, and quizzes (for practice) and tests (for assessment).

An "opening page" template for a module was created in a web page form for easy viewing. For this prototype, the ID and SME would search multiple sources from which to make choices and then integrate these into sections of the template structure. This template would have a clearly designated area for listing title and purpose, for signaling learning activities, for links to resources, for questions to prompt thinking, and for guidance for online discussions.

Course Layout

The course view was set up for students to see the major organization. Major links were visible at a glance: the "Course Welcome," "Syllabus," "Online Office," "Student Lounge," "Design Samples Book Assignment," and "Modules" folder. (The "Discussions" area was not a visible separate link; instead, each discussion was linked within the module to which it belonged.)

The Course Welcome had a welcome from the instructor, pointed out that learning would be online, set high expectations for students, explained use of the Online Office, previewed the module structure, gave time and day of weekly deadlines, and pointed out locations of course materials.

The Syllabus listed instructor contact information, materials for study and web activities, directions for the Online Office, course objectives, and explained how online learning time relates to class contact time, the grading scheme, expectations for academic integrity, deadlines and communication protocols, and a schedule of coursework.

The Design Samples Book Assignment had the due date posted and, within the folder, had directions to follow. Students would collect visual examples of each term introduced in the course, scan all those examples and save them in a CD, copy and mount them into a book, and make a checklist of the number of examples they had collected for each term. Each "term" would be a "concept" and this assignment would give practice in choosing and classifying new examples of the concepts.

At the Online Office, the SME posted an opening message to repeat what to post and pointed out turnaround time to expect for the instructor's response. At the Student Lounge, the SME posted an opening message explaining that this space would be for students and the instructor would never visit again.

Module Structure

Opening page—aesthetics. The opening page was created as a web page so that it would "open up" when students selected the module title. Parallel to this opening page, at the left menu, students would be able to see the menu links to the discussion and the quiz.

A table format structured page layout so that margins and placement of text and images could be controlled. A warm deep brown background was used for headers with light gold font, below which was a section of gold background over which warm deep brown text was added.

Opening page—top header. To signal "big ideas" for the module, the top header had the module number and title with a purpose statement, serving as the first "advance organizer."

Opening page—directions. Below the top header, serving as the second "advance organizer, was the "Directions" section with three parts, each marked with a checklist icon: (a) directions to study a set of examples, (b) reminder to complete the discussion for the module, and (c) reminder to take the quiz for the module. The template called for at least three examples, beginning with simpler obvious examples and progressing to more complex ones. The fashion line links could be easily updated for future years. Table 11.4 provides examples of the top header content and directions.

The complexity of modules also progressed from simple to more complex. As shown in Table 11.4, the "Art" module had fewer, but more complex examples as it shifted from the simpler obvious examples in the "Inspiration"

TABLE 11.4   Examples of Opening Page Top Header and Directions

Module 1: Inspiration	Purpose: Identify Sources of Inspiration for Fashion Styles

☑   Study the examples in the following sections to see how the sources of inspiration became part of the fashions.Example 1:   Bones

Example 2:   Cave Horse Drawings
Example 3:   Marc Jacob's "Teen Spirit" Collection
Example 4:   Dress Fashion for Women [year]
Example 5:   Sports Fashion for Men [year]
Examples 6, 7 & 8:   Lifestyle Fashion Selections [year]

More examples from your textbook.

☑   Then complete the discussion for this module before the start of the next module.
☑   Remember to take the quiz for Module 1.

Module 2: Art	Purpose: Identify the Influences of Art in Fashion Styles

☑   Compare examples of art to the fashions they inspire.

Example 1: Art Nouveau example of Gustav Klimt
Example 2: Modern Art example of Matisse
Example 3: Art Deco example of Tamara de Lampica

☑   Then complete the discussion for this module before the start of the next module.
☑   Remember to take the quiz for Module 2.

module. And, about midway through the course, students had the more complex purpose of identifying complexity, order, and novelty in apparel.

Opening page—content. Language began with a style designed to unpack concepts in a personable way. To illustrate, text for the "Inspiration" module began: "Fashion sometimes has odd sources of inspiration. In this case, bones. What kind of bones? We're not sure. But they are clearly bones..." This text was followed by an image of upper limb bones side by side with a top that looked as if the bodice had been decorated with some of those same bones.

Opening page—adjunct questions. After a few examples, the opening page displayed a bold gold and red question icon with an adjunct question to direct attention and prompt thinking such as: "How do the two dresses below match up to the Gustav Klimt art prints above? Look at colors, forms, and patterns, texture, complexity, and shapes. What can you see that's similar..." Later, a new example and question could be introduced, absent the explicit source of inspiration, such as: "...Notice the earth tones and velvet textures. What do you think the source of inspiration might have been?"

Opening page—notes. Occasionally, explanatory notes would be added, such as a quote "Art Nouveau: The Artists:" "The essence of Art Nouveau is described by sensuous lines and subtle light . . ." The style of presentation modeled the practice of citing sources.

Opening page—main points. This section header was followed by text designed to elaborate on the main points, to further unpack the meaning of main ideas, and sometimes to introduce ideas connected to the examples. For example, in the "Inspiration" module: "Choosing the right design for the time begins with research and research includes . . ." The text elaborated on the concept of "research" and its role in planning and managing fashion design.

Opening page—discussion and resources. The last section had a multicolored discussion icon of two profiles in conversation to signal directions for the discussion. Basic directions appeared next to the icon, after which came specific steps with choices and resources.

A complete set of examples of choices given to students would be too lengthy for this report, but a couple of examples can illustrate the approach. In one early discussion, students were given five sets of choices and, under each, five links to related art and fashion examples:

Choice 1   Compare the art of Frida Kahlo to fashions.
Choice 2   Compare the art of Jean Miro to fashions.
Choice 3   Compare the art of Edward Hopper to fashions.
Choice 4   Compare the art of Cy Twombly to fashions.
Choice 5   Compare the art of Jean-Michael Basquiat to fashions.

The student could view and compare options before choosing or choose only one of interest. In addition, for students who might be interested in exploring more about art for fashion inspiration, links were given to Baroque and Roccoco, Art Nouveau, Street Wise—Street Savvy—Street Wearable—On-the-Streets Fashion, Pop Culture, and Other Generation Influences.

By contrast, in a later module, students were given fewer choices but more complex tasks that required analyzing a fashion design and describing six changes to make for a classic style (decreased complexity) and then six to make for a postmodern aesthetic (increased complexity).

Table 11.5 provides abbreviated examples of basic directions. Table 11.6 provides examples of follow-up steps to basic directions.

Online Discussions

Each module had one discussion board. Directions for this area were the same as those in the "Discussion and Resources" section of the opening page. Discussion protocols were briefly described in the syllabus, including "think more, write less," with tips on how to compose a discussion message before posting it, and a reminder that content in the discussions may be addressed in a quiz or exam. At the end of a discussion, the

---

TABLE 11.5 Examples of Basic Directions for Online Discussions

Example 1—Simple

"Search the web or use the links listed below to find any fashion design that you like. Analyze your choice and decide what you think was the source of inspiration. Avoid using someone else's description unless you quote it. I really want you to think through what makes sense."

Example 2—Slightly More Complex

"I've selected a few links that show different styles. Can you find links for the styles you like and compare them to these? Look for your favorite designers by searching on the Internet. Then in your discussion, report your ONE favorite link and explain what you think the inspiration was for the design and why this is your favorite link."

TABLE 11.6 Examples of Steps for Online Discussions

Example 1   Simple Steps

Go to the discussion area for this module and complete the following steps: (1) Identify the artist and fashion style you selected; (2) explain why you selected them; (3) explain how the art or artist inspired the fashion designs; and (4) read over classmates' messages and choose to reply to at least one.

Example 2   Connection to Textbook

Go to the discussion area for this module and complete the following steps: (1) From the following images representing different principles and elements of design, select ONE style that might change the appearance of your body type (what would "flatter" or "insult"); (2) explain why the style would change the appearance of your body type; and (3) read over classmates' messages and choose to reply to at least one.

---

instructor reviewed discussion messages posted by students and provided a review of highlights.

Online Quizzes

Quizzes tended to be short answer, giving students new examples to classify. The online assessment tool had been set up to provide automated feedback on answers, directing student attention to key features that their answers should have included. A quiz usually had only a few questions, but each focused on a key concept that was studied, or had examples of fashion styles about which the students had to make some judgment or identification. The quiz would not cover the same examples as in the modules, but would present new ones.

Using new examples broadened students' exposure to fashion concepts and prompted them to grapple with concepts rather than just memorize previously encountered examples. Emphasis was given to having students explain reasons for answers, too, so that students would be more likely to elaborate on conceptual meaning and practice identifying the concept features. Table 11.7 shows a couple of examples of quiz items.

TABLE 11.7 Sample Quiz Items

Example 1—Simple

Look at the vest. It is described as a "bird of paradise" design, an "exotic African motif." Does this design work? Why or why not?

Example 2—More Complex

Your goal is to study an object, define its visual qualities, and imagine transforming the image you have of its visual qualities into a design. First, review the following quote.

"When I was a student, I spent a lot of time in museums taking notes. Now that I know more, I find inspiration in many diverse places..." *Source:* Is there a future in fashion's past? by Valentino; Russell Simmons; Time in Partnership with CNN http://www.time.com/time/magazine/story/0,9171,1101030205-419744,00.html

Next, choose your object—it could be anything—an image (photo, art print, poster), a food (tomato, dried up apple, fresh asparagus, frozen pea), a publication (book, magazine, brochure), a container (water sitting in the sunlight, crushed can on the street), notions (fabric, thread, buttons), or anything else.

But choose one object and study it for a few minutes. (Try to avoid choosing anything already listed in the Module 1 course site and text book.) As you study the object, pay attention to the visual qualities that you notice. Then think of how you might create a design from these qualities.

In the space that follows, describe your object, its visual qualities, your new design and how you created it from your visualized object.

   a.   What is your object?
   b.   What visual qualities did you observe?
   c.   What design could you imagine creating from these visual qualities?
   d.   How did you "see" this design as you studied your object?

Results

Course Template and Module Development

The template created as a prototype for the first two modules was used in developing the next eight modules, each produced and launched one or more days before students would begin study. For continued course development, the ID often collected possible examples for a module's purpose and concepts from web searches, after which the SME selected the best examples and/or searched for new ones. The SME prepared an opening page draft and sent it to the ID to review after which, in a scheduled meeting, questions or ambiguities would be resolved.

Content Updates and Gestalt of Design

In future terms, the SME integrated newer fashion lines within the modules. Although the structured course organization presented separate elements of the aesthetics of fashion design, those elements were continually integrated with the whole of the design process in applications to fashion design and the generation of solutions to fashion problems in discussions and quizzes.

Online Office and Student Lounge

Students posted questions in the Online Office where the instructor also provided answers and very few e-mails were sent. Data tracking showed that a few students used the Student Lounge—what was posted is not known, since the instructor did not visit this space.

Online Discussion Participation and Reviews

All students participated in each discussion, not just a few as happened in classroom sessions. Students applied wider multinational examples than would have been possible with the textbook alone in a classroom setting. Discussions revealed student insights about conceptual problems that the instructor was able to highlight in weekly reviews. These reviews of discussions were leveraged as a "teachable moment." For example, in one early discussion, students clearly were misusing a term, and the instructor posted a clarifying description with added examples.

Online Quizzes

In quizzes, students responded to visual design elements from diverse sources and received automated immediate feedback on answers. All students earned the maximum points for the quizzes (200 out of a total of 1,000 possible in the course)—perfect answers were not expected—the purpose was to encourage time spent in learning. Most students also earned full or nearly full points for discussion (300).

Formative Evaluation

For formative evaluation, students were asked to voluntarily answer these questions:

1. What percentage of the course material covered do you feel you actually learned?
2. To what extent do you think your aesthetics design skills have improved as a result of this course?
3. What observations, if any, do you have about what you have been learning in this course?
4. What concerns or satisfactions, if any, do you wish to express about any part of the course design, activities, or process?

Students reported that they liked the online learning; the course helped in setting and meeting deadlines; the course was well organized, interesting, comprehensive, and they expected it to be useful in the future. Most students also reported that they felt they had learned 80-90%, two reported 70%, and one reported 60%.

Collaborative Teamwork

The collaborative teamwork of the ID and SME continued in other projects about teaching and learning, such as the shared development of this case study, a presentation on cultural representations in instructional materials, and papers on the design of fashions for elderly women and for persons with disabilities.

IMPLICATIONS FOR DISTANCE EDUCATION

A systematic model of online course design often is set up as a sequence of procedures to complete as if running through a checklist and completing each step by a particular date—this could be thought of as the "PERT chart mindset." In this case, all steps had to be condensed in time. Yet, the style of collaboration illustrated a flexible consultative and personable style for beginning the ID and SME working relationship before moving into the fast track of production. The design process was systematic, flexible, and blended with social time. The meaning of significant learning for the course laid the foundation for envisioning the design of the course.

While it would have been simple to make rapid judgments about the expertise of the SME and vision of the course from a review of the textbook and syllabus content, the ID reserved judgment and instead formed a series of questions to further investigate the SME perspective and vision. The emerging vision revealed the need for concept and rule-using as well as problem-solving levels of learning, respective instructional strategies known to work for such learning, and an authentic context of fashion design.

In parallel with the emerging vision, the ID was able to kinetically and literally sketch out possible methods to achieve the vision. The kinetic process came in the form of ID and SME web searches for examples to use in building the first module. In that same time frame, the ID was able to do a pencil sketch of a possible layout for what later became the opening page.

The ID explained the time efficiencies of developing a course template for a modular structure and the advantages for learning that come with clarity of structure and organization. The ID could share knowledge about what works to help students learn concepts, apply them, and then put them together for rule-using and problem-solving applications. Presented with evidence-based options, the SME reviewed the options and made final choices. It was not unusual for the ID to say something like "Is this what you mean when you say . . . ?" Sometimes it would be, and sometimes not.

This work was not without some bumps in the road. For example, when the initial module, in which inspiration from art had been the focus, was ready for launch as the prototype, at the last moment, the SME came in worried about its complexity and felt a need for starting with a simpler set of concepts. This concern led to more dialogue to discover what would be simpler, and then to rapidly choosing "Inspiration" as the major concept for the first module, leaving "Art" for the second. This was a moment of frustration for the ID who thought it was a bit late to backtrack; both ID and SME felt the pressure of having the first module ready; the SME had the same frustration, but had come with honest thoughts. The ID would make coffee and together they would get through this stage.

Re-visioning was the right thing to do, and a new "first-module" was built using the first prototype. Both ID and SME made fast commitments to quick searching for examples, drafting embedded questions with examples to stimulate thinking, creating discussion questions and resources, and writing up the main points. The template structure prompted organized assignments for each. Then while students studied the first module, the ID and SME proceeded to make the first quiz questions and tune-up the second module for launch.

Once those first two modules were mapped out, and draft templates were filled with respective content to determine their workability, key concepts for the remaining modules could be mapped with reasonable confidence that the template would work for them, too. The ID and SME then had a set of procedures for development, including a sequence of discussion review and teaching. Only at this stage, after rapid development for the first two modules, leading to the structure for the template, did the ID and SME have check-off requirements as follows.

- Module title? And module purpose?
- Preview of series of examples? Reminders for discussion and quiz?
- Simple examples followed by more complex ones?
- Embedded questions to stimulate thinking?
- Notes to clarify meaning of foggy terms or ideas?
- Citation of sources?
- Main points of module?
- Discussion questions and resources?
- Choice in the discussions? Application of the concepts with previously unencountered examples?
- Combination of concepts to apply in rule using with design problems in discussions and quizzes?
- Test items to align with content of the modules?
- Cross-cultural and representation of both male and female? Representation of multiple lifestyles and fashion lines? Reflection of global market?

CONCLUSION

The online environment helped to address key challenges such as overcoming content limitations within a textbook, expanding opportunity and time for deeper student discussions about course concepts, and using course management efficiencies with online tools such as an online office, a visible and consistent course architecture, direct and visible links to learning activity areas, and automated feedback for quizzes.

Rapid development of the first two modules in a template format supported course production efficiency. The quality of instructional design within this course template began with analyzing the context of learning, teaching, and course content, along with determining what counts as "significant learning." Analysis of learning outcomes and instructional strategies then provided guidance for creating the template structure; its simplicity and consistency of structure supported clarity of organization.

Online teaching strategies were more complex than just linking to web sites about the multinational global fashion industry. Models of teaching, principles of instructional design, conditions of learning, principles of instructional text design, and strategies for higher order thinking were used to make materials appealing and manage interactions of students with the web resources. In this way, technology choices were aligned with instructional methods and learning outcomes while students learned within an authentic updated worldview and context of cultural diversity.

In addition, the building of the collaborative relationship of the SME and ID, with social time and caring respect for each other's areas of expertise, was a large part of nurturing the commitment and stamina for sustaining the fast-paced design and production schedule. The ID could be counted on for good coffee and the SME for good food. This blend of social sharing seemed to parallel the blended roles of ID and SME in the course design tasks.

QUESTIONS FOR ANALYSIS/DISCUSSION

The following questions could be used in an academic discussion of this case.

1. What are the problems and challenges in this case and what factors created them?
2. What insights did the instructor and instructional designer gain from pre-production instructional analysis and how did this influence the online course design?
3. What strategies of management and planning were reflected in this case, and what would be the pros and cons of alternative approaches in the time period for development?

4. How did the use of the online course design features in this case produce significant learning that would not have been feasible through using the assigned textbook in a classroom environment?
5. What was the instructor's role in "unpacking content" in the instructional materials used in the course, in the management of online discussions, and in analysis of discussion messages posted by students during each week of the course?
6. What features of the course template allowed for coherent updates of content that can be expected to change from year to year? And how do these features address student attention and motivation to learn?

REFERENCES

America.gov. (2008, August 15). U.S. minorities will be the majority by 2042, Census Bureau says: Report sees quicker growth, more diversity; Hispanics fastest growing group. *Engaging the World.* Retrieved from http://www.america.gov/st/diversity-english/2008/August/20080815140005xlrennef0.1078106.html

Andrews, D. L., & Goodson, L. A. (1980). A comparative analysis of models of instructional design. *Journal of Instructional Development, 3*(4), 2–16.

Andrews, D. L., & Goodson, L. A. (2011). A comparative analysis of models of instructional design. In G. Anglin (Ed.) *Instructional technology: Past, present, and future* (3rd ed.). Santa Barbara, CA: Libraries Unlimited.

Anglin, G. J. (Ed.) *Instructional technology: Past, present, and future* (3rd ed.). Santa Barbara, CA: Libraries Unlimited.

Art Nouveau: The Artists. (n.d.). Retrieved from http://artintheworks.com/

Berglin, L., Cederwall, S. L., Hallnäs, Jönsson, B., Kvaal, A. K., Lundstedt, L., Nordström, M., Peterson, B., & Thornquist, C. (2007). Interaction design methods in fashion design teaching. *The Nordic Textile Journal,* 26–51. Retrieved from http://bada.hb.se/bitstream/2320/3147/1/CTF_0607D.pdf

Campbell, K., Schwier, R. A., & Kenny, R. F. (2009, October). The critical relational practice of instructional design in higher education: An emerging model of change agency. *Educational Technology Research and Development, 57*(5), 645–663. doi:10.1007/s11423-007-9061-6

Davies, I.K. (1973). *Competency-based learning: Technology, management and design.* New York: McGraw-Hill.

Davies, I. K. (1981, October). Instructional development as an art: One of the three faces of ID. *Performance and Instruction Journal, 20*(7), 4–7. Retrieved from http://onlinelibrary.wiley.com/doi/10.1002/pfi.4150200706/pdf

Davies, I. K. (1991). Instructional development as an art: One of the three faces of ID. In D. Hylnka & J. C. Belland, (Eds.), *Paradigms regained: The uses of illuminative, semiotic, and post-modern criticism as modes of inquiry in educational technology: A book of readings* (pp. 93–106). Englewood Cliffs, NJ: Educational Technology.

Day, J. C. (n.d.) *National population projections.* Retrieved from https://cps.ipums.org/cps/resources/cpr/2_ps.pdf

De Young, L. (1996). Organizational support for software design. In T. Winograd (Ed.), *Bringing design to software*. New York, NY: ACM Press.

Denning, P., & Dargan, P. (1996). Action centered design. In T. Winograd (Ed.), *Bringing Design to Software*. New York, NY: ACM Press.

Dick, W., & Carey, L. (1978). *The systematic design of instruction*. Glenview, IL: Scott, Foresman and Company.

Dick, W., Carey, L., & Carey, J. O. (2009). *The systematic design of instruction* (7th ed.). Upper Saddle River, N.J: Merrill/Pearson.

Easters, D. J. (2012, March). Global communication part 1: The use of apparel CAD technology. *International Journal of Fashion Design, Technology and Education, 5*(1), 45–54. Retrieved from http://www.tandfonline.com/doi/abs/10.1080/17543266.2011.607851#preview

Evening dresses inspired by Gustav Klimt. (n.d.). Retrieved from The Artist Workshop Community website: http://www.artpapa.com/forum/DCForumID13/

Featuring Gustav Klimt. (n.d.). Retrieved at art.com website: http://www.art.com/gallery/id—a9/gustav-klimt-posters.htm

Fink, L. D. (2003). What is "significant learning"? In L. D. Fink (Ed.), *Creating significant learning experiences: An integrated approach to designing college courses* (pp. 1–26). San Francisco, CA: Jossey-Bass, 2003. Retrieved from http://www.wcu.edu/WebFiles/PDFs/facultycenter_SignificantLearning.pdf

Fink, L. D. (2007, Winter). The power of course design to increase student engagement and learning. *Peer Review, 9*(1). Retrieved from http://www.aacu.org/peerreview/pr-wi07/pr-wi07_analysis3.cfm

Fink, L. D. (2009, Fall). Preface. *New Directions for Teaching and Learning*, 119, 1–7. doi:10.1002/tl.358

Fink, A. K., & Fink, L. D. (2009, Fall). Lessons we can learn from the voices of experience. *New directions for teaching and learning*, 105–113. doi: 10.1002/tl.370

Frey, W. H. (2011, March 25). *A pivotal decade for America's white and minority populations: 2010 census, demographics, race, ethnicity, migration*. Retrieved from the Brookings Institution website: http://www.brookings.edu/opinions/2011/0325_census_demographics_frey.aspx

Gagné, R. M. (1970). *The conditions of learning* (2nd ed.). New York, NY: Holt, Rinehart and Winston.

Gagné, R. M., & Briggs, L. J. (1974). *The principles of instructional design*. New York, NY: Holt.

Gagné, R. M., & Briggs, L. J. (1979). *Principles of instructional design* (2nd ed.). Fort Worth, TX: Harcourt Brace Jovanovich.

Gagné, R. M., Wager, W. W., Golas, K. C., & Keller, J. M. (2004). *Principles of instructional design* (5th ed.). Belmont, CA: Wadsworth.

Global Fashion News. (n.d.). Available at http://itunes.apple.com/us/podcast/global-fashion-news/id187315488

Gram, T. (2010, January 5). *Instructional design: Science, art and craft. Performance X design: Designing learning, performance and effective organizations* [Web log post]. Retrieved from http://performancexdesign.wordpress.com/2010/01/05/instructional-design-science-art-and-craft/

Gram, T., & Tovar, M. (1991, Summer). An investigation of the consulting styles of training planning specialists in a government sponsored training consulting service. *Canadian Journal of Educational Communication, 20*(2).

Greenberry, A. (2004, July). *The science and art of instructional design: Ensuring elearning is not eboring.* Paper presented at the Tenth Australian World Wide Web Conference, Seaworld Nara Resort, Gold Coast. Retrieved from http://ausweb.scu.edu.au/aw04/papers/edited/greenberry

Gustav Klimt, "The Kiss." Retrieved from http://www.ibiblio.org/wm/paint/auth/klimt/kiss/klimt.kiss.jpg

Gustav Klimt, "Tree of Life." *Global Gallery, The Online Art Source.* Retrieved from http://www.globalgallery.com/enlarge/26364/

Hartley, J. (1994). *Designing instructional text.* New York, NY: Nichols.

Hartley, D. (1996). Designing instructional and informational text. In D. H. Jonassen (Ed.), *Handbook of Research on Educational Communications and Technology* (2 nb ed., pp. 917–948). New York: Simon & Schuster MacMillan.

Hazel, C. (2008, December). Slow + fashion – an oxymoron – or a promise for the future . . . ? *Fashion Theory: The Journal of Dress, Body & Culture, 12*(4), 427–446.

Hergeth, H. H. (2005). New curriculum: Textile and fashion management education training the next generation. *Journal of Textile and Apparel, Technology and Management, 4*(4).

Huitt, W. (2003). Models of teaching/instruction. *Educational Psychology Interactive.* Valdosta, GA: Valdosta State University. Retrieved from http://www.edpsycinteractive.org/topics/instruct/instmdls.html

Jacobson, N., Butterill, D., & Goering, P. (2005). Consulting as a strategy for knowledge transfer. *The Milbank Quarterly, 83*(2), 299–321. doi:10.1111/j.1468-0009.2005.00348.x

Joyce, B., & Weil, M. (1972). *Models of teaching.* Englewood Cliffs, NJ: Prentice-Hall.

Joyce, B., & Weil, M., & Calhoun, E. (2009). *Models of teaching* (8th ed.). Boston, MA: Pearson/Allyn and Bacon.

Kapp, K. M. (2011). Matching the right design strategy to the right content. *Professional and Management Development Training, 65*(7), 48–52.

Keller, J. M. (1999, Summer). Using the ARCS motivational process in computer-based instruction and distance education. *New Directions for Teaching and Learning, 78,* 39–47.

Keller, J. M. (2008). First principles of motivation to learn and e³–learning. *Distance Education, 29*(2), 175–185.

Keller, J. (2011, September 26) ARCS: A conversation with John Keller [Video file]. Retrieved from: http://www.youtube.com/watch?v=E1ugbX2EKN0

Keppell, M. (2001, June 22). Optimizing instructional designer-subject matter expert communication in the design and development of multimedia projects. *Journal of Interactive Learning and Research.* Retrieved from http://www.thefreelibrary.com/Optimizing+Instructional+Designer-Subject+Matter+Expert...-a078574812

King, F.J., Goodson, L., & Rohani, F. (1998, November). *Higher order thinking skills: Definition, teaching strategies, assessment.* Educational Services Program, Florida State University. Retrieved from http://www.cala.fsu.edu/files/higher_order_thinking_skills.pdf

King, F. J., Rohani, F., & Goodson, L. (1997, November). *Feasibility study: Statewide assessment of listening and verbal communication skills, information literacy skills, and problem-solving skills.* Tallahassee: Florida State University. Retrieved from http://www.cala.fsu.edu/files/feasibility_study.pdf

Knupfer, N. N., & McIsaac, M. S. (1992, Fall). Designing instructional materials with desktop publishing software: The effect of white-space variations on learning. *Journal of Research on Computing in Education, 25*(1), 75–88.

Kuhn, S., & Winograd, T. (1996). Design for people at work. In T. Winograd (Ed.), *Bringing design to software.* (pp. 290–294). New York, NY: Addison-Wesley.

O'Neill, G., & Hung. W. (2010, February). Seeing the landscape and the forest floor; changes made to improve the connectivity in a hybrid problem-based learning curriculum. *Teaching in Higher Education, 15*(1), 15–27. doi:10.1080/13562510903488006

Oh, E., & Reeves, T.C. (2010, December). The implications of the differences between design research and instructional systems design for educational technology researchers and practitioners. *Educational Media International, 47*(4), 263–275. doi:10.1080/09523987.2010.535326

Pew Research Center. (2012, February 21, 2012). *91.7%–minorities account for nearly all U.S. population growth.* Retrieved from http://pewresearch.org/databank/dailynumber/?NumberID=1225

Pomales-Garciá, C., & Liu, Y. (2006, September). Web-based distance learning technology: The impacts of web module length and format. *American journal of Distance Education, 20*(3), 163–179. doi:10.1207/s15389286ajde2003_4

Rachel Comey, Spring 2006 menswear. Retrieved from the Style website: http://www.style.com/fashionshows/review/S2006MEN-RCOMEY

Saxena, M. (2011). Learner analysis framework for globalized elearning: A case study. *The International Review of Research in Open and Distance Learning, 12*(5). Retrieved from http://www.irrodl.org/index.php/irrodl/article/view/954

Schön, D., & Bennett, J. (1996). Reflective conversation with materials. In T. Winograd (Ed.), *Bringing design to software.* New York, NY: ACM Press.

Schön, D. A. (1987). *Educating the reflective practitioner: Toward a new design for teaching and learning in the professions.* San Francisco, CA: Jossey-Bass.

Walsh, K. D., Crisp, J., & Moss, C. (2011). Psychodynamic perspectives on organizational change and their relevance to transformational practice development. *International Journal of Nursing Practice, 17*(2), 205–212. doi:10.1111/j.1440-172X.2011.01926.x Retrieved from http://onlinelibrary.wiley.com/doi/10.1111/j.1440-172X.2011.01926.x/pdf

Webster, J., & Ahuja, J. S. (2006). Enhancing the design of web navigation systems: The influence of user disorientation on engagement and performance. *MIS Quarterly, 30*(3), 661–676.

CHAPTER 12

EMERGING TECHNOLOGIES

Purpose and Practice
In Online Learning

Kim A. Hosler

ABSTRACT

To encourage development of instructional design skills, the author asked a group of novice educational technology graduate students to create instruction using a layers of necessity model (Tessmer & Wedman, 1990). The purpose of using this framework was to provide novice designers with an efficient (lean) model that supports development of an instructional artifact in a timely, efficient, and less complex manner. These lean instructional units were created for use in an online learning environment as standalone modules introducing instructors, faculty, and students to Web 2.0 and other technologies. The case study highlights some of the issues and challenges that can arise when novice instructional designers seek to learn and use new technologies to support online instruction. In addition, it points out the frustration that can ensue when a designer's work is critiqued and the instructor requests substantial revisions.

Real-Life Distance Education, pages 221–233

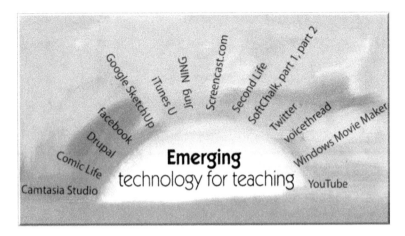

Figure 12.1 Main Web page for final emerging technology project (used with permission).

INTRODUCTION

This case study describes the artifacts and insights gained from novice educational technology graduate students creating distance learning modules about Web 2.0 and other technologies. These modules were created by 16 instructional design students taking a graduate-level Emerging Technologies special topics course. Instructional modules were created for Facebook, Twitter, VoiceThread, YouTube, ITunes U, SketchUp, Jing, Camtasia, Second Life, and Comic Life, to name a few technologies (see Figure 12.1).

The target audiences for the modules are Centers for Teaching and Learning in four academic institutions in the western region of the United States. Additionally, since the content will be posted on a web page, other instructors and faculty who teach online or desire to learn about Web 2.0 technologies may be interested in these instructional units. Students were allowed to pick the emerging technology or Web 2.0 application that interested them the most. For each technology module, students were asked to build a unit of instruction explaining how to use that technology in online higher education. The project requirements included creating the following sections for each technology:

- A description of the basic concepts and procedures involved in learning the new technology
- Quick start instructions for the technology
- The unique characteristics of the technology and why it is important to know or be familiar with that technology
- Examples of how the technology can used for education purposes

- Teaching application ideas for that technology in an online learning environment

The requirements also stipulated that each module have a consistent look and feel to create a collection of quickly accessible Web 2.0 technology overviews, instructional "how tos," and examples of the technology in online education, from one web site. To ensure consistency, students were required to create their instructional modules in Soft Chalk. SoftChalk is content authoring software for educators that lets users easily create interactive web lessons that can be used for e-learning or to supplement online courses. It does not require knowledge of html or programming languages. Once the modules were completed at the end of the semester, they were uploaded to a web page for viewing by faculty, instructors, and various centers for teaching and learning. At the completion of this case study and subsequent discussion, students should be able to

- describe a simplified (lean) or rapid approach to instructional design and how it may be implemented in the design and creation of online courses;
- critically think about and examine Web 2.0 tools and other technologies with an eye towards their applicability, usefulness, and practicality in online learning environments, from a teaching and learning perspective; and
- identify where communication broke down in the online module design process and offer suggestions for improving communication and accepting constructive feedback.

CASE STUDY

Getting Started

By the second week of class, spring semester, you could sense the student excitement about jumping into the course's Web 2.0 instructional design project. After all, this was a class in emerging technologies, and as educational technology graduate students, it doesn't get more fun than being able to experiment and play with new online tools in support of educational endeavors.

As students entered the small technology lab, they eagerly talked about the latest things they had seen on YouTube, TED, Facebook, and some of the educational technology Tweets they were following on Twitter. Just last week, Dr. Lisbonne had announced that students should begin thinking about a Web 2.0 application or other emerging technology they were interested in and how faculty and instructors who teach online could incorporate that technology into their teaching. In other words, what are some of the educational applications for these technologies? In addition to learning about the technology of their choice, students needed to use their instructional design experience to create a lesson which would teach others how to use that technology, as well as providing suggestions and examples for how that technology can augment the online learning experience. These lessons are to be created using SoftChalk.

"Well folks," Dr. Lisbonne started out as students were settling into their seats, "I have the final requirements for your emerging technology projects. Since we have a limited time frame, actually about 10 weeks, it's important that we look at how to create these instructional units in a lean and efficient manner. To that end, I'd like to introduce you to Tessmer and Wedmans' 1990 model called the 'Layers of Necessity Instructional Development Model'. I hope it will help you understand that creating instruction is an iterative process and evolves over time, but that when you are pressed for time and resources, there are several efficient options for creating good instruction. I like to call this lean instructional design because it gets at the bare essentials of crafting good instruction and focuses on what learners need to know and do, not what would be nice for them to know. It's very difficult, if not impossible to create an instructional unit that is good the first time, particularly when we have technology tools in the mix. So revising, refining, and editing are also part of a lean or efficient ID process."

Several students started to look confused. "A model?" asked Carol. "Why do we need to look at another ID model in order to start our project? I just want to dive in and start playing with YouTube or maybe even figure out how VoiceThread or Camtasia work." "I wonder what kind of educational applicability they might have and how you can incorporate them into an online class" Betsy added. Dr. Lisbonne detected the confusion and began to explain the Tessmer and Wedman model.

"I think it's important for you to know that in the real world of online teaching, faculty and instructors sometimes have to rapidly develop instructional units. The Layers of Necessity model offers us one way to consider creating instructional units when we have time and resource constraints. It's not as steeped in theory and complexity as some of the other models you may have studied."

"Essentially the Tessmer and Wedman model consists of layers and each layer is a self-contained ID model," Dr. Lisbonne explained. "For example, if time and resources constrain online course design, then use one layer of the model and in it address the most important activities needed for the instructional unit. These activities are generally goal analysis, instructional strategies development, creation of materials, and then evaluation and revision. You can have one layer or several layers depending on how much time and resources you have."

"Think of the layers in this model," she continued, "like layers you may see on a cake. Each layer represents a merged set of approaches to your instructional design, much like layers on a cake can have icing on them. However, when you put several cake layers together, you have a more complex or richer cake. The layers in a layer cake are repeated with more icing or perhaps a different filling until the cake is finished; usually three layers deep. Using this layered approach to your design frees up time as you follow a more generalized method of analyzing, designing, creating, and evaluating content for your instructional units. If you are so inclined, you can add additional layers to your instruction that contain the same elements, while going beyond the bare essentials."

Dr. Lisbonne added, "Remember, you already know that SoftChalk is the instructional delivery vehicle. However, you will still need to consider what instructional strategies to use to present your unit." With that, Dr. Lisbonne wrote the required sections for the technology instructional units on the board (see Figure 12.2).

"I have another thought too, "offered Dr. Lisbonne. "How many of you have heard of rapid instructional design?" Only two students raised their hands. "Well," Dr. Lisbonne continued, George Piskurich wrote a book titled, *Rapid Instructional Design: Learning ID Fast and Right*, that discusses how to take some purposeful shortcuts in the instructional design process. Basically, he talks about combining phases of the ID process and skipping phases that are superfluous to your needs, using templates where you can, and repurposing existing instructional materials if you have access to them. I'm thinking we are already using an ad hoc rapid instructional design approach for your instructional units. First, we know our main audience will generally be higher education instructors or faculty wanting to learn more

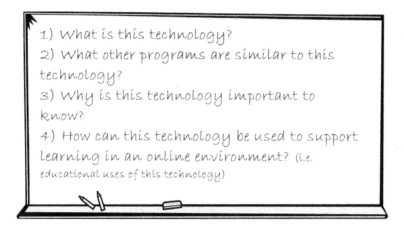

Figure 12.2. Emerging technology instructional unit requirements.

about Web 2.0 applications and emerging technologies, so we don't need a more detailed audience analysis. Secondly, I have asked you to use SoftChalk as the template for creating your lessons. To model what I'm looking for, I created a worked example about how to use SoftChalk that I created in the SoftChalk application (see Figure 12.3). Since we decided to use *Misty* as our background, along with a left-side navigation menu, and Arial 12 point for the font, you are freed up from making these visual design decisions. This gives you more time to focus on your content, rationale for the technology, examples, and instructions," she said.

Dr. Lisbonne added, "It's okay if you want to embed introductory videos or overview information about the technology within the lesson. By doing this you are re-using instructional material that you think is useful, again saving time." Dr. Lisbonne looked rather pleased that she was able to introduce ideas around speeding up the instructional design process for these novice educational technology students. Students diligently began jotting down the project requirements knowing that the semester would pass quickly, and it would soon be time for them to present their instructional module to the class, refine it, and then submit it to Dr. Lisbonne for incorporation on a web page.

Instructional Unit Presentations

Fast forward ahead to the last two weeks of the semester. Students have been independently working on their emerging technology instructional units and at the same time, learning how to use SoftChalk and implement lean or rapid instructional design strategies. Students are preparing for the

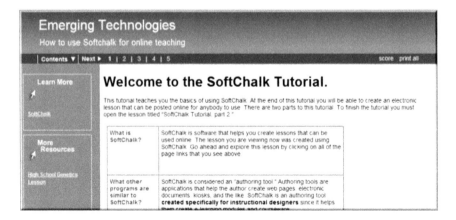

Figure 12.3. Model instructional unit of project deliverable using SoftChalk (used with permission).

presentation of their instructional modules designed to introduce faculty and other instructors to various Web 2.0 applications and emerging technologies that can support and augment their online courses.

"Okay class," announces Dr. Lisbonne. "We need to start the presentations of your instructional modules today so that everyone has a chance to present their work before the semester ends, as well as receive feedback from me and others in the class about the content of your lessons. Use this feedback to guide your revision efforts and help you polish your final submission. Once I have the final version of your module, I will upload your SoftChalk lessons onto a web page, making them accessible to other faculty and instructors. I want this to be your best work, something that you are proud to add to your vita and something that will be practical and helpful to those who teach online." With that Dr. Lisbonne asked for volunteers to go first. Carol, Trevor, and Ying Chun, after talking among themselves, decided to volunteer to go first.

"Hello. I am Carol and I will be showing you how Twitter can be used to engage online students in higher education (see Figure 12.4). First, Twitter is such a cool tool. You can use Twitter for social networking. You post your thoughts, ideas, and anything you are thinking of in something called a tweet. You can type up to 140 characters in a tweet and then friends can follow your tweets. For example if you want to know what people are saying about Michael Jackson, type his name in the search bar and all the tweets about him will appear. You can also see how 'hot' you are, or rather how influential you are on Twitter by using the Twitter Grader."

Carol continued, "Twitter is enjoyed by college students who like to use the computer and who want to keep in touch with all of their friends. You can also look up famous people who use Twitter too, like George W. Bush or Sarah Palin, or Barack Obama. I will show you a short video about how to get started with Twitter." Carol quickly launched a demonstration video about how to use Twitter. After watching the nine-minute video that explained how to establish a Twitter account and how to begin using it, Carol asked if there were any questions. She then thanked everyone for watching her SoftChalk presentation and sat down.

Next up was Ying Chun, who was very excited to share what she had discovered about Facebook. As she approached the front of the class, she began asking students if they knew some of the Facebook lingo.

"Hi everyone, I'm Ying Chun and my technology is Facebook. Have you ever been friended, or un-friended for that matter? Do you know what thumbs-up 'like' means? Do you know that over 1 billion people are on Facebook now and any one of them could be your friend? Facebook keeps you connected with friends and family and allows you to share news, information, jokes, events, web sites and just about anything you can image with them on a 24/7 basis," she exclaimed. Ying Chun proceeded to describe in

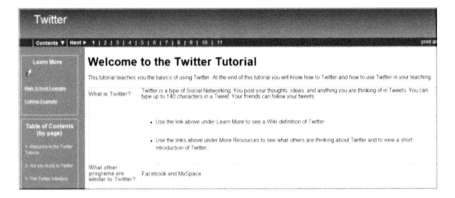

Figure 12.4 Instructional unit for Twitter as presented in SoftChalk template (used with permission).

detail what friended and un-friended mean, as well how she and her friends share information about where they are and what they are doing each day.

"And," she continued, "The 'like' button is so neat because it allows you to quickly get opinions from people who are your friends in an interactive manner. My lesson for Facebook will teach you the basics of using Facebook. At the end of this module you will be able to create a Facebook account, a Facebook group, and work with a variety of Facebook applications. By learning these things you will be able to help people use Facebook with their online lessons!" Next, Ying Chun flipped off the lights and launched an introductory video about getting started with Facebook. After the students watched the short YouTube video about using Facebook, Ying Chun thanked the class for their attention and sat down.

Trevor stood up and walked to the front of the class. His emerging technology was about Second Life (see Figure 12.5), and similar to Carol and Ying Chun's presentations, he showed the class how to get started in Second Life explaining that Second Life is a multi-user virtual environment. Like the other students, Trevor kept commenting about how neat and cool the technology was in Second Life, but how challenging it was to create an avatar. He mentioned that many universities have land or some form of presence in Second Life. He also pointed out that for healthcare, the virtual hospitals and clinics found on Second Life are very popular with students and practicing nurses and physicians. He concluded his presentation by showing us an avatar exploring a virtual explosion.

With only about 30 minutes of class time left, Dr. Lisbonne stood up and walked to the front of the class. "Okay folks," she said, "I want to take a few minutes and provide some constructive feedback about what I have seen and heard thus far. I am doing this so the rest of you can benefit from these presentations and the designs of these instructional units and not make the

Figure 12.5. Instructional unit for Second Life as presented in SoftChalk template (used with permission).

same mistakes I have observed here. Carol, Trevor, and Ying Chun, I hope you don't think I'm picking on you, but it's important we stop now and think more critically about the technologies everyone is exploring," she said.

Missing the Mark

"First off, I'm concerned that some of you may have missed the mark here," Dr. Lisbonne admonished. "The assignment called for presenting an instructional unit about an emerging technology or Web 2.0 application and how it may be used in an online teaching and learning environment. What we have seen today is a rather technocentric approach to the implementation of these technologies for teaching online, along with some marketing hype. As an education practitioner, I don't see how I can implement these technologies in an online class or for that matter, face-to-face classes. What is missing is a clear explanation about how to use the technology in a higher education context, and how that technology can enhance, support, guide, or motivate online learning in various contexts. What type of learning environments are you trying to create and how does your chosen technology support that environment? Carol, I don't see how teaching can be effective using Twitter with a maximum of only 140 characters. Where is your argument for using Twitter as a teaching tool? Doesn't Twitter privilege those who can write well and concisely? And Trevor, it's not clear from your presentation how Second Life can support online learning either. You need to do a deeper dive into the pedagogy and instructional strategies that when implemented in Second Life, may make it a viable teaching tool."

Dr. Lisbonne continued, "Remember, part of this assignment is to explain and justify how and why this technology or application may be used in an online learning environment, and why this technology is important to know. Ying Chun, where did you demonstrate how Facebook can be used as a teaching tool? Everyone needs to think more deeply about how your technology can be used in an educational manner and to support learning. Ask yourselves, have I adequately explained and demonstrated the technologies' purpose?"

At this point, Carol started to become defensive and appeared on the verge of tears. "Well, Dr. Lisbonne," she stammered, I think Twitter is an exciting and interactive tool. Many of my college friends love to use it. I think Twitter is a motivational tool for use in higher education. I don't understand what you mean when you say I need to make this more relevant to how the technology can support learning. Besides, I worked very hard on this lesson, learning SoftChalk, and setting up a Twitter account to show the class." Carol sat back in her chair and sighed dejectedly.

The class became deadly quiet and several students began to look nervously at their own SoftChalk lessons on their laptops, wondering if they too had missed the objectives for the project and had not implemented the things Dr. Lisbonne was asking for. Trevor spoke next. "Well, I for one spent tons of time trying to figure out Second Life and I think the virtual clinics show how it can be used for simulations. I can't help it if Second Life has a steep learning curve." Dr. Lisbonne politely interrupted him. "Trevor that is my point. If Second Life has a steep learning curve, then why not explain and demonstrate how online faculty may use what is already available in Second Life to support their classes? Do you think busy instructors will have time to learn all the ins and outs of Second Life to create a virtual learning experience for their students? Are there parts of Second Life with educational content that can be used by others? If so, what are those areas and how can they be implemented in an online learning environment? It may not be necessary for faculty to create original content in order for Second Life to be a learning tool, but these are the issues you need to explain in your project," she added.

Trevor looked a bit pouty and replied, "But Dr. Lisbonne, when you said we needed to explain how this technology could be used for learning in online education, I didn't think it meant looking at all the issues surrounding the technology tool."

"Well," said Dr. Lisbonne, "That's part of considering technology adoption in an online teaching environment. Is it a fad that we are trying to make into an educational tool, or are there solid rationales for using a particular technology to support teaching and learning online?"

Realizing there was time enough for one more presentation, Dr. Lisbonne looked out at the stony faced students and quietly asked if one more student was interested in presenting his or her work today. Smiling slightly, Loren offered to present his unit about YouTube.

"Well, I guess I can present my unit about YouTube today and then work on the revisions over the next few weeks," he said sheepishly. Loren opened his laptop and plugged it into the LCD projector and launched his presentation about YouTube.

"Before I get in to the nuts and bolts of YouTube, I do want to explain how YouTube can be an educational tool for online instructors. If you can get past all the crazy stuff on YouTube, you will see many noteworthy educational videos as well as the potential for you to easily create your own YouTube video for your classes." Loren opened his YouTube SoftChalk lesson. "I am going to start with the educational potential of YouTube and how it can expand and enhance online course content" (see Figure 12.6).

"First," Loren proposed, "You need to make sure the videos you ask students to view are related to the stated learning objectives and content for your course. Make sure you preview the video first for appropriate content." The class laughed, knowing exactly what Loren meant. "Next, the value of YouTube is that it provides a more interesting way for students to obtain content. It's not text-based like what you see in most online courses," he continued.

"Obviously, videos tell a story and as such, can augment your course content. I will also show you how instructors can use something called channels, which offer more control. Customizing your channel allows you to create a content repository by pointing others to content that you add to your favorites. I have a short video that demonstrates how to do this. I think channels are a good idea for online instructors because they allow them to create a content rich environment that extends beyond their own video content. Many universities maintain YouTube channels. Harvard Business Review provides specialized content from lecturers and symposiums. MIT shares video lectures from many classes. Online students can benefit from access to many interesting lectures." As Loren continued with his presentation, Carol and Travis both noticed that Dr. Lisbonne was beginning to nod her head and smile ever so slightly.

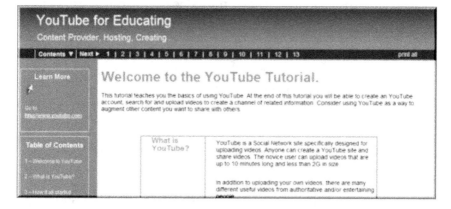

Figure 12.6 Instructional unit for You Tube as presented in SoftChalk template (used with permission).

IMPLICATIONS FOR DISTANCE EDUCATION

As this case presents, it is easy for students and practitioners alike to be caught up in the latest technology and lose sight of thinking purposefully about how these technologies can be used to support distance education. While many emerging technologies may have an affective and motivational component to them, without examining how to leverage the most educationally salient aspects of that technology, and why that technology may support learning at a distance, practitioners implementing these technologies run the risk of adding superfluous work to their courses. It is often tempting to use a technology for the sake of trying to reach students for whom the technology is ubiquitous, interactive, or perceived as "hip." As Baird and Fisher (2005) point out, course design must keep in mind the end user experience by asking questions such as, "How will the use of any particular social media element help the student achieve full cognitive development? [and] How will the use of social networking technologies facilitate learning situated in a social context?" (p. 9). It behooves online faculty and instructors to consider questions such as these to implement technology in an educationally purposeful and pedagogically sound manner.

CONCLUSION

A technocentric focus towards instruction can shortchange both students and practitioners of the media rich and interactive environments that can be created to augment online learning. The examples presented in this case illustrate how easy it is for novice educational technology students and perhaps novice online instructors to overlook ways technology can support and enhance learning. The case illustrates a loss of focus regarding the purpose for using the emerging technology in support of learning and presenting content. Additionally, practitioners and instructional designers pressed for time or with limited resources may do well to take advantage of templates, outside resources for content, and a consideration of what can be skipped, in order to advance the course design process more efficiently.

QUESTIONS FOR ANALYSIS/DISCUSSION

1. Reflecting on Web 2.0 applications and other emerging technologies, what are some things you should consider before implementing a technology tool for online teaching and learning? Create a checklist of questions an instructor or instructional designer should ask

before considering the use of an emerging technology in an online learning environment.

2. Do social networking tools like Twitter, Facebook or YouTube have the potential to deliver meaningful instructional content? Whether you reply yes or no, explain and justify your answer with examples or nonexamples.

3. When you receive feedback about your work or a presentation, what are some professional ways to handle that feedback?

4. Describe factors from this case that offer suggestions for creating effective and efficient (rapid) online instructional modules. What are some things you should consider in advance of implementing rapid instructional design or a lean approach to instructional design?

5. What additional problems do you see the students struggling with in this case other than missing the mark on the assignment?

REFERENCES

Baird, D. E., & Fisher, M. (2005). Neomillennial user experience design strategies: Utilizing social networking media to support "always on" learning styles. *Journal of Educational Technology Systems. 34*(1), 5–32.

Piskurich, G. M. (2006). *Rapid instructional design: Learning ID fast and right.* (2nd ed.). San Francisco, CA: Wiley.

Tessmer, M., & Wedman, J. F. (1990). A layers of necessity instructional development model. *Educational Technology Research and Development, 38*(2), 77–85.

FURTHER READINGS

Clark, R. E. (1983). Reconsidering research on learning from media. Review of Educational Research, 53(4), 445–459.

Collis, B., & Moonen, J. (2008). Web 2.0 tools and processes in higher education: Quality perspectives. *Educational Media International, 45*(2), 93–106.

Greenhow, C., Robelia, B., & Hughes, J. E. (2009). Learning, teaching, and scholarship in a digital age: Web 2.0 and classroom research—what path should we take now? *Educational Researcher, 38*(4), 246–259. doi: 10.3102/0013189X09336671

Hastings, N. B., & Tracey, M. W. (2004). Does media effect learning: Where are we now? *Tech Trends 4*(2), 28–30.

Kozma, R. B. (1994). Will media influencing learning? Reframing the debate. *Educational Technology Research & Development, 42*(2), 7–19

Morrison, G. R., Ross, S. V., Kemp, J. E., & Kalman, H. (2010). *Designing effective instruction.* (6th ed.). Hoboken, NJ: Wiley.

CHAPTER 13

PROMOTING INTERACTIVITY IN A DISTANCE COURSE FOR NONTRADITIONAL STUDENTS

E-Ling Hsiao and Xiaoxia Huang

ABSTRACT

In the context of an online instructional technology course designed for non-traditional students in a Midwest university in the United States, this chapter explores four types of interaction in an online learning environment: learner–content interaction, learner–instructor interaction, learner–learner interaction, and learner–interface interaction. Practical examples and strategies for promoting online interaction as well as potential challenges are described and discussed. The authors highlight possible implications for interactive online course design at the end of the chapter.

INTRODUCTION

Online learning is becoming increasingly popular. Based on the responses from more than 2,500 colleges and universities, Allen and Seaman (2010)

Real-Life Distance Education, pages 235–251
Copyright © 2014 by Information Age Publishing
235

reported that the growth rate for online enrollments (21%) far exceeds that for the overall higher education student population (2%). Although more and more learners are willing to learn online, there are remaining concerns about the methods for making online instruction effective. Online learners often do not have opportunities to meet the instructor and other learners face-to-face; therefore, it is potentially harder to facilitate interaction in the online environment as compared with the traditional learning environment. However, interaction has been consistently shown to be a key element for successful learning (Moore, 1989). Many researchers have confirmed that interactivity is a critical variable to students' online learning experience (Keegan, 1988; Moore, 1989; Swan, 2001; Woods & Baker, 2004).

According to Moore (1989, 1993), there are three types of interaction: learner–content interaction, learner–instructor interaction, and learner–learner interaction. The first type of interaction occurs when learners interact with instructional materials in different formats, such as text, audio, video, animation, and simulation. The second type of interaction takes place between learner and instructor; it emphasizes how the instructor delivers instruction, provides feedback, scaffolds learning and communicates with learners. The third type of interaction is built on the collaboration among learners either on a one-on-one basis or in group settings (Moore, 1989). Examples of learner–learner interaction include group work and course discussions.

In addition, Hillman, Willis, and Gunawardena (1994) proposed another type of interaction in the online learning environment, which is learner–interface interaction. The focus of this type of interaction is the delivery system of online courses that learners experience. Hillman and his colleagues proposed that for learners to fully interact with the course content, the instructor, and other learners, they should first be capable of using the delivery system.

The attempt to achieve online interaction is challenging because there are many interfering factors, such as learning preferences and learner characteristics (Anderson, 2004; Moore, 1989, 1993; Smaldino, Lowther, & Russell, 2007; Wanstreet, 2006). First, learners with different learning preferences construct knowledge differently and interact with content, instructor, other learners, and learning environments differently. For example, visual/verbal learners tend to learn from information presented visually in a written language format (e.g., textbooks and class notes), whereas visual/nonverbal learners prefer to learn from information presented visually in a graphical format (e.g., pictures, diagrams, flowcharts, videos, and animations). Auditory/verbal learners like to learn by listening to verbal information (e.g., lectures and discussions). Tactile/kinesthetic learners like to learn by doing because they need practical and concrete experiences

(Jester & Miller, 2000). It is essential to consider learning preferences while designing activities for online interaction. In addition, learner characteristics such as age, gender, major, prior knowledge level, and comfort level with technology may have impact on interaction design (Wanstreet, 2006). Therefore, promoting interaction in distance settings with learners of diverse backgrounds can be a challenging task, especially with nontraditional students. Nontraditional students are typically older adult learners who are full of life experiences and have lots of responsibilities (employment and family) while studying at school (Cross, 1980). Some of them may feel less comfortable with advanced technology. Such unique learner characteristics indicate that nontraditional students may have a hard time following a course schedule, adopting synchronous communication mode, or using a course delivery system efficiently. Thus, they may need more support and specific instructional guidelines for learning than do traditional students.

The focus of this chapter is a case of an online instructional technology course for nontraditional students based on the framework of the four types of online interaction previously discussed. By describing and discussing practical examples and strategies for promoting online interaction as well as potential challenges for this course, readers will be able to

- identify and apply strategies to facilitate learner–content interaction in a distance course for nontraditional students,
- identify and apply strategies to facilitate learner–instructor interaction in a distance course for nontraditional students,
- identify and apply strategies to facilitate learner–learner interaction in a distance course for nontraditional students, and
- identify and apply strategies to facilitate learner–interface interaction in a distance course for nontraditional students.

CASE STUDY

The case is to explore how to effectively design online interactivity in a distance course for nontraditional students. The title of the course is "Instructional Technology and Delivery Systems," which was redesigned and taught in the Spring semester of 2009 at a Midwest university in the United States. It was an undergraduate-level course with two sections: a hybrid section and a fully online section. This case focuses only on the design of the fully online section. The goal of this course was to teach students to identify, locate, evaluate, design, prepare, and efficiently use educational technology as instructional resources. Fifteen course topics were covered: Teaching and Media, Instructional Strategies, Visual Principle, The ASSURE Model, Computers and Multimedia, Distance Education, Online Learning, Instructional Materials and Display, Visuals, Audio, Video, Trends in Technology and Media, Virtual Reality, Concept Mapping, and Cognitive Load Theory. In addition, student were expected to apply the content knowledge they leaned by using five software applications (PowerPoint, Inspiration, Camtasia, Movie Maker, and Blackboard) to produce their own instructional products.

The course was delivered on the Blackboard course management system. In addition, a variety of tools were offered by the institution for content delivery and course communication, such as Learning Objects products (blog, wiki and podcast), Adobe products (Adobe Flash and Adobe Presenter), TechSmith products (Snagit and Camtasia) and Microsoft Office products (Word and PowerPoint). Twenty students participated in the course; most of them majored in Human Resource Development ($n = 15$), and the others majored in Technology Management ($n = 2$), Industrial Supervision ($n = 1$), Criminology ($n = 1$), and Community Health Promotion ($n = 1$). Seventeen out of 20 students taking the course were nontraditional students who worked full-time, while the others worked with one or two part-time jobs. The average student age was 32 years old, with the youngest being 23 years old and the oldest being 44 years old. There were 4 male students and 16 female students, including 9 seniors, 10 juniors, and 1 sophomore. The learning style survey (Jester & Miller, 2000) students took at the beginning of the course indicated that they had diverse learning styles (8 tactile/kinesthetic learners, 4 auditory/verbal learners, 4 visual/nonverbal learners, and 4 visual/verbal learners).

The challenges of teaching this fully online course included: (a) students came from different majors and were in different class years, which meant they might have different levels of learning experience, technology use, and relevant content knowledge; (b) most students worked full-time and the others worked with one or two part-time jobs, which meant they might have problems meeting synchronously online due to their work schedules; (c) students' ages ranged from 23 to 44, which meant they might have different levels of life experience to bring to the class; and (d) students had diverse learning styles, which meant they might have different learning preferences of interaction, such as presentation modes of course materials. It was potentially harder to facilitate the interactivity in this course due to the physical separation and unique characteristics of nontraditional students. The following part of this chapter will explore each of the four types of interaction incorporated in this course.

Learner–Content Interaction

Learner–content interaction relates to student involvement with instructional materials during the process of knowledge construction. Learning will not occur without this type of interaction (Moore, 1989). Thus, if learning content is not well designed, it will impede student understanding and learning. Learner characteristics such as age, gender, major, prior knowledge level, and comfort level with technology needed to be considered for optimizing learner–content interaction (Anderson, 2004; Kanuka, 2000; Moore, 1989, 1993; Smaldino et al., 2007). Because of the unique characteristics of nontraditional students, it was challenging to facilitate the learner–content interaction in this online course. The major course content was organized into 15 modules, each containing two types of learning: content knowledge and relevant software applications.

Content Knowledge

The textbook adopted in this course was *Instructional Technology and Media for Learning*, written by Smaldino and her colleagues in 2007. Twelve topics were included in this book: Teaching and Media, Instructional Strategies, Visual Principle, The ASSURE Model, Computers and Multimedia, Distance Education, Online Learning, Instructional Materials and Display, Visuals, Audio, Video, and Trends in Technology and Media. The instructor incorporated three additional topics that were current issues in the instructional technology field: Virtual Reality, Concept Mapping, and Cognitive Load Theory. These topics were presented in the Adobe Presenter format, one type of podcast containing narrations over PowerPoint slides (Gattis, 2008). Mayer and his colleague proposed that learning can be optimized when learners use both visual and verbal channels to select, organize, and integrate relevant information for knowledge construction (Mayer, 1997; Mayer & Moreno, 2002). Students could learn the topics at their own pace by rewinding, fast-forwarding, or pausing the files while studying the presented information. The average length of the sessions was around 10–20 minutes. In addition, the instructor offered relevant examples and resources such as images, web links and articles to facilitate student learning. Take the topic of "Visual Principles," for an example; graphics of different types of visuals (e.g., realistic, analogical, organizational, relational, transformational and interpretive) were provided for helping students understand the functions of visuals.

To foster deep understanding of the course content, multiple learning activities were provided. First, chapter forums were offered for discussing questions related to course topics, and students were permitted to start their own questions by adding new threads and replying to posts from others. The instructor joined discussions and provided feedback and resources when needed. Second, blog discussions were facilitated by the instructor for students to share their experiences and opinions on course topics. Four discussion topics were selected from the textbook for blog discussions. The first topic was about instructional strategies. Students needed to share their experiences about when and how they had used student-centered and teacher-centered approaches in instruction. The second topic was related to audio; students needed to share their experiences about when and how they had used digital audio and analog audio in instruction. If students did not have any relevant experiences, they needed to come up with strategies for using audio in instruction after reading the corresponding chapter. On the third blog, students were required to view one of the video examples posted and share their ideas about how it could be used for instruction. The last topic was related to Second Life. Students were asked to watch two videos about Second Life and post their opinions about how it could be integrated into the instruction and their own imagination of tomorrow's classroom. In addition, a wiki group project was required to explore psychological perspectives on learning. Wiki is a medium that allows a group of people working together asynchronously for a topic in an easy-to-use platform (Frydenberg, 2008; Jones, 2007; Mindel & Verma, 2006; West & West, 2009). Further, multiple assessment strategies were implemented to measure the quality of learner–content interaction. For instance, rubrics were provided for both blog and wiki activities for quality control of the interaction, and quizzes were deployed to detect students' understanding of course content.

Software Applications

Students in this course were required to use five software applications (PowerPoint, Inspiration, Camtasia, Movie Maker and Blackboard) to produce their own instructional products, including a PowerPoint presentation, a concept map, a tutorial video, an instructional video, and a mini Blackboard course site. Step-by-step software tutorials in multiple formats (text-plus-graphic, video with narrations, video with captions, and interactive Flash demonstration) were created to demonstrate the use of these applications to meet the needs of diverse learners.

First, students were instructed to use PowerPoint to produce a presentation of a topic of their own choice. It could be a topic related to their daily life or professional expertise. A series of video tutorials with captions were provided for supporting students in learning of PowerPoint. Second, the idea of concept map was introduced to students, and they needed to use Inspiration to construct a content map for a textbook chapter clarifying the internal relationship among key concepts within the chapter (e.g., the ASSURE Model). Text-plus-graphic tutorials were created by Word and Snagit for showing students how to use functions in Inspiration to complete the task. Third, students were required to use Camtasia (e.g., captions and smart focus) to produce a video tutorial for demonstrating a function in PowerPoint. Example topics students chose to demonstrate include "How to insert an image to your PowerPoint file" and "Using smart art in your PowerPoint presentation." The instructor utilized Camtasia to make video tutorials with narrations for supporting students in learning of Camtasia. Fourth, students also needed to make a video to teach their peers a particular topic by using Movie Maker. For instance, a student chose a topic called "How to jump-start a car," took photos of each stage of jump-starting a car himself, and then integrated photos with appropriate text and music into his video. Adobe Flash was used to create step-by-step interactive tutorials for supporting the completion of this project. Fifth, at the last two weeks of the semester, students needed to manage their mini projects and share with others in a Blackboard site. Text-plus-graphic tutorials of Blackboard were offered to support this course task.

All tutorials contained practical examples related to the mini- and final projects. Project rubrics and guidelines were provided beforehand for students to understand the instructor's expectation of the project outcomes. Take the Camtasia project rubric for an example, it stated clearly that students needed to include ten elements in their projects to get credits: a title clip inducing the topic and student name, background color for the title clip, one still image (e.g., graphic, photo or screen shot), at least one video clip recorded by Camtasia, one transition effect, captions to explain the procedure, an audio file, video size in 400 x 300 pixels, video in QuickTime movie format (.mov), and a clear demonstration of a function in PowerPoint. Each mini project and the final project required about two to three weeks to complete, and students were expected to spend at least two hours per week on task. After project submissions and grading, all student projects were collected and uploaded to the course site as Mini Project Gallery for peer viewing.

Challenges and Solutions

One of the challenges encountered was that initially some students with less online learning experiences were confused and did not know how to effectively study the course materials because lots of content was included in each module, including Adobe Presenter presentations, relevant examples and resources as well as software tutorials. Two weeks after the semester started, guidelines for navigating modules were added, and the problem was solved. Guidelines for navigating modules should be provided at the beginning of the course for students to know how to better study course materials in sequence while learning at their own pace. Second, as chapter forum discussions were not mandated, there were fewer posts compared to the blog and wiki activities. Most students preferred to e-mail their instructor directly when having content-related problems. Repeated questions had become a burden to the instructor. The requirement of participation in chapter forums should help to eliminate repeated questions from students. In addition, it can foster the deep understanding of course content and clarify misconceptions; students can also exchange ideas and get feedback from others on chapter content.

Another challenge was that, although most students had positive feedback on tutorials and preferred the step-by-step examples provided within tutorials, the instructor found that some students had problems following video tutorials with narrations when learning Camtasia, and the instructor needed to provide extra guidelines to help these students to complete their mini projects. Breaking video tutorials down to smaller chunks may make it easier for students to follow through when interacting with complicated software applications. In addition, adding captions to video tutorials with narrations may make the instruction clearer for visual learners.

Learner–Instructor Interaction

Learner–instructor interaction occurs between learner and instructor, emphasizing the way the instructor delivers instruction, provides feedback, scaffolds learning and communicates with learners. Since most students in this course worked full-time, it was difficult to schedule a perfect time for everyone to meet online synchronously. Therefore, the communication channels for learner–instructor interaction were mostly asynchronous in this course, including e-mails, announcements, discussion forums, course blogs, and a grade center. First, e-mail was used for information exchange between the instructor and learners; learners could choose to e-mail the instructor via Blackboard or Outlook for course-related problems. Since students were provided with a syllabus, a course calendar, weekly agendas, guidelines for navigating each module, assignment rubrics, and tutorials related to the usage of blog, wiki and Blackboard, the most common questions that the instructor received focused on the content knowledge. The instructor provided prompt feedback to individual questions within a 24-hour period. When receiving repeated questions, the instructor posted the answers to the Announcements area or the FAQs forum of the course site.

Further, the blog activities provided a virtual space for sharing experiences and exchange ideas related to course content between the instructor and learners. The instructor constantly monitored the blog discussions, answered questions, clarified misconceptions, asked students for clarification of their posts such as providing examples or more detailed explanations and offered relevant resources. The instructor also shared with students the blog rubric she used to evaluate posts from different perspectives (ideas and content, organization, and accuracy). In addition, an example of an expected post for each topic was provided beforehand to avoid low-quality posts like "Yes, I agree." High-quality responses were received and students with different backgrounds were able to share their unique experiences with the instructor (as well as the other students).

To foster instructor-student interaction, the instructor also offered synchronous virtual office hours using Blackboard Chat to communicate with students. Students were encouraged to log on to the chat room during the virtual office hours (Tuesday 4:30–5:30 PM; Friday 3:30–4:30 PM) if they needed to "talk" to the instructor.

Challenges and Solutions

Throughout the semester, most students preferred to communicate with the instructor asynchronously (e.g., e-mails, discussion forums, and class blogs) and hardly used the virtual online office via Blackboard Chat. One reason might be that most students were working full-time while taking the course, so they were not able to use Blackboard Chat during the scheduled online office hours. Setting up online office hours when most students were available (e.g., evenings and weekends) may help. Another possible reason might be that Blackboard Chat provided only text messaging, which was not appealing enough for students who preferred to talk to the instructor about their questions in other media formats such as audio or video. Using more advanced synchronous communication tools such as Blackboard Collaborate for online office hours may provide possibilities for more effective online synchronous communication between the instructor and students. In addition, since students asked questions mainly via e-mail, the same questions were asked repeatedly, which was very time-consuming for the instructor. Although there was an FAQs forum set up for students to ask general questions or questions related to course content, it was not sufficiently and effectively used. Organizing questions received from e-mails and posting the answers to the FAQs forum may help eliminate repeated questions. Further, for students who often delayed in responding e-mails or submitting assignments, the instructor tried to send out as many e-mail reminders as possible, but it did not work out well. Using multiple channels of asynchronous communication (e.g., Blackboard tools such as E-mail, Announcements, Discussion Forum, Early Warning System, and Notification) may help address this problem.

Learner–Learner Interaction

Learner–learner interaction happens "between learner and other learners, alone or in group settings, with or without the real-time presence of an instructor" (Moore, 1989, p. 4). Learner–learner interaction in this course was divided into three levels: individual, group, and class.

First, students were able to send e-mail via Blackboard or Outlook to each other for communicating course related issues or for social support. Second, for group-level learner–learner interaction, four group wiki sites were set up in the course site, with 5–6 members in each group, for students to discuss four subtopics covered in the textbook (e.g., psychological perspectives on learning: Behaviorism, Cognitivism, Constructivism, and Social Psychology). The wiki tool used in this course was the Blackboard plug-in supported by Learning Objects, which contained functions such as authorship, editing features, file sharing, access control, history tracking and archiving, and version control. Students were able to revise each other's postings and track different versions of group work. They were also able to see the contribution of individual efforts through history logs. A wiki rubric was used to evaluate this project in five categories (ideas & content, organization, accuracy, reference, and contribution to group).

Students were encouraged to assign roles for sharing responsibilities among themselves, but group members could decide on the best way working together to compose their wiki group projects. The most common model of group collaboration observed for this wiki project was (a) at the beginning of collaboration, students clarified the purpose of group project, set up goals, assigned responsibilities, shared resources and reported the work process; and (b) group members came back to put everything together on a wiki page by editing each other's posts to finish the final work. Throughout the process of collaboration, the instructor constantly checked the progress of group work, but did not get involved directly. After two weeks, all wiki sites were opened to other groups for peer viewing, and every student was required to post at least two comments or suggestions to other group wiki projects.

Finally, for class-level learner–learner interaction, students could contribute their ideas and exchange opinions through the four class blogs that were mentioned in the above section. When responding to others, students were required to identify the recipient of comments such as "to XX." Every student needed to post at least one initial post and comment on at least two other students' posts for each topic before the due dates. A total of 257 responses were posted for the blog discussions. A rubric was used to evaluate the interaction on blogs. Class-level learner–learner interaction also occurred in chapter discussion forums mentioned earlier where students exchanged ideas and questions on their textbook readings. In addition, students were permitted to view their peers' mini and final projects in project galleries and were encouraged to contribute their suggestions to others' work in mini project forums.

Challenges and Solutions

One of the challenges encountered was how to better facilitate and monitor student collaboration to keep the group on track in an online environment. One group did not perform well in the collaboration process of the wiki project because some group members did not participate sufficiently in group activities, which could be caused by the fact that this group did not assign roles among themselves for their online collaboration. Several strategies can be applied, such as making it required for assigning group roles to share responsibilities, using peer assessment strategies to evaluate individual efforts and encouraging socialization within groups to enhance group cohesion. Second, although students in general made good-quality contributions to blog discussions, on the first blog discussion, the instructor found out that some students tended to provide last-minute original posts, which made it harder for other students to make timely comments. For the following blog discussions, the instructor set due dates for both original posts and follow-up comments. As a result, last-minute posts were reduced and the interaction among students was enhanced.

Learner–Interface Interaction

Learner–interface interaction takes place between learner and the course delivery system, which affects learner interaction with course content, instructor and other learners (Hillman et al., 1994). The delivery system used in this course was Blackboard with several third-party plug-in tools such as blog and wiki from Learning Objects. Multiple strategies were implemented to promote learner–interface interaction.

First, the layout of the course site was designed in a cohesive theme including the course banner, color, navigation buttons, presentation, and document layouts, which enhanced the aesthetics of the course and reduced learner confusions. Second, a clear course-level navigation system was created for students to look for information easily while surfing the course site. The following navigation buttons were created in the Blackboard course site:

- "Announcements" button for important course-related information students needed to know throughout the semester,
- "Start Here" button including course objectives, course policies, assignment instructions, course calendar, and course navigation,
- "Contacts" button for information to reach the instructor,
- "Course Documents" button containing all course modules for the semester,
- "Tutorials" button for tutorials on a variety of technology tools used in the course,
- "Assignments" button for detailed descriptions of each assignment and a place for submitting each assignment electronically,
- "Project Gallery" button for students to review peers' mini- and final projects,
- "Communication" button for accessing the core communication tools in the course, such as Chat and E-mail,
- "Discussion Board" button for chapter discussions and FAQs,

- "External Links" button for information such as Blackboard tutorials and links to institutional resources,
- "My Grades" button for students to check their grades,
- "OS & Browsers" button for students to check if their computer settings were compatible with Blackboard, and
- "Course Surveys" button for students to provide feedback to the course.

The course navigation guide provided at the "Start Here" area included a visual map on how to search for course information within the course site when needed.

In addition, at the course module level, special guidelines for navigating individual course modules were provided to avoid student confusion. These guidelines did help students look for materials efficiently in an online learning environment. Tutorials on Blackboard, wiki, and blog also effectively supported student learning. For example, the wiki tutorial showed students how to add a new entry, edit pages, and post comments, which were required for completing the wiki project. Finally, to foster learner–interface interaction, the instructor offered technical support and provided Help Desk information to students; thus, if students could not reach the instructor when having technical problems, they could call the Help Desk for support to solve problems. In so doing, throughout the semester, the instructor received only a few questions about technical problems.

Challenges and Solutions

The only challenge that the instructor discovered was student confusion during the first two weeks when course module navigation guidelines were not provided as mentioned in the learner–content interaction section. Students reported few technical problems when interacting with the course delivery system. Most students were able to use required technology tools efficiently to interact with content, instructor, and other learners.

Student Feedback

At the end of the course, a 16-item online course survey was conducted in the Blackboard course site. The survey was a 5-point Likert scale (from 5—Strongly Agree to 1—Strongly Disagree) provided by the university. It included questions regarding the four types of interaction: learner–content, learner–instructor, learner–learner, and learner–interface interaction. In general, students provided positive feedback to this course (see Table 13.1).

Questions 1, 3, 9, 10, 11, 12, and 15 were related to learner–content interaction. The lowest rating ($M = 3.11$) was on the first question "I needed significant effort to learn the content in this course," which depended on

Table 13.1 Course Survey Results

Question Items	M
Learner–Content Interaction	
Q1 I needed significant effort to learn the content in this course.	3.11
Q3 I needed to spend a significant amount of time on class material to be successful in this course.	3.37
Q9 I spent time thinking deeply about a number of course topics.	4.11
Q10 I have a stronger understanding of the content compared to the beginning of the course.	4.58
Q11 I developed knowledge and skills that can be applied outside of the course.	4.74
Q12 I was challenged to reconsider my point of view on some course topics.	3.79
Q15 The recommended hyperlinks significantly expanded my understanding of course material.	4.42
Learner–Instructor Interaction	
Q2 I was motivated to do my best work to meet the instructor's standards.	4.68
Q4 I felt the instructor was approachable to discuss course-related issues.	4.95
Q6 I received useful feedback on my ability to meet course assignments.	4.84
Q7 The communication tools in this web course helped to keep me connected to the instructor.	4.68
Q8 The teaching strategies actively engaged me in learning the content.	4.53
Learner–Learner Interaction	
Q13 I developed positive relationships with other students from this class.	3.63
Learner–Interface Interaction	
Q5 The learning environment created by the instructor had a positive influence on my class performance.	4.63
Q14 Appropriate technology tools were effectively used to communicate the content.	4.58

individual learners' perceived difficulty level of course materials. The highest rating ($M = 4.74$) was on Question 11 "I developed knowledge and skills that can be applied outside of the course." This is positive feedback indicating the course goal was successfully achieved. In general, students agreed that they "have a stronger understanding of the content compared to the beginning of the course" and "spent time thinking deeply about a number of course topics." In addition, resources such as web site links that the instructor provided expanded student understanding of course materials.

Questions 2, 4, 6, 7, and 8 were related to interaction between learner and instructor. The ratings for these six questions were relatively higher than the others. Most students agreed that "the instructor was approachable to discuss course-related issues"; she was able to provide useful feedback, motivate and scaffold student learning and communicate with students effectively. In addition, students provided comments such as the instructor "was very helpful and very helpful through the whole class. She gave great feedback on my assignments and questions. She is a great instructor and I learned a great deal about technology and how to use things that I did not know how to use before this class."

Question 13 was about learner–learner interaction; the rating comparing to the other types interaction discussed was relatively lower, which indicates that the course activities for promoting learner–learner interaction could be improved. Probably monitoring the early stages of group work and encouraging group role assignment and socialization would help to achieve better group collaboration.

Questions 5 and 14 were related to learner–interface interaction. According to the responses to these two questions, the learning interface designed by the instructor was effective and contributed to student learning.

IMPLICATIONS FOR DISTANCE EDUCATION

Interactivity is essential for creating an effective online learning environment. When designing online courses, four types of interaction need to be considered to effectively support student learning, including learner–content, learner–instructor, learner–learner, and learner–interface interaction (Hillman et al., 1994; Moore, 1989, 1993).

For promoting learner–content interaction, multiple presentations of course content, such as text, image, audio, and video, are recommended to meet the learning needs of diverse learners. In addition, incorporating multiple presentation modes for advanced materials helps learners with less prior knowledge in the process of effective knowledge construction (Mayer, 1997; Mayer & Moreno, 2002). Instructors also need to evaluate learner–content interaction using a variety of formats (e.g., quizzes, projects, and discussions) to achieve a full understating of student mastery of course content. Further, clear guidelines of expected outcomes, evaluation criteria, course tasks, and due dates help to keep nontraditional students on track in their learning process.

For facilitating learner–instructor interaction, it can be difficult to adopt synchronous online communication modes for nontraditional students; therefore, whenever appropriate instructors need to provide multiple asynchronous communication channels between learner and instructor (e.g., e-mails, discussion forums, blogs, and others). In so doing, students can communicate with their instructor via different methods in their learning process.

For fostering learner–learner interaction, monitoring group communication from early stages, assigning group member roles, and encouraging socialization within groups are recommended because these strategies can help with group cohesion and sharing of responsibilities (Watkins, 2005). In addition, providing learner–learner interaction at different levels, i.e., individual, group, and class levels may reduce learners' sense of isolation. For example, instructor may consider using peer assessment strategy to encourage collaboration among learners.

Last, as far as learner–interface interaction is considered, instructors need to provide a clear and consistent course navigation system for creating an effective physical online learning environment. In addition, we recommend instructors provide help in different ways for better learner experience with the course site, such as tutorials on required technologies or IT contact information when students experience technical difficulties.

CONCLUSION

In the context of an online instructional technology course designed for nontraditional students in a Midwest university in the United States, this chapter explored four types of online interaction proposed by Moore (1989, 1993) and Hillman et al. (1994): learner–content interaction, learner–instructor interaction, learner–learner interaction, and learner–interface interaction. Under this framework, practical examples and strategies for facilitating online interaction were described and discussed. Problems occurred during the process of course implementation and corresponding potential solutions were also included in the chapter. By studying this case, readers may become aware of potential challenges for designing and implementing an interactive online course for nontraditional students. More importantly, to foster effective online learning, readers may want to think about what strategies and practices they would like to adopt for facilitating each type of these interactions.

QUESTIONS FOR ANALYSIS/DISCUSSION

1. What could have been done to better facilitate learner–content interaction for nontraditional students of diverse backgrounds in a distance setting?
2. What could have been done to better facilitate learner–instructor interaction for nontraditional students of diverse backgrounds in a distance setting?
3. What could have been done to better facilitate learner–learner interaction for nontraditional students of diverse backgrounds in a distance setting?

4. What could have been done to better facilitate learner–interface interaction for nontraditional students of diverse backgrounds in a distance setting?
5. What instructional technology tools and strategies could have been used to promote better online interactivity in this case?

REFERENCES

Allen, I. E., & Seaman, J. (2010). *Class differences: Online education in the United States, 2010.* Needham, MA: The Sloan Consortium.

Anderson, T. (2004). Modes of interaction in distance education: Recent developments and research questions. In M. Moore, & W. Anderson (Eds.), *Handbook of Distance Education* (pp.129–144). Mahwah, NJ: Erlbaum.

Cross, K. P. (1980). Our changing students and their impact on colleges: Prospects for a true learning society. *Phi Delta Kappan, 61*(9), 627–630.

Frydenberg, M. E. (2008). Wikis as a tool for collaborative course management. *MERLOT Journal of Online Learning and Technology, 4*(2). Retrieved from http://jolt.merlot.org/vol4no2/frydenberg0608.htm

Gattis, L. (2008). Getting started with instructional podcasting. *Journal of the Academy of Business Education, 9*(4). Retrieved from http://www.abe.sju.edu/proc2008/gattis2

Hillman, D. C. A., Willis, D. J., & Gunawardena, C. N. (1994). Learner–interface interaction in distance education: An extension of contemporary models and strategies for practitioners. *The American Journal of Distance Education, 8*(2), 30–42.

Jester, C., & Miller, S. (2000). *Introduction to the DVC learning style survey for college.* Retrieved from http://www.metamath.com/lsweb/dvclearn.htm

Jones, P. (2007). *When a wiki is the way: Exploring the use of a wiki in a constructively aligned learning design.* Paper presented at the 24th Annual Conference of the Australasian Society for Computers in Learning in Tertiary Education, ICT: Providing Choices for Learners and Learning, Centre for Educational Development, Nanyang Technological University, Singapore.

Kanuka, H. (2000, May). *Learner–content interaction: The silent but active participant.* Paper presented at the 15th Annual Conference of the Canadian Association for Distance Education, Making IT Learner Centred, Quebec, Canada.

Keegan, D. (1988). Problems in defining the field of distance education. *The American Journal of Distance Education, 2*(2), 4–11.

Mayer, R. E. (1997). Multimedia learning: Are we asking the right questions? *Educational Psychologist, 32*, 1–19.

Mayer, R. E., & Moreno, R. (2002). *A cognitive theory of multimedia learning: Implications for design principles.* Retrieved from http://www.unm.edu/~moreno/PDFS/chi.pdf

Mindel, J. L., & Verma, S. (2006). Wikis for teaching and learning. *Communications of the Association for Information Systems, 18*, 1–23.

Moore, M. G. (1989). Three types of interaction. *The American Journal of Distance Education, 3*(2), 1–6.

Moore, M. G. (1993). Three types of interaction. In K. Harry, M. Hohn, & D. Keegan (Eds.), *Distance education: New perspectives* (pp. 12–24). London, UK: Routledge.

Smaldino, S., Lowther, D. L., & Russell, J. D. (2007). *Instructional technology and media for learning* (9th ed.). Upper Saddle River, NJ: Prentice Hall.

Swan, K. (2001). Virtual interaction: Design factors affecting student satisfaction and perceived learning in asynchronous online courses. *Distance Education, 22*(2), 306–331.

Wanstreet, C. E. (2006). Interaction in online learning environments: A review of the literature. *Quarterly Review of Distance Education, 7*(4), 399–411.

Watkins, R. (2005). *75 E-learning activities: Making online courses more interactive.* San Francisco, CA: Jossey-Bass.

West, J. A., & West, M. L. (2009). *Using wikis for online collaboration: The power of the read-write web.* San Francisco, CA: Jossey-Bass.

Woods, R. H., & Baker, J. D. (2004). Interaction and immediacy in online learning. *The International Review of Research in Open and Distance Learning, 5*(2). Retrieved from http://www.irrodl.org/index.php/irrodl/article/view/186/268

CHAPTER 14

CONTINUOUS IMPROVEMENT

The Case for Adapting
Online Course Templates

Kathryn Ley and Ruth Gannon Cook

ABSTRACT

This case describes online student responses to selective semiotic adaptations in a standardized course template required for all online courses offered through a large, private Midwest university's learning management system (LMS). The instructor sought to identify online course template enhancements that could positively influence student perceptions about the course and improve course completion rates. A case study approach assessed adult student comments about the course and revealed how the enhanced factors may have influenced students' positive responses to the course and their course completion. The study incorporated data-based and theory-grounded research to analyze the LMS template and identify template adaptations that could potentially improve student online course performance and perceptions. The instructor created the enhancements, taught the online course, and collected data to conduct the study. The findings suggest students had positive experiences and all but two of the 23 students completed the course.

Real-Life Distance Education, pages 253–265

The results suggest that students may benefit from LMS template adaptations grounded in semiotic features including graphics, metaphors, and narratives.

INTRODUCTION

This study describes student responses to an online course that included selective adaptations to a mandatory, standardized course template. The case study describes how an online course instructor incorporated data-based and theory-grounded template adaptations to better meet adult student needs. All students had previously completed at least one online course with the standardized, branded university template prior to this course and all courses were part of their undergraduate degree program. The primary objective of the study was to assess whether students would respond positively to a course incorporating template adaptations that deviated from the standardized course template. The instructor sought to add or alter semiotic features. Furthermore, altering some online course template features could be justified if the adaptations positively influenced student course perceptions and resulted in a successful student completion rate. The course included adaptive features designed to improve visual appeal, navigational ease, graphic cultural relevance, and to encourage course completion. Results suggest enhancements may improve student satisfaction and result in a high completion rate. Citations in this case establish a clear audit trail for important concepts related to action and marketing research.

CASE STUDY

A large private Midwest university required all online courses offered in their learning management system (LMS) to rigidly adhere to a design template. LMS course templates allowed the educational organization to brand courses and to standardize course features and navigation, both of which should help students feel more comfortable in an online environment and help them scaffold new learning. Students appreciated finding a recognizable navigation bar consistently displayed in the same location in every course. They liked having the same template navigation features in every course. On the other hand, the course template assumed that students preferred and benefitted more from template uniformity than from template adaptations designed to address student navigation and instructional problems inherent to the template. Students did not always find the sameness created by the identical banner appealing. Courses constrained by the template had few graphics or images. Students had already mentioned these advantages and disadvantages to several online instructors at the university.

Semiotics (the study of signs and symbols in communication) and pattern learning research indicated that knowledge organization can result from experience. Some patterns can be established so that students recognize them (Brown, Collins, & Duguid, 1989; Niemi, 1997; Popkewitz, 1998; 2002), such as the patterns in online courses. Most LMS course templates organized selective features to be immediately recognizable, such as university logos in the course banners, navigation bars on the left side of the screen, and some kind of page-linking bar at the top or bottom of the screen. The university template housed courses that were predominantly or even exclusively text based. Students recognized the template course and navigation features, but often expressed their frustration that all of the courses seemed to look alike. Students might be inclined to accept the new content materials if presented in a familiar university course template. On the other hand, they find semiotic enhancements, such as graphics, metaphors, inscriptions, and media, more appealing and conducive to learning than the template presentation. A seasoned online faculty member, an academically trained designer, had taught several template courses and had identified several course attributes that some students misinterpreted, found confusing, or did not see.

Students

Twenty-three students were enrolled in the course on the first class day of the semiotically enhanced course. The adult students from 24 to 60 years of age had previously completed at least one standardized, branded university template online course prior to enrolling in the enhanced course and all courses were required in their undergraduate degree program. One student withdrew after the first week of class and one student requested an incomplete for personal reasons. The remaining 21 completed the course.

Method

A case study method that chronicled and detailed events (Ertmer & Quinn, 2003) assured that data collection would account for instructional events and document interactions. Elements of action research (Argyris, Putnam, & Smith, 1985; Avison, Lau, Meyers, & Nielsen, 1999; National Adult Literacy Database, 2006) were also included to assure a thorough and progressive investigation with data generated throughout the course. Student reflective comments traced their efforts to establish an online community using "steps... composed of a circle of planning, action, and fact-finding about the result of the action" (Lewin, 1958, p. 201).

The instructor observed and documented student reactions to determine if course template enhancements improved student perceptions and created a positive learning experience. The instructor believed changes in the LMS template or in the online course materials might positively influence the students enrolled in these courses but only systematically collected data could be the basis for an objective analysis. The challenge was to garner unbiased and sufficient student reactions to determine which adapted features students found most helpful.

Throughout the course, the instructor recorded student reactions and kept detailed records of their remarks and reactions. At the end of the course, the instructor encouraged but did not require students to write reflective comments on their course experience.

If students felt more comfortable throughout the course, they should notice the enhancements or mention feeling more comfortable in this course when compared to others they had completed with the intact template. The instructor would be able to identify course features that helped students successfully complete the course based on student comments. Ultimately the resulting analysis would suggest how to improve online instructional practices by tailoring online environments to better meet adult students' needs.

Materials

The instructor had taught many courses with the standardized template. Through personal experience and other faculty comments, the instructor had identified template features that often stimulated positive student responses or that often prompted their complaints or fomented confusion. When again assigned to teach a template course, the instructor adapted the course template with data-based course features designed that would address problematic course template and content but not alter positive template attributes. The adaptations added graphics, instructions, and student interactions but without obviously changing important LMS template features shared by other university online courses. Therefore, the adapted template layout differed subtly from the standard one used by all other online courses (Figure 14.1) and retained the original template format. The adapted course displayed text and navigation bars very similar to the original online template but with different banners, more graphics, icons, and pictures. To enhance instructor–student interactions the instructor added phone conferences. Narratives and testimonials were discretely displayed in each adapted module so as to encourage students to write about their course experiences in standard discussion conference postings.

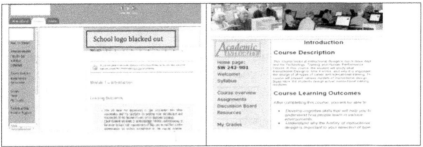

LMS Online Course Template	Graphically Enhanced Online Course Template

LMS Online Course Template	Graphically Enhanced Online Course Template

Figure 14.1 Template (left) and Enhanced Template (right) examples.

The adaptation retained required LMS course features but enhanced navigation with simple explanations and graphics. Theory-grounded (Vygotsky, 1981) graphical and metaphorical enhancements were designed to help students feel more comfortable in the course. Students were encouraged in their introductions and throughout the course to share their personal narratives (Clandinin, & Connelly, 2000), where they came from, why they were in college, and what they hoped to accomplish in the course. Social networking was encouraged through course discussion conferences and in the general discussion links, e-mail and telephone conferences.

The course also offered a slightly different perspective: Students were told that the course was set up like a virtual art gallery; all assignments would be posted to the course discussion conferences where everyone could see each other's posts. Students were instructed to communicate any private correspondence with the instructor via course e-mail to assure confidentiality. Students would post assignments or use a drop box. The instructor utilized the metaphors of an art gallery, and suggested students post assignments to the discussion conferences instead of the drop box so they would have the benefit of viewing each other's work and sharing their thoughts and ideas.

The course enhancements embedded strategic graphics, icons, and metaphors with the intention of observing whether the addition of these enhancements could augment students' receptivity to the new content materials. The rationale for the study was that if semiotic tools were effective in other interdisciplinary arenas, such as marketing and linguistics, those tools may be similarly effective in educating students. The instructor employed course graphics, metaphors, and technologies placed strategically to resonate with students' everyday life experiences, with methods similar to those utilized in electronic product marketing. Again, the intention was to have those enhancements positioned to resonate with the students' cultural experiences and habit patterns (Martin, 2008), so their comfort with familiar mental terrains could align their receptivity to new learning and help them to be more participative in the course. The electronic marketing techniques the students were exposed to daily in their lives would be mirrored in the iconic course messages and invite students' subconscious recognition just as the marketing messages do in their daily lives and optimally lead to their success in the course.

Very simple signs, symbols, and technologies, such as signposts, pictures of roadmaps, and thematic metaphors, were placed in each course module to prompt subconscious recognition and give clues to students that they were not alone and on the right path. The semiotic course design embedded semiotic features that recurred thematically with the same or similar signs and metaphors, such as pictures of people sitting around campfires, groups having conversations, etc. While maintaining the LMS course design alignment, the added subliminal sign language and metaphors resonated with the students' daily lives and cultural experiences. Again, thoughtful attention to symbolic language was designed to help students scaffold and reinforce the new course content materials. Course enhancements added semiotic structure but technologies unrelated to semiotic reinforcement, such as Wimba or wikis, were avoided.

Data Collection and Analysis

Parsing the semiotic feature influence depended upon a complete record of student remarks, observations, and anything that helped or hindered student course progress. The instructor, interacting with course students, used the same online instructional practices employed in other online classes but also recorded student reactions and kept detailed records of their remarks and student–student and student–instructor interactions. The chronicled pertinent course events and collated student comments, messages, and communications such as student conversations and interactions contributed most of the data. These essential data created a thick description of students' responses to the course and particularly to the semiotic enhancements. Immediately prior to the end of the course, the instructor solicited student course perceptions with an open-ended request, "Submit at least a several paragraph reflection of your experiences and what you have learned in this course."

The instructor classified students' comments according to function or feature: format, design, organization, graphics, and interactivities. These comments were then identified as positive, neutral, or negative. The positive comments alluded to template additions to the university course template. Neutral comments were unrelated to the course, format or enhancements, but spoke of content materials, how the students worked with other students, or how they felt they could use the lessons learned in the course. Negative comments were unfavorable statements about any aspect of the course. The instructor analyzed student responses in the context of course template adaptations to determine if the adaptations had improved the way these adult students had mediated the course content material.

More than half of the students implied or stated that this course was different and that it was one of the best online courses they had taken at university although they did not explicitly list graphics, phone conferences, or project peer feedback and interactions. The single negative comment complained about too many course assignments even though the number of assignments was comparable to the average number assignment for all degree program courses. There were ten modules, each with two message assignments, one reading assignment and one product assignment. Students submitted their reflective comments with their names unavoidably appearing on the message header and prior to receiving their course grade. This may have biased their responses (see Exhibit 1 at the end of the chapter). Of the 23 initially enrolled, 21 completed the course; the attrition rate (<9%) was well below the 40% median university online course attrition rate.

DISCUSSION

Positive student responses and a low course attrition rate provide some insight into the potential effectiveness of semiotic course enhancements. The enhanced course differed visually from the LMS course template by adding graphic and metaphoric features yet retained template format and navigation. Throughout the course, the students often and appreciatively remarked about the benefit of so many perspectives from their classmates and how this approach helped them. The students' reflections supported one intended purposes of the semiotic features, to increase student positive responses to the course.

Almost consistently positive student remarks throughout the course and in end-of-course reflective comments suggested that they appreciated the enhancements, but few alluded to specific differences, such as more graphics or interactions. While students may not have identified specific semiotic features, almost without exception, they implied this course was somehow different and many favorably compared this course to their previous online courses. Some suggested that this course was more organized even though the organization was identical to all university LMS courses. Others indicated the content was easier to understand and almost all of the students stated that they preferred this course compared to their previous online courses at the university. A few identified specific course features they liked, such as metaphors with which they could identify and the two optional phone conferences unique to this course. Several students commented how much they liked the course graphics and embedded narratives.

IMPLICATIONS FOR DISTANCE EDUCATION

This case study demonstrates that semiotic features may be added to a course template and that those features encourage successful course completion. Standardized course templates are excellent branding devices and semiotic adaptations can improve positive student reactions and lower attrition in template courses. Positive student comments suggested similar enhancements in other online courses could produce similar successful results. The case study evidence indicated online course semiotic features can effectively support student knowledge acquisition through iconic cultural representations and encourage their successful course completion.

Although enhancements may be feasible and effective, some effort would be required to embed appropriate semiotic features in an online course. Given that one instructor created and embedded the features, feasible and inexpensive adaptations may be relatively easy to implement. On the other hand, a designer or instructor would have to have the skill to determine which semiotic features would be most appropriate and effective for a given course. Sufficient planning could add existing courses into a redesign schedule so that adding the semiotic features would occur at the same time as routine revision; such a plan would avoid additional revision costs and avoid managerial, organizational, and technological issues.

Online course evaluations that draw upon thick, rich description and student interaction analysis can provide a more complete course effectiveness and student satisfaction analysis. Student course evaluations confined to a single, standardized set of forced choice options often lack the fine-grained detail inherent to qualitative data analysis. In this case, qualitative data revealed a link between features and student affective responses that even students did not articulate. Qualitative results, while not readily generalizable, suggested that online students may benefit from semiotic features directed toward continuously improving navigation and learning in online courses. Adapting LMS templates may encourage online student participation, facilitate comprehension, organize course progression, and increase student retention and course completion.

CONCLUSION

The objective of this case study was to determine if and how semiotic features might affect student online course perceptions and successful course completion rates. The students completing the course responded with positive comments about the course uniqueness thereby confirming the potential value of semiotic enhancements to LMS templates for online courses. The data-based and grounded case study method revealed positive experiences documented in student reflections and the course completion rate.

QUESTIONS FOR ANALYSIS/DISCUSSION

1. What are the advantages of a course template?
2. Why did the instructor use qualitative data instead of quantitative data to evaluate course enhancement effectiveness?
3. Why did the course instructor add enhancements to the online course template?
4. What were the added course enhancements?
5. Were the course enhancements clearly described?
6. What did students like about the enhanced course?
7. Did the case report the number of student comments and the number of students who made comments?
8. What was the evidence that the enhancements created a positive learning environment?

REFERENCES

Argyris, C., Putnam, R., & Smith, D. (1985). *Action science: Concepts, methods and skills for research and intervention.* San Francisco, CA: Jossey-Bass.

Avison, D., Lau, F., Meyers, M., & Nielsen, P. A. (1999). Action research: To make action research relevant, researchers should try out their theories with practitioners in situations and real organizations. *Communications of the ACM, 42,* 93–97.

Brown, J. S., Collins, A., & Duguid, S. (1989). Situated cognition and the culture of learning. *Educational Researcher, 18*(1), 32–42.

Clandinin, D. J., & Connelly, F. M. (2000). *Narrative inquiry: Experience and story in qualitative research.* San Francisco, CA: Jossey-Bass.

Ertmer, P., & Quinn, J. (2003). *The ID Case Book: Case studies in instructional design* (2nd ed.). Upper Saddle River, NJ: Pearson Education.

Lewin, K. (1958). *Group decision and social change.* New York, NY: Holt, Rinehart and Winston.

Martin, N. (2008). *Habit: The 95% of behavior marketers ignore.* Upper Saddle River, NJ: Pearson Education.

National Adult Literacy Database. (2006). *Action research handbook: Introduction.* Resources and Skills Development Canada Retrieved from http://www.nald.ca/clr/action/p1.htm

Niemi, D. (1997). Cognitive science, expert-novice research, and performance assessment. *Theory into Pratice, 36,* 239–246.

Popkewitz, T. S. (1998). Dewey, Vygotsky, and the social administration of the individual: Constructivist pedagogy as systems of ideas in historical spaces. *American Educational Research Journal, 35,* 535–570.

Popkewitz, T. S. (2002). How the alchemy makes inquiry, evidence and exclusion. *Journal of Teacher Education, 53,* 262–267.

Vygotsky, L. S. (1981). The genesis of higher mental functions. In J. V. Wertsch (Ed.) *The concept of activity in Soviet psychology* (pp. 144—188). Armonk, NY: Sharpe.

EXHIBIT 1: STUDENT COURSE REFLECTIONS

Student 1:

Good Afternoon—This was one of the best, if not the best online course I have taken. Dr has layed out the course work very systematically and it was extremely well organized. I can tell she put a lot of thought into the design. I enjoyed to diversity of what we learning i.e., copyright, prototyping

Student 2:

WOW. This class has been a treat; I needed a creative, fun class to get back into the rhythm of things here at XXXX. I've been away for almost a year; the birth of my daughter (1st kid) kept me away. I took this class knowing it would only be the beginning of what I want to accomplish but I have learned so much I feel confident enough to do so much more than I had originally planned. At the beginning of the class I was very frightened because I would be doing something so unique and new to me (creating a web site) and you had assured us in the phone conference of how smoothly this would run. I hadn't believed, but man, did it run.

Being away for any length of time from school can be detrimental to anyone, this class was supposed to be a nice relaxing ride into coming back into the race. It turned out that this class had more ponies under its hood than a Shelby Mustang. I have to say that this is a really fast paced class that puts you on notice immediately, the one good thing is that the class is organized in such a way that you feel like you are running downhill. I also have to add that this class has great progression from beginning to end, from the initial reading material to activities that help you learn faster, to group work that cements and proves what you've learned the subject matter. I also liked that we were asked to get information and practice on our own, the presenter gave us the tools and we got to design and make our dream site come true. It certainly did not feel like 10 weeks. This felt like a month of pure adrenaline, action packed moments that left me tired but rewarded.

There is nothing more rewarding about a class than to know that the knowledge learned in class has already been tested and has begun improvements by the end of it. Very few classes can match that. By the way please don't change the amount of homework in this class. It is perfect as it is now. The other class I just took was also wonderful and full of information that revolutionized another part of my life but was so homework intensive that much of the information I just glanced over (others have expressed the same opinion) in order to finish a task. This class runs well, quick and furious with the work it currently has. I felt that I got the most out of this class.

Student 3:

Like all courses you have the opportunity to get what you want out of it. Online courses are especially like this because there is a sense of independent study that exists. However this course was very well laid out. If you needed more information on a topic the models or other classmates would be able to point you in the right direction. This class was one of the easiest online classes I have take in regards to understanding the direction the course was taking and what was expected. Because of this it made it easy to get what I wanted out of the class.

Student 4:

For some reason this class gave me more of a real classroom experience, now being in my 2nd year @ XXXX that's definitely saying something and the interaction was the best of any of my former classes. The content of the class will stick with us all and I look forward to using the knowledge gained here in the future. As we all move on I want to thank the entire class for all the help and encouragement and definitely thank the professor, we've all learned a lot here and it was well structured so that we actually took it all in successfully.

Student 5:

Well I can't believe that the class is ending. The last 10 weeks have gone by so darn fast. I want to start by THANKING everyone including Dr. Everyone was so patient, kind, motivating, and one of the BEST groups I've come across in my 3 years here. When the class first started and we had our first conference call I thought to myself "what am I doing here right now". But through time and patients, I learned and explored areas I would probably not have. THANK YOU THANK YOU THANK YOU! I have never come across another professor like you. You have been a great professor with a great plan and agenda for us students. To all my classmates- for some of you this may be your first experience with group work and discussions and for others maybe not. I just want to stress that not every class is like this, but keep on doing what your doing in every class. You all have been so great and helpful and we need more of this. Internet classes can be difficult sometimes when it comes to staying motivated and learning materials.

Student 6:

Luckily, I got into this class, and the experience has been not only per-sonally satisfying but…every lesson we learned in here was discussed at high and low levels. When I saw the assignments, and the experience of some of my fellow classmates, I thought I had signed up for the wrong class and was way over my head. I am glad that I plugged through. I am also very, very grateful for the much more experienced and learned peers in this class that pulled many of us 'newbies' along.Thanks to all of you who provided feedback and suggestions along the way. Dr., thank you for presenting solid scholarship, a great textbook and the on-line modules that filled in any missing blanks. This class exceeded my expectations.

CHAPTER 15

EVALUATING ONLINE COURSES

Seeking Instruments and Evaluator Competencies

Joi L. Moore and Camille Dickson-Deane

ABSTRACT

Evaluating distance learning environments can be a difficult task when the evaluator does not possess the appropriate skills and knowledge for the evaluation activity. Similarly, finding an evaluation tool that can be used with different types of courses can be challenging. Furthermore, complications emerge when evaluation tools have unclear definitions, along with different units of analysis and methodologies. This chapter explores the evaluation process performed by four participants with different experiences relating to subject matter expertise, instructional design, usability evaluation, and online teaching. Although participants' descriptions of their evaluation experiences were similar, the evaluation process produced inconsistent results.

Real-Life Distance Education, pages 267–282

INTRODUCTION

As technology has improved over the decades, different forms of distance learning have emerged. With new forms of asynchronous and synchronous communication, students and instructors can form engaging learning communities that go beyond the boundaries of time and place. As instructional designers, evaluators, and researchers embrace these emerging technologies, the outcome reveals various types of learning environments that do not have the same characteristics. The design of different types of distance learning can depend on the learning objective, target audience, learning environment (physical and virtual), and type of content. In addition, it is important to know how the learning environment is used, along with the inputs and outputs to usage.

Evaluation involves the collection of information for determining the quality of a product or user performance. One aspect of quality online learning can be defined as usability, which is the efficiency, effectiveness and satisfaction of a product (International Standards Organization 9241, n.d.) as it is used during the learning process. User performance testing, concurrent and retrospective think-alouds, heuristic evaluations, and surveys are some of the different usability evaluation methods. For heuristic evaluations, an evaluator applies usability standards as it relates to a particular product and determines the ease of use and usefulness. There are several distance learning heuristic instruments that provide a myriad of assessment elements such as instructional design, visual design, and information organization (Moore, Dickson-Deane, Galyen, Vo, & Charoentham, 2008). However, these instruments have varying units of analysis, contradicting definitions of those units, and vague descriptors, which allow for multiple interpretations of the required elements. For an inexperienced evaluator, determining the overall design quality can be difficult when existing instruments are narrowly focused on a specific type of distance learning product. To add more confusion, researchers and practitioners have different perceptions of course characteristics associated with a term (Moore, Dickson-Deane, & Galyen, 2011). In the context of this case study, online learning courses take place in traditional, academic semester-based settings. They include activities and tools that support interaction among students and also interactions among students and their instructors. This type of learning does not involve any physical, face-to-face meetings. In contrast to this view of online learning, there are other e-learning and online learning products that support independent learning with self-paced tutorials and without interactions among students.

Another issue with distance learning evaluation is the competencies or knowledge of the evaluator. The learning environment is composed of instructional content and the technology that delivers and supports the learning activities (Feldstein, 2002; Zaharias, 2009). Hence, a comprehensive evaluation should assess the instructional design and learning theory, along with the technology interface (Kirmani & Rajasekaran, 2007; Zaharias & Poylymenakou, 2009). To implement this type of evaluation, an evaluator would need to go beyond the usability issues of the learning environment. Although an interface can be easy to use, there are certain design charac-teristics that can impede learning and create extraneous cognitive loads (Clark & Mayer, 2008). To assist with understanding online learning course evaluation, the case study's objectives focuses on two issues:

- Determining heuristic elements that are applicable to a semester-based online course
- Determining skills and knowledge necessary to apply heuristics

The case study illustrates how these two issues evolved during the process of evaluating a distance learning course.

CASE STUDY

Evaluation Framework

Evaluating the design of online courses is an important activity for design-ers and instructors of online courses. An effective online learning environment should have a transparent interface that allows the learner to immediately en-gage in course content and/or associated activities. This is the preference rather than a student extending too much effort searching and organizing the course content with required activities. As such, the evaluation goal was to determine the quality of the online environment for supporting the learning activities.

The Ecletic-Mixed Methods-Pragmatic Paradigm (Reeves & Hedberg, 2003) is an appropriate framework to describe the activities and outcomes of the case study. Collecting information regarding the applicability of heuris-tic elements for a specific learning environment, along with the evaluator's understanding and perspective of the heuristic involves examining multiple perspectives that triangulate results for a complex phenomena. The practical orientation of involving evaluators with different skill sets assists with exam-ining the issues that people will encounter when evaluating online courses.

Methods

Determining how to evaluate distance learning involves the utilization of appropriate instruments. For this case, the participants implemented a heuristic evaluation, which utilizes a set of accepted usability principles and rules, often called heuristics (Nielsen, 1992). From the literature review, an adaptable usability heuristic checklist by Dringus and Cohen (2005) emerged as the best tool to use for the usability evaluation process. Their checklist was focused on the usability of WebCT, a learning management system (LMS), with the purpose of evaluating all online courses. In addition, the instrument applied Nielsen (1992) as well as Reeves et al. (2002) categories as a base for the instrument design. The checklist has categories comprising approximately 160 checklist items.

As part of the data collection, the participants created reflection documents on how they approached the evaluation process. The reflection documents included a description of their personal work environment, where they implemented the evaluation, the method in which they used the checklist, and an evaluation report that identified the issues. The participants were encouraged to perform a critical reflection for analyzing, reconsidering, and questioning their experiences with the evaluation activity (Murray & Kujundzic, 2005). In addition, each evaluator provided demographic information and participated in a focus group to compare their usage of the instrument and evaluation findings for the course.

Course Description

The course topic was the multimedia platform Adobe Flash, which provides different levels of interactivity on web pages. With this online course, students developed skills and competencies for flash animation, and used Sakai, an open source course management system to view content and complete learning activities. The 15-week course included eight instructional units on specific Flash skills, and a major course activity to develop an interactive project. The instructional content was delivered via web pages with Flash project examples to support the topic. Course activities included class participation on the discussion board for specific discussion topics, along with peer feedback for projects. Students and the instructor were able to chat synchronously and send private messages.

Results

Evaluator Characteristics

The participants were graduate students in a learning technologies program and had experience with various usability evaluation projects. As such, the Adobe Flash course supported a review from different perspectives: subject matter novice, online course instructor, online course student, usability evaluation novice, and high levels of expertise in usability evaluation as well as the subject matter (see Table 15.1). In the Dreyfus and Dreyfus classification of skill acquisition (1986), an acquirer progresses through five levels: novice, advanced beginner, competent, proficient, and finally the expert level. Acquirers, normally referred to as novices can be classified based on self-perceived and decision making abilities as opposed to routinized actions (Eraut, 1994). The four evaluators completed a demographic survey to illustrate their different skills used to review the course. This survey included five specific skills for online course evaluation: (a) abilities in an LMS, (b) online instruction, (c) instructional design, (d) usability evaluation, and (e) subject mater expertise. The survey was used to illustrate the level of expertise of each evaluator as per the Dreyfus and Dreyfus Model of Skills Acquisition (see Figure 15.1). The evaluators had a myriad of experiences in online learning, and as such could take on those varying roles. In addition, these perspectives created a wider range of results to be analyzed. Focus was placed on the ability to use the instrument for identifying issues as opposed to the actual result of the online course's usability evaluation.

Based on the evaluator profiles, Figure 15.2 illustrates the evaluators' position as per their experience as a student and an instructor.

TABLE 15.1   Evaluator Profiles

Characteristics	Evaluator A	Evaluator B	Evaluator C	Evaluator D
Current education status	Masters	Doctoral	Doctoral	Doctoral
Number of online courses (instructor-led) you have taken	10	2	18	22
English as second language	Yes	Yes	No	No
Sakai Experience	Yes Intermediate to Expert	Yes Novice	Yes Expert	Yes Intermediate
Experience with other content/learning management systems:	Yes	Yes	Yes	Yes
Were you a previous student of the Flash course?	Yes	No	Yes	No
Have you taught/ designed a course in Sakai?	No	No	Yes	No
Instructional Design Experience	Yes Novice	Yes Intermediate to Expert	Yes Expert	Yes Expert
Usability Evaluation Experience	Yes Intermediate	Yes Intermediate	Yes Intermediate	Yes Intermediate

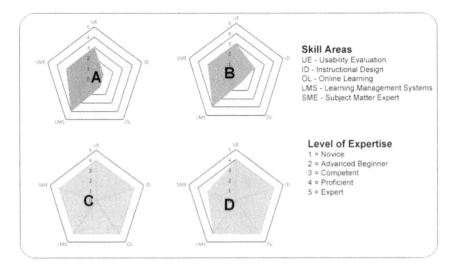

Figure 15.1 Evaluators mapped to Dreyfus and Dreyfus Skills Acquisition Model. *Note:* Total area is symbolic of overall expertise.

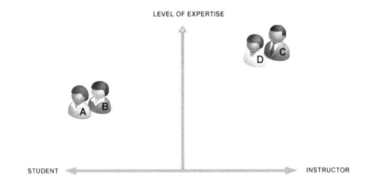

Figure 15.2 Evaluators in the evaluative dimension.

Participant Perspectives of the Evaluation Process

Reflection of a process is important for building self-awareness, examining commonalities, differences and interrelations with others, and improving future actions. The following sections provide participant perspectives of their experience.

Evaluator A

After logging into the course, I took the time and browsed the entire course environment. I paid special attention to the assignments, the units of instruction, discussion boards, etc... I then looked at the instrument and read each checklist question. Moving between the instrument and the course I tried to determine the answer to each question. As I completed the evaluation, I noticed that the checklist items that I answered "no" to indicated that there were problems intuitively with the system. I also noticed that several of the checklist items could not be answered using either a yes/no, and that the checklist items for the learner and instructor's interface were intermingled. I felt that the two interfaces should provide separate perspectives, but that's just my opinion.

Evaluator B

My view is that I need to look at the website from a learner's perspective. I opened the course and went through the sections, trying to get a sense of the course organization and navigation system. Then I chose one unit to determine how the interface assisted with the completion of the assigned course tasks. I used the checklist to study the website. It was "cognitively-consuming" as I went through each of the checklist items, so I went through the checklist double-checking each answer. Those that I did not understand I just marked them out.

Evaluator C

I took my time and explored the website first. I then used the checklist to evaluate the course; some of the questions were easy to answer because of my previous experience with Sakai, the content management system. As I answered the questions I color-coded the answers: the ones that were confusing I colored them green. I color-coded those that were not yes/no questions and those that when answered "yes," the question actually produced a negative meaning, as blue. In my usability evaluation I noticed that the instrument would sometimes use words and phrases to represent aspects or functions that were more specific to other types of learning management systems (LMSs), such as Blackboard or Moodle. For example, the checklist item "message can be easily expanded and collapsed" is not a function in Sakai. Sakai does not have a threaded discussion board and this is definitely an issue whereby being too specific creates this problem and then being too general creates an additional issue of ambiguity.

Evaluator D

I looked at the instrument and realized that there were approximately 160 questions so I used music to help me concentrate on the usability evaluation. I explored the course and the links in the course and going back and forth between the course and the instrument taking breaks because of the length of the instrument. As the usability evaluation progressed, several questions could not be answered due to wrong evaluative references or ambiguity of the question. It became increasingly difficult and disheartening to complete the usability evaluation.

After each evaluator completed the process, the entire usability evaluation team met to discuss their findings and synthesize the results. During the meeting, the team discovered that each usability evaluation report had approximately 15% of the heuristic checklist items that were either unanswered or queried. These self-perceived discrepancies led to a lengthy discussion as each evaluator felt that their own interpretation of the questions was correct based on the course that was being evaluated. The course itself was not the challenge, but the heuristic checklist that was selected and the skills required to use the checklist became the main issues. The multiple checklist items appeared to be difficult to manage and they decreased the focus required for reviewing any potential course issues. The following sections describe the main issues that the evaluators discovered.

Evaluator A

The Flash course is an instructor-led online course with interaction. The interface covers interfaces from the learner and instructor interactions, indicating a holistic approach. However, as some functions are only available from a certain perspective, it was difficult to use the same set of questions as presented in the instrument, without indicating that the questions can be applied for only one interface. Also, questions relating to the instructor interactions with the interface are dominant in many categories, especially in the categories titled interactivity, flexibility, and course management. Lastly several categories did not provide the detail to determine what is meant by "appropriate." It, "appropriate" was used to describe the item being reviewed on the checklist and the use of the word made it difficult to interpret what level of "appropriate" was expected.

Evaluator B

The instrument is a mix of student and instructor perspectives. That makes the instrument too long. People without instructional design experience cannot answer some of the questions because of the jargon used. It is an instrument mixed with assessing the usability of a course and the usability of Sakai in supporting course design. I don't have experience in managing a course and for some items I did not know whether to answer yes or no. Also, I am not confident that I know enough about Sakai. I think my limited experience with a CMS-based online learning makes it hard for me to see whether some of the items are important or common.

Evaluator C

The applicability of the tool for the type of the course is great concerning the fact that the course is instructor led. The tool does, however, include some instructional design questions, which are not necessarily appropriate for usability evaluation. Many questions were repetitive in nature. For example, "are the buttons big enough," and things like that would be covered by the accessibility standards category. By addressing accessibility standards, many of the other issues regarding usability would go away.

Evaluator D

The tool needs to be modified to provide one view of the course, not two views (i.e., strictly only the instructor view or strictly only the student view). Questions should be separated even if they are related and the instrument is absolutely too long. The length can and will alter the possible results provided by an evaluator due to the possibility of the evaluator getting tired.

Discussion

Evaluation Instrument

It is difficult to find an evaluation instrument that can be directly applied to all types of distance learning, online learning, or e-learning products. For this case study, many of the checklist elements were not applicable to the type of online course that was evaluated. In addition, there were inconsistencies in providing appropriate ratings. Another issue was the "how many" or "to what extent" type questions combined with the checklist items that focused on a yes or no response.

Several heuristic items could not be answered due to the ambiguity of the question. Specifically, items such as "Are items in the control panel appropriately arranged?" did not provide the detail to determine what is meant by "appropriate."

The large number of heuristic questions resulted in a lengthy instrument that made it difficult for evaluators to complete the task within a reasonable (e.g., 2–3 hour) time period. Also, the instrument was a mix of student, instructor, and designer perspectives. One evaluator noted that multiple perspectives made "the instrument too long, which is unnecessary."

Some checklist questions were specifically related to an e-learning product that was used as the foundation for the checklist, but they were not applicable to the online course that was being evaluated. For example, the following checklist item illustrates the reference to a function that is not available in Sakai: "Is it necessary for the designer/instructor to consistently "toggle" from "designer options" to "view" just to expand the homepage view?"

As it relates to usability of an online learning product, there were two units of analysis: course content and the LMS. Content organization can be considered a classification and instructional design activity. The checklist item "Is information presented in organized chunks to support learnability and memorability?" requires basic understanding of related instructional design principles, such as message, interface, or motivational design, along with events of instruction (Gagne, 1992). As for the LMS, the evaluators encountered heuristic elements that referred to specific features, but these features may not be applicable to all LMSs.

Evaluator Knowledge and Skills

To allow for some flexibility in the design of distance learning products, an instrument will typically have some generic criteria for different usability evaluation elements. Hence, a heuristic checklist will be somewhat vague, which directs more importance toward the knowledge and skills of the evaluator. Although all evaluators had experience as a student within an online course, there were differences in their perceptions of "good" design.

The instrument included instructional design questions relating to appropriate objectives and message design. For instance, the following heuristic item was difficult to answer: "Is cognitive load reduced by providing familiarity of items and action sequences?" Although two evaluators had some entry-level instructional design experience and had taken a related course, cognitive load was difficult to determine.

Another focus area of the instrument was to examine the capabilities of the LMS from an online instructor perspective. Heuristic items, such as "Can files easily be shared among courses?" and "Are there options to personalize the look and feel of the course?" can only be answered if the evaluator is familiar with the instructor view of the system.

IMPLICATIONS FOR DISTANCE EDUCATION

Distance education is broadly associated with any form of knowledge-exchange that occurs, once the contributing parties (i.e., mainly the learners and instructors) are geographically distant (Keegan, 1996; Moore, 1990). Older versions of distance education were mostly physical objects, such as books, hard copies of document, etc., that were mailed to learners. As technology has progressed, the definition of distance education now includes a major technological component (Conrad, 2006; Spector, Merrill, Merrienboer, & Driscoll, 2008). This technological component provides an additional complexity to the surety of distance education program quality that was not originally considered.

When discussing quality distance education, there is an ongoing area of concern; online learning (Noble, 1998). Online learning and its counterpart e-learning continue to hold the core definition represented by distance education, but now includes a heavy focus on technology. This focus describes learning as not only being geographically distant but also includes the ability to provide varying levels of accessibility, have continuous network connections, be flexible in its offerings, and include numerous interactions (Ally, 2004; Hiltz & Turoff, 2005; Oblinger & Oblinger, 2005).

The delivery method now has an expanded definition and with the expansion, considerations to the assurance of programs are of major concern to many institutions. To ensure that a distance education program, and essentially a course are of quality, the overall user experience as it relates to learning and interacting with the course interface must be examined. As such, a usable online learning product represents intuitive interactions with instructional content without the need to determine how to use the tools to complete activities.

When reviewing online learning or e-learning products for usability, the method of evaluation should be carefully considered. The process of conducting a usability study can be categorized into two usability evaluation methods (UEMs): analytical UEMs and empirical UEMs. Determining which UEM is appropriate for an evaluation is based on the purpose of the evaluation and it should be highly considered as the results can differ based on the type of learning product (Bernérus & Zhang, 2010).

Heuristic instruments are good tools for online course evaluation because of the overall cost and time used to complete an evaluation (Alsumait & Al-Osaimi, 2009; Kirmani & Rajasekaran, 2007; Nielsen & Molich, 1990; Reeves et al., 2002). There are many heuristic evaluation instruments, but some do not identify the type of product they reference in their instructions. For this case study, Dringus and Cohen's (2005) instrument was selected and used with two objectives. First, it was one of the original instruments that addressed e-learning products, therefore investigating learning outcomes. Second, the instrument comprised of approximately 160 items suggesting that it may be a more thorough instrument than the other instruments, which typically had approximately 20 items (Oztekin, Kong, & Uysal, 2010; Reeves et al., 2002; Triacca, Bolchini, Botturi, & Inversini, 2004; Zaharias, 2006).

Although the evaluators selected the instrument and reviewed the evaluation procedure before individual implementation, the challenges that ensued left the evaluators perceiving that the process was flawed. This perception is important to the actual evaluative product because the confidence of the evaluators in delivering a completed report is just as valuable as the actual contents of the report (Costabile, De Angeli, & Matera, 2001). If the method being implemented is not clear, the confidence of the entire exercise can diminish, possibly resulting in the evaluators having a less than enthusiastic approach to the rest of the exercise (Shi, 2008). The team of evaluators thus used an instrument that was perceived as being easy to implement. This produced expectations that the final evaluation discussion on the online course would focus on the usable effects of the product. However, usability procedural challenges were the topic of discussion, which left the evaluation exercise incomplete.

The method of evaluation is not the only technique that is required for the productive evaluation of distance education products. The evaluators who are selected are also of great importance to the entire evaluation process. The more expertise the evaluation team possesses, the more the evaluation would be viewed as being successful (Cloninger, 2008; Følstad, 2007; Følstad, Anda, & Sjøberg, 2010; Lanzilotti, Ardito, Costabile, & De Angeli, 2010; Oztekin, Kong, & Uysal, 2010). When selecting usability evaluators, studies show that evaluators with a higher level of evaluation expertise are the better choices. Also, evaluators who have the specific domain knowledge that is being investigated are further seen as even better choices. The knowledge in the subject matter provides the expertise to appropriately evaluate the product within context (Følstad, 2007; Hwang & Salvendy, 2007).

Novice usability evaluators can pose serious challenges to the evaluative process by not having the necessary experience. They can be more at a disadvantage because the time that is spent learning the process can detract from the activity at hand (Hwang & Salvendy, 2007; Law & Hvannberg, 2008). In addition, usability evaluation is a cognitive activity that involves detecting and assessing design problems (Hertzum & Jacobsen, 2001). Regardless of subject matter or usability experience, an evaluator's cognitive style may contribute to the inconsistencies among different evaluators with similar experiences (Ling & Salvendy, 2009).

An additional challenge that can complicate the process is that evaluators with more usability evaluation experience will typically highlight usability issues rather the utility of the tools in the product (Nørgaard & Hornbæk, 2006). This suggests that selecting evaluators who have only evaluation experience can be detrimental to the process. This is especially important for the field of distance education where learning outcomes are the focus. The use of the tools with the environment to assist with learning outcomes are just as important as only being able to use the tools.

Ensuring the quality of distance education products completes the development and implementation cycle. The evaluation planning process needs to be aptly informed with suitable methods and experienced evaluators. This plan should also be tempered not only with the applicable knowledge but consideration should be given to the quantity and quality of the services provided and how these services will achieve the goal of quality.

Another important aspect of online course evaluation is the instructional design expertise, which includes application of instructional strategies and overall content organization and presentation. In many cases, course materials are organized based on an individual instructor's mental model and preferences (Moore, Downing, & York, 2009). A popular organization scheme is hierarchical classification, in which materials and resources are arranged in a hierarchy of classes, divisions, and subdivisions

(Kim & Moore, 2009). An LMS will typically support a hierarchical approach of folders that contain similar content, such as assignments or readings. The LMS features that limit choices for navigation paths and force a more compartmentalized way of organizing information can affect content organization, which can result in unnecessary frustration among students in finding course content.

CONCLUSION

The evaluators' skill levels as well as knowledge of certain terminologies formed barriers to the success of the evaluation. Often, the terms "online course" and "e-learning course" are used interchangeably, but they represent different characteristics for some practitioners and researchers (Moore, Dickson-Deane, & Galyen, 2011). For this case, the evaluators used these terms in their descriptions based on their perceptions of the meaning. Providing definitions for these terms may misconstrue their general meaning as interpreted by the evaluators during their investigation. Hence, the evaluators' expectations of the course characteristics as they relate to online or e-learning was another factor when applying the selected instrument to the course.

In summary, the evaluator reflections reveal several issues with usability evaluation. First, the evaluator experience is important for providing valid and meaningful results in regards to issues. Second, the number of instrument checklist items and applicability to the course can cause evaluator fatigue, which can impact the outcomes. Third, competencies related to instructional design and strategies are necessary for determining the appropriateness of learning activities and how they are presented. Fourth, specific LMS experience is important for understanding capabilities and whether activity designs are impacted.

QUESTIONS FOR ANALYSIS/DISCUSSION

1. What type of experience and knowledge is needed to accurately evaluate an online course?
2. How important is usability as an element to be considered when designing online courses?
3. What factors will impact the result of a usability evaluation?
4. How important is an evaluator's experience with an evaluation tool to the outcome of the usability evaluation?
5. To provide an accurate and complete evaluation of an online course, should the evaluation team consist of usability, subject matter, and instructional design experts?

REFERENCES

Ally, M. (2004). Foundations of educational theory for online learning. In T. Anderson (Ed.), *The theory and practice of online learning* (2nd ed., pp. 3–31). Athabasca, AB: Athabasca University.

Alsumait, A., & Al-Osaimi, A. (2009). Usability heuristics evaluation for child e-learning applications. *Proceedings of the 11th International Conference on Information Integration and Web-based Applications Services* (pp. 425–430).

Bernérus, A., & Zhang, J. (2010). *A Peek at the Position of Pedagogical Aspects in Usability Evaluation of E-learning System–A Literature Review of Usability Evaluation of E-learning System conducted since 2000.* (pp. 1–21). Gothenburg, Sweden: University of Gothenburg. Retrieved from http://gupea.ub.gu.se/handle/2077/23482

Clark, R. C., & Mayer, R. E. (2008). *e-Learning and the science of instruction: Proven guidelines for consumers and designers of multimedia learning.* San Francisco, CA: Pfeiffer.

Cloninger, C. (2008). *Usability experts are from Mars, graphic designers are from Venus.* Retrieved from http://www.alistapart.com/articles/marsvenus

Conrad, D. (2006). E-learning and social change: An apparent contradiction. In M. Beaudoin (Ed.), *Perspectives on higher education in the digital age.* (pp. 21–33). New York, NY: Nova Science.

Costabile, M. F., De Angeli, A., & Matera, M. (2001). Guiding usability evaluators during hypermedia inspection. In *Proceedings of IEEE Symposia on Human-Centric Computing Languages and Environments* (p. 332).

Dreyfus, H. L., & Dreyfus, S. E. (1986). *Mind over machine: The power of human intuition and expertise in the era of the computer.* Oxford, UK: Basil Blackwell.

Dringus, L. P., & Cohen, M. S. (2005). An adaptable usability heuristic checklist for online courses. *Proceedings of 35th Annual Frontiers in Education.*

Eraut, M. (1994). *Developing professional knowledge and competence.* London, UK: Falmer.

Feldstein, M. (2002). What is "usable" e-learning? *eLearn, 2002*(9), 2.

Følstad, A. (2007). Work-domain experts as evaluators: Usability inspection of domain-specific work-support systems. *International Journal of Human-Computer Interaction, 22*(3), 217–245.

Følstad, A., Anda, B. C., & Sjøberg, D. I. (2010). The usability inspection performance of work-domain experts: An empirical study. *Interacting with Computers, 22*(2), 75–87.

Gagne, R. M., Briggs, L. J., & Wager, W. W. (1992). *The principles of instructional design,* (4th ed.). New York, NY: Holt, Rinehart and Winston.

Hertzum, M., & Jacobsen, N. (2001). The evaluator effect: A chilling fact about usability evaluation methods. *International Journal of Human-Computer Interaction, 13*(4), 421–443.

Hiltz, S. R., & Turoff, M. (2005). Education goes digital: The evolution of online learning and the revolution in higher education. *Communications of the ACM, 48*(10), 59–64.

Hwang, W., & Salvendy, G. (2007). What makes evaluators to find more usability problems?: A meta-analysis for individual detection rates. *Human-Computer Interaction, 4550,* 499–507.

International Standards Organization 9241. (n.d.). *Usability Definition.* Author.

Keegan, D. (1996). *Foundations of distance education.* (3rd ed.). London, UK: Routledge.

Kim, K.-S., & Moore, J. L. (2009) Task oriented information organization and retrieval in online learning. In P. L .Rogers, G. A. Berg, J. V. Boettcher, C. Howard, L. Justice, & K. Schenk (Eds.) *Encyclopedia of distance Distance and online Online learning Learning* (2nd ed., pp. 2023–2031). Hershey, PA: IGI Global.

Kirmani, S., & Rajasekaran, S. (2007). Heuristic Evaluation Quality Score (HEQS): A measure of heuristic evaluation skills. *Journal of Usability Studies, 2*(3), 61–75.

Lanzilotti, R., Ardito, C., Costabile, M., & De Angeli, A. (2010). Do patterns help novice evaluators? A comparative study. *International Journal of Human-Computer Studies, 69*(1–2), 52–69.

Law, E. L., & Hvannberg, E. T. (2008). Consolidating usability problems with novice evaluators. *Proceedings of the 5th Nordic Conference on Human-computer Interaction: Building Bridges* (pp. 495–498).

Ling, C., & Salvendy, G. (2009). Effect of evaluators' cognitive style on heuristic evaluation: Field dependent and field independent evaluators. *International Journal of Human-Computer Studies, 67*(4), 382–393.

Moore, J. L., Dickson-Deane, C. & Galyen, K. (2011). E-learning, online learning, and distance learning environments: Are they the same? *The Internet and Higher Education, 14,* 129–135.

Moore, J. L., Dickson-Deane, C., Galyen, K., Vo, N., & Charoentham, M. (2008). e-Learning usability instruments: What is being evaluated? *Proceedings of E-Learn 2008 Conference,* Las Vegas, NV.

Moore, J. L., Downing, R., & York, D. (2009). Organizing instructional content for web-based courses. Does a single model exist? In A. Orellana, T. L. Hudgins, & M. Simonson (Eds.) *The perfect online course: Best practices for designing and teaching* (pp. 341–358). Charlotte, NC: Information Age.

Moore, M. G. (1990). Background and overview of contemporary American distance education. In *Contemporary issues in American distance education* (pp. xii-xxvi). New York, NY: Pergamon Press.

Murray, M., Kujundzic, N., (2005). *Critical reflection: A textbook for critical thinking.* Québec, Canada: McGill-Queen's University Press.

Nielsen, J. (1992). Finding usability problems through heuristic evaluation. *Proceedings of the SIGCHI Conference on Human Factors in Computing Systems* (pp. 373–380).

Nielsen, J., & Molich, R. (1990). Heuristic evaluation of user interfaces. *Proceedings of the SIGCHI Conference on Human Factors in Computing Systems: Empowering People* (pp. 249–256).

Noble, D. F. (1998). Digital diploma mills: The automation of higher education. *Science as Culture, 7*(3), 355–368.

Nørgaard, M., & Hornbæk, K. (2006). What do usability evaluators do in practice?: An explorative study of think-aloud testing. *Proceedings of 6th Conference on Designing Interactive Systems* (pp. 209–218).

Oblinger, D. G., & Oblinger, J. L. (2005). Educating the Net generation. *EDUCAUSE.* Retrieved from http://net.educause.edu/ir/library/pdf/pub7101.pdf

Oztekin, A., Kong, Z. J., & Uysal, O. (2010). UseLearn: A novel checklist and usability evaluation method for eLearning systems by criticality metric analysis. *International Journal of Industrial Ergonomics, 40*(4), 455–469.

Reeves, T. C., Benson, L., Elliott, D., Grant, M., Holschuh, D., Kim, B., Kim, H. et al. (2002). Usability and instructional design heuristics for e-learning evaluation. *Proceedings of World Conference on Educational Multimedia, Hypermedia and Telecommunications* (pp. 1615–1621).

Reeves, T. C, & Hedberg, J. G., (2003). *Interactive learning systems evaluation.* Englewood Cliffs, NJ: Educational Technology.

Shi, Q. (2008). A field study of the relationship and communication between Chinese evaluators and users in thinking aloud usability tests. In *Proceedings of the 5th Nordic Conference on Human-computer Interaction: Building Bridges* (pp. 344–352).

Spector, J. M., Merrill, M. D., Merrienboer, J. V., & Driscoll, M. P. (2008). *Handbook of research on educational communications and technology* (3rd ed.). New York, NY: Erlbaum.

Triacca, L., Bolchini, D., Botturi, L. & Inversini, A. (2004). *MiLE: Systematic usability evaluation for E-learning web applications.* In L. Cantoni & C. McLoughlin (Eds.), Proceedings of World Conference on Educational Multimedia, Hypermedia and Telecommunications (pp. 4398–4405). Chesapeake, VA: AACE.

Zaharias, P. (2006). A usability evaluation method for e-learning: focus on motivation to learn. *Proceedings of CHI '06 Extended Abstracts on Human Factors in Computing systems* (pp. 1571–1576).

Zaharias, P. (2009). Usability in the context of e-learning. *International Journal of Technology and Human Interaction, 5*(4), 37–59.

Zaharias, P., & Poylymenakou, A. (2009). Developing a usability evaluation method for e-learning applications: Beyond functional usability. *International Journal of Human-Computer Interaction, 25*(1), 75–98.

CHAPTER 16

ONLINE DOCTORAL MINOR IN CONFLICT RESOLUTION

A Case Study in Instructional Design

Linda Agustin Simunek, Tatjana Martinez, and Judith Slapak-Barski

ABSTRACT

This is a case study in progress on course media enrichment by three colleagues at the Abraham S. Fischler School of Education of Nova Southeastern University. The first two authors teach in the conflict resolution minor of a Doctor of Education degree distance education program, and the third is an instructional designer and teacher education specialist. The authors collaborated in identifying new generation instructional technologies for course media enrichment to transform a course to be more student-centered. Using the systematic approach posited by Dick, Carey, and Carey's (2005) model of instructional design, they conducted a front-end analysis of the instructional goals, performance objectives and activities, learning tasks of the students, and their characteristics, skills, needs and goals. Based on these analyses, they implemented media-enrichment strategies. The course media enrichments represent a significant improvement on a previously text-based online course.

Real-Life Distance Education, pages 283–307
Copyright © 2014 by Information Age Publishing

INTRODUCTION

The Abraham S. Fischler School of Education ("Fischler") of Nova Southeastern University, located in North Miami Beach, Florida serves 12,000 online students from all over the world. This case study is based on a 3-credit hour graduate survey course, "Theories and Principles of Conflict Resolution," in the conflict resolution minor of the Doctor of Education Degree (EdD) program.

Fischler graduate students are predominantly adult learners enrolled in either a master's or doctoral degree program in education. The students who enroll in the conflict resolution minor are in the EdD program and have chosen concentrations in either organizational or educational leadership. The typical student in the doctoral program with a concentration in educational leadership is one who is either a teacher aspiring to go into academic administration, or an administrator aspiring to move ahead in the academic institution. The student who is enrolled in the organizational leadership EdD program is aspiring to be a leader in his or her current organization: i.e., hospitals, health agencies, or governmental agencies, armed forces, departments of corrections, and other employment settings. Based on the premise to be "guides on the side" rather than "sages on the stage," the authors collaborated in making this online course more engaging and meaningful.

CASE STUDY

The following sections are organized using the instructional design phases proposed by Dick, Carey, and Carey (Dick, Carey, & Carey, 2005).

Analysis

Review of Instructional Goals

The front-end analysis of the course to determine its readiness for media enrichment entails the assessment of how well the course learning outcomes align with the goals of the conflict resolution minor and the Ed.D. program goals. This process requires course faculty to have a working knowledge of Bloom's Taxonomy of Learning Domains: cognitive, affective, and psychomotor (Chapman, 2006); principles of adult learning; principles of curriculum design, development, implementation and evaluation, and the philosophies and theories of teaching with special focus on theories of problem-based and inquiry learning (Bloom, Engelhart, Furst, Hill, & Krathwohl, 1956; Chapman, 2006). An initial review of the literature on models for designing and delivering technologically-assisted instruction revealed that the various instructional development models stipulate a process of (a) analysis, (b) design, (c) development, (d) implementation, and (e) evaluation (Dick, Carey, & Carey, 2005; Sonwalker, 2001a).

Course instruction is guided by the learning theory of constructivism that posits that knowledge is constructed or created from a "social" perspective such as economic, social, and political environment (Vygotsky, 1962) or from a "psychological" perspective at the individual level (Richardson, 2003). The learner in this course takes center stage in the learning process; the learner is guided rather than directed. Marincovich (2000) indicates that this approach to teaching has its roots in the constructivist theory of learning, also known as the problem-based approach to teaching. Here, the learner creates meaning from personal experiences or problems and the meaning becomes formal knowledge within the group. This approach synthesizes both the social and the individual emphases of creating knowledge using both aspects. Tobin and Tippins (1993) see this approach as a hybrid approach that focuses on knowledge as personally constructed and socially mediated.

In the spring 2010 term, the Fischler School began preparing for regional accreditation; the team of faculty in the minor in collaboration with the Academic Director met several times to update course objectives in each of the conflict courses. Applying principles of curricular continuity, sequence, vertical, and horizontal integration, the alignment of course objectives with the overarching goals of the conflict resolution minor and the EdD program were evaluated. Key behavioral outcomes were identified and learning activities were reviewed to assess the progression of problem solving skills from beginning skills on the first course to more complex skills in the last course in the conflict resolution minor course sequence.

The team's review of the Theories and Principles of Conflict Resolution course led to a consensus that the course objectives were properly aligned and reflective of objectives of the minor and of the EdD program. For the EdD and the conflict resolution minor goals, as outlined in the Fischler *Catalog and Student Handbook*, see Appendix 1.

This case study analyzes Theories and Principles of Conflict Resolution, which is the first course in this minor. This course presents the major theories and principles of conflict resolution. It provides an overview of the nature of conflict and analyzes problem-solving strategies applied to different conflict scenarios. Combining individual and team approaches, students formulate action plans for different scenarios based on a theoretical framework of conflict resolution.

The course is presented online using the Blackboard learning management system. It uses Blackboard Collaborate sessions for class chats in small groups of students. Collaborate is a web conferencing tool, which offers faculty and students the flexibility to interact with each other at different geographical locations. The professor uses the chats for overview of the course and direct instruction through PowerPoint presentations. Students post weekly asynchronous written responses, which embody the virtual equivalent of face-to-face class discussions. Weekly postings are based on carefully selected readings that address the theories and principles being studied. Students are asked to analyze past conflicts in the light of the new content learned, critique conflict resolution strategies chosen in the past, and analyze how past approaches can be enhanced by applying principles from the new content learned. Each student is then required to respond to two other students' posts expanding and making suggestions of new ideas and concerns.

There are three required written assignments; two are individual assignments presented asynchronously, and one is a team effort that culminates with a synchronous oral presentation of a conflict resolution plan to the class through Collaborate. Teams are identified during the first week of class. Throughout the term, the teams meet virtually through Collaborate classrooms to select a topic, plan, discuss, and develop the third assignment. The assignment must present research on a current national or international conflict and provide action plans to resolve the conflict chosen. Finally, student teams present their final written assignment including a conflict resolution plan as a research project that they present to the class using PowerPoint presentations. It is expected that by completing the required readings, submitting the weekly postings and responses, and submitting the three written assignments, students' coconstructed knowledge, skills, and insights enable them as leaders to create solutions of conflict situations they encounter in their professional and personal lives.

The student includes in each posting two cited resources from the required texts, other resources recommended in the syllabus, other peer reviewed articles, and/or academically recognized resource that may apply to the conflict or the way the conflict was resolved (i.e., cognitive domain). The student demonstrates or integrates the conflict theories and/or principles that best describe the conflict chosen. In addition, the student is asked to analyze the conflict depicted and decide if any of the theories of conflict resolution apply to the particular situation and provide an alternative manner of resolution, if needed.

The cognitive domain involves knowledge and the development of intellectual attitudes and skills. For example, the first learning outcome identified below, expects the student to be able to examine the principles and theories of conflict resolution that the student has encountered in different systemic settings during the course of the student's life experiences. The outcome expects the student to read the text assignments and recall (i.e., cognitive domain) examples of personal involvement in a conflict that had taken place in the workplace, the family, and the community.

Finally, the student is asked to read and respond to two other classmates' postings adding comments that may clarify, challenge, or substantiate the other's findings and identify emotional responses elicited by the conflict and suggested solutions (i.e., affective domain). These cross- responses include referenced citations as well as life experiences. The process of posting responses to questions and cross-responses to peers' postings requires the student to demonstrate the full panoply of Bloom's learning domains. For example, in the cognitive domain, the student is asked to recall the theories and principles learned, and to integrate new learning with antecedent knowledge gained from experience. This synthesis and integration of knowledge are put to meaningful use by describing a better way of resolving the conflict at issue. The affective domain is reflected in the student's attitudes of neutrality, trust, openness, time, and space management, desire to maintain open communications, objectivity in assessing disputant's interactions, and adopting ethical strategies for de-escalating the conflict. The psychomotor domain is reflected in the student's listening skills, body language, and physical manipulation of environmental factors that affect the climate for conflict resolution (Bloom, Engelhart, Furst, Hill, & Krathwohl, 1956). For a complete outline of learning activities and outcomes specific to the course, see Appendix 1.

The review of course content is in keeping with the observation that "... the content is the basis for course delivery. The quality of the content has to be good to begin with. Mediocre content cannot be made better just by the infusion of the pedagogical styles or multimedia enhancements" (Sonwalkar, 2001b, p. 1).

Analysis of Student Learning

This course relies on the theory that knowledge is acquired by knowledge construction and that it is more lasting and meaningful when the student is engaged in the construction of this knowledge (Mayer, 2004; Palincscar, 1998). Hemlo-Silver, Duncan, & Chinn, (2006) agree that learning is facilitated when students are provided with "extensive scaffolding and guidance" (p. 99). Problem-based learning (PBL) and inquiry learning (IL) are the teaching/learning approaches used in the course because they provide the learner with many forms of scaffolding that allow the learning to be student centered and less teacher-centered.

Adults as learners are self-directed and bring with them the knowledge of experience gathered in a lifetime; they are practical, goal oriented, and they need to see the relevance of what they are learning to their work and responsibilities (Knowles, 1990). The PBL and IL emphasize scaffolding the learning process and engaging students by helping them make sense of the theories and principles of conflict resolution by applying them to their own experiences with conflicts and their resolution. Using PBL and IL, students manage their own exploration and analysis of conflict situations, and provide collaborative opportunities with their peers as well as guidance from a facilitator (Conlan, Grabowski, & Smith, 2003). Students in this course articulate their thinking and reflect on their learning in various ways (Hemlo-Silver et al., 2006). Lieb, 1991, suggests that the adult learner also needs to be motivated; among the sources of motivation listed by Lieb are the need for social relationships, the need to improve self and mankind, and the need to continue learning. For the most part, the adult learners enrolled in the EdD program at are also seeking to fulfill other needs late in life, such as licensing requirements prompted by a promotion, job enrichment, or a need to adapt to job changes. They also need to balance the learning process with their already busy lives that include family, work, and community service. Lieb, (1991) states that the best way to help the adult learner in the process is to "enhance" the process and lessen the "barriers" (p. 2). This course review is an attempt to strengthen the learning process, to find more flexible and accessible ways to deliver learning through media enrichment that may also serve as ways to lift some of the barriers they face. The authors believe that is the reason the process of review and evaluation of online courses like this course is an ongoing process of formative and summative evaluations and updating skills and delivery options.

For the most part, this is the case in the course in review. Thus, media enhancements to this online course are expected to increase the learners' flexibility to acquire knowledge from different modes, such as, auditory, visual, tactile, and kinesthetic. In so doing, the course will begin its media transformation journey and join other media enriched courses as a part of a hypermedia-based education system.

Learner Characteristics

The students in the course are adults motivated by expectations of enhancing their careers and acquiring more knowledge and skills that will propel them to the next level in their professional lives. They choose the Fischler School because it offers them flexibility, academic quality, and support.

The majority of the students in the course are predominantly women of diverse cultural backgrounds with varying competencies in oral and written communication skills in English. At the time students are able to start taking the minor subjects, they have had the core courses required in the doctorate. Thus the course faculty expects students to be able to apply critical thinking skills, to problem solve, and able to work in teams as well as independently. They come with knowledge of the recent trends and major issues facing education and our society. More importantly, they understand the need to become better problem solvers and want to learn more about conflicts, how they evolve, how they differ, the theories and principles proposed by social scientists, and above all, the strategies used for resolving conflicts.

Even though the students come from diverse cultural backgrounds, one thing that they find commonality in is that their experiences are full of conflict scenarios and conflict resolution theories of their own. In addition to completing a requirement, they may take the conflict resolution minor not only to learn new ways to manage and/or resolve conflicts but also they learn from the experiences of others to become better problem solvers in their worlds. Through collaboratively solving problems, reflecting on their experiences, and engaging in research and investigation in a virtual learning environment, they are breaking barriers and becoming better leaders in schools, organizations, and the world they live in.

Distance education learners are challenged with having to balance their studies, work, and family demands. Online delivery enables students to access course materials any time and any place they have access to the Internet. Adequate technological hardware is a requirement. Students must have a working knowledge of the *Publication Manual of the American Psychological Association* as the standard of procedure for academic writing; an awareness of the academic policies related to plagiarism, netiquette, copyright and fair use, and the use of Blackboard.

The adage "Tell me, and I will forget; Show me, and I may remember; Involve me, and I will understand" (Confucius, as cited in Oxendine, C., Robinson, J., & Willson, G., 2004); aptly captures the problem-solving and inquiry learning strategies in the Conflict Course.

Course Enrichment Challenges

The review of the existing course syllabus based on the systemic intructional design model ADDIE described by Dick, Carey, & Carey (2005) brought to light the following potential hypermedia elements:

- Audio support for PowerPoint presentations
- Video- and audio-casts of simulated conflict scenarios, as well as alternative conflict resolution methodologies
- Addition of modules on demand on key constructs within the course, including conflict, conflict resolution alternative dispute resolution strategies, power, trust, hierarchy of human needs, interpersonal skills, active listening skills, interviewing and questioning skills, and a sample of an agreement form between disputants
- The addition of the use of web cameras for a two-way viewing between students and faculty during Elluminate Live (now Collaborate) sessions

- Include media streaming of podcasts as mini-lectures or benchmark lessons presenting key information to students as needed to emphasizing escalation, de-escalation, intractable conflicts, and the role of third parties in resolution strategies
- Course faculty also recognize the need to collaborate with other conflict resolution departments within the University, such as the Law School, the Alternative dispute Resolution Clinic, the School of Social Sciences and Humanities' conflict resolution graduate program, and workshops and symposiums offered regarding violence prevention and bullying in the schools and workplace

The authors were eager to determine how a course that was developed originally by recreating a classroom-teaching format into an online course with then-current technologies could be enhanced by a new generation of instructional technology. A number of factors converged to motivate the authors to conduct a summative assessment of performance objectives of the online introductory course in conflict resolution. The institutional setting is renowned as a pioneer in distance education. A second factor is the ongoing college-wide evaluation of learning outcomes based on regional accreditation standards. Additionally, the award of a U.S. Department of Education Title V-B federal grant aimed at promoting warm connections, enhancing academic success, and facilitating timely doctoral degree completions of students pursuing an EdD degree through course media enrichment and other activities, served as impetus to explore ways to make existing courses more engaging and more student-friendly.

The Fischer School has the distinction of graduating the highest number of minority students earning doctoral degrees in education. In keeping with this reputation, current faculty is conscious of the need to be innovative in planning student-centered course delivery. The authors further felt the need to translate into action the paradigm that an online course faculty is a "guide on the side" rather than the traditional "sage on the stage" (King, 1993, p. 30), as well as the importance of establishing social presence to facilitate interpersonal connectedness and build a sense of community among learners at a distance (Aragon, 2003).

Design: The Dick, Carey, and Carey Systems Model of Instructional Development

The International Society for Technology in Education (ISTE, 2000) identifies "several higher-order thinking skills and digital citizenship as critical for students to learn effectively for a lifetime and to live productively" (p. 1). Technology standards for teachers (ISTE, 2000), call upon faculty to facilitate and inspire student learning and creativity; design and develop digital-age learning experiences and assessments; model digital citizenship and responsibility and engage in professional growth and leadership. Technology standards call for administrators to convey a vision for technology infusion and support faculty efforts to obtain intramural and extramural funding for technology-enabled learning initiatives.

The authors considered the taxonomy of instructional development approaches, and adopted the Dick, Carey, and Carey (2005) model for media enrichment. The Dick, Carey, and Carey model consists of reductionist and iterative processes: assess needs to identify goals; conduct instructional analysis; analyze learners and contexts; write performance objectives; revise instruction; develop assessment instruments; develop instructional strategy; develop and select instructional materials; design and conduct formative evaluation and instruction, and design and conduct summative evaluation. Gustafson and Branch (2002) note that "the Dick, Carey, and Carey model" has become the standard to which all other ID models and alternative approaches to design and development are compared (p. 79).

In this course, the student learns content, strategies, and self-directed learning skills by solving problems collaboratively, specifically using PBL. Students develop these skills by engaging in the weekly discussions and responses based on relevant problems or questions and apply conflict resolution theories learned. Students further engage in communicating these skills and content learned and apply them in individual written assignments. These assignments are based on relevant situations and scenarios dealing with their everyday lives. For example, in the first written assignment, students are called upon to explain the conflict resolution policies in their current work environment or one that they may be familiar with; to discuss a specific conflict situation and how it was handled by the administration; finally, students are asked to critique the process integrating the theories and principles of conflict resolution learned. The teacher facilitates the learning process by giving input and provides some content knowledge (Hemlo-Silver et al., 2006). Scaffolding tools help students tackle problems and find solutions, which may have been too difficult for them to find answers previously, without the aid of scaffolding (Quintana, Reiser, Davis, Krajcik, Fretz, Duncan Kyza, Edelson, & Soloway, 2004, p. 338).

The PBL and IL approaches to learning are not only key tools to help students become skilled problem solvers; they also provide the support needed to allow the assimilation of complex tasks with the support from the collaborative efforts of other students and the facilitator (Hemlo-Silver et al., 2006). The scaffolding process of inquiry learning and problem-based situations with the aid of the guidance of the facilitator assists the learners to make sense of the theories and principles of conflict resolution being presented. Scaffolding helps gain clarity and confidence on how to apply them to their everyday work and personal life situations. These skills are important and meaningful in particular to the adult learners engaged in learning conflict resolution skills in this course.

Upon completion of the course, the students' summaries and reflections on the course state that as they move on with their doctoral courses, they are taking away with them a body of knowledge of the theories and principles and a mental model of problem solving and inquiry in facilitating the transformation or resolution of conflicts. They value the higher order thinking and critical thinking skills required for analyzing individual, group, and systemic conflicts. They recognize the significance of power, trust, open communications, justice, and the acknowledgement of ripeness as key elements of the negotiations between disputants. They view conflict as an integral part of life that requires all of their perceptual fields to capitalize the learning opportunities provided by conflicts.

Development: Distance Education Course Development and Enrichment by a Team

The development phase of this project will start with the selection of appropriate media elements to enrich the course. There is a wide spectrum of media available to enrich courses, including text, graphics, audio, video, animations, and simulations responsive to the learning styles preferred by a learner to understand the information and turn it into useful knowledge (University of Wisconsin, 2005).

First Media-Enrichment Method: Introductory Video

According to research findings, one critical barrier that blocks students' success in online learning and hinders their persistence in online learning environments is the feeling of isolation and lack of connectedness in online instruction. These feelings, in turn, affect students' overall satisfaction with the distance learning experience (Billings et al., 2001). One method of addressing those feelings of isolation, which has recently gained attention, is the use of introductory videos in distance learning environments. Introductory videos help establish instructor immediacy, a special kind of social presence. "Social Presence is defined as the degree to which a person is perceived as a 'real person' in mediated communication" (Aragon, 2003; Gunawardena & Zittle, 1997, p. 9). Establishing social presence in a distance learning environment contributes to creating a level of comfort in which students feel at ease around the instructor and other participants. "Instructional immediacy is defined as behavior that brings the instructor and the students closer together in terms of perceived distance" (Baker, 2004).

The instructor for this course will utilize an introductory video in which she will provide a general course introduction (similar to the one that an instructor typically gives during the first day of a face-to-face class). Through a well-designed introductory video, the instructor is able to provide structure and guidance to distance learners by efficiently communicating course information to a large number of students. At the same time, students are able to see and hear their instructor, which helps create social presence, which in turn promotes a level of comfort among online learners and helps them feel at ease in the online classroom (Aragon, 2003). In addition, introductory videos can help alleviate the problem presented by the fact that most students do not read the syllabus, which often causes students to be confused and, eventually, fall behind. By drawing attention to the importance of reading the syllabus in their introductory video, instructors may be directly increasing students' chance for success, by communicating key points through a medium that students may actually use (Lewis, Moreno, & Large, 2009).

Second Media-Enrichment Method: Webquest

A Webquest is an inquiry-oriented lesson format in which students use the Internet as a source of information and knowledge, and conduct research on the Internet to find out the answers to questions about the course content. Webquests are associated with higher order thinking skills, and consist of distinct sections, including: introduction, task, process, evaluation, conclusions, and credits and references; which are further explained below (Dodge, 1997). Webquests can be created using various programs, including common word processing software such as NotePad, Microsoft Word, as well as other software, such as Dreamweaver and others. Webquest templates are available to educators in pre-designed formats, which generally can be easily edited.

- Introduction: This section introduces the activity to students, and it should be written with the student as the intended audience. This is where a motivational introduction grabs the reader's interest and prepares students for the work ahead. The Introduction section is also where "the Big Question" is posted (the essential or guiding question around which the whole Webquest is centered.
- The Task: This section clearly describes what the end result of the learners' activities will be. For example, the task could be a product to be designed, a problem to be solved, a position to be formulated or defended or any other task that requires learners to process and transform the information they have gathered. This is also the section where specific tools needed to complete the final product should be listed (e.g., a particular software product).

- The Process: This section lists the steps that learners will need to go through, to complete the task described above. The steps are usually written in the "you" voice, as if talking directly to the students. For example, the first step might read, "First you'll be assigned to a team of three students…" and the second step might read: "Once you have selected a role to play…" and so on. Learners will access the online resources identified by the instructor as they go through the Webquest process. The instructor may also post a "Resources" section here, with a set of links for students to review, as a way of developing background information, among others. In the Process section, the instructor may also provide some guidance on how students should organize the information gathered (e.g., flowcharts, summary tables, concept maps, or other organizing structures). The advice could also take the form of a checklist of questions to analyze the information with, or "things to notice or think about."
- Evaluation: This section describes to the learners how their performance will be evaluated. The instructor should specify whether there will be a common grade for group work, or whether each student will receive an individual grade, among other items.
- Conclusion: This section summarizes what students will have accomplished or learned by completing this activity or lesson. Here, instructors may choose to add some rhetorical questions or additional links to encourage students to extend their thinking into other content beyond this lesson.
- Credits & References: This section lists books and other analog media used as information, as well as the sources of any images, music or text retrieved from online sources to be used in the Webquest, including hyperlinks to the original source. Also, if the instructor wishes to thank or credit anyone who provided resources or help, this is the section to do so.

The Webquest created specifically for this course can be found in Appendix 2.

Third Media Enrichment Strategy Selected: Trigger Video

A trigger video is a short visual scenario recorded in video format to be used to stimulate a situation as it relates to the course content (University of Wisconsin, 2005).

Implementation

For this course, the authors have identified three initial projects to media-enrich course content: an introductory video, recorded by the instructor with the support of the project's instructional design team, a we-bquest lesson devised by the instructor and the instructional designer, and a trigger video. All the above-mentioned finalized projects will be uploaded to the Title V-B Faculty Toolbox, an electronic repository of instructional content that results from the collaboration between the project's instructional design team and the Fischler faculty. The introductory video and the webquest were presented in the course during the summer of 2012, and the trigger video was implemented during the winter of 2013.

Evaluation

The process of aligning course goals and learning outcomes with those of the Minor and the EdD degree program, was guided by an analysis of the course learning domains as described by Bloom's taxonomy (Chapman, 2006). Bloom's taxonomy domains served as guideposts in planning meaningful and relevant learning activities and the level of behavioral changes congruent with expected doctoral level learning outcomes. Its use facilitated the authors' evaluation of the course content, whereas media rich enhancements were expected to facilitate the learner's development of knowledge and intellect (i.e., cognitive domain), attitude and beliefs (i.e., affective domain); and ability to use physical skills effectively (i.e., psychomotor domain). Finally, the authors intend to consider whether the establishment of social presence was accomplished, and whether students expressed a perceived sense of community in online learning environments as a result.

For future consideration, the team recommends the use of a point value checklist, the Quality Matters rubric (2011–2013), for quality assurance review of course media enrichment. This rubric assigns point values on standards related to eight course variables: accessibility, learner support, course technology, learner engagement, resources and materials, assessment and measurement, learning objectives and course overview, and introduction. This rubric can be accessed at http://www.qmprogram.org/files/QM_Standards_2011-2013.pdf

IMPLICATIONS FOR DISTANCE EDUCATION

Although this case study focused on the premedia course enhancement phase of distance education courses, the authors' knowledge and insights on the multidimensional process of course media enrichment were strengthened. The authors were introduced to an array of instructional development models. These models need to be rigorously validated as to their effectiveness in promoting student-centered learning within the paradigm of course faculty serving as "guides on the side" rather than "sages on the stage" (King, 1993, p. 30).

A working knowledge of distance education and instructional technology jargon facilitate effective collaborative working relationships. Administrators of distance education programs must have a vision for the infusion of technology-enabled learning, digital citizenship, and global connectivity. Distance students and faculty are challenged to examine the way they teach, work, and learn in an increasingly connected digital and global society. Technology standards are a compendium of skills that empower digital distance learners and faculty to be competitive and successful in a global and digital world.

CONCLUSION

The second decade of the 21st century ushers in revolutionary changes in educational technology compelling distance education faculty to examine pedagogical strategies that will promote student-centered strategies. The zeitgeist of e-learning demands that course faculty acquire a working knowledge of technology standards for students, faculty, and administrators and a mastery of instructional design models, adult learning principles, and teaching philosophy.

According to Sonwalkar (2001a), there is a need of a shift to create a teaching delivery model that has the "asynchronous technological interface in mind" (p. 2). Sonwalkar (2001a) believes that up to now we have taken the pedagogy of teaching in a face-to-face classroom and applied it to an online learning setting. In doing so, this online classroom becomes restrictive and it places a burden on the teacher's ability to facilitate the learning process. If we agree that the cognitive domain is complex and that competence in this area is different in individual learners, then there is a need to take advantage of the benefits of a "hypermedia-based education system" (Sonwalkar, 2001b). A systemic model such as that of Dick, Carey, and Carey (2005) serves as road map in the collaboration between faculty and media specialists in front-end analysis and the ongoing quality assurance of technology-enabled instructional delivery systems. The learning curve for media enrichment, albeit the time demands, involves an exciting process and opens up a new world of delivering student-centered instruction.

QUESTIONS FOR ANALYSIS/DISCUSSION

1. Which learning models are preferred by distance learners for translating received information into meaningful knowledge?

2. Which multidimensional pedagogical processes promote success in technology-enabled learning?
3. Which media elements promote engagement and active learning among students whose primary language is not English?
4. How can media enhancements customize and personalize learning activities to address students' diverse cultural backgrounds?
5. Which course variables are reviewed for quality assurance based on a pre-established assessment tool such as Quality Matters?
6. What are potential funding sources for educational technology infusion in distance education institutions?
7. What formative and summative assessment measures are used for evidence-based revisions of course media elements?
8. What resources should be applied for learner success in the revised course?

ACKNOWLEDGEMENTS

The authors acknowledge the critical input of: Vesna Beck, Director of Academic and Faculty Support/Program Professor; Karen Bowser, Executive Director, Professional Development/Program Professor; Gary Scott Brown, Instructional Design Project Manager; and Mary Ann Lowe, Associate Dean/Program Professor, of the Abraham S. Fischler School of Education at Nova Southeastern University.

REFERENCES

Abraham S. Fischler School of Education of Nova Southeastern University. (2011–2012). *Catalog and Student Handbook.*

American Psychological Association. (2010). *Publication Manual of the American Psychological Association* (6th ed.). Washington, DC: Author.

Aragon, S. R. (2003). Creating social presence in online environments. *New Directions for Adult and Continuing Education, 57*–68. doi:10.1002/ace.119

Baker, J. D. (2004). An investigation of relationships among instructor immediacy and affective and cognitive learning in the online classroom. *The Internet and Higher Education, 7*(1), 1–13.

Billings, D. M., Connors, U. R., & Skiba, D. J. (2001). Benchmarking best practices in web-based nursing courses. *Advances in Nursing Science, 23*(3), 41–53.

Bloom, B. S., Engelhart, M. D., Furst, E. J., Hill, W. H., & Krathwohl, D. R. (1956). *Taxonomy of educational objectives: The cognitive domain.* New York, NY. Longman.

Brown, G. S. (2010). *Recommendations for media enrichment* (Unpublished monograph). The Abraham S. Fischler School of Education at Nova Southeastern University.

Chapman, A. (2006). *Bloom's taxonomy—Learning domains.* Retrieved from http://www.businessballs.com/bloomstaxonomyoflearningdomains.htm

Conlan, J., Grabowski, S., & Smith, K. (2003). Adult Learning. In M. Orey (Ed.), *Emerging perspectives on learning, teaching, and technology.* Retrieved from http://projects.coe.uga.edu/epltt/

Deutsch, M. & Coleman, P. T. (Ed.). (2006). *The handbook of conflict resolution: Theory and practice.* San Francisco: Jossey-Bass. ISBN: 0787948225.

Dick, W. O. Carey, L., & Carey, J. O. (2005). *Systematic design of instruction* (6th ed.). Boston, MA: Allyn & Bacon.

Dodge, B. (1997). *Some thoughts about Webquests.* Retrieved from http://webquest.sdsu.edu/about_webquests.html

Gunawardena, C. N., Nolla, A. C., Wilson, P. L., Lopez-Islas, J. R., Ramirez-Angel, N., and Megchun-Alpizar, R. M. (2001). A cross-cultural study of group process and development in online conferences. *Distance Education, 22*(1), 85–121.

Gunawardena, C. N., & Zittle, F. (1997). Social presence as a predictor of satisfaction within a computer mediated conferencing environment. *The American Journal of Distance Education, 11*(3), 8–25.

Gustafson, K. L., & Branch, R. M., (2002). *Survey of instructional development models* (4th ed.). Syracuse, NY: ERIC Clearinghouse on Information.

Hemlo-Silver, C. E., Ravit, G. D., & Chinn, C. A. (2006). Scaffolding and achievement in problem-based learning: A response to Kirschner, Sweller, and Clark. *Educational Psychologist, 42*(2), 99–107.

International Society for Technology in Education (ISTE). (2000). *Standards for global learning in a digital age.* Retrieved from http://www.iste.org/standards.aspx http://instructionaldesign.gordoncomputer.com/IDRoles.htmlKemp, S. (2007).

Introduction Image. Retrieved from www.google.com

Kim, B. (2006). *Social constructivism* Retrieved from http://projects.coe.uga.edu/epltt/index.php?title=Social_Constructivism

King, A. (1993). From sage on the stage to guide on the side. *College Teaching, 41*(1), 30–35.

Knowles, M. S. (1990) *The adult learner. A neglected species* (4th ed.). Houston, TX: Gulf.

Lewis, D., Moreno, M., & Large, J. (2009). Introductory videos: An analysis of student use patterns. *Journal of the Research Center for Educational Technology, 5*(3) 68–79.

Lieb, S. (1991). *Principles of adult learning.* Retrieved from http://honolulu.hawaii.edu/intranet/committees/FacDevCom/guidebk/teachtip/adults-2.htm

Marincovich, M. (2000). Problems and promises in problem-based learning. In O. S. Tan, P. Little, S. Y. Hee, & J. Conway (Eds.), *Problem-based learning: Educational innovation across disciplines.* Singapore: Temasek Center for Problem-based Learning.

Mayer, R, E. (2004). Should there be a three-strikes rule against pure discovery learning? *American Psychologist, 59,* 14–19.

Nova Southeastern University. (2012). Conflict resolution minor [syllabus]. Retrieved from http://www.schoolofed.nova.edu/doctoral/syllabi/minors/conflict_resolution.htm

Oxendine, C., Robinson, J., & Willson, G. (2004). Experiential learning. In M. Orey (Ed.), *Emerging perspectives on learning, teaching, and technology.* Retrieved April 11, 2013, from http://projects.coe.uga.edu/epltt/

Palinscar, A. S. (1998). Social constructivist perspectives on teaching and learning. *Annual Review of Psychology, 45,* 345–375.

Pruitt, D. G., & Kim, S. H. (2004). *Social conflict: Escalation, stalemate, and settlement* (3rd ed.). Boston, MA: McGraw-Hill.

Richardson, V. (2003). Constructivist pedagogy. *Teachers College Record, 105*(9), 1623–1640.

Quintana, C., Reiser, B. J., Davis, E. A., Krajcik, J., Fretz, E., Duncan, R. G., Kyza, E., Edelson, D., & Soloway, E. (2004). A scaffolding design framework for software to support science inquiry. *Journal of the Learning Sciences, 13*(3), 337–387.

Sonwalkar, N. (2001a). *Changing interface of education with revolutionary learning technologies: An effective guide for infusing technology enabled education for universities and corporations.* New York, NY: iUniverse.

Sonwalkar, N. (2001b). *A new methodology for evaluation: The pedagogical rating of online courses.* Retrieved from http://campustechnology.com/articles/2001/12/a-new-methodology-for-evaluation-the-pedagogical-rating-of-online-courses.aspx

Tobin, K., & Tippins, D. (1993). Constructivism as a referent for teaching and learning. In K. Tobin (Ed.). *The practice of constructivism Constructivism in science Science education Education* (pp. 3–21). Mahwah, NJ: Erlbaum.

University of Wisconsin (2005). *Instructional Design at ITS: Glossary.* Retrieved from http://www.uwex.edu/ics/design/glossary.htm#l

USDOE Title V-B PPOHA—Promoting Post Baccalaureate Opportunities for Hispanic Americans. P031M094009 Duns No. 002971240

Vygotsky, L. S. (1962). *Thought and languageLanguage.* Cambridge, MA: MIT Press.

WebQuest–quick overview at YouTube. Retrieved from http://www.youtube.com/watch?v=o4rel5qOPvU

WebQuest template. Retrieved from http://webquest.sdsu.edu/templates/lesson-template1.htm

APPENDIX 1

The Doctor of Education (EdD) Program

The Doctor of Education (EdD) offers students a menu-driven approach to customizing their doctoral degree with eleven different concentration options, flexible curriculum choices, and multiple instructional delivery options. The five main components of the degree are the Core Seminars, the Concentration, the Research Elective, the Electives/Minors, and the Applied Dissertation. The EdD is designed to offer students a curriculum with a solid foundation in leadership, research, and the study of current trends and issues, while customizing each student's program of study to meet their individual professional and personal goals. Students may elect to take their core seminars online or at one of our many instructional sites throughout the US, while concentration and elective courses will all be delivered completely online. (Abraham S. Fischler School of Education at Nova Southeastern University [Fischler, 2011–2012, p. 150]).

Doctor of Education Degree (EdD) graduates will be able to:

1. Demonstrate knowledge learned in the program by applying it to real settings. (Knowledge)
2. Conduct an independent research investigation that contributes to the general body of knowledge in a specific field or profession. (Research)
3. Solve diverse problems using information and skills acquired in the program to create solutions. (Problem solving)
4. Make informed decisions based on ethical and legal principles. (Ethics)
5. Formulate scholarly arguments supported by academic resources. (Communication) (Fischler, 2011–2012, p. 150)

Conflict Resolution Minor

The conflict resolution minor is designed to empower emerging leaders for the roles of mediator, facilitator, and negotiator. This minor examines theories of conflict and conflict resolution and provides opportunities for problem-based practice to enable leaders to use information and skills acquired to create solutions. Course content is research-based and infuses best practices in education. Students seeking a minor in conflict resolution must take the courses in sequence (Fischler, 2011–2012, p. 164).

Courses in the Minor: (15 CREDITS) the Conflict Course Sequence Is as Follows:

1. EDD 7811 Theories and Principles of Conflict Resolution
2. EDD 7810 The Nature of Conflict in Society (Prerequisite is EDD 7811)
3. EDD 7812 Strategies and Models of Mediation and Negotiation (Prerequisite is EDD7810)
4. EDD 7813 Managing Organizational Conflict (Prerequisite is EDD 7812)
5. EDD 7814 Special Topics in Conflict Resolution (Prerequisite EDD 7813. This course EDD 7814 is the last course in the minor (Fischler, 2011–2012, P.164)

EDD 7811

The Learning Outcomes in EDD 7811 expects that the students will achieve the following objectives:

1. Examine the principles and theories of conflict and conflict resolution in social, interpersonal, and systemic settings (Knowledge and Comprehension).
2. Examine how human behavior, interpersonal dynamics, culture, and ethical factors influence a conflict situation (Application).
3. Compare the dynamics of simple, complex, and apparently intractable conflicts (Application and Analysis).
4. Apply the principles and theories of conflict resolution to an existing intergroup conflict, the conflict and the strategies used to resolve the conflict, including an action plan to resolve the conflict (Application, Analysis, and Synthesis). (Nova Southeastern University, 2012).

The students are expected to meet the Learning Outcomes by completing the following activities:

1. Nine postings and responses that comprise the weekly discussions with professor input. These discussions follow the problem-based learning and inquiry learning approaches to learning. The student is expected to analyze specific social, interpersonal, and systemic conflicts from their experiences and apply principles and theories from the texts and other resources that provide the new content being acquired through their own research. Other resources include peer reviewed journal articles found online through the various online resources provided by the University.

2. Two individual written assignments allow the student the opportunity in the first assignment to describe the existing policies and procedures of an organization they are familiar with, discuss a known conflict scenario, and propose a resolution to that conflict. In the second assignment the student is asked to view a movie (12 Angry Men), discuss the conflict dynamics (i.e., human behaviors, interpersonal dynamics, culture, and ethical factors) observed; discuss the escalation and de-escalation present in the film, and analyze the results using the conflict theories.

3. Participate in several chats to present course overview and introduction; the theory of problem-based learning and its application to this particular course; the second chat is discuss previously viewed videos that depict scenarios addressing specific conflict dynamics and the conflict resolution theories, i.e., escalation, de-escalation; cooperative and competitive theories in analyzing human behaviors and interpersonal dynamics; and creativity and change in intractable conflicts.

4. Team approach to analyzing an existing international or national conflict and developing an action plan to be developed throughout the term is the third assignment. The team members are assigned at the beginning of the term. Teams work in Elluminate Live online classrooms to formulate the topics, analysis of the literature, integrate the conflict resolution theories and principles content of new knowledge acquired in the course, and compose an action plan that incorporates creativity and change factors.

Formative and summative evaluation processes are present throughout the course. The continuous flow of weekly postings and discussions and the two individual written assignments formulate the basis for the formative evaluation process. The third and final assignment presents a summative evaluation as it encompasses all of the aspects of conflict analysis and resolution proposal. The final and summative evaluation is made up of the on-going developmental team meetings (using the online Elluminate Live classroom and sessions recorded), a written report of the assignment, an oral presentation to the class incorporating an outline of the findings of the team findings using a power point presentation, including responding to class questions posted prior to the oral and final presentation of the team project.

APPENDIX 2

ESCALATION AND DE-ESCALATION WEBQUEST
Designed by Dr. Tatjana Martinez
for Edd 7811
Principles and Theories of Conflict Resolution

INTRODUCTION

You have read the scenario assigned to you depicting a vehicular incident and the chain of events that cascaded into a conflict, which resulted in terrible personal and community loss and polarization. The conflict presented in this scenario could have probably been avoided or de-escalated along the way, to avoid the tragic result of this case.

You have been selected by the Mayor because you represent one of the stakeholder groups involved in the conflict. Accordingly, you have been assigned to help the Mayor prepare a Press Release to address these events. The whole community is awaiting the Mayor's plan to help this community move forward with a sense of trust, unity, healing, peace, and understanding. Your whole message should be built around the theories and principles of conflict resolution and transformation identified in your texts (Deutsch, M. & Coleman, P. T. [Ed.] [2006]). The handbook of conflict resolution: Theory and practice. San Francisco: Jossey-Bass. ISBN: 0787948225 and Pruitt, D. G. & Kim, S. H. (2004). Social Conflict: Escalation, stalemate, and settlement (3rd ed.). Boston: McGraw-Hill. ISBN: 0072855355) and in the other resources recommended for your research.

As you prepare your article, you will focus on the transformational opportunities this tragic event make possible in preserving the community and learning from past errors to bring about positive change. You will identify the escalation process that led to the riots in the community and what, if any stalemates could have been identified to begin de-escalation along the way.

The Task

Compose a Press Release that the Mayor will publish in the local media, explaining the process of transformation and healing. As part of the Mayor's Peace Coalition Advisory Team, you will need to provide a scenario analysis using one of the escalation models described in your text (Contender-defender model; Conflict-spiral model; or the structural change model). Consider what parts did culture, contentious tactics, right and wrong, negative framing of issues, strong group identity, and blame play in this escalation.

Point out that the four police officers and the victim had several opportunities to prevent the violent events that had ensued. Provide specific examples to demonstrate how the process of de-escalation could have been implemented early on to prevent the many tragedies that arose from this case. Consider opportunities missed by the victim, the police officers, police commissioner, the courts, etc.; whether there was a perception of common ground or whether an assertion of personal rights and interests prevailed; whether the parties involved ever perceived a way out and that the conflict was intolerable; and, whether a solution is possible even among enemies.

Finish your Press Release with a proposal or action plan for a peaceful solution where each of the stakeholders in the community (i.e.: the justice system, the police department, elected officials, businesses and the community as a whole) have a role to play in using this experience as an agent of transformation for rebuilding trust and harmony in this charred community. Consider a possible formula that will satisfy both sides; opening the possibility for the sides to exchange and identify interests and priorities; search for alternatives jointly for their mutual welfare; and diminish the fear of the other party gaining ground.

THE PROCESS

To accomplish the task, you will need to meet with the members of your team. The team will now be the Mayor's Peace Coalition Advisory Team ("Team"), comprised of a member from each of the community stakeholders.

1. Each member of the Team will pick a stakeholder to represent (i.e.: one of you will represent the Police Department, another Justice System; someone else will represent the business community, etc.).
2. Compose a document detailing the name of each student in your group and which stakeholder the student will represent (i.e.: John Smith: Police Department).
3. Once you have picked which stakeholder you will represent, you will present to your Team an analysis of the problem using one of the following models: Contender-defender model; Conflict-spiral model; or the structural change model. Include or identify escalation, contentious tactics and entrapment. Include the following resources in your research:
   a. http://www.jstor.org/page/journal/socialproblems/about.html
   b. http://jtp.sagepub.com/content/10/1/59.short

    c. Social Psychology Quarterly, Published by: American Sociological Association ISSN: 01902725 http://www.jstor.org/stable/2786833?seq=2

    d. http://www.tandfonline.com/loi/rnpr20

    e. http://about.jstor.org/content-collections

    f. http://www.ssrn.com/

    g. Journal of Conflict Resolution: http://jcr.sagepub.com/

4. Once you have analyzed the problem, you will provide specific examples to show how the process of de-escalation could have been implemented from your stakeholder's point of view (i.e., what could the justice system have done to ameliorate the situation, what could the police department have done differently, etc.). Make sure to include stalemates, ripeness, and trust building.

5. Make sure to include the following sources in your research:

    a. Negotiation Journal, On the Process of Dispute Settlement, http://www.springerlink.com/

    b. http://www.colorado.edu/conflict/peace/example/kries7527.htm

    c. Journal of Peace Research, Published by: Sage Publications, Ltd. ISSN: 00223433, http://www.jstor.org/stable/10.2307/425586

    d. http://onlinelibrary.wiley.com/advanced/search

    e. Chicago Journal of International Law, http://heinonline.org/HOL/Page?handle=hein.journals/cjil6&div=41&g_sent=1&collection=journals

6. Once each group member (or stakeholder) has presented their proposal, the team will include every stakeholder's ideas and propose a unified plan to use this opportunity to implement lasting change in the community to prevent further events of this nature.

7. The final product should be a Press Release that encompasses a peaceful solution within an efficient and practical plan of action that can be implemented in a realistic timeframe.

Evaluation

Each stakeholder/team member of the Peace Coalition will be responsible to submit an individual finding and proposal and indicate how this was incorporated into the final product. Each team member will be evaluated individually (see Table 16.1) and will receive individual grades for the final product.

TABLE 16.1   Evaluation Rubric

TASK	Beginning 1	Developing 2	Accomplished 3	Exemplary 4	Score
Task #1 & # 2: Organization of the Team and distribution of tasks and the timely submission of individual work.	Description of identifiable performance characteristics reflecting a beginning level of performance.	Description of identifiable performance characteristics reflecting development and movement toward mastery of performance.	Description of identifiable performance characteristics reflecting mastery of performance.	Description of identifiable performance characteristics reflecting the highest level of performance.	
Task #3: Analysis of the problem Application of a selected escalation model and explained the Case in terms of this model successfully & convincingly.	Description of identifiable performance characteristics reflecting a beginning level of performance.	Description of identifiable performance characteristics reflecting development and movement toward mastery of performance.	Description of identifiable performance characteristics reflecting mastery of performance.	Description of identifiable performance characteristics reflecting the highest level of performance.	
Task #4, #5 & #6: Development of de-escalation action plan.	Description of identifiable performance characteristics reflecting a beginning level of performance.	Description of identifiable performance characteristics reflecting development and movement toward mastery of performance.	Description of identifiable performance characteristics reflecting mastery of performance.	Description of identifiable performance characteristics reflecting the highest level of performance.	
Task #7: Action Plan presented in a timely manner, including resources, with a realistic and efficient plan	Description of identifiable performance characteristics reflecting a beginning level of performance.	Description of identifiable performance characteristics reflecting development and movement toward mastery of performance.	Description of identifiable performance characteristics reflecting mastery of performance.	Description of identifiable performance characteristics reflecting the highest level of performance.	

Conclusion

By completing this assignment, you have analyzed the escalation and de-escalation cycles; over commitment and entrapment; perceived stalemates in the de-escalation process; and the transformational possibilities available for positive change and healing. In formulating de-escalation strategies, you have applied the fundamental social psychological processes, such as, emotions, biases, attributions, power, self-control, violence, group involvement, and other processes affecting conflicts, culminating in the creation of a theory-based Peace Action Plan.

Credits

A special thanks to the contributions of the instructor, Dr. Tatjana Martinez; the USDOE Title V-B Instructional Designer II and Teacher Education Specialist, Judith Slapak-Barski; and Dr. Linda Simunek, the USDOE Title V-B Grant Project Director in the creation of this WebQuest.

REFERENCES

Deutsch, M. & Coleman, P. T. (Ed.). (2006). *The handbook of conflict resolution: Theory and practice.* San Francisco: Jossey-Bass. ISBN: 0787948225.

Fischler (2011–12). *The Fischler school of education and human services catalog and handbook.* Ft. Lauderdale, FL: Nova southeastern University.

Introduction Image. Retrieved from www.google.com

Pruitt, D. G. & Kim, S. H. (2004). *Social conflict: Escalation, stalemate, and settlement* (3rd ed.). Boston: McGraw-Hill. ISBN: 0072855355.

Webquest–quick overview at YouTube. Retrieved from http://www.youtube.com/watch?v=o4rel5qOPvU

Webquest template. Retrieved from http://webquest.sdsu.edu/templates/lesson-template1.htm

CHAPTER 17

APPLICATION OF NING IN A GRADUATE LEVEL COURSE AND ITS EFFECT ON STUDENT USE

Monica W. Tracey, Kelly L. Unger, and Matthew Schwartz

ABSTRACT

The influx of the Internet and online tools in education combined with learn-ers' increased interests in online learning are driving universities and K–12 school districts to meet the desires and needs of their student populations. This chapter illustrates the use of an online social networking tool that re-placed a learning management tool in a higher education course. Four main areas are highlighted. First, the case includes a description of the process one professor used to blend a graduate level course adding an online component. Second, it illustrates the process of selecting online instructional tools used to facilitate online communication. Third, the case provides documentation of student perception of the use of the social networking tool, Ning, compared with other online instructional tools. Finally, an illustration is provided of the application of Ning by one graduate in his high school classroom as a result of his experience from this graduate course.

Real-Life Distance Education, pages 309–321

INTRODUCTION

The influx of the Internet and online tools in education combined with learners' increased interests in online learning are driving universities and K–12 school districts to meet the desires and needs of their student populations. To adapt, higher education faculty and K–12 teachers are now encouraged or required to incorporate an online learning component into courses. When designing courses, instructors should choose easy-to-use tools that assist in online facilitation of instructional strategies and activities to increase student interaction, collaboration, and motivation. When selecting tools, educators need to be knowledgeable of and creative with social and technology trends. Online social networking and collaboration tools allow for imaginative course design (Mason & Rennie, 2008).

One way to facilitate online learning activities is through the use of a learning management system (LMS). Most LMSs provide an online location for instructors to post lectures, assignments, and course materials for students. Students can submit work and interact with the instructor and other students through e-mail and discussion boards. There is another area of online learning tools, however, that are transitioning from entertainment and social purposes toward education. These include "Read-Write Web" tools, also known as Web 2.0 tools. DiNucci (1999) was the first to use the term Web 2.0 when discussing the web in its infancy stage as pages of content loaded into a browser window, usually known as Web 1.0. The term Web 2.0, however, did not find popularity among the masses until it was used by O'Reilly at the first Web 2.0 conference in October, 2004 (O'Reilly, 2005). These tools are distinguishable from Web 1.0 tools, because they allow users to interact with the web without having any computer programming knowledge or experience. Average or novice users can participate by creating and sharing their thoughts and ideas directly to the web and with others. O'Reilly (2005) states that "One of the key lessons of the Web 2.0 era is this: *Users add value.*" While allowing users to share their own content, and add their own value, the tool is crucial for collaboration and interaction. From an educational aspect, the design of the course is a necessary component for a successful collaborative online learning experience (Mason & Rennie, 2008). Increased student participation in the entire education process increases through the use of Web 2.0 tools, enriching the design and implementation of the course.

This chapter highlights four main areas. First, the case includes a description of the process one professor used to blend a graduate level course adding an online component. Second, it illustrates the process of selecting online instructional tools used to facilitate online communication in the blended graduate course. Third, the case provides documentation of the results of a survey of student perception of use of the social networking tool, Ning, compared with other online instructional tools. Finally, an illustration is provided of one graduate student's experience from this graduate course and his application of the Ning to his high school classroom.

CASE STUDY

Throughout this chapter we lead you through one professor's journey of blending face-to-face and online instruction that led to the migration from a university selected LMS, Blackboard, to the Web 2.0 social networking tool, Ning. This migration resulted in studying graduate student perceptions of Ning compared with other online instructional tools. Using Ning with her courses, the professor witnessed a cascading effect when one of her students began to use the tool in his own practice with high school students. This case study demonstrates how the social networking tool, Ning, can be used to facilitate online instruction in higher education and high school classrooms.

Preparing for the Blend

Transitioning to online instruction is not always the easiest task, especially for a professor who is a novice to online instruction. The professor in this study used a "blended" approach to courses to assist both herself and her students with easing into online teaching and learning. Though the term is widely used, "blended instruction" is ill-defined (Oliver & Trigwell, 2005). Three commonly used definitions include

- the integrated combination of traditional learning with web-based online approaches (drawing on the work of Harrison;
- the combination of media and tools employed in an e-learning environment; and
- the combination of a number of pedagogic approaches, irrespective of learning technology use—drawing on the work of Driscoll (as cited in Oliver & Trigwell, 2005, p. 17).

Of the three definitions above, this study defined "blended" as a style of teaching where the class sometimes meets face-to-face, and other times meets in an online environment. Those who select a blended approach to instruction typically find benefits in both the face-to-face and online environment for learners and instructors (Osguthorpe & Graham, 2003). Selecting specific weeks to facilitate class online allowed the professor to experiment with some of the online pedagogy and features without feeling overwhelmed by moving her teaching completely online. Students, through the blended approach, had the opportunity to learn how to work with a learning management system (LMS) and experience online learning at a slower pace, not overwhelmed with the soft skills necessary to be successful in online learning. This professor, at the beginning of the Fall 2009 semester, blended two of her courses, to meet students face-to-face 75 percent of the semester, and 25 percent in the online class environment. In this blended approach, the face-to-face meetings at the beginning of the semester helped to establish social presence and identity with others in the class, and provided an opportunity for the professor to discuss how the online sessions would be facilitated in Blackboard.

The first online class for the semester was held during week 3, and students logged into Blackboard to participate in the class discussion. The professor selected this social learning approach, because discussions for online learning in higher education are a standard practice throughout universities (Mason & Rennie, 2008). Two discussion prompts were created to stimulate thoughtful discussions about the weekly readings and content. Students had 7 days to complete an initial posting and respond to two other students' postings. All postings were to be completed by Saturday at 5:00 p.m. of the online week. The professor was astounded by the difficulty in reading the responses. The discussion board function in Blackboard was challenging to use as it allowed the professor to read only one student posting at a time. The challenges experienced with the technology reduced the quality of responses and were extremely time consuming. The professor concluded that if it was difficult responding to the student postings, students were probably feeling the same frustration, in turn reducing the quality of their responses to other students' postings.

Utilizing the Layers of Negotiation Model, a constructivist instructional design (ID) model, the professor elicited feedback from the students during the next face-to-face meeting. The Layers of Negotiation Model is a model that incorporates all stakeholders in the process of knowledge construction using reflection and the examination of information multiple times for multiple purposes, and the social negotiation of shared meanings (Cennamo, 2003). This model, used throughout the rest of the course, provided a way for the professor to gather input regarding the online activities and instruction from the students, and adapt the instruction to best fit their needs. It also aligned with Duffy and Cunningham's (1996) components of constructivism in that altering the instruction based on student feedback supported the students' active process of constructing their own knowledge and experiences rather than acquiring it. The feedback uncovered their frustrations, so the professor extended the time requirements for the next postings, and altered student response requirements to one other student instead of two. Another iteration of the Layers of Negotiation Model exposed continued frustration from students with Blackboard, leading the professor to redesign the discussion process to reduce user constraints. Not wanting a reduction in learner motivation for the course, the professor needed to assess whether to change learner attitudes and behaviors, or the environmental conditions (Keller, 2009). Knowing learner motivation is affected by internal human behaviors and external environmental conditions (Keller, 2009) it became clear that the external condition, the current LMS tool, was deterring learner motivation. In an effort to solve this problem, the professor migrated from Blackboard to the social networking tool, Ning, for the remaining online weeks.

Incorporation of Ning: Higher Education

Ning has similar features of other social networking sites where users have their own profile that can be customized by adding pictures and videos, list personal information, such as interests and hobbies, and can change the background to a design they prefer. It is appealing to students because it provides a level of personalization, socialization, and opportunities for communication and interaction (Karabult, Lindstrom, Braet, & Niederhauser, 2009; Martinez Aleman & Wartman, 2009; Mason & Rennie, 2008; Mazer, Murphy, & Simonds, 2007). This personalization component is currently not possible in Blackboard. When creating a social network with Ning, the professor had control over the design and who had access to it and its content and discussions. Educators like this feature because it keeps the network private; assessable to only those involved in the learning. The discussion forum was used for collaborating on various course content related topics. The chat feature provided a means for instant professor-to-student and student-to-student communication.

The professor watched as the Ning social network became a central focus of the course, not only for the online discussions, but for personal interaction among the students. Students began taking pictures of the face-to-face classroom activities and posting them for studying purposes, and when working on online assignments. One course required a group project, and students used the group feature within the tool to establish individualized groups to share, collaborate, and work on their projects. One of the assignments required students to find an online video that demonstrated a learning theory. Students were able to embed the videos directly on the Ning social network. One student then used a voting tool so students could vote on the best posted video. Using Ning served a multiple purpose. First, it allowed the professor to facilitate a more interactive environment with the content and the students. Second, the professor modeled the use of the tool to facilitate learning to students who are practicing instructional designers and educators, who in turn can utilize NING in their own practice.

Results of Survey

Data were collected to determine student perception of the success of the Ning social network after fall 2009 and winter 2010 semesters. After grades were submitted, a graduate research assistant contacted via e-mail the students who had used Ning in these courses, explaining the study and asking for their voluntary participation in an online survey. The survey focused on student perception and motivation in using Ning for classroom collaboration and learning. The survey consisted of open-ended and multiple-choice questions about their experience using Ninb in the course. A constant comparative analysis and coding was used to analyze the qualitative data to find themes that emerged from the data. Of the 45 (n=45) students, only 4 (9%) had used the Ning environment prior to taking this professor's courses, and 2 of those students used it for a course in higher education. The survey asked the students to compare the Ning environment with other online instructional tools.

Ning Compared to Blackboard

Students were asked if they had experience with the LMS, Blackboard, and, if so, to compare it with the Ning environment. All 45 students reported having exposure to Blackboard, and 69% ($n = 31$) of the students indicated the Ning was superior to Blackboard. One student commented, "The NING is very user friendly, easy to navigate and the layout of the NING is less complicated than Blackboard" (Student 5). Another stated, "The discussion threads were much easier to follow and read in the NING than on Blackboard" (Student 11). Another student went further to say, "NING allows for more personalization and socialization between the students and instructor. It is easier to find and locate information, and the discussion threads were much easier to follow than Blackboard. Blackboard is quite boring and was difficult for reading and following discussions" (Student 15). A fourth student agreed with finding the NING "easier" to use than Blackboard, but also added, "It's a current... tool that I not only learned the course content on, but also learned a new technological tool that I can use in my own practice" (Student 22).

While the majority of the students responded more favorably to Ning than to Blackboard, 4 students liked the Blackboard platform better. Of these 4 students, 3 liked the discussion feature in Blackboard better, finding it "easier to see and read" (Student 20), and found Ning "somewhat tedious with scrolling through all the repeated responses" (Student 8). A student who liked Blackboard better claimed, "I see Blackboard as school and NING as social" (Student 12).

Ning Compared to Moodle

The survey asked students to compare Ning with the LMS platform, Moodle. Sixteen of the 45 students reported experience with using Moodle. Approximately 44% ($n = 7$) of these students found Ning to be a better on-line learning tool than Moodle. The students who responded to liking Ning better commented on it being more "user friendly" (Students 2 and 25) and "easier to use" than Moodle (Students 9, 23, 31, and 32). Four students also found these two tools very similar.

The Moodle environment was favored by 2 of the students, with one claiming "Moodle allowed me to create course content. I'm not sure if we had this capability using the NING" (Student 38). Here the student is suggesting that Ning does not have an available feature to work collaboratively on creating one document where all students can contribute. This student is correct. While students have the capability to post any content, and others can then create a post attached to the initial post, there is no way for students to work collaboratively on one document or post in Ning.

Ning Compared to Wikis

Approximately one third ($n = 15$) of the students had previously used a wiki, and were asked to compare it to Ning. Only 10 of the students provided a descriptive comparison of the two tools. Four of them said they couldn't compare the tools, because they have different uses and applications (Students 13 and 21), and wouldn't use wiki for an LMS (Student 9) or for discussions (Student 38). The other 6 responses were split, with 3 of the students finding the "NING is better" (Student 20) and "more versatile" (Student 36). Other students found wikis to be easier to follow (Student 39) because Ning made it difficult to communicate (Student 23).

Ning Compared to Other Tools

The survey provided students the opportunity to list other tools they have used other than Ning, Blackboard, Moodle, and wikis, and to compare those tools to their experience with Ning. Students listed Google Sites and Documents, Skype, Dim Dim, Notapipe, Cacoo, Etherpad, Sharepoint, and Wimba, as other tools they have used. When asked to compare to Ning, one student said, "Google docs and websites are easy to work on, but can't compare to the NING because in the NING we didn't build content together" (Student 37). Sharepoint was suggested to have "Many more features and applications" (Student 36) than Ning. One student suggested "Like NING sometimes multiples tools are required for audio when IM [instant message] is not enough" (Student 25).

Incorporating Ning: High School

One graduate student, a high school computer applications, programming, and web design teacher, began to incorporate Ning into his own classroom practice after being exposed to the tool in this professor's course. He, too, used Ning as part of a blended approach to his courses. His students attended class in the computer lab, and instead of distributing paper-based instructions or handouts, he posted the materials to Ning. Benefits of posting the information online include: (a) assists in reducing costs associated with printer ink, paper, and time assembling and distributing; (b) prevents paper copies from being misplaced or lost; and (c) provides students with anywhere/anytime access to all instructional material and assignments.

The teacher created three separate Ning networks with a unique website address for each of his classes. They were private networks where only he could approve the members who requested to join. The Ning website address was written on the board and he explained how it was private. The students were to type in the web address and then sign-up for the Ning social network. He approved each student so they had access to the network. Once all the students were approved, he made them log into it to make sure everyone knew how to complete this task. After the students had logged onto the computers, an instructional activity on Ning was used as a warm-up for the class period. The teacher informed the students that they could log into Ning from home in the same way they did when in the computer lab at school. He perceived the students' reaction to the new online tool as good. At this point, most students did not really understand what the class Ning social networks were for, but shortly after its introduction they saw how important it was for the class.

The teacher posted class content on each Ning network, including assigned readings, worksheets, links to related websites, and assignment descriptions and rubrics. He discovered that posting material was easy and straightforward and it created a central place for all the class information. Each unit or section had a bolded and underlined title so students could find it easily. As the class progressed, the information grew creating a nice linear flow of the class materials.

Another feature that both the teacher and students enjoyed was the teacher posting pictures and videos on class topics. Using videos and graphics that were already created by others was an efficient means of providing the teacher with instructional-mediated materials. These videos also exposed the students to other experts using the same technologies and techniques they were being taught in class, providing reinforcement for what the teacher was teaching, and demonstrating the importance and use of these technologies, techniques, and concepts by others outside of the classroom. One assignment was to find a video about a topic and post it on the Ning network. Through contributing class content, students had a greater sense of ownership. The teacher also had students add pictures on the Ning network of projects they had created in class. This allowed students from different classes to see the work others had created.

To keep students on task with the completion of their assignments, the teacher used a Google Calendar. Each day, he posted a class topic on the calendar. If the student clicked on the topic, details on that day's assignment were visible. He updated it daily, and posted exams a week in advanced. The teacher embedded the calendar into the Ning network using the text box feature. Once a text box was added to the Ning network, he switched to HTML mode and pasted the code for the Google Calendar. The calendar also provided absent students a means to see what they had missed in class, and could be viewed if they were at home or the next day at school during the class warm-up.

The aspect of Ning that was most engaging to students was the individual personal profile page used by each student in a personal way, further providing that sense of ownership. The teacher found students logging onto the Ning network after school and in the evenings just to check their page. This created a desire for the students to use the tool designed for the class. This age group of students loved sharing photos of themselves, family, friends, and places they had traveled. One benefit of using a social networking tool in a high school classroom is that it provides an opportunity for a teacher to establish best practices for using social networks outside of the classroom. They can mentor the students on what should be posted and what is inappropriate. It also demonstrates that social networking tools can be used for educational purposes as well as connecting socially.

This teacher took advantage of the chat feature by holding an open study time the night before a test so students could ask questions in the chat room. He informed the students he would be on the Ning network from 8–9 p.m. the night before exams, and that if they had any questions they should sign in to ask. Most evenings six or seven students would join the chat to say hello and see if the teacher was really there. Students would pop in for a few minutes, ask their questions, and then pop out. The Ning chat was similar to a discussion in class where a student would ask a question and then the teacher would help lead them to the correct answer. A correlation was not statistically made, but he found that the students who used the study chat sessions did well on their tests.

Overall, through soliciting informal feedback and observation, the teacher found that many students saw Ning as a benefit. Students liked the ability to go online and see what they missed when they were absent. He also found that students preferred reading information on the computer rather than in paper format. If he gave students a choice between reading a physical packet or reading the same material online, they chose online. Many students liked a central location where all the class information was located. The students further enjoyed having a safe place where they could interact with other classmates.

IMPLICATIONS FOR DISTANCE EDUCATION

The cases discussed throughout this chapter demonstrate four key points for distance educators. The first is that detailed plans must be established before blending instruction that includes an online instructional component. Before implementing a blended course, distance educators need to decide how the course is going to be blended. Is it going to be face-to-face for some sessions and online for other sessions? Will it be face-to-face with students working independently on a computer? What activities in the course are best to facilitate in the online environment? What are the guidelines for online discussions?

Along with deciding which learning activities will take place in which environment, the second activity for both professors and teachers is to select online learning tools that are most conducive for the course content and student needs. Throughout this chapter, Ning was selected as the tool of choice, but distance educators must experiment with a variety of tools to best meet the needs of their students. Finding the best tool can be difficult, but as with the professor in this case, soliciting informal feedback from her students proved to be beneficial since the majority of the students were also frustrated with Blackboard. She also had to be open to learning a new tool. Had she been afraid to migrate to Ning, the students' knowledge acquisition may have been hindered due to the use of the initial course tool. It is not about simply using an online tool; it is about finding the best tool to address the instructional need, leading to the third important factor.

The third key point is to plan instructional activities carefully and be proficient with the tool to implement the activity effectively. The instructional activity examples in these cases used Ning, although many of these features can be implemented with different tools. For example, the chat feature for holding pretest night study sessions could be used in Google Chat or Skype. The key point is to understand which tools and features work best for the chosen instructional activity.

Finally, as you facilitate discussions, distribute content, and receive feedback, it is critical to remember that students are also observing how the instructor is using the tool. In the professor's case the graduate student was able to observe and participate in instructional activities that she had implemented in higher education; not only was she teaching the course content, but she was also modeling Ning and its uses for instruction to the students. Modeling the use of Ning cascaded down to high school students through one of her students, a high school teacher. As the high school teacher used the tool with his students, his students then observed and participated in activities that they could then use outside of the classroom. While data were not collected on the high school students' use of Ning outside the course, it is possible to assume that some students have created their own Ning networks for a hobby, family, sports team, or extracurricular groups. We can also hope that the rules and guidelines he established for using Ning increased the knowledge of appropriate social networking behavior.

CONCLUSION

This chapter illustrated the use of an online social networking tool that replaced a learning management tool in a higher education course. It demonstrated how to blend a graduate level course adding an online component, and highlights the importance of selecting online instructional tools that are most conducive for the course content and student needs. To assist distance educators in online tool selection, the results from a graduate student survey on perceptions of the social networking tool Ning were compared with other online instructional tools. The modeling of Ning in the graduate course cascaded to high school students as one graduate student applied the social networking tool in his classes. This chapter further illustrated that selecting a tool for an online learning environment where users can contribute is very important for a successful online learning experiences.

QUESTIONS FOR ANALYSIS/DISCUSSION

1. The professor found Ning to be easier to use then Blackboard from an instructor's perspective, and enjoyed using Ning. How do you believe her perspective of Ning influenced the students in the courses?
2. How did the use of a constructivist ID approach impact the student educational experience?
3. In this case, the informal feedback from the graduate students aligned with the professor's negative perceptions of Blackboard, so they switched tools. What would you do as an educator if you received positive feedback from your students regarding Blackboard, even though as the instructor you did not like the tool?
4. The instructor decided to step away from the university-purchased Blackboard tool. What are the benefits and challenges a distance educator faces when using a tool that is not supported by the employer?
5. The instructor chose to begin experimenting with online instruction using a blended approach with face-to-face classes and a few online classes. What are other ways to blend face-to-face and online instruction in higher education? High school?

6. Imagining that you are teaching a class of high school students who will be using a social networking tool throughout the course. At the beginning of the course it is important to establish rules and guidelines. Create a set of guidelines and rules for your students. What are the repercussions for students who disobey the guidelines and rules? How would your list differ for adult students?

REFERENCES

Cennamo, K. (2003). Design as knowledge construction: Constructing knowledge of design. *Computers in the Schools, 20*(4), 13–35.

DiNucci, D. (1999). Fragmented future. *Print, 53*(4), 32.

Duffy, T. M., & Cunningham, D. J. (1996). Constructivism: Implications for the design and delivery of instruction. In D. H. Jonassen (Ed.), *Handbook of research for educational communications and technology* (pp.170–198). New York, NY: Macmillan.

Karabulut, A., Lindstrom, D., Braet, D., & Niederhauser, D.S. (2009). Student level of commitment and engagement with Ning as a learning management system. In I. Gibson et al. (Eds.), *Proceedings of Society for Information Technology & Teacher Education International Conference 2009* (pp. 2564–2569). Chesapeake, VA: AACE.

Keller, J. M. (2009). *Motivational design for learning and performance: The ARCS model approach.* New York, NY: Springer.

Martinez Aleman, A. M., & Wartman, K. L. (2009). *Online social networking on campus: Understanding what matters in student culture.* New York, NY: Routledge.

Mason, R., & Rennie, F. (2008). *E-learning and social networking handbook: Resources for higher education.* New York, NY: Routledge.

Mazer, J. P., Murphy, R. E., & Simonds, C. J. (2007). I'll see you on "Facebook": The effects of computer-mediated teacher self-disclosure on student motivation,affective learning, and classroom climate. *Communication Education, 56*(1), 1–17.

Osguthorpe, R. T., & Graham, C. R. (2003). Blended learning environments: Definitions and directions. *Quarterly Review of Distance Education, 4*(3), 227–233.

O'Reilly, T. (2005). What is web 2.0: Design patterns and business models for the next generation of software. Retrieved from http://www.oreillynet.com/lpt/a/6228

Oliver, M., & Trigwell, K. (2005). Can "blended learning" be redeemed? *E-learning, 2*(1), 17–26.

FURTHER READINGS

Cacoo: http://cacoo.com/

Dim Dim: http://www.dimdim.com/

Etherpad: http://etherpad.com/

Google Documents: http://docs.google.com/demo/edit?id=scADBs97miRKhZG5 Ie9DTHeOl&dt=spreadsheet#document

Google Sites: http://www.google.com/sites/help/intl/en/overview.html

Moodle: http://moodle.org/

Notapipe: http://notapipe.net/

Skype: http://www.skype.com/intl/en-us/home

Sharepoint: http://sharepoint.microsoft.com/en-us/product/Pages/default.aspx

Tracey, M.W., & Unger, K.L. (2010). Increasing motivation through 2.0 tools. *Academic Exchange Quarterly, 14*(4).

Unger, K.L., & Tracey, M.W. (2011). Modeling online teaching and learning to pre- and in service teachers through the use of the Web 2.0 social networking tool NING. In D. Polly, C. Mims, & Persichitte, K. (Eds.), *Creating Technology-Rich Teacher Education Programs: Key Issues.*

Wiki: http://www.wiki.com/

Wimba (now Blackboard Collaborate): http://www.blackboard.com/collaborate

PART IV

DEVELOPING PROGRAMS

CHAPTER 18

SAXOPHONE

Creating a Global Videoconference Project

Al P. Mizell

ABSTRACT

If you woke up in 1995 and were told you had to figure out how to use the then-current technology to connect two-dozen schools around the world so the students could see, hear and respond to one another—and you had to do it so the schools didn't have to pay to participate, how would you do it? That was the challenge that faced us and this chapter is a description of how we found a way to do it.

As you follow the story, you'll see how we created a solution by using our new, instructional, two-way, PictureTel compressed video systems to connect middle and high schools around the world. We started with just two schools—one in the United States and one in Sweden. This evolved into a global project that became known as "SAXophone." The SAXophone project was a ten-year endeavor that connected some two dozen middle schools and high schools from around the world in monthly videoconferences jointly exploring a different topic each month. Schools decided if they wanted to participate or not each month, based on how the announced topic fit into their curricu-

Real-Life Distance Education, pages 325–335
Copyright © 2014 by Information Age Publishing

lum plans for the month. The schools recommended the topics with final decisions on topics resulting from the availability of experts to conduct the sessions. Generally, six to ten schools participated each month. The schools had class assignments to complete before each session so they were prepared for the interactions with the experts. The project was unique in that it was for early adopters of technology, involved expensive video equipment, required access to an ISDN phone line, and willingness for teachers and administrators to allow their students to participate in a global project in addition to their normal curriculum plans.

Topics ranged from joint musical concerts to meeting with the authors to discuss their books to sharing the students' original poetry, and even traveling virtually to the Johnson Space Center to "walk" through the mock-ups of the International Space Station with a real astronaut. Several articles and book chapters described the project until it ended after ten successful years.

INTRODUCTION

Marshall McLuhan (1964) introduced the concept of the global village that helped us see what was happening with worldwide, inexpensive communication through technology. However, at the time we did not envision that it would result during our lifetimes with our students being able to see and talk with students across the ocean and around the globe.

When I wrote a chapter on the use of compressed video for the *Encyclopedia of Distance Learning* (2005) that was edited by Howard et al., I began the chapter with this observation: "To get even more structured interactions with students in other parts of the nation or the world, and to have high-quality picture and voice exchanges, compressed video systems connected via broad bandwidth ISDN phone lines are being used" (p. 317). I was reflecting on how far we had come in the ten years since we began the SAXophone project. I had a cabinet full of SAXophone brochures and videotapes of the many interactive sessions we had conducted over the years. I wanted to write a chapter that documented the work we had done and the many students and teachers who had been impacted by this innovative use of this new technology. It foreshadowed today's world where we see youngsters holding their personal phones up to engage in two-way video calls and conferences with their friends and not seeing anything unusual or unique about it. Yet, those of us who have lived through the development of this phenomenon are constantly impressed as we observe it and recall what it was like in "the old days." Hopefully, this case study will help you relive part of the excitement and challenges of that development.

I wrote the chapter mentioned above in 2005 to describe the project we had created in1995 to connect students around the world via compressed video. "**S**tudents **A**round the World e**X**changing over the **phone**," known as the SAXophone project, was created to provide middle and high school students around the world with an opportunity to meet and interact with students from other cultures and societies over a ten-year period beginning in 1995. The SAXophone project was sponsored by Nova Southeastern University and the Broward County, Florida BECON Distance Learning Center. Their support enabled it to survive with volunteers doing the coordinating but with no funding other than what each participating school provided for their own equipment and to cover the phone costs for their connections.

CASE STUDY

The Fischler Graduate School of Education and Human Services (Fischler School) of Nova Southeastern University (NSU) purchased ten PictureTel videoconferencing units in 1994 to further their work with distance learning between the main campus and remote locations. I was serving as Director of Technology for the Fischler School and constantly seeking ways to make new uses of the technology that we used in our graduate courses with educators from a variety of backgrounds. In June 1994, the first use of the new video technology was to conduct a summer, week-long, intensive workshop connecting three remote class sites (Ft. Lauderdale, Phoenix, and Las Vegas). I was impressed with this creative use (especially the ice breaker when all the students placed one of their shoes in a pile at each site and other students tried to guess which shoe belonged to which student) and it set me to wondering how else compressed video could be used.

As owners of these new PictureTel units, our faculty automatically became members of the PictureTel User Group. This group met each year to share ways that the equipment was being used, to gain ideas for new uses, to meet other users so we could network with them, and to find out what new developments were coming. I was able to attend the September 1995 Annual Conference in Nashville, Tennessee. During lunch one day at the conference, I happened to sit at a table with two individuals who became instrumental in helping create the SAXophone project. As we talked, the conversation turned to ways to use the compressed video equipment that each of us had recently received. The result was the creation of a project that began during lunch, as I have more fully described in a *Distance Education Report* (1997). This was when Bent Kroon from the Swedish Military College, Thomas Ziegler, Computer Center Director at Ulster BOCES in New Paltz, New York, and I agreed to try to connect with each other from our home locations, using the new NSU bridge as soon as we returned home from the conference. Ted Detjen, now retired Assistant Director at BOCES, was appointed by Ziegler to replace him as the BOCES participant. Although it hadn't been too difficult to connect two or three institutions over ISDN lines within the United States, it turned out to be a real challenge for us to connect from Florida to Sweden. In fact, it took over three months to make the international connections work, but then these three (i.e., Florida, New York, and Sweden) sites finally connected.

After Kroon and I met a few times using the PictureTel units, he told me that one of his staff members had a son in the nearby Swedish high school. The boy had told his teacher about the connections that Kroon and I had made using compressed video. The teacher asked if there was some way for his students to connect with some U.S. students. Since the videoconferencing units were seldom used during the day, I asked my wife, who was the director of the University School, if I could work with some of her teachers to help their American students become pen pals with the Swedish students. Our next step would be to see if we could get them to meet over compressed video. My wife agreed and the two groups of students became pen pals. Kroon offered to let the Swedish class come to the Swedish War College to use their video equipment and we agreed for the University School students to come to the Fischler School to use our equipment.

I'll never forget the first time the University School students met each other online and saw who their pen pals really were. One student exclaimed, "Oh, look, that's Emil, he's my pen pal!" There were exclamations and excitement all around on both sides of the ocean as pals met for the first time in virtual space.

We needed to have a name for the project so we originally called it "SAXophone." We made the name up as an acronym from the participating countries—"Swedish and American students eXchanging over the phone." However, as the project grew and additional countries joined in, we wanted to keep the acronym the same but with a slightly different meaning. So we renamed the project by making the new name reflect the purpose that we, the initial group of teachers and students, had envisioned for it: "Students Around the world eXchanging over the phone."

We held our first formal session on December 11, 1995 when students in New York, Sweden, and Florida each gave brief presentations, including skits, songs, and descriptions of their major winter holidays. We were able to incorporate document cameras into the session to show close-up images of typical foods, icons, photographs, etc. Our second formal session was held on February 27, 1996 when the same three groups of students described a typical "Day in the Life" of students from each culture.

In the second year of the project, as additional schools heard about the project, some of them became involved. Soon, we had schools from England, Sweden, Finland, Poland, Norway, Greece, Germany, Japan, the UAE, Costa Rica, Japan, and the Unites States all participating in one or more of the sessions. One of our participants, Randy Palmer, contributed to Chapter 11 of the text, *Teaching and Learning with Technology* (Lever-Duffy et al., 2003). In the chapter, Randy described the project in the following words: "With opportunities such as those provided by SAXophone, students come together as an international learning community in our global village" (p. 373).

PictureTel (which has now become PolyCom) not only sold us the video-conferencing equipment and hosted the annual Users' Group conferences, but they worked with us in planning the project and in helping provide leaders for some of the sessions. For example, they paid the rather large honorarium for Eliezer "Elie" Wiesel, author of the book, *Night,* to spend over an hour with our students engaging and motivating them as they discussed the novel and its impact.

Reactions to the Topics

As mentioned in the Introduction, we offered a wide range of subjects with different topics each month. A copy of the announcement of topics for 1999 was prepared by our administrative assistant, Ruth Chernet; it is included as Appendix A. Probably one of the most popular topics was the session where students read and discussed their original poetry reflecting their feelings. Equally engaging were the emotionally charged session with Holocaust survivors, a simulation game involving the global environment and oil drilling, and the concert that included a symphonic presentation from England and a rock band from a New York alternative school. The impact of the project on preconceived notions is best illustrated by this 17-year old from the United States who said, "...that kids would get an idea that there are other ways to work things out than the way [they are done] in the United States." From across the ocean, a student from Sweden said, "We will understand each other better."

After several years participating in the regular SAXophone events, the coordinator at a New York high school developed a quiz format over compressed video that could expand the offerings in the project. He invited several high schools to compete two or three times during the year to see if the concept would work. It did, and a series of formal quiz sessions were included in the next year's schedule. The New York school, Wallkill High School, volunteered to serve as the host school. They developed and enforced the competition rules, developed a series of questions of varying difficulty, assigned the items 5-, 10-, or 20-point designations in a variety of academic subject areas, and provided scorekeepers and a moderator to ask the questions and judge the accuracy of the answers.

Participating schools provided teams of four students with a designated captain. Each participating school's team took a turn at selecting the category and difficulty level of the question their team wanted to answer. The team members conferred and the captain or appointed team member gave the official answer for the team within the time limit indicated. If they missed, the same question went to the next school and so on until, in a 60- to 90-minute session, four to six teams could participate in three rounds of questions to identify an overall winner.

Interested schools could sit in to observe as the supporting "audience." A middle school teacher from Costa Rica and another from New Jersey offered to develop a middle school version of the Quiz Bowl. The teacher from New Jersey (Williamstown Middle School), with help from other teachers in her school, ran the first middle school competition. They learned from the experiences of the high school competition and developed more complete rules and added fun elements. For example, schools were encouraged to develop minicommercials for their state, county, school, and so on to present at the breaks between rounds.

The middle schools that contributed a minicommercial developed their presentations as they desired. One such commercial was a description of the school; another was a humorous poem with different parts read by different students. Yet another was a satire on regular commercials. The main thing was that their creativity and willingness to present to a broad audience was appreciated by all and added a light touch to the session while involving students who were not team members in the Quiz Bowls over compressed video.

The End of the Project... or the Beginning?

NSU and the New Paltz, New York BOCES hosted the project using their video bridges until 2003 when course usage became too heavy. At that time, The Broward County BECON Center agreed to host the project. However, by January of 2006, their bridge also became so busy that they could no longer support the project. Without support, it seemed to me that the time to retire the project had arrived. The project did impact the many participants. These effects are described by a colleague who worked with me on the project, George Kontos, in our article in *TechTrends* (1997). In January 2006, the SAXophone project was closed.

However, even though we had to close the SAXophone project, NSU agreed to keep the Web page in its archives with active links. You may go there by using the URL: http://web.archive.org/web/20070430025835/ http://www.fgse.nova.edu/saxophone/ and then clicking on the various tabs to see the resources, etc. that we found useful at the end of the project and kept updating for a few years after that.

On this website that is now in the archive, we explained the closing of SAXophone because its time had come and new opportunities had become available. Another reason that led to the decision to close was that the University had to reassign the administrative assistant who handled the many details, the paperwork, and the many phone calls. Perhaps this case study will encourage the reader to move out from today's accepted practices and create something new that in the next ten years will be historical as well but will also help lead the way to new technologies and their innovative uses.

IMPLICATIONS FOR DISTANCE EDUCATION

As more K–12 schools find themselves under emerging legal requirements to make sure their students experience one or more courses via distance learning before they can graduate, the more valuable experiences, similar to SAXophone, will be to those students. Working online in two-way audio and video communication with their peers around the world, students will find formal distance learning to simply be an extension of their previous experiences. Polycom, Inc. continues to encourage the use of video globally by sponsoring new projects that are similar to the original design of the SAXophone project. *School Buyers Online* released the following news report on March 10, 2010:

> Pleasanton, CA—(Marketwire)—An increasing number of primary and secondary schools are leveraging videoconferencing for classroom-to-classroom collaboration as a way to expand their curriculum and give students memorable learning experiences by interacting with students and teachers in other cities, states and countries. Each year hundreds of schools get their first experience through Read Around the Planet, a free, annual videoconferencing event sponsored by Polycom, Inc. (NASDAQ: PLCM), the leading provider of visual communications solutions, and Two-Way Interactive Connections in Education (TWICE), Michigan's K–12 videoconference organization. In its ninth year, Read Around the Planet 2010 took place between Feb. 22 and March 5 and involved more than 58,000 students in six countries.

CONCLUSION

In 1995, before the widespread use of the Web, the use of compressed video to connect elementary and secondary students was in its infancy. Yet, by modifying the use of early and expensive videoconferencing equipment from its academic role to that of bringing global connectivity to schools without charge showed the world how valuable this tool could be. As we use today's tools, like Skype and ooVoo, to share in 6 and even 12-way videoconferencing, it is hard to imagine that in those earlier days, it took thousands of dollars' worth of equipment and digital phone lines to achieve similar results. Of course, even today, you get what you pay for. So, it is still true that if we use more expensive cameras and software, the quality of the sound and images will be higher than what we can get for free. But, pedagogically, we can achieve similar results whether we spend next to nothing or hundreds or thousands of dollars.

However one choses to make it happen, connecting youngsters around the world with their peers is worth the effort. It will pay off for the teacher and for the students. It will also help advance the field of distance learning. Teachers will find their students anxious to put forth that extra effort to be able to present a great musical concert, share original poems, gather and analyze important data in a worldwide science experiment, ask pertinent questions of world-renowned experts and authors, and to write the best essays to share that are error-free. Teachers will be happy to see the enhanced motivation and active involvement that the medium inspires without thought of the grade as a motivator. By introducing youngsters to the use of compressed video at a young age, they may be expected to be ready participants in distance learning as a natural way to learn.

May this case study inspire you, the reader, to look around your own setting and see what new technologies are being used that you might repurpose to expand their value to make distance learning even more effective and valuable—as well as exciting!

QUESTIONS FOR ANALYSIS/DISCUSSION

1. What are the minimum items of equipment and other resources that you would need to operate a project connecting six schools in different parts of the world for monthly videoconferences?

2. What resource would you choose to use for your host if you were to create your own equivalent of the SAXophone project? To find out, investigate the different sources available to host a videoconferencing project today. List them in increasing order from the least expensive to the most expensive. Include a brief summary describing each source and their cost.

3. Do you agree that having young students participate in videoconferencing projects with external resources and other schools will make it easier for them to engage in distance learning later on? Support your response with references to the literature that led you to your conclusion.

4. What companies other than Polycom, Inc. and Cisco provide equipment and support for projects like SAXophone? Give your opinion of the level of support each gives.

5. If you were planning a compressed video project, which of the companies in the above question would you approach and why?
6. Do you think SAXophone was ahead of its time or do you believe it may have helped lead the way?
7. What lessons have you learned from the description of the SAXophone project that could be helpful to you?

REFERENCES

Kontos, G., & Mizell, A. P. (1997). Global village classroom: The changing roles of teachers and students through technology. *TechTrends, 42*(5), 17–22.

Lever-Duffy, J., McDonald, J., & Mizell, A. (2003). *Teaching and learning with technology.* Boston, MA: Allyn and Bacon.

McLuhan, M. (1964). *Understanding media: The extensions of man.* New York, NY: McGraw-Hill.

Mizell, A. (1997). SAXophone: Enhancing the global village via compressed video. *Distance Education Report, 1*(3), 1–3.

Mizell, A. (2005). Compressed video for the global village. In C. Howard, J. Boettcher, L. Justice, K. Schenk, P. Rogers, & G. Berg (Eds.), *Encyclopedia of distance learning, 1,* 317–322. Hershey, PA: Idea Group Reference. doi:10.4018/978-1-59140-555-9.ch048

School Buyers Online. (2010). Polycom programs spur classroom video collaboration globally. Retrieved from http://www.schoolbuyersonline.com/doc.mvc/Polycom-Programs-Spur-Classroom-Video-0001.\

APPENDIX A

Video Conferencing Opportunities

The Saxophone Project provides for school exchange programs in a variety of instructional topics. For schools and communities (business partnerships) having ISDN videoconferencing capabilities, this might be of interest.

SAXophone

   Welcome to the fifth year of SAXophone, our global videoconferencing project!! Through the use of videoconferencing, young people across the world will meet to discuss the following topics. Our schedule is established for the entire year; it should help you plan which sessions your school can participate in and enable you to make your reservation now. Remember, the number of ports available in most of our events is limited to eight so you should reserve immediately. You may preregister for any event by emailing with a cc.

   The overall theme for the year is: Looking Back to Make a Better Future.

SAXophone XXXI

Topic:	SAXomail (Students All over the world eXchanging over email)
	Student Council exchange project utilizing email, snail mail & video.
Coordinators:	Teddy Kjendlie & Al Mizell
Bridge:	Nova Southeastern University

SAXophone XXXII

Topic:	Students Around the World
	Cultural exchange program with students in Japan.
Coordinator:	MaryAnn Butler-Pearson
Bridge:	Ulster BOCES

SAXophone XXXIII

Topic:	Environmental Solutions
	A look at energy sources, nuclear power, and environmental solutions.
Coordinators:	Ulla Rodestam-Orsell & Rene Carver
Bridge:	Nova Southeastern University

SAXophone XXXIV

Topic:	A Poetic Look at Holidays
	An opportunity for students to share and comment on their original poetry focusing upon holidays

CHAPTER 19

FACULTY DEVELOPMENT

Features and Guidelines to Improve Online Course Communications

Kathryn Ley

ABSTRACT

Most evidence suggests online college and university students value interactions with their online instructor. On the other hand, redundant, superfluous, and inefficient online student communications can unnecessarily overwhelm instructors and undermine learning. This case describes how an instructional designer-instructor minimized redundant and superfluous communications and replaced almost all inefficient student-instructor communications with learning support interactions. The designer-instructor created online course features and communications grounded in theory and research from learner self-regulation and cognitive load to support learning. The designer-instructor created and formatively evaluated the features and communication guidelines using data from online courses and faculty colleagues trained to use both. The case documents the changes in the features and guidelines as they evolved during an iterative, three-year training process culminating in the faculty development materials presented with the case.

Real-Life Distance Education, pages 337–357
Copyright © 2014 by Information Age Publishing

INTRODUCTION

Dr. Fairly's experience teaching online entailed communication challenges unique to asynchronous learning environments yet common among online instructors (Vaughan, 2007; Mupinga & Maughan, 2008). The volume and nature of asynchronous online communications was especially daunting for online novices—both instructors and students. Fairly, an instructional designer and tenured faculty member in a graduate instructional technology program, had been designing and teaching online courses since arriving at her tenure-line position a few years previously. Teaching graduate online courses gave her a perfect opportunity to turn theory and research into practice. She could explain much of the volume and the nature of online communications based upon theory, research, and experience. The theory, garnered from studies on high- and low-achieving students' self-regulation (SR; Butler & Winne, 1995), and on extraneous cognitive load (ECL; Merriënboer & Sweller, 2005), informed her teaching and guided her course design.

SR theory and research explained learning as a function of specific activities associated with better academic performance. Online instructional features and course guidelines that engaged online learners in SR activities associated with higher achievement could systematically support online student SR (Clark, Nguyen, & Sweller, 2006; Leahy, Chandler, & Sweller, 2003; Ley & Young, 2001).

Cognitive load theory (van Merriënboer & Sweller, 2005) suggested two sources of ECL that are especially problematic for online courses. Learners who discover the same information in two or more places must then confirm information from different locations is the same; they experience ECL redundancy effects. Learners who must consult two or more information sources to retrieve and to integrate complementary information are coping with ECL split attention effects. Both effects challenged online learners but could be easily remedied with appropriate course design features and guidelines. Design could potentially eliminate split attention and redundancy effects for learners and help online instructors revise materials since updating information in two different places is more difficult than in one.

Fairly knew from experience that online communications were different from traditional classroom communications. The very nature of online communications rendered them more problematic than traditional classroom communications. Online communications required instructors and students to compensate for lack of visual and audio cues that accompanied traditional classroom interaction. Online miscommunications took longer to untangle without synchronous exchanges enhanced with audio and visual cues the classroom instructor and learner used to facilitate communications. Text communications are inherently more complex and time-consuming; humans are hardwired to take longer to read than to listen and longer to write than to speak.

Course communications affected SR and ECL. Whether student-student and student-instructor communications facilitated or impeded learning depended upon their effect on SR and ECL. Online communications features that supported SR and removed ECL could simultaneously help online students and their instructors. Communications guidelines and course features could easily direct learner attention to progress monitoring without introducing ECL if carefully designed. Likewise, prominent, conveniently accessed course communications could encourage student progress monitoring, a critical SR activity.

Fairly began incorporating communication features and guidelines consistent with SR and ECL theory and research (Bol & Garner, 2011; Kalyuga, 2011; Ley & Young, 2001; Roodenrys, Agostinho, Roodenrys, & Chandler, 2012; van Merriënboer & Ayres, 2005). She added communication features designed to induce learner SR activities. Added features organized online course materials, prompted active progress monitoring, and provided students evaluative and corrective information to guide their learning efforts and successfully meet course requirements. Specific online course features systematically organized information and communications, prompted students to compare their course progress to assignment requirements, and induced students to reflect upon how effectively they were studying. Features, such as a single-page assignment table displaying chronologically listed assignments with name, due date, point value, and submission location inherently aided student progress monitoring. An online student could easily confirm in one location, four essential assignment attributes, what, when, where, and worth. Class assignment status notices consistently published in the same single location prompted progress monitoring without adding ECL. Frequently updated future assignment reminders and past assignment status appeared when students accessed the course. The progress-monitoring notices listed forthcoming assignments and announced when assignments were under review, points were posted, and feedback e-mailed.

The unavoidable notices could capture learners' attention with immediate, constant updates on course progress and allowed students to conveniently compare what assignments were past and forthcoming to what assignments they had completed and which they still had to complete. Fairly increased routine, specific advice about effective learning activities and suggested completion milestones. Notices might advise learners which interim activities could lead to successfully completed assignments and which wasted effort. Poorly self-regulated students are much less able to discriminate between effective and ineffective learning processes; they fail to monitor and evaluate if what they did actually led to successfully completed assignments and exams. Corrective feedback on their submitted assignments implicitly provided students with information about how effectively they were studying. Online students could compare what they were doing to instructor-advised learning activities, successful assignment attributes, and test scores.

She derived, revised, and improved the features and guidelines in her online courses offered over many semesters thus continuously decreasing ECL barriers and increasing embedded SR support. The volume of redundant, unnecessary, and anxiously unhappy student communications decreased with continuously improving communication features and guidelines. Students rarely submitted late assignments or offered excuses about confused/forgotten due dates or technical problems. The online course features and guidelines had reduced ECL, systematically embedded SR support, and promoted SR communications such as corrective feedback. Proactively designed SR support and reduced ECL averted online students' questions about where assignment instructions were, when assignments were due, how to submit assignments, and other procedures. Now that she spent so much less time answering questions about submitting course assignments and locating or retrieving course materials, Fairly had more time to evaluate student assignments and provide individual feedback. In short, embedded SR and reduced ECL had created a more productive learning environment.

Other online instructors at the university complained about the same communications challenges that Fairly had largely overcome with embedded SR support and reduced ECL. She was certain her colleagues teaching online at her university could also benefit from both. Convincing faculty would be simple once they believed continuing current practices took more time and effort than an attractive alternative. They had to believe adding and using communication features and guidelines would save them more time and effort than continuing without them. Faculty would adopt the features and guidelines if they believed restructuring course communications would benefit them and their students and the accrued benefits would outweigh the adoption and implementation effort.

Faculty would recognize the value of changing how they structured online communications if the change would solve their frustrating communications problems. An effective change strategy would match an instructor's specific online communication problems to appropriate solutions an online instructor could easily adopt and implement. Whatever her approach, an effective change strategy would have to appeal to faculty. Training could present the problems and solutions but training required faculty time. Perhaps she could develop and formatively evaluate and revise training materials that faculty would eventually be able to access online. Faculty would be able to solve their own online course challenges without training; they could use a job aid to add the learning support and communication-facilitating features and tools. A job aid seemed to be an easy, convenient, alternative to training. A job aid could provide readily available solutions to any online instructor whether or not they wanted to attend training.

CASE STUDY

At the turn of this century, institutions began offering online courses, and Fairly, eager to design online courses, had accepted a faculty position in a 7500-student suburban commuter university. The university served upper division and graduate students who were predominantly nontraditional, working residents from the immediate community. Surrounded by developed communities, lacking campus housing and intermural sports, the university could not attract any more students than the 7,500 whose campus class commute time was feasible given their work and home locations. The university, one of four in a regional system, had few options to add satellite campuses; the regional and State board assigned each university a service area that gave them the exclusive right to offer courses or programs in any facilities in its assigned area. Online courses were new, few, and not included. If the university were to grow, attracting online students would finesse the urban commuter time-barrier and the assigned service area restriction.

Fairly was a good fit; she was eager to design online courses and the university's instructional technology graduate program was adding faculty to make a fully online program reality. The university had licensed WebCT, a learning management system (LMS), as part of a plan to deliver online courses and, eventually, online programs. Online courses would be one of the few mechanisms for increasing enrollments in the nascent instructional technology program that was beginning to offer online courses. With stimulus funds to encourage faculty participation, the engineering and education deans offered faculty a course release or compensation for each online course a faculty member would voluntarily develop.

The early faculty volunteers could ask their assigned instructional designer to help them create online course materials and negotiate the LMS technology. Several of the university's designers had recently graduated from the university's instructional technology program. The relatively inexperienced designers had to learn how the LMS worked and everyone, faculty and designers, was discovering what worked and what did not work in online courses. Software engineering and instructional technology faculty were among the very first to volunteer to design and teach online courses. Both groups had eager early adopters with technical and design skills that most faculty in other programs lacked. Their deans were also the first to give participation incentives such course releases and compensation for developing courses. These two programs became the first and, for a few years, the only programs at the university to offer students a fully online degree option.

More and more instructors were teaching online and the technology support staff trained them in LMS procedures, such as uploading files, recording grades, threading messages, creating discussion boards, etc. Technology training by the technology support staff was poorly attended unless mandated. Faculty regarded the button-clicking sessions about arcane LMS procedures as confusing, irrelevant, or both. The button-clicking skills for online LMS mechanics did not address online instructional issues such as teaching courses in which almost all class communications were written and read instead of spoken and heard. The few faculty teaching online agreed that the online students' continuously arriving emails and questions took much more time to answer than did traditional classroom questions. Considerably more up-front development time dropped dramatically once a course was ready to offer but student-instructor communications time did not.

Administrative Support for Training Online Faculty

To test her ideas about applying theory to practice to help online instructors, Fairly applied for faculty development leave. She proposed to train faculty with materials that would evolve into an online job aid. She would train faculty to use features and guidelines that would support online SR and reduce online ECL. Using training feedback, Fairly proposed to formatively evaluate, iteratively revise, and continuously improve draft materials until confident faculty could use the materials as a job aid without training or a trainer's explanation. Faculty could use it as a stand-alone job aid. The administration granted her leave request to train colleagues and convert the training materials she would develop into an online job aid.

Two training goals stipulated the desired training outcomes. Faculty participants would be able to decrease the amount of time and effort spent on organizing, locating, and retrieving instructional information and engaging in avoidable, redundant, or unnecessary communications with online learners. Faculty would have more time to spend on teaching because they would save time with the solutions they would learn. They would have more time to teach because they would waste less time moderating ECL effects and functions they could supplant with embedded SR support.

The job aid, an SR support and ECL reduction selection tool would be a print training aid distributed during training. The formative evaluation process would develop the print training aid into an online job aid for faculty. The job aid would enable faculty to readily identify online course features, policies, and activities that effectively, efficiently, and feasibly addressed problems exacerbated by ECL and poorly self-regulating learners.

She knew online instructors would be more willing to change how they helped students if they perceived the change as an improvement worth their time to implement and to maintain. The best way to develop a job aid would be to design and formatively evaluate the job aid would be to obtain feedback from online faculty. The job-aid design development plan was simple. Faculty would receive the draft aid as part of a training session in which Fairly would collect formative evaluation data. After each time she conducted the training session, Fairly would revise and improve the job aid.

Online Faculty Voluntary Attendance

Fairly wanted faculty to voluntarily attend training so she had to appeal to an obvious and compelling need—the gap between their traditional classroom time demands and online teaching time demands. The training sessions had to convince faculty that quick, easy, feasible, solutions offered an obvious, immediate, time-saving payback. Training would enable her to test and revise an online job aid to replace the training.

The training would have to appeal and attract as many faculty participants as possible since training was voluntary. A faculty listserv conveniently distributed Fairly's e-mail invitation (Figure 19.1) to which volunteers sent a reply reserving one of six training sessions. The invitation subject line gained faculty attention immediately because it addressed a common and commonly perceived online faculty instructional problem—the amount of time online instruction took. The training offered colleagues a compelling opportunity—a chance to eliminate their most time-wasting online communications and simultaneously help their online students. The e-mail invited faculty to voluntarily participate in a short, convenient training session that would be well worth their time. The e-mail invitation subject line "Saving Time teaching online . . . in just one session" preceded a message body in the style of for-profit training marketing materials (Figure 19.1). Fairly encouraged faculty participation in the invited sessions with personal, timely reminders. As soon as they reserved a session, each faculty member received an individual e-mail reply responding to their request and a reminder email within 24-hours prior to their scheduled session.

Fairly sent the e-mail invitation to 58 faculty whom the WebCt administrator verified had LMS shells for web-supported, web-enhanced, or web-only courses. She expected faculty who taught web-only or web-enhanced courses to be most likely to attend because they replaced most, or all, traditional classroom sessions with online activities and communications. Three full professors of business immediately reserved a session in response to the invitation. Fourteen more soon reserved one of six session times and two more asked for a different time. Eighteen of the 19 attended one of seven

> ### Saving Time Teaching Online
> ### Never Waste Hours of Time Teaching Online Again
>
> - Does writing student feedback and comments on their work take hours?
> - Do you spend time answering the same student questions over and over? Or answering student questions when they have the answers available online?
> - Do students have trouble keeping track of when and where assignments are due?
> - Do you often wonder how you can help them learn better and help yourself teach online more effectively and efficiently?
>
> Then I invite you to STOP wasting time online -- help yourself teach and help your students learn more efficiently with WebCT. Attend just one session to learn methods that WORK. These are methods I have taught at national conferences and now offer to you, my faculty colleagues, for the first time – and at NO CHARGE. You will learn how to
> *give students fast, efficient audio feedback;
> *organize and name assignments so students NEVER forget due dates;
> *establish a learning community that supports and motivates students;
> *replace reprimands with reminders
> . . . and more – spend two hours NOW and save hundreds in the future.
>
> WHO can attend? Any faculty scheduled to use WebCT in Spring to teach either online or web-enhanced courses.
> WHAT? One 2-hour training session taught by a Professor in Education. I have eight years of online teaching experience, two decades designing and teaching courses, and a PhD in instructional design.
> WHERE? The library training room inside the U Library, Building.
> HOW? Email or call me to reserve the session you want to attend
> WHEN? Next week - any ONE of the following times/dates*
> 1. Tues November 13th - 9:30 a.m. -11:30 a.m.
> 2. Tues November 13th - 1:30 p.m. -3:30 p.m.
> 3. Thurs November 15th - 9:30 a.m. – 11:30 a.m.
> 4. Thurs November 15th - 1:30 p.m. - 3:30 p.m.
> 5. Fri November 16th - 9:30 a.m. - 11:30 a.m.
> 6. Sat November 17 - 10:00 a.m. -12:00 p.m.
> *Please, only covered drinks allowed – no food in the Library training room.
>
> Reply to this email with the session number (one of the six offered) or send me an email to reserve your space; for more information call me.

Figure 19.1 Faculty development email invitation.

fall semester sessions and 23 more attended a single session immediately prior to the spring semester. About 10% of attendees anticipated future online courses but had not yet taught online. In less than two months, 41 (20%) of the full-time faculty at her university voluntarily attended training.

After the university sessions, Fairly expanded her trainee sample to faculty using other LMSs at other institutions. She invited community college faculty who taught on a different LMS platform a convenient session on their campus. Eleven, about a third of the invited online instructors, voluntarily attended the session. Twenty-eight attendees at a regional distance learning conference session provided even more formative evaluation feedback from faculty teaching online at diverse institutions. Eighty faculty had voluntarily attended one of Fairly's faculty development sessions at the regional conference, the community college, or her university by the end of the Spring semester. Eight faculty from a university session allowed Fairly to collect data about how they conducted online communications during the Spring semester after attending training.

Faculty Development Training Design and Development

Training preparation followed a standard design sequence: compose objectives that corresponded to the desired outcome, and then develop instruction. Two training objectives enabled faculty to benefit from applied ECL and SR theory. The first objective was to enable faculty to embed SR support in their online courses, and the second, reduce ECL in online courses. Based on SR and ECL literature and several years' experience applying the theories to online teaching, Fairly drafted a list of online features and guidelines that she had incorporated into her course to help learners in all online classes. The features and guidelines supported SR activities and reduced ECL redundancy and split-attention effects in online courses. The list guided training design and was developed into the job aid.

The training session was designed to guide faculty through each part of the job aid, from challenges to options and implementation strategies sequenced by challenge frequency. The introductory activity provided challenge frequency data that determined the order in which each option was presented. From experience Fairley had determined which challenges would probably be the most frequent among her colleagues.

The opening training activity established training relevance, introduced the training purpose, and captured trainee attention. The activity also provided formative evaluation data for the job aid and became the session standard introduction. The one-page introductory activity checklist (Figure 19.2) they received upon entering the session conveniently assessed faculty needs, tacitly revealed the session topics, and actively engaged faculty with the topics. Fairly handed the five who arrived at the first training session the checklist, "Which of the following online problems do you want to solve?" The checklist itemized 10 problematic online communications including redundant questions, questions answered in course materials, inappropriate messages, assignment due date questions, vague questions, filenames for assignment submissions, and requests for individual feedback.

All five of the first faculty trainees checked two or more of the communication behaviors; five checked students asking questions already answered online; five, students asking for individual feedback; four, different students

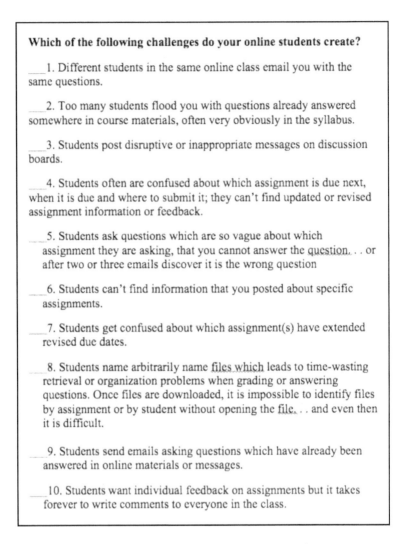

Which of the following challenges do your online students create?

_____1. Different students in the same online class email you with the same questions.

_____2. Too many students flood you with questions already answered somewhere in course materials, often very obviously in the syllabus.

_____3. Students post disruptive or inappropriate messages on discussion boards.

_____4. Students often are confused about which assignment is due next, when it is due and where to submit it; they can't find updated or revised assignment information or feedback.

_____5. Students ask questions which are so vague about which assignment they are asking, that you cannot answer the question. . . or after two or three emails discover it is the wrong question

_____6. Students can't find information that you posted about specific assignments.

_____7. Students get confused about which assignment(s) have extended revised due dates.

_____8. Students name arbitrarily name files which leads to time-wasting retrieval or organization problems when grading or answering questions. Once files are downloaded, it is impossible to identify files by assignment or by student without opening the file. . . and even then it is difficult.

_____9. Students send emails asking questions which have already been answered in online materials or messages.

_____10. Students want individual feedback on assignments but it takes forever to write comments to everyone in the class.

Figure 19.2 Faculty development introductory activity checklist.

e-mailing the same questions; four, too many students emailing questions already answered in the course materials or the syllabus; two, students asking vague questions and assignment file names which were uniquely individual and meaningless; each of the remaining four items received one check. Faculty responses verified that all items on the introductory activity checklist represented perceived faculty online problems relevant to the training and the job aid purpose although some were more pervasive than others. After the first five sessions, she had sufficient challenge data to verify and cluster challenges and then order them by challenge frequency. Options were ordered by the most frequently voted challenge that it resolved. Placing more common challenges at the beginning of training captured attention from the most faculty. The challenge that received the most faculty votes was placed in the first row on the table. Regardless of frequency, other challenges resolved by the same option were clustered with the most frequent challenge in the same row. Therefore, options and implementation strategies appeared only once in the matrix and challenges solved by the same options were placed together in the same row.

After the initial training, Fairly asked the director of the university professional development center to review the material. The director suggested two revisions: (a) replace *problems* with *challenges*, thereby enabling faculty to acknowledge challenges instead of admitting to problems and (b) replace *solutions* with *options*, a term connoting a range of ameliorating possibilities. These changes were made in the checklist, the job aid and the presentation slides. By the end of the five original small group sessions session, Fairly revised materials to include an option not yet formally in the training materials although it was described in the training session. The revised materials added an option that reduced avoidable ECL generated by text. The new, unique guideline option replaced written communication with synchronous duplex audio. An eleventh challenge checklist item that corresponded to the new guideline option was added: miscommunications unresolved by further text communications.

The third large group session venue, a regional distance learning conference session, yielded 23 more introductory activity checklists. The anonymous checklist responses continued to confirm faculty at other institutions experienced the same online communication. Every checklist item was selected by one or more faculty at each session, and these additional data verified content relevance. Community college and conference session attendance and needs assessment data confirmed online faculty from other institutions experienced the same online communications challenges as faculty at Fairly's university and the community college.

The standard training session sequence, established with the first session, remained the same: introductory activities followed by challenges, options, implementation and examples. When they arrived at a session, attendees were asked to complete the checklist. After collecting the completed checklists, Fairly welcomed participants, distributed the job aid as part of the training, and commenced an illustrated 45-minute presentation in which she introduced the most common challenges clustered by options to address the challenge and then the implementation activities.

The first job aid draft (Figure 19.3) clustered challenges with a solution and implementation strategy. Implementation strategies anticipated faculty

Online Problems with Solutions and Implementation

1. Multiple students in the same online class email you asking the same questions.

Solution 1: Dedicated Q/C discussion board that all student assignment questions.

Implementation 1: Syllabus policy requiring all course questions must be posted on Q/C board (or in person, or by telephone) but never email: state that this is to promote a learning community and equity of information throughout the class

Implementation 2: Repeating email on discussion board in message beginning with the phrase "Here is a great example of a question that should be post on the Q/C board since everyone should see my response" Always delete any student identifier in the email message you have copied to the discussion board message.

Implementation 3: Respond to any email by telling the student, he/she will find the answer on Q/C discussion board.

2. Too many students flood you with questions already answered somewhere in course materials, often very obviously in the syllabus.

Solution: Dedicated Q/C discussion board

Implementation 1: Whenever answering any assignment question about where, when, and how many points for an assignment tell them WHERE to find the answer without giving the answer.

3. Students post disruptive or inappropriate messages on public discussion boards.

Solution: Remove any such message immediately. To keep a record, move to a private disc board which only you can see.

4. Students often are confused about which assignment is due next, when it is due and where to submit it; they can't find updated or revised assignment information or feedback.

Solution 1: Assignment Table with columns for month number, due date, submission location code, and system for the assignment

Implementation 2: Create and chronologically sequence discussion board message that are for submitting specific message assignment.

Implementation 3: Create and chronologically sequence assignment or drop box titles for individual assignment submissions.

Solution 2: Every week announce next few assignments on the course homepage as a reminder

Implementation 1: List next few assignments with due dates in chronological order with brief reminder or notice of any updated information and where to find the updated information in the course

5. Students ask questions which are so vague about which assignment they are asking, that one cannot answer the question.

Solution 1: Require students are intuitive, standardized assignment names (such month number, due date) whenever referring to an assignment. Example: 10_4

Implementation 2: Syllabus communications policy should specify that students should include the standardized, intuitive assignment name in all messages subject lines when asking about a specific assignment on the discussion board or in email.

6. Students (and sometimes you) can't find information that you posted about specific assignments.

Solution 1: Use a dedicated INSTRUCTOR-only message board for any all, and only your messages to the class and begin every subject line for discussion board message with the standardized assignment name (such month number, due date, 11_1/7) or, if not an assignment, three or four words to specify the message subject

Implementation 1: Syllabus policy should specify that only YOU, the instructor should post messages on the instructor message board; student messages will be removed and must be reposted by the student.

Implementation 2: Syllabus policy should state that you will use YOUR instructor message board for all important communications about assignments. The policy should identify your other primary communication methods such as instructor answers on Q/C board and instructor homepage reminders – do NOT use email.

Implementation 3: If REMOVE any student message posted to instructor board immediately, quickly and discreetly; assume the student will repeat correctly if it is important.

Implementation 4: Syllabus policy should specify that students are responsible for reading. All confusing messages posted on the homepage, instructor message board, the Q/C board and in email!

7. Students (and sometimes you)

Solution 1: KEEP the original assignment name followed by the extension date whenever referring to the assignment; NEVER change the original due date – JUST extend with parenthetical notice

Implementation 1: Refer to the assignment only by original month number, due date followed by the extended time period or due date. Example: 10_4 (students until Nov 6

Implementation 2: Announce the extension on the homepage beginning with the original assignment (e.g., 10_4)

8. Students name arbitrarily name files which leads to time-wasting retrieval or organization problems when grading or answering questions. Once files are downloaded, it is impossible to identify files by assignment or by student without opening the file… and even then it is difficult.

Implementation 1: Syllabus policy requiring all assignment files begin with a seven character code, the month, due date and the student's last and first initials (or first two letters of last name for students with same initials in same class)

Implementation 2: Assignment instructions or syllabus policy which specifies a credit penalty if misnamed.

9. Students send emails asking questions which have already been answered in online materials or messages.

Solution: Dedicated Q/C discussion board.

Implementation 1: Syllabus policy which encourages students to answer each other's Q/C questions

Implementation 2:

Solution: Respond with WHERE to find the answer

Implementation 1: Respond professionally, kind and gentle reminder telling all where the answer is located in the course materials – avoid giving the answer unless you quote the material directly after you tell the location

Implementation 2: Be polite and considerate when directing students to the appropriate materials to answer the question but avoid giving the answer.

10. Students want individual feedback on assignments but it takes forever to write comments to everyone in the class.

Solution: Audio feedback in pdf files

Implementation 1: convert student assignments to one pdf file with all or one for each assignment and add audio feedback

Implementation 2:

Figure 19.3 Faculty development job aid to support sr & reduce ecl–first draft.

who may have attempted similar options without success; effective solution-options depended upon implementation.

The job aid format quickly evolved from challenge sections with option and implementation strategies to an outline by challenge (Figure 19.4) to a table (Figure 19.5) that visually separated each challenge cluster with its associated options and implementation strategies.

The outline job aid that listed each challenge had proven awkward so the aid was arranged by option to avoid repeating option and implementation strategies with each challenge resolved by the same option. To eliminate

---

Options For The Challenges Your Online Students Create

CHALLENGE #9 Students email questions answered in online materials.

Option: Dedicated Q/C discussion board.

Implementation 1: Syllabus policy which requires questions posted on dedicated discussion board Students email questions answered in online materials.

Implementation 2: Syllabus policy encourages students to answer each other's Q/C questions Students email questions answered in online materials.

Implementation 3: Acknowledge/reward students helping students – when a student offers a helpful response to any Q/C question, thread a discussion board message to the helpful message thanking the student for assistance.

CHALLENGE #10 Students want individual feedback

Option: Audio feedback

Implementation 1: Convert student assignments to one pdf file with all or one for each assignment and add audio feedback.

Implementation 2: Reply to email questions about grades with audio message.

CHALLENGE #1 Multiple students email same questions

Option: Dedicated Q/C discussion board for all student assignment questions.

Implementation 1: Syllabus policy requiring all course questions must be posted on Q/C board (or in person, or by telephone) but never email; state that this is to promote a learning community and equity of information throughout the class

Example Syllabus Policy: Ask your questions about the course requirements, content, assignments, etc., either in-class or on the Questions/Comments Discussion Board. Why? Equity -- everyone in the class is entitled to the same information and they have the opportunity to hear or read it if you use one of these two methods.

Message content. ANY and ALL questions about the course on the Questions/Comments board; only questions about your grade or your personal difficulties meeting course requirements should be in email.

Example Email Policy: Please use WebCT email only for emails about your grades and unique personal circumstances. If you forget and email questions about the course or assignments, I will post the question and response on the questions/comments discussion board.

Note: Delete only student name/id from their message and include the message in your disc board response.

Figure 19.4 Faculty development job aid revision by challenge.

Options to Meet the Challenges Your Online Students Create

Challenge	Options / Implementation
1. Different students in the same online class email you with the same questions. 2. Students flood you with questions already answered somewhere in course materials, often very obviously, in the syllabus. 9. Students send emails asking questions which have already been answered in online materials or messages.	Option 1: Dedicated Q/C discussion board for all student assignment questions. 1, 2, 9. Options 1a: Students-Helping-Students board. Implementation 1: Include a syllabus policy requiring all course questions be posted on a dedicated question/comments (Q/C) discussion board (or in person, or by telephone) but never email; state that this is to promote a learning community and equity of information throughout the class. Implementation 1a: Include a syllabus policy requiring all course questions be posted first on the students-helping-students board at least 12 hours before posting on the two-helping-students board at least 12 discussion board (or in person, or by telephone) but never email; state that this is to promote a learning community and equity of information throughout the class. Implementation 2: Repost every email question that violates your syllabus policy on a discussion board message beginning with the phrase "Here is a great example of a question that should be posted on the Q/C board since everyone should see my response." Always delete any student identifier in the email message you have copied to the discussion board message. Then respond to the violating email question about future assignments by telling the student, he/she will find the answer on Q/C discussion board. Implementation 3: Include a syllabus policy encouraging students to answer each other's Q/C questions. Implementation 4: Acknowledge/reward students helping students; for example, when a student offers a helpful response to any Q/C question, thread a discussion board message to the helpful message thanking the student for assistance.
3. Students post disruptive or inappropriate messages on discussion boards.	Option: Remove any such message immediately. To keep a record, move to a private disc board which only you can see 3. Implementation 1: Include a syllabus policy should state the instructor reserves the right to maintain a productive learning environment and promote a learning community and will remove any messages or information counter to those goals. Implementation 2: Remove any messages or information counter to those goals (usually anything that is inconsistent or cruel to other students. Note: usually it is completely unnecessary to do anything else. Offenders come soon enough.
6. Students can't find information that you posted about specific assignments.	Option: Use a dedicated INSTRUCTOR-only message board for any, all and only your messages to the class. 6. Implementation 1: Begin every message subject line on your dedicated discussion board with the standardized assignment name (such month, number, due date, 11-07) or if an assignment, three or four words to specifying the message subject. Implementation 2: Include a syllabus policy that you will use YOUR instructor message board for all communications about assignments. Then publicly identify your other primary communication methods such as instructor answers on Q/C board and instructor homepage reminders - do NOT use email. Implementation 3: REMOVE any student message posted to instructor board immediately, quickly and discretely; assume the student will repost correctly if it is important. Implementation 4: Include a syllabus policy that students are responsible for reading All instructor messages posted on the homepage, instructor message board, the Q/C board and in email.
7. Students confused about assignment() extended or revised due dates.	Option: KEEP the original assignment name followed by the extension date whenever referring to the assignment. 7. Implementation 1: Refer to the assignment only by original number_date followed by the extended time period or due date. Example: 10_4 (submit until Now is submit late penalty). Implementation 2: Announce the extension on the homepage beginning with the original assignment (e.g. 10_4) Implementation 3: NEVER change the original due date - JUST extend with penalty/feedback.
8. Students name arbitrarily name files which leads to time-wasting retrieval or organization problems when grading or answering questions. Downloaded, files may be impossible to identify assignment or by student without opening the file.	Option: Use a file-naming protocol which intuitively names the file with the assignment and student. 8. Implementation 1: Publish assignment instructions or syllabus policy which specifies a credit penalty if file-naming protocol not followed. Implementation 2: Include a syllabus policy that requires all assignment files begin with a secure character code, the month, due date and the student's last and first initials (or first two letters of last name for students with same initials in same class). Example: 10_04nk
4. Students are confused about which assignment is due next, when it is due and where to submit it; they can't find updated or revised assignment information or feedback.	Option 1: Assignment Table with columns for month number, due date, submission/location code, and points for the assignment. 4. Option 2: Every week announce next few assignments on the course homepage as a reminder. 4. Option 3: Announce any important information on the instructor message board and on a course homepage reminder. 4. Implementation 1: Whenever answering any assignment question about where, when, and how many points for an assignment refer the responded to the assignment table but also directly answer the question. Implementation 2: Create and chronologically sequence discussion boards for submitting specific message assignment. Implementation 3: Create and chronologically sequence assignment or drop box titles for individual assignment submissions.
5. Students ask questions which are so vague about which assignment they are asking, that you cannot answer the question, . . . or you discover after two or three emails discover it is the wrong question.	Option: Require students use which assignment they are asking about a specific month number, due date) whenever referring to an assignment 5. Implementation: Include a syllabus policy that requiring students use the standardized, intuitive assignment name in all message subject lines when asking about a specific assignment or an email. Implementation: When students do not use the standardized, intuitive assignment name when asking about a specific assignment, begin your reply with "I assume you are asking about [insert name here]" or ask the student to confirm assignment by standardized name.
10. Students want individual feedback on assignments but it takes forever to write comments to everyone in the class. 1. You reply to a message only to receive more questions about the same issue.	Option: Audio feedback. 10. Option: Use telephone for communications after any initial email miscommunications. 11. Implementation 1: Convert student assignments to one pdf file with all or one for each assignment and add audio feedback. Implementation 2: Reply to email questions about grades with audio message. Implementation 1: Reply to any 2nd email about the SAME issue from the same student with "Help me help you by calling me", or "Lets switch to synchronous listening and speaking instead of asynchronous writing and reading."

Figure 19.5 Faculty development job aid revision—challenge matrix.

redundancy, presenting options with all associated challenges in a table format was more effective for at least two reasons. The table format eliminated redundant text because options and implementation strategies were now listed once instead of under each challenge. The table displayed each option with multiple advantages; visually, one could see at a glance which options solved the most challenges and therefore held a greater potential return on invested effort to add it. The new revised job aid format remained the same after the initial five sessions; minor text revisions added clarity. The table format presented a challenge-option-implementation matrix that clustered 11 challenges with one of nine options. Challenge item numbers and text on the introductory activity corresponded to item numbers and text on the matrix.

From the first training session, faculty saw examples projected on a screen of how the options appeared in online course materials such as syllabus content and LMS displays. Faculty found examples presented with options useful because they requested electronic copies that could be replicated or adapted. Almost immediately, examples (Figure 19.6) were added to the electronic documents for which print copies were distributed at training.

This enabled quicker adoption since faculty did not have to compose guidelines or consider how to apply implementation strategies; instead they had only to copy or adapt examples. Three types of materials supported training sessions after the initial formative evaluation data from the first five sessions: the checklist, the challenge-option-implementation matrix job aid (Figure 19.5), and job aid examples. Examples changed from the university large group session to the community college LMS for the second large group session.

The formative evaluation process included five small group sessions followed by three large group sessions. During the process, Fairley revised materials based upon several factors. During and after training Fairley would make notes on materials whenever faculty asked questions or she realized the materials could be clearer or more useful. She would then revise the materials prior to the next training. After the five initial formative evaluation sessions and the third large group session (university, community college, and distance learning conference), she no longer received faculty questions or noted content or format issues that indicated gaps or required revision. Faculty questions could be answered with the information addressed in materials or they were asking questions about their unique circumstances. Such circumstances were either impossible to anticipate or feasibly address in materials without sacrificing job aid accessibility and parsimonious utility.

The original purpose of training was to develop a stand-alone job aid that faculty could use independently and access online. The job aid would lack some advantages face-to-face instruction afforded. For example, faculty

EXAMPLE Course Features and Guidelines

Instructor Discussion Board — All of my communications to the class will be posted on the Instructor's Discussion Board or on the homepage.

Questions/ Comments Discussion Board — Ask your questions about the course requirements, content, assignments, etc., first on the Students Helping Students Discussion Board to allow your classmates the opportunity to help you; if your question is not satisfactorily answered within 12 hours, then post the question on the Questions Discussion Board, not in email. Why? Equity — everyone in the class is entitled to the same information at the same time. If the assignment is due in less than 48 hours, call me (see next).

WebCT email: Please use WebCT email for all emails about your grades, your progress, your work, etc, but never for questions about the course. If you forget and do email a question about the course, I will post the question and answer on the discussion board.

Example of Announcements Page

HPR Student Announcements
Create Announcement
Announcements

7_12 Your progress report :
Status: Sent July 7, 2008 7:42 AM
see syllabus instructions

7_14 your contribution :
Status: Sent July 7, 2008 7:44 AM
Everyone submits something to help others: see syllabus assignment instructions

7_21 HPR N1 Interventions. What do you know? :
Status: Sent July 7, 2008 7:45 AM
Follow syllabus instructions carefully ... ask questions if you need clarification

7_26 The major assignment for the semester :
Status: Sent July 7, 2008 7:46 AM
Attend to the criteria and ask questions if you need clarification.

7_28 guidance :
Status: Sent July 16, 2008 12:47 PM
Need some advice - read my comments and guidance in my discussion board announce...

You folks found an amazing number of job boards! Now you must find sources for a your planner

Jul 21 chat 7p : room 1 :
Status: Sent July 17, 2008 10:15 AM
Class,
As of you should be working on drafts of the three sections required for the assign...

If you have questions about 7_28, you may post them on the instructor message b
stay for 15 minutes or until I have answered all questions whichever takes longer.

EXAMPLE – This is a one-page assignment table gives you and your students one chronological list of what is due, when, where, and a place to check when you have finished grading or they have submitted the assignments in the far right column (done).

Assignment Table

Mo	Dt	/Wk		Sub*	Pts	done
Aug	22	/ 1	Introduce yourself	DD	10	10
	25		Ask a question	D	B	
	26		Syllabus Orientation	Q	10	
Aug	27	/ 2	Quiz – Chapter 1 Introduction to Research	Q	15	
Sep	1		Quiz – Chapter 2 Quantitative, Qualitative, and Mixed Research	Q	15	
	2		One exp/quasi exp study reported in scholarly refereed journal article.	DD	150	
	4	/ 3	Quiz – Chapter 3 & 18 Research Questions; Preparing Proposals	Q	15	
	9		Research questions, hypothesis, abstract from your 9_2 study	DD	100	
	10	/ 4	Research questions, hypotheses, abstract		B	
	11		Quiz – Chapter 5 Measurement & Assessment	Q	15	
	14		Quiz – Chapter 7 Sampling	Q	15	
	16		Participant sampling/assignment procedures in your 9_2 study	DD	100	
	17	/ 5	Quiz – Chapter 4 Ethics	Q	15	
	23		Ask a question	D	B	
	24	/ 6	Quiz – Chapter 8 Research Validity	Q	15	
Oct	1	/ 7	Quiz – Chapter 6 Data Collection Methods	Q	15	
	8	/ 8	Methods/design		-	
	15	/ 9	Quiz – Chapter 15 & 16 Descriptive & Inferential Statistics	Q	15	
	21		Methods/design from your 9_2 study	DD	100	
	22	/ 10	Quiz – Chapter 9 Experimental	Q	15	
	23		Ask a question	D	B	
	29	/ 11	Quiz – Chapter 10 Quasi-experimental	Q	15	
	30		Quiz – Chapter 11 Non-experimental (e. g., correlational)	Q	15	
Nov	4		Lit review & research questions, hypotheses for your proposal	DD	100	
	5	/ 12	Peer review 11_4	DD	50	
	11		Sampling/Procedures for your proposal	DD	100	
	12	/ 13	Peer review 11_11	DD	50	
	18		Design for your proposal	DD	200	
	19	/ 14	Peer review 11_18	DD	50	
	26	/ 15	Research Proposal – Questions due Q/C Board			
Dec	3		Research Proposal	A	800	
			Total pts		2000	

*Submission location codes: D – Q/C disc brd, DD – due date designated disc brd, DD – peer evaluation submitted to DD for evaluated assignment, A – assignment encl, Q – quiz brd, LAS – List association system on Subt page. Sub column identifies WHERE you will submit the assignment.

Figure 19.6   Faculty development job aid examples sr support & ECL reduction.

training session attendees could ask an expert online faculty instructor for advice. The instructor could provide timely, relevant, and useful options for resolving their online challenges given their instructional environment. Novice online faculty could benefit from their expert colleague's individual guidance and identify an optimum solution a novice might not consider. Training had a distinct advantage over the job aid alone in other ways. The faculty instructor was a credible model offering realistic guidance and encouragement to adopt and adapt the features and tools they received with the job aid and examples.

At the end of the semester following training, nine university faculty agreed to answer questions about the how and if they were using any on the online aids. All participants had adapted or were using two or more options for saving time by supporting SR and minimizing ECL. Three of the eight were using six of the nine options; two, four options; one, three options; two, two options. The two who used the fewest options were teaching web-enhanced courses which had some face-to-face meetings. Only one option was adopted by all participants, using a dedicated discussion board for students to ask questions about course content and completing assignments instead of e-mailing the instructor. Five of the eight had syllabi with an explicit policy reserving e-mails for personal requests. Five reminded students with public messages about future assignment due dates. Three had applied their policy to remove disruptive messages from the public discussion board. Three used some form of assignment table which displayed assignments in chronological order with assign points, due date, and submission location. Three required students use a standardized file-naming convention when submitting assignment files. Four provided audio feedback to students assignment converted to pdf files; two wanted to use audio feedback but did not have the software; only one suggested that audio comments were as time-consuming as written comments, and therefore not worth the trouble. Two used homepage announcements to prompt students about assignments. None of them had asked students to switch to synchronous telephone communications since none had found students written communications warranted it.

Faculty had innovated communications techniques that furthered the class as a learning community; at least two were using a "student-helping-student" message board, one had a syllabus policy to use this board as a prerequisite to asking the instructor. Four of the eight faculty identified the most time-consuming online teaching task took the same amount of time in their face-to-face courses: evaluating student's submitted assignments. All nine faculty surveyed the semester after receiving training reported that grading papers, which was the same for online as face-to-face classes, was their most time-consuming instructional activity.

IMPLICATIONS FOR DISTANCE EDUCATION

There are several implications of this case that confirm existing literature on faculty development. For example, certain factors motivate faculty to engage in faculty development. A faculty organization sponsoring the training, former participants recommending the training, and a faculty trainer can add credibility and boost willing faculty participation. Faculty are willing to listen to a credible trainer who speaks from relevant experience; that is, another online faculty member. The faculty trainer easily attracted faculty to attend voluntary training sessions; almost two dozen attended the session sponsored by a formal faculty support organization. Word-of-mouth promotion by faculty who participated in earlier sessions may also have motivated participation.

Another factor affecting faculty development is explicitly tying the faculty development purpose to a documented and relevant need. Faculty training that clearly addresses a problem that faculty perceive is a problem will attract their voluntary attendance. Faculty laboring under undesirable conditions are much more open to answers because dissatisfaction with the status quo stimulates change. In this case, the problem was the amount of time online instruction took; the gap between faculty time wasted and avoidable time wasted was a need the training addressed. The initial training invitation offered an alternative to this undesirable condition that undermined online teaching. Every invitation and even the title of the training promised to resolve this pressing faculty problem. Training objectives and announcements stated positive and desirable instructional outcomes for faculty who attended. The invitation promised resolution to problems they were experiencing and they willingly responded to faculty development invitations.

Systematically designed training and online support materials may require only minor revisions. The first design step was a needs assessment. In this case, Fairly had identified instructional communications problems attributable to poor learner SR and ECL in her online courses. Features that could compensate for poor SR and remove ECL were added and tested in courses. The training and job aid objectives addressed the need documented from personal experience, professional literature, and relevant theory. Systematic design to determine needs and objectives assured acceptable materials almost immediately and formative evaluation data from small group training sessions was used to refine instructional materials.

Faculty development to build their online teaching skills should include how to provide SR support and minimize ECL. Data collected from faculty who participated in these sessions clearly indicated they had the same kinds of problems that these particular features had already resolved in multiple courses. Furthermore, faculty were interested enough to voluntarily attend sessions to learn how to ameliorate the effects of poor self-regulation and online ECL. Although many online faculty members find ways to resolve some problems exacerbated by poorly self-regulating students and ECL, faculty development can decrease the learning curve. Furthermore since faculty resist teaching online in part because of the time it may require, offering faculty easily-adopted/adapted time-saving solutions may assuage anxiety fomented by the prospect of constant counterproductive student interactions.

This faculty development process implies faculty development can occur at many points on a continuum of commitment and effort from both the trainer and trainee. At the lowest commitment and effort, a job aid with examples could be distributed to online faculty. At a slightly higher level would be to offer examples from the LMS that faculty would receive with the job aid matrix. At the highest level, faculty training sessions with both the job aid matrix and relevant LMS examples would be available. Although the features and guidelines can be implemented through standard LMS features such as discussion boards, e-mail, and announcements areas, supplementing the training with LMS-specific examples accompanied by the button-clicking procedures might be helpful for faculty preparing to teach online for the first time.

CONCLUSION

Faculty development success depended upon several factors. Features were adopted if faculty saw them as feasible, immediate options to their perceived online challenges. Hence dedicated discussion boards which were easily added to courses and course syllabus procedures managed online communications effectively with little implementation effort. Some adapted the students-helping-students discussion board and the student questions/comments message board. Some liked the assignment table or announcements.

They were less likely to adopt a feature that required more intensive or continuous effort or for which they were satisfied with their own approach. Options that required revisions to online features every semester were not adopted. Faculty did not adopt the assignment naming convention that used one label incorporating the due date into the name. This feature required additional and potentially extensive changes in most online courses every semester since every time the assignment name was used for a discussion board name, drop box name or other tool linked by assignment by name, the date component had to change. Options that offered low-value benefits were not adopted. The file naming convention enabled an instructor to tell which assignment and whose it was in less than seven characters, but faculty either did not value that level of organization, found student compliance more challenging than the organizational benefits, or may have had other organizational methods they considered sufficient. Faculty members with extensive online experience did not adopt features as readily and were more resistant to change what they did. Others were already using variations of some features. Their response would be consistent with the literature that indicates that online experience enables faculty to improve their efficiency managing online communications over time.

QUESTIONS FOR ANALYSIS/DISCUSSION

1. How was the need for improving online communications documented?
2. Why did faculty voluntarily participate in training?
3. Why might faculty have adopted the features and guidelines to support SR and to reduce ECL?
4. What might be other barriers to adapting the features and guidelines?
5. What other features, guidelines, student or faculty activities might support SR?
6. What other features, guidelines, student or faculty activities might reduce ECL?
7. How was training success measured and documented?

REFERENCES

Bol, L., & Garner, J. K. (2011). Challenges in supporting self-regulation in distance education environments. *Journal of Computing in Higher Education, 23,* 104–123. doi:10.1007/s12528-011-9046-7

Butler, D. L., & Winne, P. H. (1995). Feedback and self-regulated learning: A theoretical synthesis. *Review of Educational Research, 65,* 245–282.

Clark R. C., Nguyen, F., & Sweller, J. (2006). *Efficiency in learning: Evidence-based guidelines to manage cognitive load.* San Francisco, CA: Pfeiffer, Wiley.

Kalyuga, S. (2011). Cognitive load theory: How many types of load does it really need? *Educational Psychology Review, 23*(1), 1–19.

Leahy, W., Chandler, P., & Sweller, J. (2003). When auditory presentations should and should not be a component of multimedia instruction. *Applied Cognitive Psychology, 17,* 401–418.

Ley, K., & Young, D. B. (2001). Instructional principles for self-regulation. *Educational Technology Research and Development, 49,* 93–105.

Mupinga, D. M., & Maughan, G. R. (2008). Web-based instruction and community college faculty workload. *College Teaching, 56*(1), 17–21.

Roodenrys, K., Agostinho, S., Roodenrys, S., & Chandler, P. (2012). Managing one's own cognitive load when evidence of split attention is present. *Applied Cognitive Psychology, 26,* 878-886. doi:10.1002/acp.2889

Vaughan, N. (2007). Perspectives on blended learning in higher education. *International Journal on E-Learning, 6*(1), 81–94.

Van Merriënboer, J. J. G., & Ayres, P. (2005). Research on cognitive load theory and its design implications for e-learning. *Educational Technology Research and Development, 53*(3), 5–13. doi:10.1007/BF02504793

Van Merriënboer, J. J. G., & Sweller, J. (2005). Cognitive load theory and complex learning: Recent developments and future directions. *Educational Psychology Review, 17*(2), 147–177.

FURTHER READINGS

Gannon-Cook, R. (2010). *What motivates faculty to teach in distance education? A case study and meta-literature review.* Lanham, MD: University Press of America

Wolcott, L. L., & Betts, K. S. (1999). What's in It for Me? Incentives for faculty participation in distance education. *Journal* of *Distance Education, 14*(2), 34.

Wolcott, L. L., & Shattuck, K. (2007). Faculty participation: Motivations, incentives, and rewards. *Handbook of Distance Education,* 377–399.

CHAPTER 20

PROFESSIONAL DEVELOPMENT AND TRAINING FOR DISTANCE INSTRUCTORS IN HIGHER EDUCATION

Xiaoxia Huang, E-Ling Hsiao, and Les Lunce

ABSTRACT

The purpose of this chapter is to describe and discuss a case of faculty development and training for distance instructors in a medium-sized university in the Midwest of the United States. The faculty development and training model includes five key elements: professional development workshops, customized training and consultation, online course development and support, instructional technology support, and faculty learning communities. Each of the elements and its impact on faculty development is described and discussed in detail. In so doing, we hope readers will (a) identify and apply best practices and processes of professional development and training for distance instructors, (b) identify challenges of professional development and training for distance instructors and corresponding solutions, (c) identify and apply strategies for diffusion and adoption of instructional technologies among distance instructors, and (d) identify and apply strate-

Real-Life Distance Education, pages 359–376
Copyright © 2014 by Information Age Publishing
359

gies to evaluate the effectiveness of professional development and training programs for distance instructors.

INTRODUCTION

Recent years have seen the increasing popularity of distance education in higher education institutions. According to a national survey on distance education at degree-granting postsecondary institutions conducted by the National Center for Education Statistics (NCES), during the 2006–2007 academic year, 66% of responding 2-year and 4-year Title IV eligible, degree-granting institutions offered online, hybrid/blended, or other types of distance education courses. The estimation of total enrollments in credit-granting distance education courses is 12.2 million (Parsad & Lewis, 2008). As distance education plays an increasingly significant role in higher education, it presents unique challenges for instructors as distance education "requires special techniques of course design, special instructional techniques, special methods of communication by electronic or other technology, as well as special organizational and administrative arrangements" (Moore & Kearsley, 1996, p. 2), which can present a steep learning curve to instructors new to distance education.

To ensure the quality of distance education, it is important to support instructors in their professional development and training. Since the emergence of faculty development and training as a new and distinctive field in the 1960s, the field has seen rapid growth (Ouellett, 2010; Schönwetter, Dawson, & Britnell, 2009). Faculty development is a "process which seeks to modify the attitudes, skills, and behavior of faculty members toward greater competence and effectiveness in meeting student needs, their own needs, and the needs of the institution" (Francis, 1975, p. 720). Changing faculty's attitudes, skills, and behavior in relation to distance education can be challenging as it involves a shift from the face-to-face paradigm to the distance education paradigm. A solid, well-planned professional development and training program for distance instructors is essential to enable them to achieve the level of competence and effectiveness required for quality distance education.

The focus of this chapter is a case of faculty development and training program for distance instructors at a public regional university in the Midwest of the United States. Founded in 1865, this university has an enrollment of 11,494 students as of 2010, with 9373 undergraduates and 2121 graduates. A significant number of the student population is first-generation and low-income students. The student body consists of 78.3% in-state students, 17.1% out-of-state students (52 states and territories represented), and 4.6% international students (56 countries represented). The average class size is 33 students. The university employs around 500 tenure and tenure-track faculty and about 1000 full-time staff. It offers more than 100 majors at the Bachelor's, Master's, Doctorate, or Education Specialist levels in five colleges: College of Arts & Sciences, College of Business, College of Education, College of Nursing Health & Human Services, and College of Technology.

Like many institutions in higher education, distance education at the university is becoming increasingly important due in part to its flexibility, convenience, and accessibility. Currently more than 30 undergraduate or graduate degrees and professional development programs are offered via distance education, including those offered entirely via distance and those requiring minimal campus visits. Distance courses are offered mainly via the Web, and Blackboard is the course management system used by the university.

One goal of the university's strategic plan is to recruit and retain highly qualified and skilled faculty. In alignment with this strategic plan, faculty development and training for distance instructors at the university is facilitated by the Center for Instruction, Research, and Technology (CIRT). The major mission of CIRT is supporting faculty in the creation of optimum teaching and learning environments. CIRT is composed of 10 units, including Academic Programming, Graphic Design, Instructional Design, Learning Spaces Support, Grant Support, and Visualization. Working together with the CIRT administration, the Instructional Design area is the main unit responsible for professional development and training of instructors for face-to-face, hybrid and online courses. The original team of four full-time instructional designers has recently been reduced by half due to budget constraints. There are four graduate students assisting the instructional design team, each working 15–20 hours a week. Instructional designers conduct faculty workshops on topics related to instructional technologies and strategies, coordinate and consult with instructors to support the design, development, and delivery of face-to-face, hybrid, and online instruction, and provide technical assistance to instructors who encounter problems with instructional technology tools. The instructional design team also works with CIRT administration in facilitating the formation of faculty learning communities to promote faculty collaboration and sharing of knowledge on teaching and learning improvement.

The next part of the chapter will describe in detail the faculty professional development and training model currently employed at CIRT. In general, based on observations, workshop surveys, program documents/reports, and feedback from instructors, the CIRT model of faculty development and training programs has had positive impact on distance instructors. However, there are also issues or questions to consider to improve the program. By studying and analyzing this case, we hope readers will be able to: (a) identify and apply best practices and processes of professional development and training for distance instructors, (b) identify challenges of professional development and training for distance instructors and corresponding solutions, (c) identify and apply strategies for diffusion and adoption of instructional technologies among distance instructors, and (d) identify and apply strategies to evaluate the effectiveness of professional development and training programs for distance instructors.

CASE STUDY

The faculty professional training and development model currently employed at CIRT mainly consists of the following key activities: (a) workshops related to instructional technologies and instructional strategies, (b) one-on-one customized sessions or consultations based on instructor needs, (c) instructional software support, (d) online course design and development, and (e) facilitation of faculty learning communities. Each element is described below in detail to give readers an in-depth look at the case.

Workshops are frequently used for faculty development in higher education. A well-planned and conducted workshop can have a significant and long-term impact on participants (Bland, 1980). CIRT offers the *Passport to Faculty Development* program each fall, spring, and summer semester, which consists of a variety of professional development workshops related to instructional technologies and strategies. Workshop topics are developed based on research in the area and needs assessment through conversations with faculty and feedback from previous workshops. Example workshop topics include: online teaching strategies and best practices, synchronous and asynchronous communications, e-learning design tools, Web 2.0 technologies, web-based assessment, and teaching with the Blackboard CMS. Objectives for each workshop are carefully planned in an effort to address the learning needs of the instructors.

The instructional design team plans and conducts most of the workshops. In addition, each semester CIRT invites other professionals on campus to conduct workshops related to their areas of expertise, for example, library resources. Workshops are designed to provide hands-on experience for participants and engage them in the learning process through strategies such as demonstrations, reflections, discussions, and hands-on activities. In so doing, the workshops aim to focus on knowledge increasing, skills building, problem solving, and systemic change (Brooks-Harris & Stock-Ward, 1999). Workshops are usually conducted in the CIRT conference room, which is equipped with 2 presentation computers (one of which is a Sympodium), two projectors, one Tegrity recorder, and 24 laptops for participant use. Most workshops run for 1.5–2 hours. In addition, 1–3 day workshops focusing on a specific topic in depth are offered, for example, *teaching in an online environment series* ranging from managing online content, delivering online content, to assessing online learning. Many workshops are conducted more than once over a semester to give faculty different choices of dates and times for a particular topic. There are 2–3 workshops offered each week on average. To encourage more instructors to attend the workshops, an incentive of $300 is provided for tenured, tenure-track, and special purpose faculty who complete five workshops during a semester. At the end of each workshop, participants complete an evaluation survey sharing their thoughts on the workshop quality, their learning, and their future plans on how to apply what they have learned.

In addition to workshops, instructional designers provide customized training and consultation for instructors who are not able to attend the workshops or who have specific needs on a topic related to teaching and learning. Customized training and consultation on a one-on-one basis is an effective mode of faculty development as it focuses on each individual faculty member's specific needs with the consideration of his or her unique backgrounds and learning styles. At the same time, individualized focus can be time-consuming. Indeed, one-on-one consultation has been claimed to be "the most time-consuming, yet most rewarding" activity in faculty development and training (Lewis, 2002, p. 59). At CIRT, customized sessions usually range from 1 to 2 hours. If more time is needed, additional session(s) are scheduled.

Workshops and some one-on-one consultations are more aligned with the stages of *knowledge, persuasion,* and *decision* of an innovation-decision process; however, not until faculty implement the technologies in teaching and learning does *overt behavior change* occur (Rogers, 2003). Further, since technology is an integral part of distance education, in order for faculty to continue using the technologies they have adopted, post-adoption technology support is essential for professional training and development for distance instructors. A wide variety of instructional software are supported by CIRT, including: the Blackboard CMS; the Learning Objects package of blog, wiki, and podcast; a synchronous communication tool, Elluminate Live! (now Blackboard Collaborate); the Tegrity Campus 2.0 lecture capture tool; interactive multimedia design tools Adobe Presenter and Lectora Publisher, and many others. The instructional design team provides documentations, online tutorials, and FAQs, in addition to one-on-one consultations, to support the post-adoption use of technologies. The instructional design team also works with the Help Desk of the university to provide support such as trouble-shooting and problem-solving to aid distance teaching and learning. In so doing, we hope to promote not only the awareness of instructional technologies, but also the actual use of these technologies in distance education.

Another integral part of distance education support is collaboration with faculty in systematically designing and developing online courses. Any instructor can request help from instructional designers for online course development, whether redesigning an existing online course, converting a face-to-face course to an online course, or designing and developing a complete new online course from scratch. Some instructors come to the online course design and development help voluntarily; others were under contract with the Office of Distance Services. Online course development is a team-based process. Instructional designers work extensively with faculty from the initial planning stages to the full development of hybrid or online courses, which usually is a semester-long project. Instructional designers meet regularly with instructors to plan the design and development of the courses as well as discuss and suggest effective technology tools and online teaching strategies as appropriate. Whenever necessary, instructional designers provide faculty with training in the use of technology tools. In addition to collaborating with faculty regarding the interface design, content design, activities design and assessment design of a particular course, instructional designers coordinate with the graphic designers, programmers, video production, or 3D visualization staff at CIRT when the respective expertise is desired for developing the course.

If a course design and development project is under contract with Distance Services, instructors need to complete a 10-week "Good Online Teaching and Learning" program facilitated by CIRT and instructional designers. The purpose of the program is to engage participants in discussing a variety of important topics in distance education, such as assessment and copyright issues, and to better equip the instructors with the knowledge, skills, and tools needed for quality online education. The program is delivered via different communication modes, including face-to-face meetings, online synchronous meetings, and online asynchronous communication via Blackboard. Once an online course under contract is developed, instructional designers evaluate and approve the course before its delivery to students. Courses are evaluated based on criteria related to course organization, use of technology, learner support and resources, instructional design and delivery, interactivity, and assessment. An incentive of $2,000 is provided to instructors whose courses meet the minimum requirements delineated in the evaluation rubric.

In the interest of providing an engaging professional development experience, CIRT also actively sponsors the formation of formal learning communities for faculty. Faculty learning communities (FLCs) are cross-disciplinary groups engaged in an active, collaborative, year-long program, structured to provide encouragement, support, and reflection (Cox, 2002). CIRT's instantiation of FLCs is derived from the concept of communities of practice such that both novice and expert are actively engaged in the practice of teaching and learning (Hsu, 2004; Pringle, 2002). Wenger (1998, p. 145) has defined communities of practice as "an interaction between experience and competence." The emphasis in FLCs is towards the mentor/mentee relationship rather than the master/apprentice relationship characteristic of most communities of practice (Wenger, 1998). In a well-functioning learning community, the novice gains competence by engaging with the seasoned expert (Wenger, 1998).

FLCs are also grounded on the concept that learning is essentially experiential and social (Wenger, 1998). Effective FLCs are inaugurated by the agreement of community members upon a clearly defined set of goals. Goals should include providing professional development opportunities for both new and seasoned faculty, promoting intercollege and cross-discipline collaboration, encouraging discussion of best practices as well as facilitating knowledge creation and dissemination (Lock, 2006; Wazienski, 2007). FLCs also constitute a forum where faculty can discuss the scholarship of teaching and learning as documented by Aucoin (2009). A commitment to competence, respect for expertise and collaborative investigation on the part of novice and expert are essential to achievement of the FLC's goals (Wenger, 1998).

FLCs are formed at the beginning of each fall and spring semester and may continue throughout the academic year. CIRT strives to include FLC members from the widest possible array of colleges and disciplines within the university. FLCs typically consist of five to seven invited faculty members who have expressed interest in a particular topic and/or who are conducting active research relevant to that topic (Code, 2005; Offutt, Smart, & Pearson, 2009). Restricting FLC size to five to seven invited faculty lends a collegial yet informal atmosphere to group activities as well as facilitating opportunities for all members to participate equally. Topics are both suggested by CIRT administration and solicited from faculty. Past learning community topics have included concept mapping, gender matters in the professoriate, social networking and building an online community. FLC members may select to meet face-to-face and/or online (Hsu, 2004). Synchronous online meetings are conducted using the Elluminate Live collaboration software. Asynchronous collaboration is carried out through the Blackboard CMS. Integration of online synchronous/asynchronous and face-to-face communication modalities facilitates equitable and democratic participation and contribution on the part of all community members (McConnell, 2009; Pringle, 2002).

Faculty collaboration through FLCs is facilitated by active discussion, critical thinking, and presentation. Each FLC member is expected to make a presentation to the community, complete a reflective activity, and contribute actively to the body of knowledge germane to the topic under investigation (Aucoin, 2009). To motivate already busy faculty to add another activity to their calendars, each participant receives a $500 stipend for full participation in the program, payable upon completion of FLC goals and submission of an FLC report.

Satisfaction, Challenges, and Potential Solutions

In the previous section, we have described the key activities consisting of our professional development and training program for distance instructors. Assessing the effectiveness of the program is critical for its improvement and accountability. We have collected some information that helps us to make an initial assessment of the program. General quantitative data collected each academic year includes the number of workshops, one-on-one consultations, online course design and development projects completed, as well as the number of participants. Qualitative information about our program is mainly garnered through workshop surveys, observations, program documents/reports, and informal feedback from the instructors. Generally speaking, we have received positive feedback regarding the professional development and training model. However, there are also challenges posed at the same time.

Satisfaction

For each professional development workshop, participants rate from 5 (Strongly Agree) to 1 (Strongly Disagree) on their perceived learning ("I understand and can describe the basic technologies and/or concepts covered in this program"; "I can use and/or apply the technologies and/or concepts covered in this program") and facilitator performance ("The facilitators were open to comments and questions from the participants"; "The facilitators were helpful in addressing specific questions and issues that arose during the program"). Participants are also asked about their overall impression of the workshop ("Would you recommend this program to other faculty members?"), their reflections on the learning ("Please share your reflections, i.e., how you will use these technologies and/or concepts in your teaching"), and additional comments for program improvement ("Please feel free to provide any additional comments and suggestions for improving the program."). In general, participants provided positive feedback to our workshops. We received an average of more than 4 points for each question on perceived learning and facilitator performance, and more than 98% participants indicated that they would recommend the programs to their colleagues. Example instructor comments include:

> "I will use this technology when I teach online for the first time. It offers lots of ways to convey course content and involve students in active learning."

> "I am excited to learn more about Elluminate and to use this technology in my classroom to better accommodate distance students."

> "I plan to design lessons using Lectora for my classes. The rich multimedia content as well as the ability to gather all resources in one location will help me organize my course content as well improve the learning process."

"I am thinking about ways in which I can tailor the use of blogs and wikis to my class based on what was presented today. I believe I can use blogs effectively for generating individual responses to current business articles on strategy in my classes. Wikis would be useful in group projects that students do in my classes...Based on what I have learnt today, I think using wikis for group projects would make the member contributions more transparent to the instructor and thereby help with the problem of fairness in grades assignment for group projects...Thanks for a good workshop. The presentation was clear, well-organized and the pace was just right."

Similarly, instructors who have had one-on-one consultations or online course design and development with us often commented on the helpfulness of these programs. However, as mentioned previously, we have also encountered challenges that we hope can be addressed to improve our professional development and training model.

Low Workshop Attendance

First, although instructors who attended the workshops generally provided positive feedback, the workshop attendance rate has been relatively low. The average number of participants is 2–3 instructors per workshop for the spring and fall semesters, although the attendance rate rises slightly for the summer semester. An average of six faculty members completes five or more workshops a semester.

Several reasons could have contributed to the relatively low attendance issue. First, faculty schedule conflict is a problem. Faculty members are busy with teaching, research, and service activities, and very often their schedule is in conflict with the workshop schedules. One strategy CIRT is planning is to reach out and offer tailored sessions in different departments or colleges when most instructors are available, such as during a department or college meeting. A few sessions have been conducted in this way upon requests and the feedback has been very positive. To effectively promote this strategy, however, department chairs or deans will need to be willing to serve as the change agent who encourage faculty in incorporating instructional technologies and strategies in their teaching (Rogers, 2003). Second, lack of awareness of the workshops can be another reason for low attendance. In the past, CIRT printed *Passport to Faculty Development* program booklets and sent a copy to each faculty's office to promote the awareness of the workshops. Due to budget cuts, the printing of program booklets was stopped. Instead, CIRT mails out a postcard every semester reminding faculty of new and repeated programs. In addition, instructors can access online information posted in the university calendar and CIRT's website. However, this requires more initiative from faculty to look for the information. Third, many workshops are repeated every semester as they involve fundamental skills regarding distance education. Instructors who are innovators and early adopters may already have taken the workshops. It will take more deliberate effort to encourage *late majority* and *laggards* (Rogers, 2003) to attend the workshops.

Limited Staffing for One-on-One Consultations

In addition, many instructors have expressed their preference for customized sessions over group workshops because of the tailored focus on their specific needs and questions. This should not be a problem when the instructional design area is fully staffed. However, it can be challenging with only two instructional designers on staff. The instructional designers conduct about 300 customized sessions a year. Sometimes it is difficult to handle when more requests are received. To help address the problem, instructional designers have trained their graduate students to help with one-on-one customized sessions. However, students graduate or leave, and recruiting and training new students to be able to independently handle consultations takes time. As an alternative, instructional designers are working with the CIRT Academic Programmer on a project to build a searchable and interactive online knowledge base to replace the static-html online tutorials that are provided. This knowledge base will include constantly updated FAQs, a searchable database containing up-to-date online tutorials and resources, a place for users to ask questions, and other relevant information. CIRT is also considering ways to more effectively use the CIRT liaison program. CIRT invites a faculty member from each college to be a CIRT liaison. The liaisons' main responsibility is to advise CIRT administration on issues of relevance to faculty. CIRT liaisons also serve as the first contact point for colleagues by providing suggestions and feedback on distance learning issues. We are considering better engaging the liaisons to help their colleagues in integrating technology into teaching and learning.

Dealing with Technology Upgrade/Replacement

Another challenge we have encountered is related to helping faculty adjusting to the environment for technology upgrades or replacements. Technologies change constantly, and upgrades or replacement of technology tools that enhance online instruction is inevitable. However, the change might not always be understood and welcomed. For example, the change oftentimes means instructors need to relearn the technologies, which is another thing added to their already busy schedule. Also, both instructors and students may need time to get used to the new change, which seem to "take away" the time they could have used to focus on the course content.

CIRT has been concerned with making the transition smoother for distance instructors by helping them adjust to new environments. For example, the university recently upgraded from Blackboard 7 to Blackboard 9 to address some problems in the earlier Blackboard version. For this upgrade, several campus global e-mails were sent out during the six months before the upgrade informing instructors about the change. Notifications also appeared in official university online publications. In addition, CIRT conducted a user group, provided online tutorials, face-to-face workshops, and customized sessions on Blackboard 9. These activities and training opportunities notwithstanding, it remains problematic for some instructors to adjust to the new Blackboard environment. For example, some instructors complained about the Blackboard upgrade saying they did not know about the change, and we found out later that they usually ignored campus global e-mails and university online publications. A more effective mass communication channel is needed to inform faculty about the upgrade. Also, other instructors said they underestimated the scale of the change since they tended to think an upgrade usually meant minor changes; therefore they did not prepare early enough to address the change. A demonstration site for faculty to access well in advance of the upgrade should help. In addition, faculty who participated in the user group should be encouraged to distribute relevant information to assist colleagues dealing with the upgrades.

Changing Behaviors of Late Adopters

Still another challenge is related to how to more effectively change the behaviors of late adopters regarding the use of technologies in distance education. As mentioned briefly earlier in the chapter, instructors who are innovators and early adopters often attend our workshops and training or seek other relevant information after they become aware of a technology. They are representative of instructors who are interested in integrating the introduced technologies into their teaching once they see the value and advantage. However, there are instructors who are reluctant or do not feel comfortable learning or using the tools. For example, for online course design and development, we have seen high-quality online courses developed using our model. Instructors, especially those new to distance education, have found going through the process of systematically building an online course to be of significant benefit. However, the main challenge is that some instructors are not comfortable or willing to go beyond the minimum requirements and try suggested technologies or strategies even though they agree that the suggestions will improve the course. Common reasons mentioned include limited time, heavy workload, and not being technology savvy. Our concern has been how to better assist this group of instructors. One strategy we are considering is to invite instructors who have successfully developed a high-quality distance course in the discipline to share their experiences and solutions. This approach should encourage and motivate other instructors to try similar strategies or technologies.

The challenge of changing the behaviors of late adopters is also reflected in our FLCs program. At this time we invite instructors to join FLCs as there are not enough volunteers. Ideally, by bringing together a diverse group of faculty, FLCs facilitate cross-fertilization, exchange of ideas, generation of new theories and inter-disciplinary collaboration (Lock, 2006; Wazienski, 2007). Participants benefit through the exchange of questions and solutions to research and classroom issues (Hartman & Cassidy, 2006). As the culminating activity of participation in an FLC, faculty members are expected to return to their respective colleges with new knowledge and insights to share with colleagues. These enlightened colleagues will in turn be motivated to participate in future FLCs further expanding a network of new knowledge and best practices. However, this has yet to happen. We hope that faculty will increasingly see the value of participation in and contribution to FLCs, thereby stimulating formation of active learning communities among our faculty. We recommend that deans and chairs extend a course reduction to encourage faculty participation. In addition, we recommend that deans and chairs offer faculty promotion and tenure credit for participation in active research. Ongoing and completed FLCs should also receive recognition in appropriate university publications. Ultimately, we would like to see all faculty at our institution actively engaged with and contributing to a cross-discipline learning community. The potential for cross-fertilization, exchange of ideas, generation of new theories and inter-disciplinary collaboration will ultimately benefit our students by providing a more relevant and active learning experience. For a learning community to be optimally effective and achieve its goals, ongoing, active contribution and participation by all members is integral.

Rogers' (2003) theory of rate of adoption of an innovation may provide guidance for addressing the challenges presented to our faculty development and training program for distance instructors. According to him, rate of adoption is influenced by several factors such as perceived attributes of an innovation, type of innovation decision, communication channels, and extent of change agents' promotion effort. Considering these factors should help instructors more readily adopt our professional development and training program and benefit their distance instruction and student learning.

Further Assessment

In this section we have discussed the benefits, challenges, and potential solutions of our professional training and development model based on our observations and data collected. However, current information is not sufficient to draw conclusions about the impact of our program as it has only allowed us to primarily look at the short-term impact on participant attitude and perceived learning. To more accurately assess our program, we also need to look at the long-term impact on faculty behavior change in relation to distance education. For example, what actual changes in instruction does our program bring about? Does that translate into positive learning experience for our students? To answer these questions, we need to look at not only the changes in instructor attitude and skills, but also their behaviors as perceived by students and how that affects student learning (Francis, 1975). We received some positive feedback from instructors about student responses through informal contact. However, a more systematic method to evaluate the impact of our faculty development and training program is needed.

The first step towards meaningful assessment of a professional development program is the definition of clear and concise goals and outcomes and aligning the program goals with the institutional goals (Jansen, Kreijns, Bastiaens, & Stijnen, 2010; Plank & Kalish, 2010; Schönwetter et al., 2009). In addition, to determine the success of a professional development program requires both formative and summative assessment. Zygouris-Coe and Swan (2010) stress the importance of multiple and ongoing assessment modalities to evaluate what faculty experience throughout a professional development program. Recommended assessment methods include surveys, e-portfolios, observation of participant interaction, focus groups, individual interviews, and reflective activities. Assessment should also include a measure of self-efficacy or confidence with technology as part of the summative program evaluation (Osman & Duffy, 2005). Timing of assessments and appropriate use of assessment tools are critical for acquiring meaningful data regarding program success. Another key to successful assessment is recognition of program participants as stakeholders who seek a role in shaping their professional development experience (Zygouris-Coe & Swan, 2010). Successful assessment of a 3-year faculty professional development program is documented in Teclehaimanot and Lamb (2005). A number of assessment models for professional development programs have been documented in the literature, as in Ostashewski (2010) and Plank and Kalish (2010).

IMPLICATIONS FOR DISTANCE EDUCATION

As higher education institutions move increasingly towards offering distance education opportunities, developing an effective professional development and training model for distance instructors becomes ever more critical. Faculty development and training can help distance instructors enhance the quality of instruction in nontraditional methods, which will subsequently impact distance student learning. By describing and discussing the key elements in the model currently used in a medium-sized public state university, we hope readers can learn from our case what has worked and how improvements can be made. Through this case, we hope readers can

- identify and apply best practices and processes of professional development and training for distance instructors,
- identify challenges of professional development and training for distance instructors and corresponding solutions,
- identify and apply strategies for diffusion and adoption of instructional technologies among distance instructors, and
- identify and apply strategies to evaluate the effectiveness of professional development and training programs for distance instructors.

Successful faculty development and training programs require careful planning based on institutional goals and an institution's strategic plan. A needs assessment to ascertain instructor needs and expectations is integral to program growth. Also, instructional designers need to realize that there is no "one size fits all" solution. Therefore, it is important to incorporate a variety of activities into a faculty development and training program. At the same time, when institutional budgets are constrained, program developers also need to think about how best to support faculty while keeping the cost down.

Workshops are one of the more traditional elements of faculty development and training (Ouellett, 2010), targeting a group of faculty at one time and in one place. Workshops can continue to be effective training modalities for today's distance instructors as long as they are focused on instructors' needs. An effective alternative is for instructional designers to reach out and conduct tailored sessions with individual colleges or departments "on their turf." One-on-one consultations are a traditional yet favored format for many instructors. However, providing one-to-one consultations can be problematic in that they can be costly and time consuming. Collaboration with faculty in designing, developing, and delivering online courses is an important part of distance education support. Although workshops and individual consultations are effective, faculty new to distance education often find the most benefit from working with an instructional designer to complete a formalized online course design and development program where they progress through the design and development process together. Technology is an integral part of distance education. It therefore follows that technology support plays an important role in faculty development for distance instructors. Institutions should make a commitment to providing faculty with access to and support of current and emerging technologies for effective distance education. Instructional technology support is also critical if instructors are to adopt and sustain appropriate technologies in their teaching. Finally, In the interest of providing an engaging professional development experience, institutions are strongly encouraged to actively sponsor the formation of formal faculty learning communities (FLCs) for instructors to share and disseminate knowledge and find support from their peers.

Another goal of this chapter has been to increase reader awareness of the potential challenges inherent in faculty development and training. For example, how can we motivate instructors to actively participate in the program when they already have a busy schedule teaching, researching, mentoring, and engaging in other academic activities? How do we better convince instructors who fall into the categories of late majority and laggards (Rogers, 2003) to try strategies and technologies that they have never tried before? How do we make the transition smoother when software upgrade or replacement is inevitable? How do we balance cost/time and individualized focus in faculty development programs? To overcome the potential challenges, instructional designers must act as change agents and carefully plan, effectively promote, efficiently deliver, and continuously assess the program. An effective faculty development and training program for distance instructors not only changes knowledge and skills, but also behaviors of instructors to better meet the needs of different stakeholders (Francis, 1975).

CONCLUSION

In the context of distance education, this chapter described and discussed a case of faculty development and creation of a training model in a medium-sized university in the Midwest of the United States. The model consists of five key elements: (a) workshops related to instructional technologies and instructional strategies; (b) one-on-one customized sessions or consultations based on instructor needs; (c) online course development and support; (d) instructional software support; (e) and facilitation of faculty learning communities. For each element, we discussed what has worked for us and what we saw as improvements that are needed. By studying this case, we hope readers see a faculty development and training model "in action," and think about how this case can help them design faculty development and training programs for distance instructors. As distance education gains popularity in traditional postsecondary institutions, it is important to better prepare faculty for this new trend by providing effective faculty development and training programs.

QUESTIONS FOR ANALYSIS/DISCUSSION

1. What do you see as good practices and effective strategies for professional development and training for distance instructors in this case?
2. What do you see as challenges for professional development and training for distance instructors in this case?

3. What could have been done to motivate more instructors to attend the Professional Development workshops in this case?
4. What could have been done to help instructors adopt appropriate instructional technologies and/or instructional strategies for effective delivery of instruction?
5. What could have been done to help instructors better adjust to the environment when technology upgrade or replacement is inevitable?
6. What could have been done to encourage the formation of learning communities among instructors?
7. What could have been done to effectively assess the impact of faculty development and training for distance education instructors?

REFERENCES

Aucoin, R. (2009). The intersection of technology and the scholarship of teaching and learning: A review. In T. Bastiaens et al. (Eds.), *Proceedings of World Conference on E-Learning in Corporate, Government, Healthcare, and Higher Education 2009* (pp. 2263–2268). Chesapeake, VA: AACE.

Bland, C. (1980). *Faculty development through workshops.* Springfield, IL: Charles C Thomas.

Brooks-Harris, J., & Stock-Ward, S. (1999). *Workshops: Designing and facilitating experiential Learning.* Thousand Oaks, CA: Sage.

Code, K. P. (2005). Exploring large-scale teaching technologies-Results from a faculty learning community. In G. Richards (Ed.), *Proceedings of World Conference on E-Learning in Corporate, Government, Healthcare, and Higher Education 2005* (pp. 50–53). Chesapeake, VA: AACE.

Cox, M. (2002). The role of community in learning: Making connections for your classroom and campus, your students and colleagues. In G. S. Wheeler (Ed.), *Teaching and learning in college* (pp. 1–38). Elyria, OH: Info-Tec.

Francis, J. (1975). How do we get there from here? Program design for faculty development. *The Journal of Higher Education, 46*(6), 719–732.

Hartman, S., & Cassidy, M. (2006). Using a scenarios-based faculty learning community for faculty development. In C. Crawford et al. (Eds.), *Proceedings of Society for Information Technology & Teacher Education International Conference 2006* (pp. 677–678). Chesapeake, VA: AACE.

Hsu, E. (2004). Re-considering on-line and live communities of practice. In R. Ferdig et al. (Eds.), *Proceedings of Society for Information Technology & Teacher Education International Conference 2004* (pp. 4446–4450). Chesapeake, VA: AACE.

Jansen, S., Kreijns, K., Bastiaens, T., & Stijnen, S. (2010). The influence of guidance on the quality of professional development plans. In D. Gibson & B. Dodge (Eds.), *Proceedings of Society for Information Technology & Teacher Education International Conference 2010* (pp. 98–105). Chesapeake, VA: AACE.

Lewis, K. G. (2002). The process of individual consultation. In K. H.Gillespie, L. R. Hilsen, & E. C. Wadsworth (Eds.), *A guide to faculty development: Practical advice, examples, and resources* (pp. 59–73). Bolton, MA: Anker.

Lock, J. (2006). A new image: Online communities to facilitate teacher professional development. *Journal of Technology and Teacher Education, 14*(4), 663–678.

McConnell, N. (2009). Learning portals for faculty development. In I. Gibson et al. (Eds.), *Proceedings of Society for Information Technology & Teacher Education International Conference 2009* (pp. 1266–1268). Chesapeake, VA: AACE.

Moore, M., & Kearsley, G. (1996). *Distance education: A systems view.* Belmont, CA: Wadsworth.

Offutt, S., Smart, K., & Pearson, D. (2009). One faculty member's story–How to learn to do what you don't know how to do? In I. Gibson et al. (Eds.), *Proceedings of Society for Information Technology & Teacher Education International Conference 2009* (pp. 1291–1295). Chesapeake, VA: AACE.

Osman, G., & Duffy, T. (2005). Online teacher professional development and implementation success: The learning to teach with technology studio (LTTS) experience. In G. Richards (Ed.), *Proceedings of World Conference on E-Learning in Corporate, Government, Healthcare, and Higher Education 2005* (pp. 407–413). Chesapeake, VA: AACE.

Ostashewski, N. (2010). Online technology teacher professional development courses: Design and development. In D. Gibson & B. Dodge (Eds.), *Proceedings of Society for Information Technology & Teacher Education International Conference 2010* (pp. 229–233). Chesapeake, VA: AACE.

Ouellett, M. (2010). Overview of faculty development. In K. Gillespie & D. Robertson (Eds.), *A guide to faculty development* (2nd ed.) [Kindle DX version]. Retrieved from Amazon.com

Parsad, B., & Lewis, L. (2008). *Distance education at degree-granting postsecondary institutions: 2006–07* (NCES 2009–044). Washington, DC: National Center for Education Statistics, Institute of Education Sciences, U.S. Department of Education.

Plank, K., & Kalish, A. (2010). Program assessment for faculty development. In K. Gillespie & D. Robertson (Eds.), *A guide to faculty development* (2nd ed.) [Kindle DX version]. Retrieved from Amazon.com

Pringle, R. M. (2002). Developing a community of learners: Potentials and possibilities in web mediated discourse. *Contemporary Issues in Technology and Teacher Education, 2*, 218–233.

Rogers, E. M. (2003). *Diffusion of innovations* (5th ed.). New York, NY: Free Press.

Schönwetter, D., Dawson, D., & Britnell, J. (2009). Program assessments: Success strategies for three Canadian teaching centers. *Innovative Higher Education, 33*(4), 239–255.

Teclehaimanot, B., & Lamb, A. (2005). Technology-rich faculty development for teacher educators: The evolution of a program. *Contemporary Issues in Technology and Teacher Education, 5*(3/4), 330–344.

Wazienski, R. (2007). Using faculty learning communities to integrate WebCT technology into a curriculum. In R. Carlsen et al. (Eds.), *Proceedings of Society for Information Technology & Teacher Education International Conference 2007* (pp. 1160–1163). Chesapeake, VA: AACE.

Wenger, E. (1998). *Communities of practice: Learning, meaning and identity.* Cambridge, MA: Cambridge University Press.

Zygouris-Coe, V., & Swan, B. (2010). Developing and evaluating online teacher professional development communities on a large scale. In J. Sanchez & K. Zhang (Eds.), *Proceedings of World Conference on E-Learning in Corporate, Government, Healthcare, and Higher Education 2010* (pp. 584–592). Chesapeake, VA: AACE.

FURTHER READINGS

Simonson, M., Smaldino, S. E., Albright, M., & Zvacek, S. (2008). *Teaching and learning at a distance: Foundations of distance education* (4th ed.). Upper Saddle River, NJ: Prentice Hall.

Weigel, V. B. (2002). *Deep learning for a digital age: Technology's untapped potential to enrich higher education.* San Francisco, CA: Wiley.

CHAPTER 21

DESIGNING AND MAINTAINING AN ONLINE DEGREE PROGRAM SERVING A DIVERSE STUDENT POPULATION

Karen Kaminski

ABSTRACT

Faculty in a well-established and highly successful online master's program are faced with some difficult questions to answer and decisions to make. While they have collaborated to provide an up-to-date curriculum and applied learning experience for their students, scarce resources have increased outside pressures to increase revenues while reducing expenses. The faculty are taking a fresh look at the program and keeping an open mind regarding change. Given foundational information regarding program design, learner centered philosophy, and decisions that have made the program a success, this study asks the reader to weigh many different variables while incorporating their prior knowledge and experience to present what they believe is the best path to take for the future of the program.

Real-Life Distance Education, pages 377–389

INTRODUCTION

Many institutions of higher education are turning to distance learning to reach new or underserved populations and/or to generate revenues (Perry, 2010). Budgets are declining, grant money is becoming more difficult to secure, and departments are looking for new ways to bring in discretionary monies. One solution is to reach additional students through a distance learning model. Frequently a large portion of tuition revenues from distance programs flow directly to the department, college, or community that is offering the program. These revenues are not typically tied to base-budgets and can be used to cover additional expenses or held in reserves for special projects. This case study investigates an online master's degree program that was originally developed with the needs of distance learners in mind and has since become a foundational revenue generating aspect of the unit. This Master's degree in Adult Education is historically one of the oldest and longest running programs in Education at the University. While the on-campus program is celebrating a 25-year milestone, the online version of the program was developed in 1998 and has become a successful distance program with an average of 150 active students in any given semester.

A strength of the program is that the underlying principles and theories for teaching and learning cross multiple disciplines. Students attracted to this degree work in a broad range of fields including corporate/business training, Adult Basic Education/General Education Degree/English as a Second or Other Language in the community or at a local college, community college faculty, high school teachers and teacher coaches, athletic coaches, health care educators, emergency services trainers, and many more. The students admitted reside around the world and the majority work full-time and have many responsibilities beyond their studies. Often the students' goals are to increase their knowledge and skills in facilitating learning specifically to enhance their performance in their current work or gain a promotion. A smaller number of students are working toward a career change. Students who are making a career change may not be certain where they want to work but know they want to facilitate adult learning based on their area of expertise.

The faculty follow Bloom's mastery learning model (Eisner, 2000; Richey, 2000), allowing students to revise and resubmit their work until they have demonstrated the knowledge and skills desired. While this creates additional work for the faculty, as a team they have agreed this model provides the best experience for the community of learners. Hours of faculty collaboration and consideration have been dedicated to the design and facilitation of each course to help all learners reach their goals. This includes a curriculum-mapping project, obtaining feedback from students, and constant investigation into updating curriculum to meet learners' needs. Over the years, the program has developed a strong reputation among students and the adult education profession. Student feedback indicates appreciation for the individualized attention and states that the applied nature of the course work leads to a better understanding of the content, increased recognition in their workplace leading to promotion, and the opportunity to network and obtain new positions.

Revenue generation was a secondary goal when the distance version of the program was developed. The annual budget is built to cover a 10% overhead to the University. Of the remaining 90% of tuition revenues, 35% goes to the outreach branch of the University and 21% to the School of Education. The School keeps 21% of this and the remaining revenues cover all the costs of instruction and expenses of the program.

While the faculty use feedback and research in the field to update the course content (Partnerships, 2010; Pindus, 2007; Rovai, Ponton, & Baker 2008) and a personalized approach to learning, they have generated considerable ownership in what they have developed. When external pressures suggest change, it is natural for faculty to become defensive and protect what has been accomplished. This case presents the foundation that supports such a successful program and investigates best practices, varied perspectives, and reflection for change. Readers who use this case study will be able to:

- Substantiate a model, based on research and best practices, for distance-delivered curricula
- Develop a process for student-based feedback for curricula updates
- Discuss the pros and cons of cohort-based programs and a set curriculum
- Analyze proven practices to determine change

CASE STUDY

The distance delivered Master of Education–Adult Education and Training was initiated by two faculty who developed the online versions of the traditional courses and collaborated regarding required content, sequencing of courses, and textbooks. The content is based on the national standards for Adult Education established by the Commission of Professors of Adult Education (Commission, 2012) part of the American Association of Adult and Continuing Education.

The content in the program did not fit a traditional lecture format; therefore, the faculty did not use the then common "tape a live lecture and post it" process. Interactivity through computer mediated communication was key to the success. The course sessions were designed to be discussion-based where the instructor and/or students post questions and student responses are based on their experience, their readings, and additional examples from the literature. The faculty encouraged student-to-student discussion and collaboration, steering the conversations when needed. They were pioneers in using WebCT 12 years ago, a learning management system (LMS) that provides password-protected access to course content, discussion, and assignments. The primary tools within the LMS that were employed included discussion, e-mail, and grade book. The syllabus and schedule for each course appear as links on the home page. The design was intentionally kept simple and effective to ensure easy access and minimal technology challenges for the learners.

To earn the degree, students complete 33 credits or 11 courses; eight of these were required courses and three electives of the students' choice. The typical student completes two courses each fall and spring semester, and one or two courses each summer term, for two years of study. A number of students complete one course each semester taking four years to finish and moving to a new cohort their third and forth year in the program. Therefore, courses are offered once each year, supporting a semi-cohort based model. While cohort based distance learning has proven successful (Fenning, 2004), nontraditional students require flexibility in their schedules, the ability to study part-time, and potentially stop out for a semester or longer. While some students may never become part of a cohort for more than a year, the cohort groups of students study together throughout the program, share information, communicate outside of class, and provide a lot of support and encouragement for each other. This model simplifies advising and student planning as the course sequence is set for the first year and electives do not come into play until the faculty knows the students and the students have experience in graduate school. Students receive information on forms such as their program of study and their application for graduation as a group within class sections and work individually with their advisor for individual mentoring. This allows advisors to spend more time focused on instruction and supporting specific and unique learner needs. The faculty found it important to closely track all students' progress through the program and, therefore, created a master spreadsheet that includes student name, contact information, admission term, location, advisor, courses completed, and a column to indicate when formal documents such as the program of study and application for graduation are completed and processed. Each faculty has access and can refer students to their advisor or answer simple questions.

The online course schedule is identical to the on-campus traditional course schedule. This results in the need to offer two or three sections of each course in the same semester. While faculty in the Adult Education program specialize in specific research areas, they need to be able to teach all courses in the program. This ensures that each faculty member has a good understanding of the entire program, the learning the students have experienced prior to their courses, and the ability to build on prior learning. Application of learning is integrated throughout the courses, helping students reach the program goals and their personal learning goals. Students customize assignments to fit their needs and apply their learning to work, community, church, or their related environment. Students post their work to the open discussions in the learning management system, allowing peers to provide feedback and learn from the shared experiences. A number of students opt to take their electives in their specific content area or other related areas such as business, sociology, psychology, additional research course work, additional technology application, etc. The content offered within the program is based on feedback from the learners regarding additional content that provides depth in their specific areas of need. For ten years these two faculty worked together to build the reputation of the program. As they were successful, and enrollments continued to increase, they experimented with different class size limits. They quickly determined that the best class size was 15–20 students. More than 25 and the discussions were unmanageable, becoming difficult to provide individual feedback. Fewer than 10 and the discussions were not as robust. In recent years, they found they were offering two or three sections of the core content courses to be able to serve all the students. Initially these additional sections were taught by part-time adjunct instructors. They quickly realized that the increase in workload was not limited to instruction. To support the additional advising, in 2009 two additional full-time nontenure track faculty were hired to teach, advise, and provide administrative support, increasing the team to four. When considering faculty hires, it was important to find individuals who followed the same philosophy of experiential, applied, and mastery learning on which the program was based.

These four faculty members recently completed a curriculum mapping project, creating a spreadsheet that identifies the objectives, content, assignments, and desired outcomes of each course. With their collective experience, they collaborated to remove any overlap in content that had emerged, ensure all primary program objectives were covered, and the sequencing of the courses was still appropriate for scaffolding learning. Minor changes were made based on the mapping. For example, the introduction to research course was moved from the third to the second semester of study to allow students to apply the tools and skills in their subsequent course work. Faculty also investigated new and updated textbooks, other learning resources, and made changes as appropriate.

With recent advances in information and communication technologies, as a team they determined that literacy in this area is important when preparing learners for the workforce. Hence teaching, learning, and communicating with technology would be modeled in practice. Technology integration across the curriculum was more appropriate than offering a separate course on the use of instructional technologies for teaching and learning. They identified technologies to incorporate into the appropriate assignments. Depending on the instructor and the content of the course, they initiated the use of class-developed wikis, Ning, podcasts, video presentations, blogs, and much more. In addition, they support student use of free software such as Prezi and narrated PowerPoint for presentations. Most students choose to complete a portfolio rather than a thesis. This initially was print based; now the students create a digital portfolio and presentation.

Feedback informs the faculty that the reason students initially decide to apply to this program includes the prompt response they receive to their request for additional information beyond what was available on the program Web site. Potential student queries go directly to the faculty, who have a goal of responding to all requests within 48 hours. This personal attention results in a high admission rate as the faculty are familiar with the potential student and their fit before the application is completed and those who are not a good fit are directed to more appropriate opportunities. While students typically begin their studies in the fall semester, applications are reviewed on a rolling basis permitting response to the students within weeks of application. Students admitted to the program indicate the faculty are responsive to their needs, are willing to spend time getting to know each individual learner, and are able to customize learning for their specific needs. Transfer students indicate they receive more feedback and support from these faculty than in their previous university experience.

The Challenges

The university has not escaped the plight of many institutions across the country that are trimming their budgets and focusing their offerings. While some departments in the institution already made vertical cuts, the School had already lost a number of faculty positions and thousands of dollars due to budget reductions. Not surprising, the dean asked all of the departments to consider how they could consolidate. Faculty members are nervous and concerned about their future. While this Adult Education Program had a strong on-campus student population, distance students and faculty who teach in the program are often invisible to the on-campus faculty.

Ideas Start to Flow

Initial ideas included eliminating 20% of the courses on the books, assuming this will result in fewer courses offered; sharing courses and resources with other programs when appropriate; and reducing or eliminating the number of adjunct instructors hired to teach sections. This request initiated a flurry of activity. Each specialization obtained current lists of courses including those that have not been offered in recent semesters. They compared their own program of study and the curriculum in other areas. Many meetings were scheduled and unique, innovative, and even crazy ideas were brought to the table.

As in any stressful situation, program areas were reluctant to offer plans that tightened their belts more than their peers'. Some started to scrutinize what others were doing, sometimes more so than focusing on their own best practices. This particular program became a target because of the difficulty for others to succinctly describe the student population and the nature of their work.

Narrowing

Can the program become more focused? Another program in the unit that also offers on-campus and distance versions requires a set sequence of courses with no elective options. In meetings, the chair of the other program suggested that the "no elective" approach was the most effective and efficient way to manage courses and reduce costs. This is certainly something to consider, yet there are a few things that are important to note. This other program has a narrowly focused curriculum where students all work in the same general field making it easier to standardize courses. For those students who request exceptions from the set curriculum, additional paperwork is necessary that requires signature and approval through three levels of administration. Would eliminating student options truly save dollars?

Another suggestion for this program was to become more specialized, meeting the needs of a narrower population base. Administrators have a difficult time understanding the purpose of a program that crosses many fields and, therefore, a difficult time understanding it and explaining it to others. The team was asked to more clearly define the student population, their goals for earning the degree, and the job opportunities available to them. Is it possible to identify terminology that is clear yet all encompassing to maintain the diversity in the program or is it prudent to truly narrow the focus? If the latter, which focus is best?

Expanding

At the same time, financial officers indicated the need to increase enrollments in the distance-based master's programs to help support the expenses within the department and college. They wanted programs to reach out to broader populations and increase class sizes. The program receives 65% of the tuition revenues from distance students and the unit as a whole takes a third of this to support general operating expenses. The remaining two-thirds of the revenues are used to cover all expenses of instruction, advising, and administrative support within the program.

At first glance, the requests to narrow and expand appear to be conflicting. How can the program both narrow and expand at the same time? Consideration needs to be given to many aspects including the advantages of cross discipline learning and the additional learning that occurs from shared experiences. One of the strengths that would be impacted by a narrow focus is the broad range of experiences shared in the classes. Yet there are limits. Some of the faculty taught online courses with close to 30 students and shudder at the thought of doing so again. The faculty ran budget scenarios to determine how offering additional sections would increase expenses if it would it be possible to attract enough students to create a third section. They wondered if they could maintain quality, successfully retain larger numbers of students, and still be proud of their work.

Students

Another aspect all programs were asked to consider was the nature of the students admitted to programs. Faculty were asked to ensure they are only enrolling high quality students who are likely to succeed in graduate school. They were to review admissions policies and consider more stringent guidelines for admissions. One idea was to begin requiring the GRE for admission. With an average student age of 45, this program team is concerned that requiring current GRE scores will severely reduce the number of applications to the program. The GRE is a good tool for students who have just completed an undergraduate degree. Potential students who have not participated in formal learning for many years are already nervous about returning to school, much less taking a standardized test to gain admission. Nationally, similar programs do not require the GRE and students might be likely to go elsewhere. The faculty asked if this is a good reason not to require such a measurement.

Another idea was for all faculty in the department to review applications and/or approve acceptance into all programs. This could potentially increase cross ownership and responsibility in helping all students succeed. Though with hundreds of applications submitted to the various programs each year, this would consume many hours, could create competition for resources, and with a common application deadline it would significantly delay notification to students and severely tax the personnel in the Graduate Programs office who process all the applications, thereby making it difficult to provide prompt and clear student support.

Steps

The chair of this program is feeling stretched in many different directions. It is clearly impossible to try to meet all of the requirements and pressures while protecting the foundational student centered philosophy that makes this an exceptional degree. Yet defending all aspects of the existing program would be the wrong strategy politically. The challenge is to select which direction to take and to justify the decision to administration and students.

The faculty in the program started meeting to discuss the challenges and determine a plan of action. One easy decision was to reduce the credit requirements from 33 credits to 30 credits, moving one of the original required courses that met about 50% of the student's learning needs, to an elective course. They will now offer one hybrid section of this course for both on-campus and distance students, eliminating the need for two sections and one adjunct faculty member. The other requests were not as easy to resolve. The faculty members are invested in the work they perform, the program they built, and the student-centered model they use.

There are many variables to weigh. For example, some of these variables are maintaining a high quality program and the institution's reputation, the applied nature of the program, advising, communication, and revenue generation. Faculty did not want to mechanize processes simply to allow for increase in enrollments and increased revenue; they repeatedly stated "we are not a diploma mill." These options were considered:

- Increasing marketing to increase enrollments and, therefore, revenues. Yet this must be balanced with the additional costs of instruction, advising, and support resources.
- Replace one or more of the electives in the program with a required course. Required courses have higher enrollments than electives and, therefore, this would increase revenues. Yet this change would also require an on-campus section, which is another additional cost.
- Narrow the focus of the program to reduce the size and resources required for delivery.

All options require additional time and resources to implement. With reductions, jobs may need to be eliminated while increases may require heavier workloads and reduced services. In addition, the paper work for curriculum changes can take months to process through the unit, the college, and the university for approval.

IMPLICATIONS FOR DISTANCE EDUCATION

There are multiple purposes for deciding to offer degree programs for distance learners. One primary reason is to reach new or isolated audiences. More recently, many institutions do so with the primary purpose of generating new revenue. While we consider the needs of our program, college, or institution, we should acknowledge who the different stakeholders are and what their individual goals are for the distance program. There may be conflict between faculty and administrative purpose, yet with open communication we should be able to meet the needs of both.

This case presents the foundational development of an online degree program and a number of internal and external pressures for critical review and potential change. Although revenue generation is a significant factor for distance programs, there are many variables to weigh. In addition to considering the best practices for learning, one needs to consider the politics, social pressures, and institutional pressures.

There are two primary distance learning facilitation models. One has been around for over 100 years: correspondence study. Although many online degree programs would not consider themselves correspondence because they run their courses on a semester basis and students are entered in the same course in the learning management system (LMS), the facilitation style of the instructors mirror that of correspondence. Students access readings and homework assignments in the LMS, complete the work, and post it back to the system. The faculty, or often a graduate teaching assistant, will grade the assignments and post feedback for the students. There is little direct instruction or communication between students

Another model uses a facilitative, discussion-based process where students participate in threaded discussions regarding the readings and assignments; they discuss with peers in the class, complete team projects, and share their work. This second model requires a much greater time investment on the part of the instructor and the students. Our Adult Education program in this case study follows this second model and, therefore, generates a significant connection with the students and more ownership in the entire program. Conflict can come when administrators or faculty in other programs do not understand the impact this investment has on learning, underestimate the time it takes to be an effective online instructor and to support distance students, and they minimize the importance of supporting these programs. As distance learning administrators or faculty, we need to continue to educate stakeholders and help them understand the different facets of distance learning.

A student-centered distance learning model takes many aspects into consideration. Supporting nontraditional students who may have been out of formal education for many years, helping them to meet specific personal goals for adults returning to school, and who have many responsibilities in addition to learning. We need to focus on how to motivate students at a distance, engage them in discussion and learning, help them transfer their learning to their real-life settings, and reflect on the process. This takes considerable time and effort.

Often we hire adjunct or nontenure track faculty to teach in our distance programs. These instructors may not be invited to attend faculty meetings or be included in larger decisions. Transparency, community building, and internal marketing can make these faculty more visible and reduce some of the challenges that they face.

Finally, it can be very tempting to simplify. We can mechanize processes, hire inexpensive support staff to field general questions and provide basic advising, and as I heard one instructor say, "flush students through." This would make everyone's work easier, including the student's. One question we receive frequently from distance learners is "will I get the same education as if I were on-campus"? To respond to this question, we need to consider what the campus experience is like and how isolated our distance learners may feel. In a meta-analysis, the "No Significant Difference Phenomenon" (http://nosignificantdifference.org) informs us that years of research have indicated that outcomes from distance learning are not different from on-campus learning. In fact, we have evidence that in some instances, distance learning exceeds that of on-campus (Means, Toyama, Murphy, Bakia, & Jones, 2009). If we want to provide the same level of learning, rigor, and experience as we do on-campus it takes time and effort. In addition, as we have discussed above, programs may come under fire from administration or peers and you may need to educate others about the processes and purposes that the program established. It is important, but sometimes difficult, to remain open-minded and positive.

CONCLUSION

This case presents the foundational aspects for a successful distance graduate program. We have over 120 graduates over the past five years. The faculty members collaborate regularly to maintain a student-centered focus with current curriculum. This program admits students from a broad range of backgrounds who work as trainers and formal or informal educators in a variety of settings. Faculty consider the learners as their primary stakeholders and students consistently express gratitude and share personal and career rewards upon completion of their studies.

The institution has many stakeholders in addition to the learners. This includes the administration, faculty in the program, the unit, and the college, support staff, and the community. There are many political, social, cultural, and financial aspects that must be considered when decisions are made. The current climate is one of change and competition for scarce resources. There is a natural resistance to change, bolstered by a belief that time has been well spent and that the program is already the best that it can be. External pressures may be conflicting, making it even more difficult to respond. This requires a fresh look, an open mind, and creative ideas. Recommendations for change need to be supported by sound reasoning that recognizes the concerns of all constituents.

It is important to listen, network, and build collaborations on an ongoing basis. While we are often challenged to market the success of our programs to internal audiences, doing so can build confidence and understanding among peers. When difficult times arise, one can count on these relationships for support and cooperation.

QUESTIONS FOR ANALYSIS AND DISCUSSION

1. Identify the primary and secondary problems in this case.
2. Who are the key stakeholders and how do they impact the decisions made?
3. Generate a list of program evaluation data that you may want to collect to help make or support your decisions.
4. Compare and contrast having a fully set curriculum versus allowing students to take elective courses and transfer courses into the program from other institutions.
5. Applying best practices in distance education, develop a model of instruction that facilitates learning for a broad range of experiences/fields and engages all learners allowing them to apply their work directly to their field of interest.
6. Given the varied pressures placed on programs (increase enrollments/revenues; tighten admission standards; reduce course offerings; meet the needs of students; while maintaining quality) suggest specific recommendations the chair and faculty might use to make the best decisions for the future of the program.

REFERENCES

Commission of Professors in Adult Education. Retrieved from http://web.memberclicks.com/mc/page.do?sitePageId=85442&orgId=cpae

Eisner, E. W. (2000). Benjamin Bloom Prospects: The quarterly review of comparative education. *UNESCO: International Bureau of Education, 30*(3).

Fenning, K. (2004, Winter). Cohort based learning: Application to learning organizations and student academic success. *College Quarterly, 7*(1).

Means, B., Toyama, Y., Murphy, R., Bakia, M., & Jones K. (2009). *Evaluation of evidence-based practices in online learning: A meta-analysis and review of online learning studies.* Washington, DC: U.S. Department of Education.

Partnership for 21st Century Skills. (2010). Retrieved from http://www.p21.org/

Perry, M. (2010). Colleges see 17 percent increase in online enrollment. *The Chronicle of Higher Education.* Retrieved from http://chronicle.com/blogs/wiredcampus/colleges-see-17-percent-increase-in-online-enrollment/20820

Pindus, N. M. (2007). *Expert's corner: Adult education and workforce development can be key assets in local economic development.* Retrieved from http://www.urban.org/publications/901035.html

Richey, R. (2000). Legacy of Robert M. Gagné. *International Board of Standards for Training, Performance and Instruction.* Retrieved from http://www.ibstpi.org/Products/Legacy_Gagne_TOC.htm

Rovai, A., Ponton, M. K., & Baker, J. D. (2008). *Distance learning in higher education: A programmatic approach to planning, design, instruction, evaluation, and accreditation.* New York, NY: Teachers College Press.

FURTHER READINGS

Caffarella, R., S. (2001). *Planning programs for adult learners: A practical guide for educators, trainers, and staff developers,* (2nd ed.). San Francisco, CA: Wiley.

Ertmer, P., & Quinn, J. (2006). *The I.D. casebook: Case studies in instructional design* (3rd ed.). Upper Saddle River, NJ: Pearson.

Jonassen, D. H. (2004). *Learning to solve problems: An instructional design guide.* San Francisco, CA: Pfeifffer.

Conceição, S. C. O. (2007). *New directions in adult education.* Retrieved from http://www3.interscience.wiley.com/journal/114204635/issue

CHAPTER 22

THE PUBLIC ADMINISTRATION PROGRAM AT CHURCHAMPTON COLLEGE, UK

Angela D. Benson and Andrew Whitworth

ABSTRACT

The program discussed in this chapter began as part of an initiative known as the UKeU. Though this initiative collapsed before the first students were enrolled, the program survived with characteristics that reflected the values of the initiative. However, the program had to overcome several challenges in order to begin operation. Of top priority, a new LMS had to be found at very short notice. This was achieved through exploiting social networks. The program also had to administratively adjust itself to assume duties that were originally to be carried out by the UKeU. Over time, through active professional development and a managerial style that emphasized creativity and critical inquiry into the team's activities, the program team built a knowledge base around their activities that allowed them to develop a strong identity as a quality distance education program.

Real-Life Distance Education, pages 391–404
Copyright © 2014 by Information Age Publishing
391

INTRODUCTION

This case focuses on the Public Administration Program (PAP) at Churchampton College, a medium-sized institution in England with a strong reputation for quality teaching and learning. PAP runs a set of three fully distance Master's degrees aimed at public administrators and civil servants in the UK and abroad. The issues particularly addressed by this case and illustrated by PAP are administration and management of distance education, professional development and evaluation, and learning management systems. As a result of reading and discussing this case study, readers should:

- Explain how fundamental choices, such as the selection of an LMS, will shape activity throughout the life of a distance education program, even where such choices were made because of random events, "serendipity" and the existence of social networks
- Discuss the value of reviewing and learning from experience, and thus building a repository of applied knowledge about the LMS-in-use: but also how this might place a distance education program in a position of tension vis-a-vis its host institution
- Explain how e-tutoring can be managed using a fairly strict division of labor and procedural rules such as course templates, but how these can also be relaxed over time in response to internal evaluations

CASE STUDY

Program Origins

PAP was originally developed as a face-to-face program run on behalf of a UK government department. Over a period in the early 2000s, certain trajectories began to converge in a way that encouraged the development of a distance version of the program. The government department remained the principal client and sought a more flexible version of the program. While PAP was happy to continue to deal with this client, they were also looking for ways to widen their market. Churchampton were interested in moving the program online, but it had no policy mechanism by which the substantial start-up funds required could be sourced internally. Instead, the principal catalyst was the planned launch of the "UKeU" (UK e-University). As Conole, Carusi, De Laat, Wilcox, and Darby (2006) say:

> The UKeU was initiated in response to a perceived need for the UK to be a key player in packaging UK Higher Education internationally in a distance education format.... The UK e-University business model was based on a critical

mass of high quality learning materials being available on-line. These materials would be wrapped around by learner support and administrative mechanisms, commissioned in response to an identified demand, or offered by institutions and other organizations wishing to contribute to the e-University. (pp. 3–4)

In other words, the UKeU aimed at bringing together distance education expertise from around the country under a single umbrella. A range of institutions would provide the instructors, syllabi, and course materials; UKeU would be responsible for marketing the programs, and also providing a centralized LMS, which was to be built by a major software provider. The PAP team, therefore, submitted a bid to become one of the original providers of a UKeU program. In 2001, they received UKeU funding in the form of a loan, which was to be paid back over 7–10 years.

Once funding was awarded, course creation for PAP began under the leadership of the UKeU. Course content and design was conducted by teams of subject matter experts from the United States and the United Kingdom. Once complete, the courses were then packaged for online delivery by an outside consulting organization hired by the UKeU.

However, a crisis developed before the courses were put online. Due to fundamental tensions between the academic and corporate missions of the umbrella UKeU organization (Conole et al., 2006), the UKeU collapsed before the first cohort of PAP students commenced their studies. Churchampton, like several other recipients of UKeU funding, was able to renegotiate the loan as a grant, and, thus, the program itself survived: but the institutional collapse took with it the putative Sun system that was to be PAP's LMS.

This meant that there was a pressing need for PAP to find a replacement LMS, literally within weeks. Debbie, the PAP team's teaching and learning manager, had a "good relationship" with the people at Sun, who were giving her "off the record statements" that "they should find another platform, fast." Blackboard and WebCT (still separate firms at the time) were both approached, but while content creation and transfer to a new LMS was not perceived as a problem by either vendor, PAP realized that there was no hope of drawing up contracts quickly enough. Churchampton was supportive, but as Debbie described, "couldn't help because this [distance education] was something beyond the ken of the university at this time."

Fortunately for the PAP team, Yuji, a colleague in the Mathematics department at Churchampton, who was doing some work with the open source course management system, Moodle, heard of their dilemma and e-mailed Debbie. "I hear you're in a need of a platform," he wrote. "I've got this thing. Do you want to see it?"

Debbie's response was an enthusiastic "yes." She recalled, "I went across [to see him] not knowing what I was going to find and then I saw this thing [Moodle] and just thought, 'Wow! This is lovely.'"

After a review of the system features, which Debbie found aligned well with PAP's needs, Yuji suggested they use Moodle and Debbie agreed. Yuji then helped the PAP team set up a server and transport all existing PAP course materials across to it in time for the first cohort of 13 students to start their studies on schedule in September 2003.

Program Evolution

Though the UKeU was no longer in existence, its planned policies and procedures for course development and program operation lived on in the early days of PAP. Over time, PAP relaxed some of the UKeU structures and developed policies and procedures specific to the needs of its students and staff.

Program Structure

From its initial single degree offering in 2001, PAP has grown to three online master's degree programs: Public Policy and Management; Public Administration; and Policy Management and Government. Each of the three programs requires approximately three years of coursework to complete. The PAP programs are flexible in structure though, allowing students to select different and shorter study paths, depending on their interests and needs. A student can opt to go the certificate route by completing only the first year of study, which consists of three required foundational modules. A student can receive a diploma by completing one year of study beyond the certificate year. During this year, the student completes three elective modules in chosen areas of interest. Students desiring the master's degree must complete a third year of study, which includes an elective module and an independent project. PAP currently has 16 modules shared across the three degree programs.

Roles/Administrative Staff

In the early start-up days, PAP operated with a thin staff consisting of Clare, the Director of Studies, and an administrative officer. The group outsourced its major functions. According to Clare, "we relied heavily in the early stage of the project on a contract with external providers at the University of Oxford who provided instructional design advice and helped us design the program from its very outset."

The next person to join the PAP team was a project manager to oversee the content development of the modules. This person coordinated the work of the team of contractors, content experts from the US and UK, who jointly developed the course materials for PAP courses. The fourth person hired to make up the core PAP team was Debbie, the teaching and learning manager, who assumed the instructional design responsibilities originally provided by the University of Oxford. Since there were no full-time PAP faculty members, Debbie also hired and trained the group of part-time adjunct tutors who taught the PAP courses. Tutors were trained online and invited to participate in a yearly face-to-face conference where they reflected on their practice as a group.

Today, PAP has grown from an administrative team of four to a team of nine: a Director of Studies, two program directors, three teaching fellows, a teaching and learning manager, a program and recruitment manager, a student support officer and a web developer. PAP still maintains a strict division of labor for completion of program tasks. The two program directors oversee the teams of content experts, paid as consultants, who create the teaching materials according to the course creation compliance documents. Three full-time teaching fellows join the adjunct tutors in teaching the PAP courses. The teaching and learning manager acts as point person for instructional design and technology support issues. The program and recruitment manager is dedicated to marketing the program and recruiting new students. The student support officer is the primary admissions contact for students. She is responsible for maintaining student records and providing advising services to students. The web developer is contracted to serve as a software developer and technical support interface between PAP staff and Moodle.

Student Composition

Since the initial enrollment of 13 students in 2003, PAP has graduated more than 100 students and has a current enrollment of approximately 225 students. While initially the PAP students were primarily from the UK, the program has evolved to include large numbers of students from other European, Asian, and African countries. The current enrollment consists of students representing 55 different countries. Because of PAP's commitment to enrolling students from low- and middle-income countries, the program provides substantial tuition discounts to students from these countries. PAP is currently recruiting about 70 students each year.

A large majority of PAP students are full-time government employees whose tuition is covered by their employer. For this reason, retention tends to be high, around 85–95%. The age group skews older. According to Fran, the PAP student support manager, there are "not many younger students in the program, many are in their 50's and 60's." In addition, a high proportion of students do not have a first degree. These students are accepted into the program based on their professional work experience. Because many of the PAP students have never taken an online course before, they are required to attend a weeklong online course orientation prior to starting the program.

Budget

Though originally funded by the UKeU, PAP has had to evolve to a position of self-sufficiency. Thus, marketing and recruiting, a function that was to be originally provided by the UKeU, has become a very important PAP function. According to Clare, PAP is:

> ...moving into somewhere where it's going to start to break even. It's getting there...there's two separate things here, one of which is the start-up costs which were substantial, and without them I'm not sure we would ever have got off the ground, but given the fact that that resource was provided up front...It didn't cost, it cost time and input and intellectual instead, but actually there was a substantial grant to help get the modules written and to pay the people at Oxford that we worked with. We paid every author a substantial sum for each module. We paid a huge sum of money across to the people at Oxford. We paid the BBC, anyway, big cost...we are now starting to break even, but only just. It's a pretty tight business plan. We do run to a business plan.

Clare set enrollment benchmarks before growing the administrative staff:

> We'd like to bring in more support but we can't quite afford it at the moment. It's always a cost. The money's a pressure. It's expensive to deliver I would say because there are four of us fulltime on this [program]. Student numbers are getting to a point where I feel more confident about the future. We need to keep on recruiting at the levels we're recruiting at the moment, hoping to keep on increasing that actually...but if we could recruit about 100 [students] a year then we'd be able to relax more...at the moment we're getting an intake in the Summer, Spring of about 20, 25 and an intake in the Summer of about 55.

Course (aka Module) Design

PAP has a standardized model for the task of course design and subsequent tutor practice. Heavy and rigorous use is made of compliance documents such as course development guides, tutor contracts, and student guides, all which have their origin in the original UKeU course specifications. These actions and operations yield a structured and controlled course environment in which students face a consistent interface and operation in each module. Since students are not technology experts and the course is not technology-related, this standardization is considered a positive characteristic. Debbie describes the standardized course model this way:

The initial, original model was 11 weeks [of study] on Moodle... within each week, you get a little learning objective, an HTML page, about six or seven per unit per week. And then you have a discussion, a forum set in each of those weeks. And in each forum there is one discussion topic. Every week has a single discussion that the students all had to engage in for that topic, and that was all based on the learning objective of that unit.

However, this standardization led to limited tutor decision-making when teaching a course. Only recently have tutors been given the flexibility to adjust the rules under which the teaching (as opposed to the LMS) operates, through a loosening of the course standards. Debbie explains:

> ... we'd like them [tutors] to be able to feel freer to use some of Moodle's tools so that they, they can set up a quiz if they want. There's no reason why not! They can set up a poll if they want to. They can set up an extra discussion if they want to. So we want to allow them to use the technology a bit more to do their teaching their way, if you like. At the moment they do it all in pretty much exactly the same way.

Along with loosening the reins on the tutors with respect to using the tools of the LMS to modify their individual courses, the PAP team is also moving students from didactic assignments to more collaborative assignments. Debbie explains:

> They [students] had to, initially it was very typically, things like "read this paper, and discuss it." We've refined that a little bit, because that's a bit too broad. But that will typically be it, all the way through they do a "read some stuff, discuss it, read some more stuff, discuss it" and off they go, right the way down, and that was fairly unbroken, and then they do an assignment at the end, a written assignment, 3,000 words. And what we've done in the last couple of years is just try and break that up a little bit and start using a bit more, we're trying to get students to work more together, more collaboratively together, so we're trying to get them to problem solve things together, and we're trying to get them to work jointly to create presentations together and that kind of thing.

Learning Management System

Because Churchampton doesn't provide University technical support for Moodle, PAP has always been responsible for providing technical support for the system. In the early days, Debbie and Yuji, her colleague in the Mathematics department, served as the technical support team. According to Debbie,

> He did all the back end support because I simply don't have the skills to do that... he hosted it for us in the Math department. Since then, simply because it was too much to expect the guy to do, we have an external hosting

service, Starserv Learning, who are one of the Moodle approved host services, they host for us and also I've paid for a short period of support with them as well... They also offer development so if I need anything developed they can do that for me as well. So they offer everything that I need, basically. But I'm the front line for here, I support my team and I support students, that's me. If anything goes beyond that then I go up to Starserv and talk to them about it.

Debbie has hired external contractors to handle Moodle software fixes, develop additional features, and incorporate them into the local Moodle system. These changes are also submitted to moodle.org for possible inclusion in the Moodle kernel. PAP staff work hard to try and have local changes incorporated into the kernel, so that upgrades to new "global" versions of Moodle do not disrupt local practice.

The use of Moodle is prescribed, and no other technological tools are used in any significant way to mediate teaching and learning tasks in PAP degree programs. However, more recently, "top down" community influences have come to the fore. Churchampton recently chose Blackboard as the campus LMS despite the lobbying of PAP staff (and Yuji) for Moodle. Subsequently, PAP has been directed to transfer to Blackboard. PAP staff were forced to make a case for why they were yet to adopt it. A variety of objections were raised. According to Gordon, an online teaching fellow, "Blackboard will lead to a different way of working... I have reservations." Francesca was "against the idea [of moving to Blackboard], but admits she "hasn't seen it and is being swayed by Debbie, Erik [the marketing and recruitment manager] and Clare." Yuji voiced the strongest objection. According to Debbie:

> Yuji particularly was very disgruntled with that choice and let it be known that he was very annoyed that Blackboard had been chosen. He felt that strongly for financial and pedagogical, actually we agreed with him, [but] we kept a bit quieter about it. For financial and pedagogical reasons we should have chosen something like Moodle and had that. Because he's a coder, he hasn't got the fear. "Let's just get some more coders in and we'll make it go, we'll make it work!" And I know he's right, we could have done it, but there was no infrastructure, no skill base in the University to do that, so it fell over on that particular [point]. But we looked at Blackboard and, its communication tools suck, they just do, and it's just not up to anything sophisticated as what Moodle does. And by that I mean the discussion boards primarily."

Nevertheless, PAP came under heavy pressure to adopt Blackboard from senior management at Churchampton. They were considered a "flagship" distance education program, and it was believed that they needed to be on board with the campus solution. The administration also cited Blackboard's ability to interface with the university's administrative systems and Moodle's inability to do so as a key reason for the request to move to Blackboard. The result of this contentious process is that PAP has been allowed to continue its use of Moodle, though not indefinitely. Debbie explains:

> We got accused of being change-averse...there were also people saying, "why've we spent all that money on Blackboard when PAP are using that free [software]?" So he [the director of IT responsible for Blackboard] was having to defend his corner....We got the [Blackboard] sales guy in first...and showed him the difference between Moodle and Blackboard and why we wanted to stay with Moodle. And he agreed, he said "Yep, you're absolutely right....Blackboard can't compare, it just doesn't offer the same functionality"...we ended up being given a stay of execution, and that's all it is....He wants to persuade Blackboard to do what Moodle can do, so he can shift us over.

IMPLICATIONS FOR DISTANCE EDUCATION

The PAP case provides several practical insights for distance education practitioners. The PAP experience shows the political challenges distance education programs face, even those as well-planned and well-funded as PAP. As part of the UKeU initiative, PAP was positioned as a model for distance education practice; instead, it became a victim of distance education politics when the initiative collapsed. PAP's response to this collapse illustrates the importance of fluidity in distance education programs. Those on the outside looking in sometimes view distance education programs as turnkey systems that, once turned on, continue in operation without much interference or effort. PAP shows that is not the case. Distance education programs must be fluid organizations that respond to change and evolve to meet the changing needs of their stakeholders. PAP was fluid enough to recover from the collapse of the UKeU. They scrambled to find a replacement learning management system and were able to meet their target program start date. Their start-up days were not what they expected, given the absence of UKeU support and resources, but PAP adjusted. Their fluidity was further shown in their ability to relax their initial policies and procedures, whose origins were in the UKeU initiative, to better serve their stakeholders.

The PAP case also shows the importance of distance education programs being fiscally responsible. Like PAP, today's distance education programs are expected to be self-supporting. For many programs this means responsibility for a budget that must cover staffing, marketing and recruiting, and student support services. As with PAP, the primary income stream for these programs is revenue from student enrollments. This close tie between program solvency and student enrollments forces distance education programs to be responsive to student needs. The modular design of the PAP program (e.g., giving students certificate, diploma, and degree options) is one example of PAP addressing student needs to increase student enrollment.

Another insight to be gleaned from the PAP case is the importance of distance education program identity and purpose. PAP had a vision of who they were as a distance education program. They were committed to diversity in their student enrollment as evidenced by their reduced tuition for students from low- and medium-income countries. They never lost sight of their responsibility to serve students to the best of their ability. This focus was evidenced in the fight they waged to keep Moodle as their learning management system when the administration at Churchampton wanted them to move to Blackboard.

There are insights to be gained from looking at the PAP case through a theoretical lens as well. PAP was one case study within the present authors' project, "Technology at the Planning Table" (TPT), which examined several distance education programs in both the UK and US (see Benson & Whitworth, 2007; Benson, Lawler, & Whitworth, 2008; Whitworth & Benson, 2010. These were investigated using a framework that originated in Cervero and Wilson's work (1994; 1998) on planning practices in educational organizations, which had been used in Benson's prior study (2002) of "NetEd," a distance education program based in the Southeastern US. The TPT project developed this interest- and negotiation-based framework by focusing particularly on how the technologies in use—usually, though not exclusively, an LMS—changed over time as a result of these negotiations, and how our subjects, individually and collectively, learned about the affordances of the technology and of the social systems that had grown around it.

A key conclusion of this project is that systems-in-use in distance education can be responsive or directive (Benson & Whitworth, 2007). Responsive technologies are open to transformation as the result of learning that takes place within a team. This learning results in change, not just in the source code and other technological capabilities of an LMS, but the whole "digital habitat" (Wenger, White, & Smith, 2009) within which the team exists. The tools that the team uses can respond to learning, but so can the rules that govern behavior and the roles, or divisions of labor, through which day-to-day work is organized (Benson et al., 2008).

Originally, PAP's system was directive. The UKeU had rules in place that governed the tools that could be used and the divisions of labor through which the team worked. When the UKeU collapsed, a significant tool—the original LMS—went with it, but the rules and divisions of labor stayed in place. The course authoring and e-tutoring system were clear examples of this. Distance education can be managed through such clearly demarcated divisions of labor and procedural rules: PAP's establishment and relative success shows this to be true.

However, partly as a result of the LMS (Moodle) that it adopted serendipitously and partly because of a managerial style, or ethos, that encouraged creativity and critical enquiry into how the LMS is used in the local setting as opposed to a situation where all technical control is centralized up to the institutional level, the PAP system became more responsive over time. As we have said previously (Benson & Whitworth, 2007):

> Although . . . divisions of labor do exist, the expertise to change the technical parameters of the system has not been delegated out of the activity system. The subjects are therefore able, not just to learn about the LMS, but to adapt it, in response to their learning.

The code, interface, and other technological aspects of the system are easier to change because of Moodle's open source nature, and having these changes incorporated in the Moodle kernel means that the team's local context is not "lost" each time the central system upgrades. Though the changes would not be as potentially disruptive, this would in the end be little different from how PAP "lost" a large portion of its context with the disappearance of the UKeU system. But responsiveness is also a feature of the social aspects of the system. Divisions of labor and rules have been relaxed over time and tutors given more freedom to experiment with design features such as course templates. This responsiveness and the team culture of critical enquiry into the management, design, and practice of online learning are two sides of the same coin, and mutually interdependent. Yet, at the same time, the team recognized that the student body required high levels of assistance with the technical aspects of distance education. Features, such as standardized course templates and highly managed induction, were rules less open to change, though still agreed-on by the team.

This culture has enabled the team to develop what we have called "technostructural knowledge" (Whitworth & Benson, 2010). This recalls Mintzberg's (1989) model in which the technostructure is that part of the organization tasked with the planning and controlling of the work of others. Technological knowledge (cf. Mishra & Koehler, 2006), an understanding of how to use ICTs and other technologies in teaching, is important, but to really understand the role of a LMS in working life requires a broader perspective; one that also appreciates the system's impact on a team's internal and external communicative relationships and on its ability to learn, and transform the system as a result of its learning.

PAP empirically illustrated its high level of technostructural knowledge by being able to defend itself against the proposed change of LMS. They not only had a conscious awareness of why change would be detrimental, but were able to "speak the language" of the technostructure; to build a case against the change in terms that the technostructure valued and understood. The tools that are wielded by a team of distance educators in the prosecution of its daily tasks go beyond just technologies and are also manifest in things like tacit knowledge and experience. It is their experience with Moodle that has helped PAP develop a rules- and tools-based argument against this change. But note also that the form of teaching they have developed is itself partly a function of Moodle's technical capabilities. It is therefore unsurprising that any activity system into which a particular technology, or other practice, was fully integrated would be "change-averse"; that this is wielded against PAP as a criticism shows the dislocation between micro- and macro-level perspectives in this case.

CONCLUSION

The previous section outlines the authors' interpretation of the PAP case; readers of this chapter can use the discussion questions that follow as a means of exploring their own views. Our conclusion is that PAP is a rich case for illustrating the interplay between rules, roles and tools in defining the activity of a team of distance educators. Ultimately, responsiveness is not just a technical characteristic of a system but a function of its human elements as well; here, largely driven by a management style that valued creativity and critical enquiry while still retaining a core (and market-based) value of high levels of implicit and explicit student support. On the surface, it may seem a paradox that PAP's responsiveness has in fact allowed it to resist change, but underneath, what is being seen here is a system that has embedded the results of its own learning into its rules, roles, and tools and become strong and sustainable as a result.

QUESTIONS FOR ANALYSIS/DISCUSSION

1. The demise of the UKeU could have been the demise of the PAP online programs. Why do you think PAP succeeded despite the situation in which it found itself? What can other distance education programs learn from PAP in this instance?
2. From the *institutional* perspective, is it desirable to have a program of PAP's size and prestige using an LMS that is not the institutional system? What are the advantages and disadvantages of allowing programs to deviate from institutional policy in this way?
3. What are the advantages and disadvantages of strict divisions of labor within a distance education team? Do they risk retarding organizational learning? Should procedural rules be used to strictly control the form of different courses within a program, or is it better to encourage variety and academic autonomy here?

4. What constitutes the difference between a responsive system and a directive one? Is this distinction inherent in the LMS itself (the software), or is there more to it than this?

5. The goal of the PAP program was to become financially self-supporting. What are some challenges to distance education program becoming self-supporting?

6. The PAP program was a true distance education program in that it enrolled students from 55 different countries. Do you think this diversity is common in distance education programs? What impact do you think the diversity of the student body has on the program?

7. Initiatives like the UKeU that provided start-up funds for distance education programs were plentiful in the early 2000s, but not so much today. Do you think start-up funds are still a barrier to starting a new distance education program? What do you think are the barriers?

8. Though PAP offered only three master's degree programs, they were able to serve nine sets of student interests: certificates in each program, diplomas in each program, and master's degrees in each program. How were they able to do this when they only offered 16 different courses? What can other programs learn from the PAP approach?

REFERENCES

Benson, A. D. (2002) Using online learning to meet workforce demand: A case study of stakeholder influence. *Quarterly Review of Distance Education,* 3/4. 443–452.

Benson, A. D. & Whitworth, A. (2007). Technology at the planning table: Activity theory, negotiation and course management systems. *Journal of Organisational Transformation and Social Change,* 4(1), 65–82.

Benson, A., Lawler, C., & Whitworth, A. (2008). Rules, roles and tools: Activity theory and the comparative study of e-learning. *British Journal of Educational Technology,* 39(3), 456–467.

Cervero, R. M., & Wilson, A. L. (1994). *Planning responsibly for adult education: A guide to negotiating power and interests.* San Francisco, CA: Jossey-Bass.

Cervero, R., & Wilson, A. (1998). *Working the planning table: The political practice of adult education.* San Francisco, CA: Jossey-Bass.

Conole, G., Carusi, A., De Laat, M. F., Wilcox, P., & Darby, J. (2006). Managing differences in stakeholder relationships and organisational cultures in e-learning development: Lessons from the UK eUniversity experience. *Studies in Continuing Education* 28(2), 135–150.

Mintzberg, H. (1989) *Mintzberg on management.* London, UK: Collier Macmillan.

Mishra, P., & Koehler, M. J. (2006). Technological pedagogical content knowledge: A framework for teacher knowledge. *Teachers College Record,* 108(6), 1017–1054.

Wenger, E., White, N., & Smith, J. D. (2009). *Digital habitats: Stewarding technology for communities.* Portland, OR: CPSquare.

Whitworth, A., & Benson, A. D. (2010). Technostructural knowledge: Making pedagogy count in the technology-rich university. Presentation at the Research-Informed Teaching conference, University of Staffordshire, UK, July 13, 2010. Retrieved from http://prezi.com/reh_xjjkevbp/.

CHAPTER 23

HYBRID FLEXIBLE LIBRARY INSTRUCTION (HYFLI)

Brandon C. Taylor and Rosalind L. Fielder

ABSTRACT

The Hybrid Flexible Library Instruction (HyFLI) model is a novel way to provide library instruction for students who take courses on campus, off campus and/or online., This HyFLI pilot project aimed to expand access to library instruction regarding finding books and articles for students at a Minority Serving Institution in the United States. The pilot project involved offering library instruction sessions simultaneously live online and live in person as well as providing access to recordings of the live sessions. The findings indicate that of the 12 participants in this pilot project, six participants participated in a live in-person HyFLI session, five participants participated in a live online HyFLI session and only one participant participated in an online-recorded HyFLI session. All participants reported favorable overall ratings for their HyFLI sessions. Thus, further research seems warranted regarding the HyFLI model's viability for expanding access to library instruction and other student learning and development opportunities and services.

Real-Life Distance Education, pages 405–417
Copyright © 2014 by Information Age Publishing
405

INTRODUCTION

This pilot project proposed to use the HyFlex (Beatty, 2011) course design model to develop and offer hybrid flexible library instruction (HyFLI) sessions for students whose course instructors did not schedule an instruction session for their class. Our plan was to conduct a pilot project for creating and offering HyFLI sessions, observe, and then analyze the observations, findings and results from the pilot project. The context of this pilot project is a medium-sized, public, urban, mainly commuter, primarily baccalaureate, Midwestern university in the United States that is also a predominantly Black institution/minority serving institution. The vast majority of the students at this institution are nontraditional students who typically are older, often have a full-time job, and may be supporting a family. HyFLI is needed at this institution to meet the library instruction needs of students whose instructors have not or typically do not bring their classes to the library for formal bibliographic instruction and other instruction services (e.g., students in distance learning courses and students at off-campus/satellite sites). Students who missed a library instruction session scheduled for a class could also benefit.

The objective for the pilot project was to expand access to library instruction using a web conferencing platform (Elluminate, now known as Blackboard Collaborate). The HyFLI session is a one-hour session focused on accessing and searching library catalogs and databases in which students can participate live in person (i.e., in the same room as the instructor) or live online via a web conferencing platform. In other words, the live online students, the live in-person students, and the instructor can hear, talk to and interact with each other during the same session. In addition, on-demand/asynchronous online library instruction (i.e., a recording of a live session) is also an option available to students.

The theoretical perspective that guided the study is Beatty's (2011) HyFlex course design theory. The Hyflex course design theory has four main principles: (a) learner choice; (b) equivalency (i.e., all learning participation modes have equivalent content, activities, resources, etc); (c) reusability (i.e., content, activities, resources, etc. from one option can be used for another option; and (d) accessibility (i.e., facilitate students' ability to effectively participate in various participation modes).

Review of Literature

A review of literature regarding using the Hybrid Flexible (HyFlex) model for library instruction revealed few citations. Thus, this literature review focuses on recent literature related to synchronous or live, online library instruction, and live library instruction at extension/satellite campus sites. Like this pilot project, the reviewed literature suggested that live online library instruction could be an option for addressing the problem of providing equivalent library instruction to students in distance learning courses and/or in courses at extension/satellite campus sites (Kontos & Henkel, 2008; Lietzau & Mann, 2009; Richard, 2006). Kontos and Henkel (2008) foresaw an expansion of library instruction via web conferencing technology at their institution in the future. Prior to the study, their library offered library instruction via 60-minute one-shot sessions on the main campus as well as asynchronous web-based tutorials. The former were not usually accessible to students in online courses and/or students enrolled in courses at extension/satellite campus sites. The latter were regarded as inadequate to meet the needs of an undergraduate population that had multiplied nearly seven times in one year, three-quarters of whom were distance education students.

The librarians in the Kontos and Henkel (2008) study used a web conferencing platform similar to the one used in this HyFLI pilot project for the synchronous online library instruction sessions. One of the perceived strengths of the project was the same user-friendly web conferencing platform that was already widely used across the campus. Thus students were more likely to be familiar with it. Kontos and Henkel note that a "second presenter" (p. 6) was advantageous based on their own experiences despite the fact that the majority of undergraduates were enrolled in online courses. Overall, Kontos and Henkel deemed the project as a success based on the level of enthusiasm and positive feedback from participants in the live online library instruction sessions. However, they noted a number of technical issues related to network connection type and speed, and hardware issues. Kontos and Henkel experienced low attendance patterns, with no more than 5 students at each session. They attributed that to insufficient familiarity with computer technology and limited experience navigating within a "sophisticated electronic environment" (p. 8) among the undergraduate student population; they expected that dynamic to shift over time.

Librarians in Lietzau & Mann (2009) experimented with web conferencing technology for synchronous online library instruction in several different instructional situations: instruction sessions for a fully online graduate short-course, individualized research consultations with doctoral students in an online program, and a series of workshops for faculty as well as online doctoral students on a web-based bibliographic management software application. They experimented with two different web conferencing platforms. By and large, course instructors and instruction librarians who were involved in the project concurred that synchronous library instruction was beneficial, particularly the student-instructor (and student-to-student) exchange that is facilitated by various features available on the web conferencing platforms employed.

Richard's (2006) study described her efforts to provide live in-person library instruction for students at off-campus sites. However, the study is also relevant to research focused on live online library instruction. The study emphasizes the importance of providing distance education students with the same access to library resources and superior services afforded to students enrolled in courses that meet on the main campus.

The aforementioned studies suggest that live online, live in-person and asynchronous online delivery modes are viable options for expanding access to library instruction. The HyFLI model contains the delivery modes noted in the review of literature. Thus, the literature review supports exploration of using the HyFLI model to expand access to library instruction.

CASE STUDY

This section of the case study will describe the problem, methods used, and evaluation.

Problem

The overall problem of this pilot project was that prior to this study, library instruction sessions were only offered on the main campus to students whose instructors made appointments to bring their classes to the physical library for library instruction. Although library instruction sessions were offered in the library by appointment during normal library hours on Monday through Saturday, few if any of the faculty teaching online classes or classes at extension sites scheduled library instruction sessions for their courses. Although the distance learning program is relatively small, it has been continually growing and represents a few hundred course sections per year. Thus, a significant number of students have not been afforded the opportunity to participate in any library instruction sessions prior to this pilot project. It should be noted that not all of the classes on the main campus have participated in library instruction sessions. There is considerable evidence of the need for library instruction. This is no less true for online students.

According to the National Forum on Information Literacy, Inc. (National Forum on Information Literacy, 2013), "Simply put, information literacy is the *key* competency needed to enhance K–16 academic performance, engage patient personal responsibility, improve workplace performance and productivity, and compete effectively in a dynamically evolving world marketplace" (para. 2). However, some deficiencies in information literacy still exist even among college graduates. The most recent National Assessment of Adult Literacy (NCES 2007) data reported that about a third of college graduates were proficient in certain aspects of information literacy. Library instruction is a key component for enhancing and improving information literacy. There are a number of factors that contribute to the problem of inadequate access to formal library instruction in the case of distance learners, such as physical space, equipment, and scheduling. The extension campus sites of the university in this study, like those of some other institutions, often lack the physical space and the equipment to provide on-site library instruction (Richard, 2006). In addition, there might even be a perception of a conflict of interest regarding having library instruction during regular class times (Richard, 2006). However, these factors are not unique to the university in this pilot project.

Methods

To promote the HyFLI pilot project, the reference and instruction librarian who collaborated on the project disseminated flyers via the official communications/public relations channels in the library and on campus. In addition, the librarian created an online registration/sign-in form. Registration forms were used to determine whether or not the registered participants for each session were predominantly undergraduate students, graduate students, or even faculty. The forms were also used to gather information concerning participants' academic major, graduate program, or teaching department. Based on the information gathered from the registration form, there were 24 registrants: 4 freshman, 1 sophomore, 2 juniors, 3 seniors, 12 graduate students, and 2 faculty. Registrants were from three colleges: Arts and Sciences (7), Health Sciences (10), and Education (7). All that information informed the librarian's decision concerning the instruction level and topic for each session. In addition, there were registrants for each instruction delivery mode: Live In Person (13), Live via Elluminate (7), and Recorded Session (4). In stark contrast to the relatively low registration level, there were more than 500 views of the online registration form, which was only accessible from the URL provided on the flyer.

The librarian was the session instructor and an instructional technologist was the facilitator. The instruction sessions were conducted by simultaneously teaching sessions live in person in the institution's library instruction lab and live online. The online session was recorded. At the start of each session, the library instructor informed participants that the session would be recorded. They were advised to e-mail their questions to the session instructor if they preferred that their question not be recorded; they would receive a response after the session. In the event that some online participants had no prior experience using the web conferencing platform, all were instructed on how to raise and lower their virtual hand and to type questions in the chat window. The instructional technologist facilitated the library instruction sessions by lending his technical and instructional expertise to the library instructor and the session participants. The librarian and instructional technologists had various planning sessions and debriefing sessions regarding the HyFLI sessions.

The HyFLI sessions were approximately 60 minutes in duration. The sessions used the same general format as the library's typical live in-person instruction session conducted for classes brought to the library by their instructor. During each session participants were instructed on how to find materials related to a particular topic using the institution's OPAC (Online Public Access Catalog) and the OPAC of the library consortium with which the institution is affiliated, to identify books. Participants were also instructed on how to use relevant online bibliographic databases to find articles (e.g., Academic Search Complete, Medline Plus with Full Text, CINAHL, Library, Information Science & Technology Abstracts with Full Text, Education Research Complete, ERIC). In addition, students were guided through the process of refining the original search strategy, advised on strategies to identify the most relevant materials from among the items in the results set, and taught how to use key tools included in each electronic resource. All searches were conducted in real time and participants were encouraged to replicate the library instructor's search at their workstations. Participants were also shown how to navigate the library web site and advised on how to identify relevant databases based on the academic discipline(s) most closely related to the topic at hand. The search topic varied between sessions and participants were encouraged to participate in a brainstorming exercise to identify related search terms. The following are some examples of the topics used: the death penalty and youth, traumatic brain injury in children, electronic publishing, and teaching middle school math.

The HyFLI sessions were conducted using a web conferencing platform, the institution's library instruction lab, and a wireless lapel microphone. The library instruction lab is a computer lab equipped with LCD projector, a podium containing a computer and audio/video controls, and approximately 30 student computers. The wireless lapel microphone was worn by the library instructor and the wireless microphone base was connected to the microphone jack of the instructor's computer (using an additional cable and adapters), which allowed the instructor to have the option to move away from the podium to further engage and interact with the live in-person HyFLI participants.

The primary features of the web conferencing platform used for the HyFLI sessions were the audio feature, chat feature, application sharing feature, whiteboard feature, web tour feature, and recording feature. The audio and chat features were used for primary communications. The application sharing feature was used to demonstrate navigating the library website and conducting searches for books and articles. The web conferencing platform enabled live instruction sessions to be recorded, stored and accessed online. Thus, the recorded or on-demand online instruction sessions were recordings of the live instruction sessions in which the instructor interacted with and engaged live online and in-person participants, provided a tour of the library website, and discussed and demonstrated search strategies for locating books and articles.

The HyFLI session provided a variety of interaction and communication options. The live online instruction participants could communicate via their computer microphone and the audio feature or type messages using the chat feature of the web conferencing platform. The live in-person participants could hear and talk to the instructor. However, the live in-person participants' comments had to be repeated or paraphrased by the instructor so the live online participants could hear the questions and comments from the live in-person participants. In addition, the live in-person participants could hear the live online participants if they talked via the web conferencing platform microphone feature. Moreover, depending on where the live in-person participants were sitting or whether or not they were logged into the online session, they could see the chat messages from the live online participants. Since the live instruction sessions took place in the library instruction lab, the live in-person participants had the option of logging into the online session. However, the live in-person participants typically did not log into the online session. The instructional technologist facilitated the live in-person and the live online library instruction sessions, assisting participants and the library instructor.

The HyFLI pilot project had a number of challenges, including technical and scheduling challenges. Some technical challenges during the instruction sessions were related to network connection issues. Although the web conferencing platform used during the pilot project can operate with 28.8 kbps dial-up connections, depending on the various network conditions at the time of a given online session, there were network connection issues that caused the loss or latency of audio, loss or latency of application sharing, exiting out of the online session, and so forth. These problems were also reported in other studies (e.g., Kontos & Henkel, 2008; Lietzau & Mann, 2009), which employed different web conferencing software than the platform used in the current study. Some of the other technical challenges included finding the right sequence and rhythm for toggling back and forth between application sharing, presentation mode, and the default mode during the sessions as the default communication interfaces were not visible during application sharing in presentation mode. Another challenge for the HyFLI sessions was the scheduling of the sessions. It was not clear which days and times, if any, would be best to schedule sessions. Thus, in this pilot project instruction sessions were scheduled on a number of different days and times during the first few weeks of the fall semester. Scheduling might explain, at least in part, the low participation rate (12 participants) relative to the significant number of presumably interested parties gauged by the number of views of the online registration form (i.e., 500). Polling students enrolled in online classes very early in the academic term to both assess interest in library instruction and pinpoint times when the most students could potentially attend might address the scheduling problem. Polling proved effective in determining a feasible instruction schedule in a related study (Lietzau & Mann, 2009) although the situation in that case was somewhat different. Students in all sections of a course were required to participate in two library instruction sessions. The problem was establishing the best times for groups of students for each session (Lietzau & Mann, 2009). One surprise from the HyFLI pilot project is that the advertisement for the HyFLI sessions prompted some faculty to schedule live in-person library instruction for their classes. It seemed to have heightened awareness about library instruction services at the university.

Finally, it was an ongoing challenge to confine the HyFLI sessions to the 60 minutes scheduled while trying to engage both the online and face-to-face students and addressing technical difficulties. Sessions typically lasted longer. This problem could be addressed by offering separate sessions for the catalogs and other library databases (e.g., article databases). This approach would contribute to more interactive sessions and afford time for brief active learning exercises. The sessions could be scheduled back-to-back with a break in between so that students interested in learning how to use library catalogs as well as article databases, for example, could attend both sessions the same day, time permitting. Donaldson (1999) provides support for dividing the instruction sessions into two units. Donaldson writes, "breaking down instruction tutorials into manageable sections (modules), while remaining linear and allowing for the step-by-step acquisition of skills, prevents the user from becoming overwhelmed with information" (p. 241). Although that study used recorded web-based tutorials, her assertion is still valid for HyFLI. Moreover, whereas the library instructor can read the faces and body language of participants in the instruction lab to determine if they are confused or overwhelmed, that is not possible in the case of participants in the "virtual" instruction lab. The instructor must rely on the word of online participants that the material that has just been presented is clear and manageable. Quizzing both sets of participants would, of course, be a more reliable gauge of their comprehension and retention levels.

Evaluation

Towards the end of each HyFLI session, students were asked to complete an anonymous online evaluation form before leaving the instruction lab. The evaluation form included the following questions:

1. University Status (Freshman, Sophomore, Junior, Senior, Graduate/Professional Student, Faculty, Staff)
2. Which date did you attend? (drop-down menu with list of dates)
3. Which type of session did you attend? (Live in Person, Live via Elluminate, Recorded Session)
4. Were the concepts of the instruction session clearly explained? (Lowest 1 to Highest 10)
5. Was the information presented at a level that was understandable? (Lowest 1 to Highest 10)
6. Do you feel that because of this session you have a better understanding of the research process? (Lowest 1 to Highest 10)
7. Was this a valuable learning experience? (Lowest 1 to Highest 10)
8. I would like instruction on: (comment box)
9. What improvements do you suggest for this session? Other Comments? (comment box)
10. Select a number from 1 to 10 to rate this library instruction session overall.

Questions 4–10 are questions commonly used for student evaluations for all library instruction at the institution. The instruction evaluations had an overall rating scale from 1 to 10, with 10 being the highest. The rating of the participant in the recorded instruction session was 10.0, the average rating of the live in-person session participants was 9.8, and the average rating of the live online participants was 9.4. Thus, all of the participants rated the instruction sessions very positively. In contrast, the average rating of students who participated in the librarian's standard library instruction sessions, which are face-to-face sessions, during the same academic term, was 8.4. Similar content was covered in the standard sessions as the HyFLI sessions. Therefore, despite the low number of participants, this HyFLI pilot project was considered a success based on the feedback of instruction participants. However, due to the small number of participants, the results of this HyFLI pilot project are not generalizable and thus should not be interpreted as such. The response from library and course faculty to the HyFLI pilot project was very positive as well. Some course faculty made participating in one of the HyFLI sessions an assignment for their students and some librarians referred students to a HyFLI session. One course instructor even attended a HyFLI session with some students and planned to request a live online library instruction session for her entire class. One librarian stated that the HyFlex model as demonstrated by the HyFLI pilot project appears to be a good model for all library instruction.

IMPLICATIONS FOR DISTANCE EDUCATION

The HyFLI pilot project has a number of implications for distance education. For example, this pilot project demonstrates how the HyFlex model could be used to remove some of the major barriers to distance education cited by many educational institutions. Three commonly reported barriers to distance education include faculty acceptance of distance education, distance education course development costs/effort, and student discipline in distance education (NASULGC-Sloan National Commission on Online Learning, 2007). This is especially true at Minority Serving Institutions like the Historically Black Colleges and Universities (HBCUs) and Predominantly Black Institutions (PBIs). The HyFlex instructional model used in this pilot project could remove the barrier of faculty acceptance of distance learning by allowing the faculty to teach in their natural style and use many of the same teaching best practices and techniques for both the live in-person students and online students.

In addition, the costs and effort to create and teach distance education courses using the HyFlex model used in this pilot project is also significantly less than creating and teaching an asynchronous distance education course because it allows the faculty to use existing best practices, techniques, content, and related resources with little or no modifications to simultaneously teach live in-person and live online sessions, and via recorded live online instruction sessions. For example, the library instructor in this pilot project only had to make minimal changes to the existing library instruction content and teaching techniques for the HyFLI sessions.

Finally, the HyFlex model used in the HyFLI sessions could be used to address lack of student discipline by one or more of the following methods: (a) requiring active participation from each student during the live (in-person and online) sessions; (b) requiring a student to participate in one or more of the live (in-person and online) sessions if a student is not effectively participating or performing at the desired levels by only participating in the recorded/on-demand online sessions; and (c) creating small learning communities/teams where each small learning community/team has students from the live online, live in-person, and recorded/on-demand sessions. Moreover, during the course of the study, the reference and instruction librarian became aware of a potential new use of the web conferencing platform used in this pilot project to enhance library services to distance education students.

The application sharing feature of the web conferencing platform could be used to enhance telephone reference services by allowing librarians to virtually demonstrate to callers how to navigate the library web site to find information they need as well as guide them step-by-step through the process of conducting database searches and identifying relevant materials in real time. In effect, the student would be shifted to a virtual reference desk maintained on the institution's web conferencing platform. In addition, pre-scheduled one-on-one research consultations with a reference librarian could be conducted in the same manner. In both instances, the entire interaction could be recorded and saved for review. The virtual reference consultation idea has already been tested in a related study (Lietzau & Mann, 2009).

CONCLUSION

The HyFLI pilot project tested the feasibility of expanding access to library instruction from exclusively live in-person instruction to simultaneous live online and asynchronous online instruction by integrating web conferencing technology into the institution's library instruction program. Participants were offered three instruction options: live in-person, live online, and recorded sessions. The study assessed which option was preferred most by students and whether there were significant differences in student ratings of the instruction session across the three instruction modes. Although, there was only a small number of participants (12) in the HyFLI pilot project, each instruction session had participants who had never attended a library instruction session before and whose professors had not scheduled their class for library instruction.

Session attendees participated via each of the instruction delivery options, six participated in a live in-person session, five participated in a live online session and one participated in a recorded instruction session. Therefore, there seemed to be a preference for live instruction sessions. In addition, all participants rated the library instruction sessions very favorably regardless of instruction mode. Moreover, feedback from both librarians and course faculty was also very positive. There has already been some discussion about fully integrating HyFLI sessions into the institution's library instruction program and adding a position for an instructional design librarian. However, there are a number of things that we would do differently and recommend to others wanting to implement a hybrid flexible model for library instruction.

First, we would make sure that more stakeholders (e.g., adjunct faculty, advisors, counselors, and student support staff) are aware of HyFLI opportunities, not just students and full-time faculty. This should significantly increase the number of students participating in HyFLI sessions. Second, we would modify the library instructor's audio notification preferences in the web conferencing platform to have a particular sound played for a specific activity, like a chat comment, so that the instructor can not only see the chat comment notification, but can also hear the chat comment notification. That should facilitate the instructor's ability to respond to the live online session participants while he or she is teaching. Third, we would suggest using a web conferencing product like Elluminate Live! (now known as Blackboard Collaborate) to organize, script, and package content and activities (Blackboard, 2011) prior to instruction sessions. Fourth, we would train and provide job aids for the student workers who would be assisting the instructor and students with the web conferencing platform during HyFLI sessions (e.g., assisting students/instructor with basic facilitation like starting/stopping the recording and making sure everyone has minor troubleshooting) as basic facilitation during the HyFLI sessions does not necessarily require a full-time instructional technologist. Finally, similar to another study (Richard, 2006), we would prepare a set of materials to assist participants with retaining the ideas and information that were introduced during the HyFLI sessions. However, we would create them in an electronic rather than print format. For example, an online "pathfinder" (p. 420) could be developed using a software product like Springshare LibGuides, which is a web-based content management system specifically designed for libraries to create those types of resources. A LibGuide would have the added benefit of enabling the library instructor to embed direct hypertext links to relevant library online resources (e.g., library catalogs, articles databases, online reference references).

Documents like a PowerPoint presentation or an instruction session outline could be uploaded into the LibGuide. A PDF version of the documents would make them more widely accessible, particularly via mobile devices, like smartphones and tablet devices. Those devices are more widely available to students at the institution where the current study was undertaken than are laptops and desktop computers. The online guide could be printed by participants who prefer a paper copy of the guide. In addition, a link to the recorded session could be included in the guide for review as well as brief online tutorials focused on the individual online resources presented during the instruction session. Some of these recommendations are also relevant for credit/non-credit courses, faculty development/staff training, other student development sessions, and similar activities.

QUESTIONS FOR ANALYSIS/DISCUSSION

1. What are some of the reasons library instruction in various delivery formats is needed?
2. What are some of the affordances of offering hybrid flexible (HyFlex) instruction?

3. What are some of the challenges of offering hybrid flexible (HyFlex) instruction?
4. How would you plan to offer hybrid flexible (HyFlex) instruction in your field and/or organization?
5. Discuss managerial/administrative, organizational, and technological issues and resources related to this pilot project.
6. What are some of the emerging technologies and open source technologies that could be considered in solving the problem(s) related to the pilot project?
7. Although there were only 12 participants in this HyFLI pilot project, there were more than 500 views of the HyFLI sessions' online registration form, which was only accessible from the URL provided on the flyer. What are your thoughts regarding the large difference in the number of HyFLI session participants and number of hits on the HyFLI registration web page?

REFERENCES

Beatty, B. (2011). *HyFlex course design.* Retrieved from http://itec.sfsu.edu/hyflex/hyflex_home.htm

Blackboard. (2011) *Elluminate plan!* Retrieved from http://www.elluminate.com/Products/Elluminate_Learning_Suite/Elluminate_Plan!/?id=78/

Donaldson, K.A. (1999). Library research success: Designing an online tutorial to teach information literacy skills to first-year students. *The Internet and Higher Education, 2*(4), 237–251. doi: 10.1016/S1096-7516(00)00025-7

Kontos, F., & Henkel, H. (2008). Live instruction for distance students: Development of synchronous online workshops. *Public Services Quarterly, 4*(1), 1–14. doi:10.1080/15228950802135657

Lietzau, J. A., & Mann, B. J. (2009). Breaking out of the asynchronous box: Using web conferencing in distance learning. *Journal of Library & Information Services in Distance Learning, 3*(3), 108–119. doi:10.1080/15332900903375291

NASULGC-Sloan National Commission on Online Learning. (2007). *Online learning as a strategic asset: A survey of NAFEO college and university presidents.* Washington, D.C.: NASULGC-Sloan National Commission on Online Learning. Retrieved from http://www.aplu.org/NetCommunity/Document.Doc?id=1881.

National Forum on Information Literacy. (2013). *What is NFIL| National Forum on Information Literacy.* Retrieved from http://infolit.org/about-the-nfil/what-is-the-nfil/

Richard, D. (2006). On the road again: Taking bibliographic instruction off-campus. *Journal of Library Administration, 45*(3), 411–425. doi:10.1300/J111v45n03_07

CHAPTER 24

CHALLENGES IN PUTTING A DOCTORAL PROGRAM ONLINE

Al P. Mizell

ABSTRACT

In this chapter, the author shares the development of the first two online doctoral programs in education, the EdD in information science (DAIS) and the EdD. in computer education (ED/CED). These two online programs were created in 1983 and offered around the country with their first classes begun in late 1983 and early 1984. Development of formal, online graduate programs, which could be accessed from anywhere in the world, in the early '80s led the way to today's proliferation of distance learning opportunities from kindergarten through graduate school as well as in industry and the military.

INTRODUCTION

According to various sources, distance learning began with the Pitman Shorthand training program as a postal service correspondence course in 1852. From there, the Colliery School of Mines developed a distance learning program on mine safety in 1890 in Wilkes-Barre, PA. It evolved into

Real-Life Distance Education, pages 419–431

419

the International Correspondence Schools for iron and rail workers (Casey, 2008). Since they had over 2.5 million students by 1923, the potential for distance learning was obvious many years ago. But using the postal service for asynchronous training did not have the flexibility, versatility, capability, or interactivity that we expect in distance learning today.

Radio broadcasting in the 1920s meant that instruction could be delivered almost instantaneously instead of having to wait for the Post Office to deliver the material. Also, according to Casey (2008),

> The history of online education extends back further than you may think, with the very first virtual classroom environments being created in the 1960s. University of Illinois scientists created a classroom system based in linked computer terminals. There, students were able to access informational resources while listening to a professor whose lectures were brought in remotely, via some form of television or audio device. (p. 1)

The University of Iowa began using television in 1934 to deliver distance learning but it was in the 60s when the use of TV for distance learning expanded (Casey, 2008). We all remember the expansion of instructional television (one-way) for the delivery of K–12 schools. In fact, I was teaching science in the 60s and found that the number of places I could find a science teaching position had been significantly reduced as a consequence of the large TV science classes.

The next logical step was to take the teaching to the students at a distance. To follow that part of the story, we need to look at the creation of a new type of university in 1964. From this beginning, we'll see how learning in a face-to-face setting at a distance evolved into learning at a distance with the instructor and students separated both in space and even in time.

It was in 1964 that, what was then called, Nova University of Advanced Technology was chartered as a graduate institution in the physical and social sciences. The historical evolution of the name is described (NSU, 2010) as follows:

> In 1970, the New York Institute of Technology (NYIT) partnered with Nova University of Advanced Technology, but it wasn't until 1973 that Nova officially changed its name from Nova University of Advanced Technology to simply Nova University. This affiliation would not last however, and in 1985 the two institutions terminated any federation between NYIT and Nova. In 1993, Nova University set in motion a merger between itself and The Southeastern University of the Health Sciences. Once the merger took place a new name was required and the powers that be settled on what became the Nova Southeastern University that we know today. ("History")

In 1971, under the leadership of the new university president, Abraham S. Fischler (1970–1992), the university developed and offered the first doctoral distance education program in the nation. This was their initial entry into the area of distance education. By establishing cohorts in different geographical locations and flying the professor in for weekend classes once a month, Nova became the first fully accredited distance learning institution. The technologies used in these cohort-based doctoral programs were the jet plane, U.S. Mail, and the telephone.

Then, in early 1983, John Scigliano and I, two Nova professors, met with President Fischler. Our proposal was to create and offer an online doctoral program using the newer electronic technology that was then available. The technology used in this first program included a 28-pound, transportable, Zorba computer with a built-in 5" black and white screen and a 5¼ inch floppy disc drive plus an acoustic, 300-baud modem to call into the university computer from almost anywhere in the world. The equipment was to be provided to each student, along with basic software, as part of their $900 annual tuition in the proposed three-year program. This avoided the challenge that could come from students having different computers and software; thus, this removed a potential problem for the program that could cause a significant concern for the program administrators. After five years directing the computer education doctoral program, compressed video was introduced at the university. This is another technology that is important in distance education. However, in this chapter, I will focus only on the two online doctoral programs. See Chapter 18 on compressed video for a description of that technology's use in distance education. The details presented in this chapter mainly come from the author's memory and may only be approximations in some cases.

CASE STUDY

In 1983, Scigliano proposed a Doctor of Arts program with a major in information science (DAIS) for library and computer majors. I proposed a Doctor of Education program, with a major in computer education (EdD/CED) for educators at all levels. Fischler suggested that I work on the development with Scigliano since Dr. Scigliano was familiar with the UNIX operating system and that was the operating system used on the Nova computers. To develop online tools for the students would require creating them within the UNIX system.

The first challenge to their proposals was obtaining acceptance from the university administration. President Fischler appeared to be supportive of the concept but when he took it to the deans of the various schools at Nova University, there was intense opposition. The majority of the deans felt that the use of technology for distance learning would make both the program and the necessary support systems so expensive that they would bankrupt the university. However, the President maintained his usual, forward-thinking approach and faith in the future; he approved both programs, giving them his full support. Later, he supported the creation of a new center for computer-based learning to house both programs.

However, even with presidential support, planning the marketing, developing the curriculum, and creating a budget were all challenges facing the program developers. Since few people owned their own computers in the early 80s, we decided to include providing each student with a Zorba computer that they could use at home, on the road, and carry to their week-long institutes twice a year. We were able to arrange to purchase a group of Zorbas for $300 each. Thus, we could remove a potential problem if one student bought a Zorba, another bought a KayPro, etc. With everyone using the same operating system and software, we could provide one set of instructions for everyone.

The New York Institute of Technology (NYIT) had formed a federation in a consortium with Nova University at a time when Nova faced severe financial challenges. NYIT's financial support enabled Nova to develop and expand its undergraduate program at that time. Thus, it now seemed logical for us to propose that NYIT cosponsor the new doctoral online programs; this would provide the all-important marketing funds we needed to help recruit students for the two new programs. NYIT agreed and provided funds that enabled us to conduct a significant marketing campaign.

Planning the Marketing

From the $10,000 that NYIT made available, we developed joint marketing for the two new doctoral programs. We designed flyers and brochures for each program and created a pull-off postcard poster to send to schools. We bought mailing lists of technology leaders in the schools and districts and did mass mailings of our recruitment materials. We scheduled presentations at national and regional conferences to generate excitement to help get the word around. We received some of the postcards even years after we had sent them out. It seemed that some schools left them up on their staff bulletin boards and they were seen by new staff—even years later.

Planning the Program

Our first task was to plan our objectives and break them into individual courses. Even though the concept of online courses was relatively new and there was not much available in the literature to guide us, we believed in blended learning. Therefore, we planned a three-year doctoral program with a major in computer education consisting of eight six-credit courses online plus six week-long, face-to-face institutes. Students would normally be scheduled to take two courses each semester for two years. The third year was to focus on doctoral practicums where students attempted to solve a real-world problem using technology. The students had to agree to meet twice a year, face-to-face, for a summer and a winter academic institute. We believed that the institutes were essential to build relationships and mutual support. We found that meeting online before the first institute enabled students to begin to get to know each other without any of the usual prejudices that can occur when people see each other for the first time. I recall at the first institute when John saw Tony for the first time and exclaimed, "You're Tony? I thought Tony was a guy!" They became friends from then on. Everyone was surprised to meet Chris to find that he was in a wheelchair—no one had any idea before that meeting. The disability had no impact on Chris's success in the program, nor in forming friendships with his cluster mates.

Each winter institute was planned in conjunction with a national technology conference. The Association for Educational Communications and Technology (AECT) met in different cities each fall, so our location for the winter institutes varied each year. Later, students voted to switch to the Florida Educational Technology Conference (FETC) for our Winter Institutes because they felt the sessions there were more focused on best practices rather than so much on research. Students attended formal conference sessions during the day and began work in their two new courses in the evening. It was exhausting but fulfilling. The summer institutes were held on the Nova main campus in Fort Lauderdale for one week each summer to help them identify with the university. Workshops and classes were held during the day in the summer with field trips or social activities offered in the evenings.

We established a formal advisory board for the program that consisted of nationally known educational leaders (such as Sam Postlethwait from Purdue, David Thornburg from California, and Sylvia Charp, Editor-in-Chief of *T.H.E. Journal*). The entire Board was always hosted at the summer institute where they sat in on the classes and workshops, presented some of the material, had individual and small group meetings with all of the students, and conducted extended Board meetings as they evaluated the program and provided us with formal recommendations for improvements.

Instruction at summer institutes was similar to the winter institutes. However, once past the first institute, the time at each of the remaining institutes was divided between a day to end the two current courses and then a day to take a proctored, formal exam in each course. The students spent the remainder of their institute instructional time meeting with their new professors and beginning their two new courses that would last for the next six months.

Developing the Curriculum

Once the course topics were identified, we formed development teams including those who we planned to hire as instructors. Most of these were current Nova instructors or adjuncts so they had extensive experience in their subject areas. However, they now had to convert those experiences to an online format. We provided them with templates for their student guides and instructional development models and guidance, but they also had freedom to modify the models as needed. As an experienced instructional designer, I was able to help them follow a formal instructional design model. We were responsible, at Nova, to have the materials word processed, printed, and available for distribution at the next institute.

Program and Support Challenges

Since this was a new experience for most of the participants, we had to spend the initial time in their first course making sure they could use their new Zorba computers and that they knew how to connect their phones into the acoustic couplers that we also provided. They also had to know how to dial in to the university 800 number to connect to one of the university modems so they could use our mainframe and software and avoid any long distance charges. One of the university's information technologists created our own learning management system (LMS). It was somewhat primitive but it was one of the first such systems and had to be developed in the UNIX programming language. It was named the ECR, or Electronic Class Room and it was amazingly rich in features for its time. It included the equivalent of today's whiteboard and chat room and files could be shared.

Primitive as it was, the ECR was a real step forward and placed our program light-years ahead of most institutions. In fact, many institutions decried the use of online technology in any form (just as many of our deans at Nova had done). We did not bankrupt the university as had been forecast and many of those same critics of online credit courses are today's largest providers of online learning. Nova was just ahead of its time. Today, however, some other institutions have leapfrogged over Nova and are making even more creative uses of technology for distance learning than we are now doing. But, with NSU's reputation for being on the cutting edge, who knows what the future will hold? Remember that in the 80s, there was no Internet or Microsoft Windows. Although ARPANET was in use, it wasn't until 1990 that there were 300,000 hosts and the ARPANET ceased to exist. It was 1991 when Tim Berners-Lee developed, and CERN released, the World-Wide Web; from this time on, use of the Internet began to become commonplace. The operating system in common use in the 80s was called C/PM—there was no MS Windows at that time. Each manufacturer created his or her own version of C/PM (Marshall, 2013). Generally, if you used a KayPro machine to create a file, you could not read it on a Zorba or any other make of computer that was available at that time. In fact, the Zorba was the first machine to enable you to save your file in any one of five different versions of C/PM, so you could read it on another make of computer.

The digital research website contains the following description of the origin of CP/M, the first PC operating system:

> In 1974, Dr. Gary A. Kildall, while working for Intel Corporation, created CP/M as the first operating system for the new microprocessor. By 1977, CP/M had become the most popular operating system (OS) in the fledgling microcomputer (PC) industry. The largest digital research licensee of CP/M was a small company which had started life as Traf-O-Data, and is now known as Microsoft. In 1981, Microsoft paid Seattle Software Works for an unauthorized clone of CP/M, and Microsoft licensed this clone to IBM which marketed it as PC-DOS on the first IBM PC in 1981, and Microsoft marketed it to all other PC OEMs as MS-DOS.

Then, learning how to connect their external, acoustic modem (meaning there were two cups to place your handset down into) to their current phone system (before the days of the wall telephone jack) was a new and novel experience. Traveling with a 28-pound, "transportable" machine and modem to institutes was also a challenge. One of our other challenges was the need to repair or replace machines that went bad during the time when students were working from home.

When students work online in a doctoral program, they have to be able use the library. Nova was always ahead of the curve in providing online catalogs, full-text materials available digitally, online reference librarians, etc. Our library had to devote significant funds to obtain licenses to give students access to research sources and services, from LEXUS to electronic journal subscriptions, with search and print capability. The library also had to be able to fill book and article requests online just as they would with campus students. These services have always been outstanding. Library orientation, online or at institutes, has always been one of Nova's special strengths.

Creating a Budget

Projecting a cohort (cluster) of 20 students in 1983 with tuition of $900 each, produced a budgeted, annual program income of $18,000.

Considering the director's full-time salary, an assistant director, an administrative assistant, and all of the adjunct salaries, it was obvious that running only one cohort would never cover all of the expenses. A second cohort, scheduled to begin in the second semester, was needed. Along with the income from NYIT, the program could survive the first year. By starting two additional clusters in year 2 while continuing the first two clusters, expenses could be covered. We projected that we needed to maintain four simultaneous clusters (i.e., 80 students) as a minimum for the program to be financially viable.

Importance of the Cohort Concept

Creating a cohort, or group, of 18–20 students, who would go through the entire three-year program together, was of crucial importance in student retention. At first, outsiders questioned the possible "warmth" of an online program. How could students get to know each other and the instructor? It was hard to believe, but we found that students became better friends and supporters of one another in the online format than they had in traditional classrooms.

One example of this cluster support was in the fourth cohort when the wife of one of the students ran off with their church choir director, leaving our student with their child. He was devastated and e-mailed the cohort that he was going to have to drop out. Immediately, he was bombarded with replies encouraging him to not make any hasty moves and they would support him. He replied that he couldn't handle all the new expenses on one income so he couldn't pay tuition. At the university, we discussed it and stretched our budget to create a "cohort buddy" position that covered most of his tuition. He assumed the job of looking after the other cohort members and staying ahead of such problems so we could help other students avoid or handle their own challenges as they arose. This not only enabled him to find the support he needed from colleagues around the world, who had lived through similar experiences, but he was able to complete the doctorate. We found the "computer buddy" position so valuable that we introduced it into our other cohorts. Saving even one student provided us with enough "unlost" funds to cover the positions.

In other clusters, positive relations formed and marriages ensued. There were also some difficulties. For example, one new couple shared their passwords—against the rules. When they had arguments and broke up, the young woman called in to report she could no longer get into her account to do her work. Her "ex" had changed her password. We had to become involved since it affected her academic performance. The young man repaired the damage, although he later dropped from the program.

At summer institutes, students constantly evaluated the program positively—especially their opportunities for the up-close interactions they enjoyed with the national names in the field who served on our Advisory Board. Having formative data collected throughout the program and summative data at the end of each year, we were able to work with the Advisory Board members to constantly improve the program and react to the students' creative suggestions. The Board presented us with a written report and recommendations at the end of each institute.

Overcoming Difficulties

Following the first year of successful operation, a master's in computer education and a master's degree in DAIS were developed and added to the doctoral programs in a time-saving, combination program that led to completion of both the master's and doctoral degrees. This saved up to a year in time and tuition. The next year, a 36-credit educational specialist degree in computer education was developed; it used many of the doctoral courses but did not require the doctoral practicum (i.e., an applied dissertation).

After five years of intense effort, we were at 60 students in the CED program but a way to attract more students had to be found for the program to become financially viable. The CED program was moved from the Fischler Graduate School of Education (FGSE) to the School for Computer and Information Science (SCIS). There, the DAIS and CED programs were combined under one director and coordinated with resources already in existence for other SCIS programs. It became financially viable at this point.

However, with the financial viability and reduced need for administrative leaders, I left the position of computer education program (CED) director and moved back to the Fischler School of Graduate Education (FSGE) to become their first Director of Technology and used the CED online delivery model to try to interest other program directors in the use of computers and in introducing distance learning into their programs. I eventually worked with them to begin moving the graduate programs in FSGE to offer an online alterative in their programs. We also developed the first center-wide network for our faculty. However, this did not happen immediately upon my return to FSGE.

I was surprised that the program directors, in such an innovative environment as Nova, did not immediately jump at my offer to incorporate computer literacy training or online work into their programs. I regularly flew around the country once a month (for three months) to teach a doctoral curriculum course, face-to-face, over the weekend at a site where the students drove in to meet with me. I suggested to that program director that we replace the middle weekend meeting with an online meeting, but he was not interested. None of the other directors seemed interested either. Finally, interest in trying the use of computers came from the director of the Child and Youth Studies program. They experimented by letting me add a three-credit, hands-on technology course to their doctoral program and we offered the hands-on course live during their next summer institute, when all of the students in the cluster came together in a central location for a week's institute. This course proved to be so popular that the students put pressure on the program director to add a second technology course. A second, more advanced, technology course was added at the next year's summer institute. Then, an entire online version of the existing program was created; it was known as the National Technology Program. A new, and separate, online degree in Instructional Technology and Distance Education (ITDE) evolved out of the National Technology Program; today, ITDE is a strong, fully online technology program for educators offering all M.S. and Ed.D. degrees.

It has been interesting to observe the integration of computer technology into the university. The journey has gone from reliance on centralized mainframes and dumb terminals when I first came to Nova University in 1978 to a fully computerized institution in the 21st century with over one-half of the 28,000 students at Nova Southeastern University enrolled in online programs. I also watched secretaries threaten to quit if they had to give up their typewriters—but, in spite of their early objections, I then saw them evolve into full-time data entry clerks. Meanwhile, the faculty moved from our first computer course offering in the 70s, using the then-new Apple II computer, to the point today that every faculty member and administrator is provided with a personal computer and now does a majority of his or her teaching and administrative duties in an online format.

The lessons learned have been leveraged throughout the university as most of the programs are now either fully online, offered in a blended mode, or incorporate some of the online resources in their classes. New programs have developed and evolved as a consequence of using technology for improved delivery of programs. Thus, working professionals around the world don't have to give up their full-time positions to pursue a graduate degree. Even the face-to-face classes have benefited from overcoming the challenges presented by online teaching. Technology use has been greatly enhanced from the online experiences and shared in the f2f environment.

Seeing how the university has evolved into one of the leading names in distance education and how many of our graduates have gone on to other institutions as leaders in the development of distance education at their institutions and districts has been especially rewarding and wonderful to look back on from today's perspective.

IMPLICATIONS FOR DISTANCE EDUCATION

Having lived through the evolution from typewriters to personal computers, tablets, smart phones, and other innovations, I believe that similar cycles are repeated over and over. Lessons learned certainly support Rogers' (2003) description of Innovators through Laggards. I felt like an innovator whose task was trying to move laggards to an early adopter frame of thinking. This may suggest that when you try to create anything new, you have to plan on a slow start and be prepared to be persistent for some time. You will enhance your chances for success, of course, if you first have support from the top.

Some of the lessons we learned from our experience in creating and operating these programs include some guiding principles for distance education that we have forgotten or ignored. However, I believe that we will return to review what we learned and find ways to update them to apply to today's learners. Some of these lessons are:

1. Form cohorts or clusters of students to go through the entire program together. They provide mutual support and encouragement.
2. Create a program that uses cutting-edge technology so the students feel they are learning for tomorrow—not for yesterday.
3. Use a blended format, combining online and sufficient face-to-face time for students to form meaningful and supportive relationships.
4. Make the program affordable in some way. This may mean including other means of gaining knowledge and experience that is less expensive than your tuition so that the overall program cost can be more attractive and competitive. For example, find a way to incorporate reputable MOOCS within the curriculum and to accept life experiences for credit.
5. Consider partnering with other agencies to help provide start-up costs but don't "give away the store."
6. Start with upper-level support if you can.
7. Be open to change and ideas from others to improve what "you've always done."

From the experiences described, readers may avoid some of the difficulties that are likely to occur if they decide to create new approaches to distance education. Hopefully, the success of this early effort will encourage the readers to consider modifying their current approaches to distance learning and to create new programs that will take advantage of new technologies as they emerge.

CONCLUSION

Distance education has evolved rapidly over a relatively short period of time. In our case at NSU, we began as Nova University in the 70s with the concept of distance learning as flying a professor to a distant location to meet with a cluster of students for full-day class meetings over the weekend. The format was to meet once a month for three months in a row. The telephone was the medium for communication and offices hours. In the 80s, our definition evolved. Distance learning now meant giving each student a computer and modem and communicating with them online at a distance using plain old telephone service lines. (Note that five years later, our definition expanded to include the use of compressed video.) In addition, a blended approach was felt to be essential to develop relationships and support. There were challenges that had to be overcome; these ranged from obtaining initial support at the top to finding funding to get the program started. We were pleased to be in on the ground floor in developing distance learning and we created two online graduate programs in the early days that served as precursors for the broad incorporation of technology in distance learning throughout the university—and , we believe, in other institutions and agencies as well.

QUESTIONS FOR ANALYSIS/DISCUSSION

1. Reviewing the evolution of these two online programs at NSU, what do you think might be the next step in the evolution of distance education?
2. Using external references (with citations), diagram a timeline for the evolution of distance learning; include your forecasts for the next five years.
3. What does a summary of the findings by research studies on the differences in learning in face-to-face and online formats reveal to you?
4. What do you see as the role of compressed video in distance education?
5. What has been the fate of former, innovative technology approaches (e.g., audio-tutorial labs, language labs, instructional television, 8 mm single-concept films)?
6. Based on your answer to the above item, what do you predict will happen in the field of distance education in the next 10 years?
7. Can you find other online doctoral programs that predate the two developed at Nova University that are described in this chapter?

REFERENCES

Casey, D. (2008). A journey to legitimacy: The historical development of distance education through technology. *TechTrends, 52*(2).

Digital Research. (n.d.). CP/M: The first PC operating system. Retrieved from http://www.digitalresearch.biz/CPM.HTM

Marshall, D. (2013). History of the Internet: Timeline. In *Net Valley: A new home for the mind*. Retrieved from http://www.netvalley.com/archives/mirrors/dave-marsh-timeline-1.htm

Nova Southeastern University. (2010). NSU Digital Collections. Retrieved from http://www.nova.edu/library/dl/about.html

Nova Southeastern University (2012). NSU Overview. Retrieved from http://www.nova.edu/overview/history.html

Rogers, E. M. (2003). *Diffusion of innovations* (5th ed.). New York, NY: Free Press.

ABOUT THE AUTHORS

In Sook Ahn serves as Associate Professor in Fashion Design at Chung Ang University in Seoul, Korea. She previously served as Associate Professor in the Merchandising and Apparel Design Program at Georgia Southern University. Her PhD is in Fashion Design and Patternmaking. She uses technology in her courses and teaching practices, and she has been an owner/manager of fashion boutiques in Korea and in the United States. In addition to studio practice and fashion seminars, In Sook has taught courses in fashion technology, computer-aided design, aesthetics for apparel, advanced pattern draft, draping, and basic and advanced sewing. Currently, she is preparing her research in developing apparel spatial visualization test model, linear measurement estimation skills with reduced scale in apparel, and spatial visualization skills of apparel industry professionals. Her scholarship interests are to expand the body of knowledge in the fashion field by conducting research and teaching in areas of emerging creativity and aesthetics from fashion design technologies, functional design, and pattern development.

Omar Alvarez Xochihua is a Computer Science Professor at Autonomous University of Baja California, México. Since 1995, he has worked as a university professor on the science faculty and currently administers the Computer Science program. He participated as Instructional Designer and Developer of the Virtual Network Engineering Laboratory. He has experience teaching online courses and implementing distance education environments. His research interests lay primarily in intelligent tutoring systems, especially in building models for knowledge representation within

Real-Life Distance Education, pages 433–445
Copyright © 2014 by Information Age Publishing
433

ill-defined domains. He is also interested in computer science instruction through using computer-based agents and distance learning technologies. He received his BS degree in computer science from the Autonomous University of Baja California, México in 1991 and his master's degree from the Institute of Technology of Monterrey, México in 1994. He received his PhD degree in Computer Science from Texas A&M University in 2012.

Michael Barbour is an Assistant Professor at Wayne State University in Detroit, Michigan, where he teaches instructional technology and qualitative research methodology. Michael's interest in K–12 distance education began after accepting his first teaching position in a rural high school. Having been educated in an urban area, Michael was troubled by the inequity of opportunity provided to his rural students and began a program to offer Advanced Placement social studies courses online at his own school and at other schools in the district. For more than a decade now, Michael worked with numerous K–12 online learning programs in Canada, the United States New Zealand, and around the world as a teacher, course developer, administrator, evaluator, and researcher. His current research interests focus on the effective design, delivery, and support of online learning to K–12 students in virtual school environments, particularly those in rural jurisdictions. Michael resides in Windsor, Ontario, Canada.

Angela Benson is an Associate Professor of Instructional Technology at the University of Alabama. Her research addresses the influence of educational technology on individuals and organizations. She has given numerous conference presentations and published several academic articles related to distance and online learning. She is the coeditor of *International Perspectives of Distance Education in Higher Education* (2012) and *Cases on Educational Technology Planning, Design and Implementation: A Project Management Perspective* (2013). Benson has designed and taught a variety of traditional and distance courses. Her professional experience includes 13 years as a systems engineer in the telecommunications industry. She holds undergraduate degrees in Math and Industrial Engineering, master's degrees in Operations Research and Human Resource Development, and a doctorate in Instructional Technology.

Lauren Cifuentes is Director of Distance Education and Associate Professor at Texas A&M University—Corpus Christi. Her expertise lies in design and development of online learning environments. Her current primary research interests are in administration of distance education and design of effective online instruction, including design considerations for collaborative environments. With NSF funding she currently investigates the relative contributions of instructors, peer-interaction, case-based experiences, and scaffolds in online learning environments. She also investigates the power of user-communities for maintaining Web 2.0 environments.

Camille Dickson-Deane received her BS degree in Computer Science from The University of the West Indies (UWI) and her MS degree in Software Development and Management from Rochester Institute of Technology. Her professional experience includes project management consultancies in the web development, banking and education fields and professional trainer/instructor for continuing education in the field of information technology, web development, business/project management. She has also worked in the field of quality assurance as a test engineer for West Group Inc., and as an analyst for First Caribbean Bank and was also a senior lecturer at the College of Science Technology and Applied Arts of Trinidad and Tobago. She is currently a program consultant and adjunct faculty member of UWI Open Campus and is an external evaluator for Barbados Accreditation Council. Her research interests include workplace e-learning, usability evaluation of distance learning products, and cultural artifacts associated with both fields.

J. Ana Donaldson is a Past-President of the Association for Educational Communications and Technology (AECT) and is a Contributing Faculty member for Walden University in the Educational Technology PhD program. She retired in 2009 as an Associate Professor of Instructional Technology from the University of Northern Iowa. Besides her years of classroom and online experience, she is a published author, keynote speaker and international presenter. She coauthored with Rita-Marie Conrad: *Engaging the Online Learner: Activities for Creative Instruction* (2004 & 2011) and the newly released *Continuing to Engage the Online Learner: More Activities and Resources for Creative Instruction* (2012). The 2011 edition was recently awarded the 2012 IAP Distance Education Book First Place Award.

Joanna C. Dunlap is an Associate Professor of Instructional Design and Technology at the University of Colorado Denver. Joni is also the university's Assistant Director for Teaching Effectiveness, working through the Center for Faculty Development to help online and on-campus faculty enhance their teaching practice. An award-winning educator, Joni's teaching and research interests focus on the use of sociocultural approaches to enhance adult learners' development and experience in postsecondary settings. Recently, her work in this area has revolved around online teaching and learning in higher education, specifically looking at social presence, student engagement and retention, and the use of social networking and media tools to support learning. For over 15 years, Joni has directed, designed, delivered, and facilitated distance and eLearning educational opportunities for a variety of audiences.

Lesley Farmer is Professor at California State University Long Beach and coordinates the Librarianship program. She earned her MS in Library Science at the University of North Carolina Chapel Hill, and received her doctorate in Adult Education from Temple University. Farmer has worked as a teacher-librarian in K–12 school settings as well as in public, special and academic libraries. She serves as SLA Education Division Chair, CSLA Research Committee Chair, International Association of School Librarianship Vice-President of Association Relations, and Editor for the IFLA School Libraries and Resource Centers Section. A frequent presenter and writer for the profession, she won ALA's 2011 Phi Beta Mu Award for library education. Farmer's research interests include information literacy, assessment, collaboration, and educational technology. Her most recent books are Youth-Serving Libraries in Japan, Russia, and the United States (Scarecrow, 2012) and Instructional Design for Librarians and Information Professionals (Neal-Schuman, 2011).

Rosalind Fielder is Assistant Professor of Library and Information Services and Reference and Instruction Librarian at Chicago State University. She is primarily responsible for reference and instruction services to undergraduate and graduate students. She coordinates the library instruction program. Throughout her tenure at CSU, she has experimented with a wide variety of Web 2.0 and instructional technologies to enhance reference and instruction services, and extend those services beyond the physical boundaries of the campus. She is chair of the Association of College and Research Libraries Law and Political Science Section Library Instruction Committee, serves on the CSU Distance Education Committee, and was recently appointed as cochair of the ACRL Distance Learning Section Bibliography Committee (2013–2015). Her research interests include problem-based learning, online library instruction, and virtual reference. She holds an MS in Library and Information Science and an MA in Political Science from the University of Illinois at Urbana—Champaign.

Ruth Gannon-Cook has been an Associate Professor in Chicago at DePaul University in the School for New Learning since 2003. She received her Ed.D. from the University of Houston, with an emphasis in Instructional Technology (2003). She also received a Certificate for Advanced Studies from the Queens College, Cambridge, United Kingdom, with an emphasis in Change Diffusion and Technology Integration. Her MS Ed in Educational Administration and her B A in Business are both from Loyola University, She has published a book, ten book chapters, and peer-reviewed journal articles. Ruth also currently serves as Secretary of the Faculty Council of DePaul University. In addition, she is currently the Editor of the *Journal of Educators Online*, an international peer-reviewed online journal.

Ludwika "Ludy" Goodson works as a Senior Instructional Designer and Consultant in the Center for the Enhancement of Learning and Teaching at Indiana University—Purdue University Fort Wayne. She consults with faculty and supports professional development workshops and resources for course design, teaching, assessment, and integration of technology. Her previous work at Florida State University, Georgia Southern University, and Embry-Riddle Aeronautical University included online course design with several learning management systems. Ludy's coauthored paper with Dee Andrews on a *Comparative Analysis of Models of Instructional Design* has been published four times, most recently in the 2011 publication of *Instructional Technology: Past, Present, and Future* (3rd ed.) edited by Gary Anglin. Her recent presentations and interests center on the scholarship of teaching and learning and collaborative investigation with Don Slater at Georgia Southern and Yvonne Zubovic at IPFW on the impact of students' confidence estimates in self-identification of knowledge gaps to support motivation.

Bruce R. Harris is Professor of Instructional Design and Technology at Western Illinois University. He earned his PhD at Brigham Young University. He has been directly involved in, both in teaching and researching, online learning for over 20 years. He has published refereed articles and presented papers at major conferences on the topic of self-regulated learning, with a particular emphasis on integrating self-regulated learning strategies in online learning environments. Harris has worked as an external evaluator and consultant for distance learning initiatives, grants involving advanced learning technologies, and large corporations and school districts. He has served on advisory boards of professional organizations and on editorial boards of refereed journals.

Kim Hosler earned a PhD in Educational Technology from the University of Northern Colorado. She has presented at AECT conferences as well as at the Sloan-C Consortium annual conference on topics ranging from student perceptions of Quality Matters, the use of text messaging to enhance online communities, to engendering cognitive presence and critical thinking in online courses. She teaches online and face-to-face classes as affiliate faculty for several universities in the Denver, CO area. In the past, she managed learning and professional development departments for technology and financial services companies. Kim's research interests include building communities in distance learning environments, mobile learning, and technology as a teaching and learning tool for use in higher education.

E-Ling Hsiao is an Assistant Professor in the Department of Curriculum, Leadership, and Technology at Valdosta State University. Prior to joining VSU, she worked for Indiana State University as an Instructional Design Specialist to assist the faculty members in the development of on-line and hybrid courses and to provide guidance in a wide variety of instructional technology applications. She received a PhD in Instructional Technology from Ohio University in 2010. Her ongoing research interests include cognitivism, problem-based learning, instructional design, interface design, and visual literacy.

Xiaoxia "Silvie" Huang is an Assistant Professor in Instructional Design in the School of Teacher Education at Western Kentucky University (WKU). She received her PhD degree in Instructional Systems from Florida State University. Before she joined WKU, she worked as an Instructional Design Specialist and adjunct faculty member at Indiana State University (ISU). Her current research interests include cognitive load theory-based instructional design, instructional design for distance courses, online teaching and learning, and the impact of technology integration in educational settings.

Karen Kaminski is the Chair of the Instructional Leadership Area of Study in the School of Education at Colorado State University. She supports two PhD Specializations: Learning, Teaching, and Culture; and Interdisciplinary Studies, and a Master of Education in Adult Education and Training. The master's is offered in a face-to-face version and a fully online version which she co-developed in 1999. Kaminski's research includes instructional design and the use of technology to enhance learning, and transfer of knowledge and skills to new settings. Prior to coming to CSU, she served as the Director of Distance Learning at the University of Northern Colorado, and earlier, an Instructional Designer at the University of Wyoming supporting faculty preparing to teach via distance delivery.

Kathryn Ley, an Associate Professor of Instructional Technology at University of Houston-Clear Lake, teaches graduate courses in instructional design, learning theory, instructional motivation, project management and grant writing, and performance technology. She has authored over 25 journal publications and presented at national and international educational and distance learning conferences for more than two decades. She currently investigates self-regulation, extraneous cognitive load, and their effects on online faculty and learners and conducts faculty workshops on online course communications. She earned a PhD in Instructional Systems from Florida State University, an MS Environmental Management–Human Resources from the University of Texas at San Antonio, and an MLS from the University of Texas at Austin.

Ying Liu is a doctoral candidate in the Learning, Design and Technology program in the College of Education at the University of Georgia and an Instructional Designer at University of Wisconsin Extension Continuing Education, Outreach, and E-Learning. She has worked as an instructor and an instructional designer in universities in both China and the United States. She is committed to helping faculty creating engaging online learning environments and fostering effective online learning. Her research interests focus on online student self-regulation, authentic learning tasks, and educational design research methods.

Patrick R. Lowenthal is an Instructional Designer at Boise State University in the Department of Educational Technology. Before moving to Boise State, Patrick spent the past ten plus years in Colorado working in online learning at a variety of institutions. He recently defended his PhD focusing on social presence and online learning. His research interests focus on instructional communication, with a specific focus on social and teaching presence in computer-mediated environments. In addition, he often writes about issues and problems of practice related to post-secondary education.

Les Lunce is an Instructional Design Consultant with the Blumberg Center for Interdisciplinary Studies in Special Education at Indiana State University. Beginning his academic background with BAs in Computer Science and Economics, Les completed his M.S. in Computer Education and Cognitive Systems at the University of North Texas in 2003. In 2007 Les completed his PhD in Educational Computing at the University of North Texas. Les's dissertation topic and his principal ongoing research interest is the design, deployment, and assessment of instructional simulations. Other research interests include virtual environments and learning spaces. Publications include articles and conference proceedings on simulations, wayfinding in virtual worlds, and multiple intelligences.

Larissa V. Malopinsky is a Senior Manager of Learning Technology and Training Operations at Otsuka America Pharmaceutical, Inc. headquartered in Princeton, NJ. She holds a PhD and MSc in Instructional Systems Technology and Information Science from Indiana University Bloomington, and a doctoral candidate in Language Education and MA/BA in Slavic Linguistics from St. Petersburg State University, Russia.

Tatjana Martinez is a full-time Program Professor on special administrative assignment at the Abraham S. Fischler School of Education at Nova Southeastern University. At the Fischler School, she teaches online courses on Conflict Resolution and Advanced School Law. As a public school teacher, she has taught all grade levels in the bilingual education programs. She has served as a school counselor and administrator, personnel director, and as a district labor and legislative relations specialist. She has served as Legal Counsel for statewide school board and superintendent associations in Florida. She has a master's degree from the University of Miami, Coral Gables, Florida, and a Doctor of Jurisprudence from Widener University School of Law.

Al P. Mizell began his educational career as a secondary science and math teacher for 12 years in Dade County, Florida. After earning his doctorate in IST at Indiana University, he spent eight years as Associate Dean of Instruction at Howard Community College (HCC) in Columbia, Maryland. In 1978, at Nova Southeastern University (NSU), as Director of Curriculum, he created the first online doctoral program in computer education and coauthored *Teaching and Learning with Technology*. He cofounded the SAXophone videoconferencing project in 1994. He has served as president and/or board member of AECT/DDL, FDLA, and ISPI's South Florida Chapter. Mizell now focuses his efforts on teaching and seeking grants to help senior citizens gain computer literacy. He is married (for 53 years) to Dr. Mary and lives in South Florida. They have three grown children, five grandchildren, and four great-grandchildren—plus their malt-i-poo, Gracie.

Joi Moore received her BS degree in Computer Science and MS degree in Management from North Carolina State University, both focusing on a minor in Management Information Systems. Her professional experience includes consulting with technology companies in Research Triangle Park, North Carolina, and teaching in the Department of Computer Information Systems at Shaw University. Moore earned her PhD in Instructional Technology from the University of Georgia—with a cognate area of Management Information Systems, wherein her primary research interest was teachers' participation in the design and usage of an electronic performance support system (EPSS). Her current research agenda is the application of appropriate design principles for technology environments that support learning and/or effectively improve a desired performance. Additional areas of research include: analyzing information architecture and evaluating performance in distance learning environments; designing performance-centered applications; and Human Computer Interaction.

Eunjung Oh is an Assistant Professor in the Foundations, Secondary Education, and Educational Technology Department at the Georgia College and State University. She earned her PhD at the University of Georgia. She has diverse professional experiences in K–12, higher education, and corporate training as a Human Resources Development (HRD) specialist, trainer, instructional designer, multimedia developer, instructor, and consultant in both Korea and the United States. Her research interests include design of online and blended learning environments to enhance students' learning experiences (e.g., collaborative group work, authentic learning tasks, critical thinking, and reflective practice), educational design research methods, and digital generation learners.

Gihan Osman is an Assistant Professor of Instructional Design and Technology at the Graduate School of Education and the Center of Learning and Teaching at the American University in Cairo. She has her PhD and MSc in Instructional Systems Technology from Indiana University Bloomington, an M.A. in TEFL from the American University in Cairo, and a BA in English from Alexandria University, Egypt. Over the past 10 years, she has worked as an instructor, designer, researcher, and evaluator of online and blended instruction in a number of universities including Indiana University Bloomington, the University of South Florida, and the Arab Academy for Science and Technology. Her current research examines strategies to scaffold critical thinking, problem solving, and knowledge construction in educational environments supported by emerging collaborative technology. She is also investigating individual, cultural, and organizational barriers that inhibit critical discourse and the transfer of learning in professional contexts.

Anthony A. Piña is Dean of Online Studies for the Sullivan University System. Tony has designed and taught numerous online and hybrid courses and has developed online degrees at undergraduate, master's, and doctoral levels. He has served as consultant to Fortune 500 corporations, small businesses, local government agencies, educational institutions and the U.S. military. Tony is Past-President of the Division of Distance Learning of the Association for Educational Communications and Technology (AECT) and has served on the AECT Board of Directors. He is author of the book *Distance Learning and the Institution*, has over 40 academic publications and over 150 conference presentations. He serves on the editorial boards of two scholarly journals. Tony earned undergraduate and master's degrees from Brigham Young University, did postgraduate work at Arizona State University, and completed his doctorate at La Sierra University. His research focuses primarily upon macro and institutional issues in online and distance learning.

Thomas C. Reeves is Professor Emeritus of Learning, Design, and Technology, Department of Educational Psychology and Instructional Technology, College of Education, The University of Georgia. He earned his PhD at Syracuse University. He was a Fulbright Lecturer in Peru and he has been an invited speaker in the U.S. and 30 other countries. From 1997-2000, he was the editor of the *Journal of Interactive Learning Research*. In 2003, he received the Fellowship Award from the Association for the Advancement of Computing in Education (AACE), and in 2010 he was made a Fellow of the Australasian Society for Computers in Learning in Tertiary Education (ASCILITE). His *Interactive Learning Systems Evaluation* book (with John Hedberg) was published in 2003, his *Guide to Authentic E-Learning* book (with Jan Herrington and Ron Oliver) was published in 2010, and his *Conducting Educational Design Research* book (with Susan McKenney) was published in 2012.

Roberta Ross-Fisher has been a professional educator and administrator for more than 30 years at the K–12 and collegiate levels, focusing in the last decade on distance learning environments. Her scholarly interests include creating positive connections between learners and facilitators in online classrooms; training and mentoring distance learning faculty; and making data-driven decisions to enhance online student learning. She has served Western Governors University in various capacities during her six-year tenure and is currently Senior Coordinator for Program Reporting in the Compliance & Accreditation department.

Julian Scheinbuks was Emeritus Professor of Biology and Director of Distance Learning at Chicago State University. He received his bachelor's degree from the University of Illinois Urbana-Champaign, and his MS and PhD degrees in microbiology from Loyola University. He taught at Northwestern University before beginning a two-decade career at Chicago State University. After his retirement as Professor of Biology, Julian founded Chicago State University's Office of Distance Learning and served as its Director until his untimely death in 2010. In his will, Julian bequeathed the equivalent of his 20-year salary—one million dollars—to the university to be used for scholarships for CSU biology majors and for the continued development of online instruction at CSU.

Matthew Schwartz began his career at Eastern Michigan University earning a Bachelor of Science in Secondary Education Computer Science. In 2005, he earned his Master's in the Art of Teaching at Marygrove College. Matt returned to school at Wayne State University where he completed the Educational Specialist Certificate focused in Instructional Technology K–12 Technology Integration in 2010. Through hard work and commitment, Matt was awarded Outstanding Student of the Year from Wayne State's Instructional Technology Department in the spring of 2011. A computer teacher at Huron High School in New Boston, MI, where he has taught since the fall of

2001, Matt teaches three classes: Computer Applications, Web Design, and Computer Programming. Matt is committed to educating his students on best practices for using Web 2.0 tools. In 2011 he became the assistant director for the MACUL organization's SIGWEB, which is a Special Interest Group for Webmasters in K–12 Learning.

Judith Slapak-Barski serves as Instructional Designer, faculty trainer and conference presenter for Title V-B at Nova Southeastern University. Judith has a Master's Degree in Education and Instructional Technology, and specializes in online learning management systems, instructional technology, and teacher education, among others. Her activities focus on improving the teaching and learning process through course enrichment and implementation of multimedia in everyday instruction, ultimately helping in the creation of enhanced instruction. Before joining Nova Southeastern University, Judith served as the Title V Teacher Education Specialist for Broward College. As a bilingual faculty member, Judith received the "Adjunct Professor of the Year" award for 2009–2010 at Broward College, a resounding display of support from her students, among other recognitions. As a member of the Academic Excellence Committee, she contributed to the creation of the Adjunct Institute, an organizational development initiative from the Office of the Vice President for Academic Affairs.

Linda Agustin Simunek is currently the Executive Project Director of the Title V-B federally-funded grant project at the Abraham S. Fischler School of Education at Nova Southeastern University. At the Fischler School, she also teaches online courses on Leadership Development, Conflict Resolution, and Law in Healthcare Education as an adjunct professor. As a Registered Nurse, she served as the founder for nursing programs at Florida International University, the International University of Nursing in St. Kitts, West Indies, at National University in Los Angeles, and, at Purdue University in West Lafayette, Indiana. She has served as a curriculum consultant to nursing programs in Kuwait, the Philippines, and in Mexico. She has served as a pro bono legal counselor to the Philippine Nurses Association of America (PNAA). She has a master's degree from De Paul University, a PhD from Loyola University, and, a Doctor of Jurisprudence degree from the University of Miami.

Brandon C. Taylor is a doctoral candidate in Instructional Technology at Northern Illinois University. He has been a Dean of Distance Learning, an Online Instructor and an Online Instructional Designer. He has distance learning experience in higher education, K–12, corporate and public sectors. His research interests include distance/mobile learning, culture and instructional design/technology, human performance improvement/ technology and assistive technology. He holds a BS in Computer Science from Prairie View A & M University and an MS in Instructional Technology from Western Illinois University. In addition, he is a Master Online Teacher, a certified reviewer for Quality Matters, Inc. and an Illinois licensed math, computer science, and technology teacher.

Monica W. Tracey is an Associate Professor of Instructional Technology in the College of Education at Wayne State University. Her teaching and re-search focuses on theory and design-based research of interdisciplinary de-sign including design thinking, designer reflection and designer decision-making. Monica was the recipient of the 2011 Association for Educational Communications and Technology Achievement Award, which recognized her commitment and outstanding leadership work in the creation of the MIAECT chapter. She was also recognized with the 2008 Design and De-velopment Award. Tracey has worked for over 25 years in design and on numerous design projects. Her work includes designing internationally and across disciplines. Recently, she directed a large-scale cross-cultural custom-ized instructional design and performance improvement project in Dubai, The United Arab Emirates. Tracey has over 30 publications on her research and practices of instructional design including a co-authored book, book chapters, and refereed journal articles.

Kelly Unger has been a professional in instructional technology for 10 years, working extensively with K–12 school districts and other adult learners, pro-viding instruction on various technologies and concepts. Kelly currently works as an End-User Change Management and Engagement Specialist on a global Information Technology team at Ford Motor Company. Her responsibilities include gathering and reporting information from 80,000 salaried global employees' current and desired uses of information and communication technologies throughout the company. She enjoys teach-ing and will continue in higher education as an adjunct faculty member, and technology professional development provider for K–12 schools. An activist for community service, Kelly was co-founder of MIAECT (Michigan Association for Educational Communications and Technology), the first statewide chapter of the international organization, AECT. She is actively involved in the Michigan Council of Women in Technology, where she as-sists with the summer technology camp and university committee.

Andrew Whitworth is Senior Lecturer at the School of Education, Univer-sity of Manchester, UK, and the Program Director for the MA: Digital Tech-nologies, Communication and Education, a research-based program that promotes a critical and reflective view of the impact of technology- and information-rich environments on both working practices and everyday life. He is the author of *Information Obesity* (2009) and many articles on both e-learning design and information literacy.